Parties and party systems

Volume I

Parties and party systems

A framework for analysis

Volume I

GIOVANNI SARTORI

CAMBRIDGE UNIVERSITY PRESS

CAMBRIDGE

LONDON · NEW YORK · MELBOURNE

Published by the Syndics of the Cambridge University Press
The Pitt Building, Trumpington Street, Cambridge CB2 1RP
Bentley House, 200 Euston Road, London NW1 2DB
32 East 57th Street, New York, NY 10022, USA
296 Beaconsfield Parade, Middle Park, Melbourne 3206, Australia

© Cambridge University Press 1976

First published 1976

Printed in the United States of America
by Vail-Ballou Press, Inc., Binghamton, New York

Library of Congress Cataloging in Publication Data
Sartori, Giovanni, 1924–
Parties and party systems.
Includes bibliographical references and index.
1. Political parties. I. Title.
JF2051.S26   329'.02   76-4756
ISBN 0 521 21238 3 hard covers
ISBN 0 521 29106 2 paperback

Contents

Contents

Tables and figures

Tables and figures

Preface

I have been working on this book for so long that I dislike to admit it, even to myself. Looking back I discover that I began lecturing on parties and party systems at the beginning of the sixties. The original impulse was my unhappiness with Duverger's pioneering volume, which appeared in 1951. Duverger's everlasting merit was to seize a topic in want of a general theory. By 1963, however, David Apter correctly asserted, in surveying the theme, that "what is lacking is a theory of political parties." In struggling with this manuscript I have since discovered that this lack has not been remedied – indeed, it has steadily grown.

A first draft was completed in 1967 at Yale and was circulated during that year. A number of friends quoted the 1967 draft believing, as I did at the time, that the book was about to appear. I owe them my humble apologies. The draft was more theoretically cumbersome than today's book, and its design was very much concerned with systems theory and with furthering structural-functional analysis. This is not to say that I have since dropped my theoretical ambitions. The difference is that in 1967 whatever I had to say was contained in *one* volume – whereas I am now publishing the *first* of two volumes. And my theoretical thread emerges as I go along, that is, especially in the *second* volume.

Since the rest is still to come, I ought perhaps to mention here where I stand with respect to systems theory. As the complaint correctly goes, whole systems analysis, on the one hand, and empirical research and findings, on the other, fall widely apart. Presumably, however, one way of bridging this gulf is to develop the in-between level, namely, subsystem or partial system analysis. I equally take it that the party system, and more precisely the party subsystem, is crucial to this end. Parties are *the* central intermediate and intermediary structure between society and government. Furthermore, insofar as they are a *system,* parties interact and such interactions can be viewed as mechanical propensities, as structures of rewards and opportunities that go a long way toward explaining the different performances of different types of party polities. Finally, I assume politics to be an independent

ix

variable, thus implying that parties and party systems mold (beyond the point at which they reflect) the political society. That is, before treating politics as a dependent variable, it behooves the political scientist to explore how much mileage is afforded by its autonomy.

These and other theoretical ambitions emerge in the second volume. But why did the 1967 text never appear and how did the deferment affect the original design? In 1968 the so-called student revolution knocked at my door also, and four years went by in what scholars aseptically call conflict management. Only at the end of 1971, during a full year spent at the Stanford Behavioral Sciences Center, was I able to take the manuscript in hand again. In the meantime so much new material had appeared that the manuscript simply exploded in my hands. The single work had to be divided in, or, better, multiplied by two.

In the seventies it was no use contending – as Duverger was entitled to – that no general theory of parties could emerge without evidence. The evidence had since become massive – but for what theoretical use? I tried hard to substantiate the theory with findings and, conversely, the findings with theoretical relevance; but I stumbled into masses of empirical material that were neither cumulative nor comparable and, indeed, that added up to nothing. Over and over again, my efforts were defeated by a conceptual morass, or diaspora. Pluralism, representation, expression, coercion, structure, function, system, ideology, culture, participation, mobilization, all are concepts that are surely central to the party topic. As I encountered each of them, at each encounter most of my time and energy went into understanding how the concept was being used (extravagantly or fuzzily), in discussing it, and in having to justify my own choice of meaning. I thus found myself entangled to no end in preliminaries and miles away from the substance of my subject. Finally, everything had to be thrown into the wastepaper basket and I was back, feeling like Sisyphus, where I began.

These frustrating vicissitudes by no means represent an alibi for my slow pace, nor for whatever I have failed to accomplish. They help explain, however, why 25 years have gone by without replacing the classic of Duverger; they may alert us, if this is so, to the current predicament of political science qua empirical theory. It would seem that the more sophisticated we become technically, the more inept we become conceptually.

I have also been in endless trouble on sheer comparative grounds. We all blow up our own experiences and play down those of others in other countries. Human beings are Ptolemaic. Yet there must be something fundamentally wrong in a discipline that manages to bring under a same category, for example, a number of states of the United

States, the Soviet Union, and a set of embryonic African states. In any event, the problem of applying common and constant yardsticks to some 100 countries *is* a problem; each single country specialist is bound to be unhappy with the sweeping (to say the least) nature of my analyses. This is the price that one must pay for worldwide comparative endeavors.

Turning to the contents, this volume comprises two parts. Part One largely consists of a rationalization of how and why parties came about, of what they are for, and of the peril of entrusting the one polity to its parts. Despite the current dislike for abstractions such as "part" and "whole," they have, in fact, been historically the cornerstone of the debate about parties, and they do help us analytically to regain a sense of perspective. Indeed, the whole issue of factionalism – with which Part One begins and ends – has been grievously muddled, in my view, precisely from a lack of perspective.

Part Two deals with party "systems" and attempts to sort them on the basis of their mechanical tendencies or predispositions, and on the basis of the explanatory and predictive power that results. This sorting may leave me, at many points, with old-fashioned classifications. However, if classes and types are only an entrance door – as can be easily granted – the fact remains that, unless a science is entered with a systematized analytical vocabulary, all its subsequent steps are bound to be faulty. Furthermore, because it does not appear that classes and types can be replaced by indexes and algorithms, the sensible stand would seem to be that the nominal and mathematical routes have much to gain by joining forces and by putting a venerable enmity to rest. At first view I attribute a major importance to the number of parties, that is, to the numerical criterion of classification of party systems. However, a glance at the table of contents suffices to reveal that my major thread is competition. It is not by chance that this volume ends with a discussion of the Downsian model and of the direction of competition.

The second volume will investigate, in Part Three, party types, organization, and functions. The reason for dealing first with the system and with single varieties of parties, such as the mass party, only afterward is the systemic reason mentioned at the outset. Finally, in Part Four, the party topic will be placed in context and related to a set of crucial variables: Political culture and ideology, cleavages and the social system (the sociology of parties properly understood), the influence of electoral systems, and the ways and means of political engineering. The work will end by relating the party system to the political system as a whole, with particular reference to coalition government and coalition theory.

In the end, then, it will appear that I have set out to explore the *party polity* – which is not the same as the democratic polity. This work is predicated upon the assumption that if modern politics has something peculiarly "modern" about it, the novelty derives from a politically active, or politically mobilized, society, which is a new resource and also a new source of complexities. If so, modern politics requires a party channelment; the single party when not, or where not, parties in the plural.

Over the years of the laborious delivery of this book, I have been assisted by the advice and criticism of many colleagues. I acknowledge my gratitude to them in the various chapters. However, since at different points in time Leonard Binder, Val Lorwin, Hans Daalder, and G. Bingham Powell have commented upon major parts of the manuscript, my very great debt to them for their help must be mentioned here. I have also benefited more than I can say from the very stimulating discussions at the Committee of Political Sociology of the International Sociological Association during the decade in which Seymour M. Lipset and Stein Rokkan promoted the study of parties on the Committee's agenda. The Concilium on International and Area Studies at Yale University and, subsequently, the Center of Advanced Study in the Behavioral Sciences at Stanford, provided ideal settings and facilities for my muddling through. Most of the final manuscript was in fact drafted at Stanford, "on the hill," and edited at the Center by Miriam Gallaher. I am grateful for her patient (and often dissenting) assistance, as well as to the editors of the Cambridge University Press for taking care of the final styling and copyediting.

G. S.

San Giuliano, September 1975

Abbreviations

Frequently cited journals are abbreviated as follows:

AP   *Acta Politica*
AJPS   *American Journal of Political Science*
AJS   *American Journal of Sociology*
APSR   *American Political Science Review*
CJPS   *Canadian Journal of Political Science*
CP   *Comparative Politics*
CPS   *Comparative Political Studies*
EJPR   *European Journal of Political Research*
ISSJ   *International Social Science Journal*
JP   *Journal of Politics*
GO   *Government and Opposition*
MJPS   *Midwest Journal of Political Science*
PQ   *Political Quarterly*
PS   *Political Studies*
PSQ   *Political Science Quarterly*
PT   *Political Theory*
RFSP   *Revue Française de Science Politique*
RIS   *Rassegna Italiana di Sociologia*
RISP   *Rivista Italiana di Scienza Politica*
SPS   *Scandinavian Political Studies*
WP   *World Politics*
WPQ   *Western Political Quarterly*

PART ONE

The rationale: why parties?

1

The party as part

1.1 From faction to party

The name "party" came into use, gradually replacing the derogatory term "faction," with the acceptance of the idea that a party is not necessarily a faction, that it is not necessarily an evil, and that it does not necessarily disrupt the *bonum commune*, the common weal. The transition from faction to party was indeed slow and tortuous – both in the domain of ideas and in fact. The second half of the eighteenth century had just begun when Voltaire concisely stated in the *Encyclopédie*: "The term *party* is not, in itself, loathsome; the term *faction* always is."[1] With his versatile genius for synthesis Voltaire epitomized in this sentence a debate opened by Bolingbroke in 1732 and after that pursued for about a century.[2]

That the name faction was loathsome was not, from Roman times until the nineteenth century, a statement in want of proof. In the whole tradition of Western political thought there is hardly an author who has not taken the same view. The interesting part of the sentence is, therefore, where Voltaire concedes that parties might be different, that the term party does not have by necessity a negative association. Voltaire himself can hardly be credited, however, for having sustained this difference. Faction, he wrote, is *"un parti séditieux dans un état"* ("a seditious party in a state"). The term party would thus seem applicable to the factions that are not seditious. But Voltaire went on to explain, instead, that a faction is "a seditious party when it is still feeble, when it does not rejoin [*partager*] the entire State." Thus "the *faction* of Caesar shortly became a dominant party which swallowed the Republic." And the distinction is further enfeebled, if not canceled, by Voltaire's remark that "a head of a party is always a head of a faction."

A distinction with no difference, then? It would be unfair to address this criticism to Voltaire, for he only reflects the ambiguities and the perplexities of the entire eighteenth century. It is proper, therefore, to raise the question with respect to all the authors concerned: Bolingbroke, Hume, Burke, and the protagonists of the French and American revolutions. First, however, we must understand their terminology.

Etymologically and semantically speaking, "faction" and "party" do not convey the same meaning. Faction, which is by far the older and more established term, derives from the Latin verb *facere* (to do, to act), and *factio* soon comes to indicate, for authors writing in Latin, a political group bent on a disruptive and harmful *facere*, on "dire doings." Thus the primary meaning conveyed by the Latin root is an idea of hubris, of excessive, ruthless, and thereby harmful behavior.

"Party" as well derives from Latin, from the verb *partire*, which means to divide. However, it does not enter in any significant way the vocabulary of politics until the seventeenth century – which implies that it does not enter the political discourse directly from Latin. Its longstanding predecessor with very much the same etymological connotation is "sect," a term derived from the Latin *secare*, which means to sever, to cut, and thereby to divide. Since "sect" was already available and established for rendering the strict meaning of *partire*, "party" lent itself to being used in a looser and more blunted meaning. "Party" basically conveyed, then, the idea of *part*; and part is not, in and by itself, a derogatory term: It is an analytical construct. True enough, the learned society of former times – whether it spoke Italian, Spanish, French, German, or English – did understand its terminology through Latin (and Greek). Hence the etymological derivation of party from *partire*, i.e., partition, by no means escaped the seventeenth- and eighteenth-century writers. Nonetheless, "part" had long lost its original connotation. The term part enters the French *partager*, which means sharing, as it enters the English "partaking" (let alone partnership and participation).

When "part" becomes "party," we thus have a term subject to two opposite semantic pulls: the derivation from *partire*, to divide, on the one hand, and the association with taking part, and thereby with sharing, on the other. The latter association is, in fact, stronger than the former derivation. A complication must be noted, however. While "party" was entering the vocabulary of politics, "sect" was on its way out. During the seventeenth century the term sect became associated with religion and especially with Protestant sectarianism. By this route the term party took on, at least in part, also the meaning formerly conveyed – in the political arena – by the term sect. And this reinforced the original linkage of "party" with the idea of severance and partition.

The foregoing goes a long way toward explaining why "party" had, from the outset, a less negative connotation than "faction" and yet remained a close synonym for faction. There is little doubt that no eighteenth-century author, aside from Burke, really disentangled the two concepts. Yet all our authors – and notably Bolingbroke and Hume – were struggling, at some point, with a distinction that carried a difference. If as we read the literature we pay attention to the exact wording, whenever the two terms are not used interchangeably, the difference is that "faction" applies to a *concrete group,* whereas "party" is far more an *analytic partition,* a mental construct, than a concrete entity. And this explains why the distinction is quickly blurred and does not hold tight. If faction is the concrete group and party the abstract grouping, reference to the real world makes the two indistinguishable.

The foregoing also alerts us to the fact that authors who spoke of "parts" but did not use the word "party" were not really confronting the problem. This is particularly the case of Machiavelli and of Montesquieu, who are often cited as the precursors in glimpsing the *idea* of party in a favorable sense. But they did not use the *word.* The relevant passage of Machiavelli to this effect reads that the "riots between Nobles and Plebeians . . . were a first cause in maintaining Rome free," with the comment appended that in every republic one finds "two different tempers [*umori*], one of the people and one of the almighty [*grandi*]," so that "all laws made in favor of freedom result from their disunity." But Machiavelli made it quite clear, immediately after, that he was not prepared to apply this generalization to his own time nor, indeed, in his words, to the "partisans from which are the parts of the city born," for these "parts" bring the city to its "ruin."[3] Actually, when Machiavelli referred to a concrete group, he wholeheartedly subscribed to the condemnation of sects and factionalism.

Montesquieu went, prima facie, a little bit further than Machiavelli. In the *Considerations* on the causes of the greatness and decadence of the Romans, Montesquieu wrote:

What is spoken of as union of the body politic is something very ambiguous: the true one is a union of harmony, following which all the parts [*toutes les parties*] even if they appear opposed, concur to the general good of the society, just like some dissonances in music concur to the overall . . . harmony. . . . It is as with the parts of this universe, eternally linked by their actions and reactions.[4]

Now this argument is highly abstract, and the imagery – musical and cosmological harmony – is a very old one. If Montesquieu seemingly went a step further than Machiavelli, this was because he was willing to extend the point of Machiavelli from the Romans to the English of his time.[5] Yet one must go through all of Montesquieu to find a few, allusive indications of a favorable understanding of the "parts" of a republic, whereas there is no reference to parties in the crucial chapter of *L'Esprit des Lois* in which he outlines the English constitution.[6] And there is no question, on the other hand, that Montesquieu fully concurred in the general condemnation of "factions."[7]

Machiavelli and Montesquieu did not really enter the problem, then, because the crucial step – along the transition from "part" to "party"

– resided in conceiving party as an *object term,* that is, as a concrete noun that pointed to a concrete entity or agency (distinguishable from a faction). This breakthrough occurred only with Burke, almost one-half century after Montesquieu. And to perceive the distance that had to be covered before arriving at Burke one must begin with Boling-broke, the contemporary of Montesquieu who was indeed the first major author to write extensively about parties.[8]

Bolingbroke's stance is this: "Governing by party . . . must always end in the government of a faction. . . . Party is a political evil, and faction is the worst of all parties."[9] It might seem that Bolingbroke only draws, here, a difference of degree: While faction is more evil than party, both are misfortunes of the same family. But he makes it clear that the difference is also of kind, for parties divide a people "upon principles."[10] Thus, according to Bolingbroke, there is a real, not a nominal, difference between the "national parties" of the seventeenth century, which reflected a "real difference of principles and designs," and the divisions of his time, in which "national interests" were no longer concerned and are "made subordinate to personal interests" – this being "the true characteristic of faction."[11] To be sure, Bolingbroke also uses party and faction interchangeably, as if they were synonyms. But this is often consistent with his argument that the degeneration of parties into factions is inevitable; and when the two things merge, the two terms must equally be merged.[12]

It should be recognized, nevertheless, that Bolingbroke's notion of party is somewhat ambivalent, depending on whether his reference is to the parties of the Great Rebellion that led to the constitution settled in 1688 or to the "country party" of his time, i.e., the party for which he himself stood. His position with respect to the latter is most interesting. On the one hand, he is very close to legitimizing it, for "A country party must be authorized by the voice of the country. It must be formed on principles of common interest." On the other, Bolingbroke hastens to add that the country party is "improperly called party. It is the nation speaking and acting in the discourse and conduct of particular men."[13] Yet the country party is, if only for emergencies, a necessity – a necessity for a good cause. Bolingbroke concedes that there are parties "we must have";[14] but only the parties, or the coalition of parties, that join issue with the enemies of the constitution. This is the case of the country party, which upholds the constitution against its usurpation by the court faction (which is indeed a "faction"). Thus the country party is not a party among other parties (in our sense) but – as is implied by the wording – the country against the court, the subjects against a sovereign who does them wrong. If the king does no wrong, if he rules in Parliament as the constitution prescribes, then the country has no reason for becoming a party. Hence we have the

notion of a non-party party, i.e., of a party that is to end all parties.[15]
This is, in fact, *the* purpose of Bolingbroke. In the dedication that
introduces the *Dissertation upon Parties* Bolingbroke represents his
work as the "attempt to extinguish the animosities, and even the names
of those parties that distracted the nation for so long, so fatally at first,
and so foolishly at last." In short, the intent of Bolingbroke is to "reconcile parties and to abolish odious distinctions."[16]

It is fair to conclude, then, that Bolingbroke was antiparty. Since
governing by party always ends in governing by faction and since
parties stem from passion and interest, not from reason and equity, it
follows that parties undermine and endanger governing by constitution. And constitutional rule is what Bolingbroke stood for. His ideal
was an ideal of unity and harmony. Yet Bolingbroke did draw, more
than anyone before him, a distinction between factions and parties.
And his passionate and lengthy analysis, restated in numerous writings,
forcefully brought parties to the fore and obliged his contemporaries
and successors to reckon with the problem.[17] This is borne out by the
fact that Hume, shortly after, and first among the major philosophers,
took up the subject.

Hume stands halfway between Bolingbroke and Burke, though he
was closer to the former than to the latter – both in his ideas and in
time. Hume's first *Essays* on parties appeared less than 10 years after
the *Dissertation* of Bolingbroke, while Burke joined the issue in 1770,
some 30 years later. Hume is, as one would expect, less sanguine on the
matter than Bolingbroke. Only on factions is he equally vehement, for
"factions subvert government, render laws impotent, and beget the
fiercest animosities among men of the same nation."[18] On parties Hume
is more lenient. He goes, in fact, one important step further than
Bolingbroke, for he concedes that "to abolish all distinctions of party
may not be practicable, perhaps not desirable in a free government."
Yet the ideal of Hume remains very similar to the ideal of Bolingbroke:
the end of artificial and odious distinctions. In his time Hume detected
"a universal desire to abolish these party distinctions," i.e., those
"entertaining opposite views with regard to the essentials of government." He called this desire "tendency to a coalition" and saw in this
coalescence "the most agreeable prospect for future happiness."[19]
While granting that the parties of the Great Rebellion were "parties
of principle," he saw no such nature in the "new parties" that subsequently arose "under the appellation of *Whig and Tory*," for here
"we are at loss to tell the nature, pretensions and principles of the
different factions."[20]

Hume's major contribution was thus the typological contribution
outlined in the essay of 1742, *Of Parties in General*. The reader is
somewhat baffled, in this and other essays, by Hume's intermingling of

"party" with "faction"[21] – for Hume surely was less consistent than Bolingbroke in allocating the two words. It should be borne in mind, therefore, that Hume was classifying, and that the distinction between party and faction as drawn by Bolingbroke was insufficient for sustaining a classification. If party also ends in faction, it appeared to Hume – presumably – that his typology had to be of any and all political groupings. Let us say, then, that Hume establishes a typology of partisanship that begins with a basic distinction between (i) *personal* and (ii) *real* groups – the latter being the factions and/or parties "founded on some real difference of sentiment or interest."[22] While "parties are seldom found pure and unmixed," Hume suggests that "personal factions" are typical of small republics and, generally, of the past, while "real factions" are typical of the modern world. Hence Hume's analysis concentrates on the "real factions," which are subdivided into three classes: factions from (i) *interest,* (ii) *principle,* and (iii) *affection.*

In Hume's judgment, factions from interest are "the most reasonable, and the most excusable"; and while these factions "often do not appear" in despotic governments, "they are not the less real; or, rather, they are more real and more pernicious upon that very account." Instead, Hume goes on to say (and the switch to "party" should not pass unnoticed): "Parties from *principle,* especially abstract speculative principle, are known only to modern times and are, perhaps, the most extraordinary and unaccountable *phenomenon* that has yet appeared in human affairs." This novel phenomenon is far less justifiable. But here he enters, albeit by illustration, a crucial distinction between "political" and "religious" principles. The latter are Hume's real target: "In modern times, parties of religion are more furious and enraged than the most cruel factions that ever arose from interest and ambitions." The former, the parties of political principle, receive a very different treatment: "Where different principles beget a contrariety of conduct, which is the case with all different political principles, the matter may be more easily explained."[23] And this different and more tranquil understanding results quite clearly from the essay that follows, *Of the Parties in Great Britain.*

In the main, Hume accepted parties as an unpleasant consequence, hardly as a condition, of free government. And there is, doubtlessly, a world of difference between viewing parties as de facto inevitables[24] and the Burkeian view that parties are both respectable and an instrument of free government. Yet Hume provided some of the material on which Burke was to build his case. Hume's typology not only allowed a more analytic understanding of the matter but provided – as any classification does by its very nature – stable elements on which to ground further reasoning. As a political writer, Hume was by no means prophetic. His class of "factions from *political* principle" is still a far cry from what we shall come to call ideological parties; but it does provide a bridge across which the party will be perceived and conceived as a concrete group. Parties outgrow factions because they are based not merely on interests, and not merely on affect (Hume's "affection"), but also, and principally, on common principles. This is Burke. But Hume paved the way by indicating that the factions from principle were a new entity appearing on the scene of politics and that political principles had to be distinguished from religious principles.[25]

Burke's much quoted but little understood definition is: "Party is a body of men united, for promoting by their joint endeavours the national interest, upon some particular principle in which they are all agreed." Ends require means; and parties are the "proper means" for enabling such men "to carry their common plans into execution, with all the power and authority of the State."[26] Clearly, Burke's party is not only a respectable means: It is a *party* in all its difference from a *part,* i.e., a concrete agency, something as real as factions are. At the same time, factions and parties can no longer be mingled: They are made different by definition. In Burke's own words: "Such a generous contention for power [the party's] . . . will easily be distinguished from the mean and interested struggle for place and emolument" – the latter being a splendid definition of what factions are about.[27] The argument no longer is that party always ends in faction but that in such a case a party is not a party. When Burke means faction, he says faction; when he means party, he says party.

The preceding sentences are not occasional. Burke dealt with the point at length. He had a well-identified target: the king's men. And the king's men were arguing that "party was to be totally done away, with all its evil works." Burke's *Thoughts* are a meticulous refutation of such argument, which is denounced as the design of "a faction ruling by the private inclination of a court."[28] The king's men were propagating the doctrine that "all political connections are in their nature factious." Burke pointed out that this was the recipe propagated at all times by those serving "unconstitutional" ends, for it is only "in a connection," that is, when men are linked together, that "they can easily and speedily communicate the alarm of any evil design." *Connection* was, in fact, Burke's key word. "Connections in politics," he argued, are "essentially necessary for the full performance of our public duty." While these connections are "accidentally liable to degenerate into faction," nonetheless "the best patriots in the greatest commonwealth have always commended and promoted such connections."[29] Men, Burke granted, "thinking freely will, in particular instances, think differently." But this is no argument for throwing "an odium on political connections," for if a man concerned with public business "does not concur in these general principles upon which the

9

party is founded . . . he ought from the beginning to have chosen some other. . . ." And Burke concluded that "how men can proceed without any connection at all, is to me utterly incomprehensible."[30]

As has been convincingly argued, party government in Britain was not fathered by the great parties of the seventeenth century; it presupposed their dissolution and was actually fathered by the small parties of the eighteenth century.[31] Bolingbroke did find something distinctive (vis-à-vis faction) in the great parties. But the problem was to locate the distinctiveness of "party" in the small parties that were taking shape in the eighteenth-century House of Commons. And this was Burke's breakthrough. The circumstances were by no means irrelevant to such an accomplishment. Burke's advantage was to write almost a century after the 1688–1689 settlement, that is, when both the religious and the constitutional crises had clearly been resolved. Bolingbroke and Hume still had to plead for consensus on fundamentals, and thus were antiparty in principle and antifaction in substance. In Burke's time, however, it was pretty clear that the great parties fighting for or against the constitution had withered away and that the factions of the long reign of George III were merely fighting over the spoils of government. Bolingbroke and Hume saw the anticonstitutional menace coming from the *divide et impera* formula, from the king's men taking advantage of a faction-riddled, disunited, and thereby impotent Parliament. Burke understood – and this was his genius – that since Parliament could not be a monolith, it was in a far better position to resist the crown if its members were connected, i.e., organized in "honorable connections."

The essence is, then, that with Burke the axis of the argument had rotated. Bolingbroke justified "party" only as the opposition (when necessary) of the country to the unconstitutional sovereign. Burke, instead, placed "party" within the realm of government, reconceiving it as a partition that no longer was between subjects and sovereign but among sovereigns.[32] In his time there was consensus on the constitution, but there was little understanding and even less consensus as to how, and by whom, constitutional rule was to be conducted. Burke *proposed* that this might be the business of parties – if they became parties. Burke was proposing, for he actually conceived "party" before it came to exist, and indeed provided the *idea* that helped parties, with the passing of time, to outgrow factions.[33] But many decades had to pass before his insights were fully grasped.

It was not long after Burke's intellectual breakthrough that the Continent was swept by the French Revolution. The Girondins, Jacobins, and other political groups that actually propelled the events of 1789–1794 could well have used Burke to legitimize their connections and their principles, that is, their existence. They did not. Almost every political viewpoint was put forth during the vortex of those memorable five years. On one point only did the French revolutionaries remain of the same mind and speak with one voice: They were unanimous and persistent in their condemnations of parties. Throughout their verbal and eventually mortal battlings, their major reciprocal accusation was *chef de parti,* head of a party, which was the same as saying head of a faction.[34]

Condorcet, in advising the Girondins on their constitutional project, argued – against the English parties – that "one of the primary needs of the French republic is to have none." Danton declared: "If we were to exasperate each other we would end up with forming parties, whereas we only need one, that of reason." Robespierre stated that what brings about a plurality of parties is only the "personal interest"; and that "wherever I perceive ambition, intrigue, cunningness and Machiavellianism, there I recognize a faction; and it is in the nature of all factions to sacrifice the general interest." Saint-Just was even more drastic: "Every party is criminal. . . . Every faction is thus criminal. . . . All faction attempts at undermining the sovereignty of the people." Still more concisely, he stated: "In dividing a people factions replace liberty with the fury of partisanship."[35]

Three reasons are generally given to explain this unanimous chorus: First, the 1789 revolutionaries were under the spell of Rousseau; second, their God was *La Raison,* Reason; third, they were imbued with an individualistic, if not wholly atomistic, philosophy.[36] All of these reasons hold well; but we should not be forgetful of a major premise of fact: the harsh reality and virulence of factionalism. Factions have been equally condemned under entirely different assumptions. The French revolutionaries declared themselves "patriots." To them parties and factions were the same as for Halifax, the Trimmer, a century earlier, a "conspiracy against the nation." And perhaps the major lesson to be drawn from this leap back to the English mood of the previous century is that parties presuppose – for their acceptance and proper functioning – peace under a constitutional rule, not an internal war investing, among other things, the very establishment of a constitution.

If it is hardly surprising that the French revolutionaries could not accept or understand Burke, one would expect the case to be different with the Founding Fathers of the United States. However, in 1787–1788 Madison still spoke very much of "factions" and very much in the classic, derogatory sense of the word – though in a different and broader context. His definition was as follows:

By a faction I understand a number of citizens, whether amounting to a majority or minority of the whole, who are united and activated by some common impulse of passion, or of interest, adverse to the rights of other citizens, or to the permanent and aggregate interests of the community.

And his contention was that the Union would help "to break and control the violence of faction," which had been, and remained, the "dangerous vice" of popular governments.[37] The novelty is that the problem is perceived constitutionally and in the setting of how a large "republic" is best suited to control the *effects* – not to remove the *causes* – of factions. What Burke left to noble intentions, Madison confronted in terms of constitutional engineering. For the rest there is no doubt that Madison used faction in a negative sense and that faction and party were still conceived as equivalent, or nearly equivalent, terms.[38]

Madison was by no means alone in condemning what Burke had praised. In Washington's Farewell Address of 1796 – based on a draft by Hamilton – one reads:

Liberty . . . is indeed little else than a name where the government is too feeble to withstand the enterprises of *faction*. . . . Let me . . . warn you in the most solemn manner against the harmful effects of the spirit of *party*. . . . There is an opinion that parties in free countries are useful checks . . . and serve to keep alive the spirit of liberty. . . . This within certain limits is probably true. . . . But in governments purely elective it is a spirit not to be encouraged.[39]

This text is indeed far removed from the ones of the French revolutionaries; but it is equally far removed from Burke. Faction remains equal to the "spirit of party"; and where Washington concedes that parties might keep alive the spirit of liberty, he is hardly conceding more than Hume.[40] For Washington's emphasis definitely is on warning against the spirit of party.

The case of Jefferson is even more interesting. If the modern idea of party was first identified by Burke, the first modern party materialized, if only to disintegrate shortly afterward, in the United States under the leadership of Jefferson. He did organize "connections," and he did bring the Republican party program to victory by appealing, over the heads of the Federalists, to the country at large. Yet it would be wrong to assume that with Jefferson's party the message of Burke had finally struck roots. Paradoxical as this might seem, Jefferson conceived his party very much as Bolingbroke conceived the country party: as a party which was to end or, at any rate, undermine the legitimacy of partisanship, once the "republican principles" had been actuated and fully established.[41]

Meanwhile, ideas and events were moving not any faster, but more slowly, in continental Europe. It took more than 30 years for the wounds of the French Revolution to heal. Washington's "spirit of party" was, in the very same year of his address, 1796, the object of the

12

passionate denunciation of Madame de Staël.⁴² It was only in 1815 that the major French constitutional thinker, Benjamin Constant, recognized that "one cannot hope to exclude factions from a political organization, where the advantages of liberty are wont to be preserved." But he immediately added: "We must therefore labor to make factions as harmless as possible."⁴³ Constant was merely catching up with Madison. And even these words were too advanced for the Restoration, which was to last until 1830. Clearly, Burke is the turning point in the realm of intellectual history. But the turn of events is another matter. It was not until circa a half-century after his *Discourse* that parties, as he had defined them, superseded factions and came into existence in the English-speaking world.

1.2 Pluralism

When Burke came to see that parties had a positive and necessary use, there was no theory to back up his insight. Yet the soil had been tilled. The transition from faction to party rests on a parallel process: the even slower, more elusive, and more tortuous transition from intolerance to toleration, from toleration to dissent, and, with dissent, to believing in diversity.⁴⁴ Parties did not become respectable because Burke declared them such. Parties came to be accepted – subconsciously, and even so with formidable reluctance – with the realization that diversity and dissent are not necessarily incompatible with, or disruptive of, political order. In this ideal sense, parties are correlative to, and dependent upon, the *Weltanschauung* of liberalism. They are inconceivable in the Hobbesian or in the Spinozan view of politics; they were not admitted in the city of Rousseau.⁴⁵ They are only conceivable, and have actually been conceived, when the "horror of disunity" is replaced by the belief that a monochromatic world is not the only possible foundation of the polity. And this is tantamount to saying that, ideally, parties and pluralism originate from the same belief system and the same act of faith.

The question immediately arises as to what we mean by pluralism. Let us first pause to note that party pluralism was preceded by constitutional pluralism and that the latter did not pave the way to the former. Constitutionalism had praised and sought – since Aristotle – mixed government, not party government. In particular, constitutional pluralism – the division of power and the checks-and-balances doctrine – long preceded party pluralism and was constructed without, and against, parties. Constitutionally speaking, a body politic not only could but should be separated into parts; but the analogy, or the principle, was not carried over to those parts that were "parties."⁴⁶ The theory of constitutional government, from Locke to Coke, from Blackstone to Montesquieu, from the *Federalist* to Constant, had no place, and surely no need, for them. When constitutional theory was taken up by constitutional lawyers, parties were kept even more in a limbo – for parties acquired the status of public law only in the aftermath of World War II, and only in very few constitutions at that.[47]

Possibly the difficulty with extending to parties the *Weltanschauung* of liberal constitutionalism was twofold. First, parties were not parties but factions, i.e., parts *against* the whole rather than parts *of* the whole. The second difficulty was the strongly individualistic tenet of the Enlightenment. We are reminded by Talmon that "what is today considered as an essential concomitant of democracy, namely, diversity of views and interests, was far from being regarded as essential by the eighteenth-century fathers of democracy. Their original postulates were unity and unanimity."[48] That this should be the case with the eighteenth-century fathers of democracy is hardly surprising, for their referent was ancient democracy – not liberal democracy – and hardly Athenians, but rather the Spartans and the Romans.[49] What is less obvious is why the same applied to the liberal thinkers of the seventeenth and eighteenth centuries. A major explanation lies in their thoroughgoing individualism, which met the need for freeing their epoch from medieval bonds, from a tightly knit, immobile corporatist structure.[50]

Clearly, the relation between pluralism and parties is subtle and often elusive. Pluralism is a hinterland, a background factor, and its link with party pluralism is hardly a direct link. Yet party pluralism has been, very definitely, an export of the countries in which pluralism was first implanted – the Protestant rather than the Counter Reformation countries. And it is abundantly clear that party pluralism has not fared well, or for long – with very few exceptions – beyond the area permeated by a pluralistic *Weltanschauung*.[51] It is no simple step to operate a political system in which *many* parties are not disruptive of *one* polity. The difficulty of this step has been consistently underrated by Western scholars, no less than by the policy makers intent upon exporting democracy. It is important, therefore, that it should be understood in the light of its substratum.

The question remains: What do we mean by pluralism? No doubt, the word is a shorthand for an intricate wealth of connotations, a richness that has been turned into a morass since we have adopted the view that "all large-scale societies are inevitably pluralistic to some degree."[52] According to this generalization, pluralism stems from, and largely coincides with, the division of labor and the structural differentiation, which are, in turn, the inevitable bedfellows of modernization. The argument thus becomes nearly tautological, its conclusion true by definition,[53] and "pluralism" is easily extended to African settings and indeed to most of the world.[54] In my view, this is a typical instance of

14

conceptual stretching and mishandling. If it pleases us to lump together modern Western pluralism, a medieval hierarchical status system, a Hindu caste system, and an African-type tribal fragmentation, let all of this be called a state of plurality, or a *plural society;* but let us not confuse this bazaar with "pluralism" and with what we are trying to convey when Western societies are called pluralistic.

The term pluralism can be conceptualized at three levels, namely, (i) cultural, (ii) societal, and (iii) political. At the first level we may speak of a *pluralistic culture* in the same latitude of meaning as the parallel notions of secularized and homogeneous culture. A pluralistic culture points to a vision of the world based, in essence, on the belief that difference and not likeness, dissent and not unanimity, change and not immutability, make for the good life. It may be said that this is philosophical pluralism, or the philosophical theory of pluralism, in its difference from the reality of pluralism.[55] Even so, it should be understood that when philosophers have been concerned with worldly matters – as they have in their political theorizing – they were both interpreting and shaping the course of the real world. Hence what originates as the theory of pluralism is subsequently reflected, if only in part and imperfectly, in the reality of pluralism. I would thus maintain that even when we come to use pluralism as a descriptive (not normative) term, we cannot dismiss the fact that pluralism denotes societal and political structures that stem from a value orientation, from a value belief.[56] Pluralism, as it now permeates Western societies, would cease to exist if we ceased to believe in its worth.

With respect to the second level, *societal pluralism* must be distinguished from *societal differentiation.* Both are societal structures or, more exactly, structural principles epitomizing sociostructural configurations. But while any complex society turns out to be "differentiated," it does not follow in the least that all societies are differentiated "pluralistically." In my previous wording, a plural society is not a pluralistic society, for the latter is only one out of many possible types of societal differentiation.

With respect to the third level it can be said that *political pluralism* points to "the diversification of power" and, more precisely, to the existence of a "plurality of groups that are both independent and non-inclusive."[57] How this pluralism extends to those parts that are parties has been mentioned earlier. However, a number of ad hoc points now deserve elaboration.

The first relates to where the pluralistic vantage point stands vis-à-vis consensus and conflict. Bored with too much consensus and in the face of so much conflict, we are currently emphasizing that the basis of democracy is not consensus, but indeed conflict.[58] This strikes me as a reckless use of terminology that puts the pluralistic basis of liberal democracies singularly out of focus. For the term that best conveys the pluralistic vision is *dissent*. Lord Balfour spoke in the language of British understatement when he wrote that the English "political machinery presupposes a people so fundamentally at one that they can safely afford to bicker." But we are going too far in the direction of overstatement when we assert that democracy postulates conflict. Conflict was what made Hobbes long for peace under the despotic rule of his Leviathan, and was equally what made Bolingbroke and Hume and Madison and Washington seek for a "coalition of parties." Whenever conflict means what it says, parties fall into disrepute. Let it be stressed, therefore, that what is central to the pluralistic *Weltanschauung* is neither consensus nor conflict but dissent and praise of dissent. Characteristically – and this is very telling – dissent has never been understood as the opposite of consensus. Dissent draws from both consensus and conflict, but coincides with neither.[59]

Consensus may well be related to conflict – but only at different levels of belief and behavior. The important distinctions here are between (i) community level and governmental level (policies), and/or between (ii) fundamentals and issues. If there is consensus at the community level and on fundamentals – and especially on the rules for resolving conflicts – then people may well conflict over policies. But this is so because consensus on fundamentals provides the self-restraints that make conflict something *less than conflict,* as we endlessly if often too late rediscover whenever we are confronted with the reality of a people shooting at each other. Conflict over fundamentals is not a possible basis for democracy, nor indeed for any polity: Such conflict – i.e., real conflict – calls for internal war and for secession as its only solution.[60]

On the other hand, consensus should not be conceived as a close relative of unanimity. The difference might be stated thus: Consensus is a "pluralistic unanimity." It does not consist of the one mind postulated by the monochromatic vision of the world but evokes the endless process of adjusting many dissenting minds (and interests) into changing "coalitions" of reciprocal persuasion.[61] This is also to say that while "dissensus is the entropic state of societal nature, consensus is not found but must be produced."[62] And the importance of consensus – so conceived – to our present world is borne out by the fact that it is probably no fortuitous coincidence that Western party systems had no part in building the nation-state and became operative only when the crisis of legitimacy – i.e., acceptance of constitutional rule – had been resolved.[63] Perhaps the polity must exist first, perhaps unification has to precede party "partition," and perhaps this is the condition that makes parties a subdivision compatible with unity rather than a division that disrupts it. This is supported by the experience of most of the develop-

something that happened before being understood – and even less designed.

One often hears it said that during the eighteenth century the English began practicing party government.[72] But "party government" is very ambiguous. It can be used to mean party *in* government, that is, that parties enter the sphere of government as one of its relevant component elements. This is already a big step forward, for parties can be only linkages between a people and a government – as they long remained in Imperial Germany – without any real access to governmental decision making. At any rate, the party *in* government, as defined above, is a far cry from party government literally understood, that is, meaning that the party *governs,* that the governing function is actually seized and monopolized by the winning party or by a coalition of parties.

Let us distinguish among (i) the party that remains external to, and uninvolved with, the sphere of government, the ambassador party, so to speak; (ii) the party that operates within the ambit of government but does not govern; and, (iii) the party that actually governs, that takes on the governing or governmental function.[73] Let it also be noted that there are many intermediate formulas not only between but within these three cases; and especially that the distance between party *in* government and party *governance* is indeed a long distance to travel. It is quite certain that nothing resembling party governance actually materialized, in England or elsewhere, during the eighteenth century. And it is very dubious whether during the long reign of George III the English really crossed the threshold between the ambassador-type party and the party that has a place in government. Burke never saw, during his lifetime, the party he had defined. If this is so, "party government" does not apply, even in its loosest sense, for lack of a subject.

What the English did start practicing during the eighteenth century was not, then, party government, but *responsible government.* Not only does responsible government precede, in time, party government, but the latter is very much an outgrowth of the former. Responsible government consists of the responsibility of ministers to parliament. This may be called in a very loose and, again, ambiguous sense a parliamentary system, that is, a system based on the parliamentary support of government. But nothing in this arrangement entails, by necessity, a party-based system of government. This is very clear in Burke. His stance was: "The virtue, spirit and essence of a house of commons consists in its being the express image of the feelings of the nation. It was not instituted to be a control *upon* the people. . . . It was designed as a control *for* the people."[74] However, *for* the people did not imply *by* the people. Parliament was conceived by Burke as a representative body; but the representation spoken of was "virtual" far more than electoral. In this view parties were not only extraneous to the representational process but inimical to it. Burke's representative was not a delegate bound by the instructions of his electors.[75] By the same token, Burke would have been horrified by party instructions and party discipline.

On the other hand, Burke's party organized "connections" in parliament; it did not, nor was it intended to, organize members outside of parliament. This was something yet to come; and something that Burke neither foresaw nor advocated. In the terminology of Tocqueville, Burke's party was still an "aristocratic," not a "democratic" party. The difference is momentous. As Tocqueville perceptively noted: "It is natural, in democratic countries, for the members of political assemblies to have their minds [*songent*] more with their electors than with their party, while in aristocracies, they are more concerned about their party than their electors."[76] The question can be formulated, correspondingly, as follows: How do we pass from the aristocratic, in-group, parliamentary party to the electoral, out-group and, ultimately, democratic-oriented party?

With due allowance for how tortuously and unevenly this transition occurred historically, logically the sequence can be reconstructed neatly. To put it sweepingly, a government responsible to the houses also becomes, in the long run, a government responsible to the people and thereby a *responsive* government, a government attentive to, and influenced by, the voice of the people. But this is far too sweeping. How and why these developments occurred must be seen in more detail, and can be represented as in the scheme of Table 1 (with the understanding that the arrows indicate only the major causal vectors).

In and by itself, responsible government implies only that ministers must obtain funds from, and are exposed to the criticism of, parliament. But the members of parliament can well remain atomized, i.e., lack the party-type connections advocated by Burke. Since Burke did explain why it was to the advantage of the members of the Commons to unite along party lines, by now this first step can be taken for granted. Nonetheless, this leaves us with a constitutional "rule of gentlemen" *for* the people. Things remain very much as Burke would have liked them to remain, unless and until the electorate becomes meaningful in either size or quality or both. It is unnecessary to review the manifold forces that led to the first extension of the suffrage and, in England, to the 1832 Reform Act. There was, doubtlessly, growing pressure from below. As Daalder puts it: "The modern political party . . . can be described with little exaggeration as the child of the Industrial Revolution."[77] Yet the process was triggered, at the outset, from above. Probably the members of parliament felt that their voice would gain

Table 1. *From responsible government to party government*

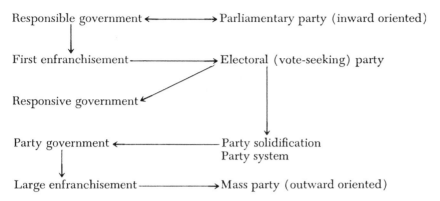

weight if their representativeness were less presumptive and more electoral. Above all, however, the electorate was involved as a result of mutual outbidding between parliament and government. A government faced by an intractable parliament would appeal, beyond parliament, to the vote of the constituencies – as William Pitt did. And a parliament is bound to retaliate on the same grounds. The process was triggered, then, by an endogenous development, by the internal dialectics between parliament and cabinet; but it gained momentum and was subsequently determined by exogenous forces.

Aside from the United States, the first waves of enfranchisement stood a very long way from universal male suffrage.[78] Yet enfranchisement stands out, regardless of the numbers involved, as a decisive turning point. It was the redistricting of the "rotten boroughs" and the entry of voters who could not be bribed, or would no longer follow the instructions of their betters, that moved the party from where Burke had placed it. The more the members of parliament need votes, the more the party-in-parliament – i.e., the aristocratic party – must develop outward tentacles, that is, the more the parliamentary party will need, if only at election time, the addition of an electoral party, a vote-collecting and, ultimately, a vote-seeking instrument. The vote-collecting party may not make much difference; but the vote-seeking party does. If votes are to be sought, grievances must be attended to, and demands must be, to some extent, satisfied.

Two feedbacks are thus implied when elections become real. One is the *solidification* of party, meaning by this that at some point parties are held together not only by "principles" but also by the electoral advantages of becoming stabilized, or more stable. Too much swinging,

21

splitting, or name changing ends up becoming a liability. It is at this point that the protoparties, or the "parts" that were formerly internal divisions of the inner (and upper) circle, become parties in our sense, that is, divisions of the country at large. And this is what Duverger implies when asserting – correctly – that "truly called parties are only a century old."[79]

The second feedback is the one that leads from responsible to *responsive* government – or, at any rate, to a combination of the two. A responsible government need not respond beyond its technical responsibility: Its standard is to behave responsibly and competently. A responsive government is, instead, a government that is required to yield to demands. If measured by the yardstick of competent and technically responsible behavior, a responsive government may well be declared "irresponsible," i.e., as abdicating its own independent responsibility. The two things are thus very different, and their balance cantankerous. Nonetheless, one can speak of a democratic party – meaning an outward, demophile orientation – only when the emphasis shifts from responsibility to responsiveness.

Logically, it would appear that it is responsive government that entails party government proper. The party can hardly meet the demands through which it competes for votes unless it can govern: hence party government. Historically, however, the sequence might well be reversed, for many circumstances impinge upon this development. The matter can be left at saying that responsive government and party government tend to be conterminous. One might also say, still more cautiously, that there is no compelling reason for party governance until parties really have to "return" electoral returns.

When all these strands come together, we obtain not only the modern party but also the *party system* as a structural requirement of the political system and thereby as one of its subsystems. While parties become parties in the wake of the first extension of the suffrage – that is, under conditions of very low participation and of very restricted enfranchisement – the same does not apply to the establishment of the party system. The party system structuring of the polity emerges only when the enfranchisement and other conditions reach a "critical mass" and involve a substantial section of the community. One has to be vague on this size requirement, because of its great variance in timing and tempo. It is clear, nevertheless, that universal or near-universal suffrage is not the necessary condition for parties to become a subsystem of the political system – England being the eminent case in point. Universal enfranchisement brings about mass parties and the "externally created" party.[80] It therefore modifies the party system but is not required for establishing it. As for the sequence, the historical record does not point to a clear or uniform progression for all the steps recalled in Table 1; but a nonreversible order does appear to exist for three major events: (i) responsible government, (ii) the "reality" of elections, (iii) the establishment of parties as a subsystem. This sequence is nonreversible in that elections and participation alone, i.e., without constitutional and responsible government, are by no means necessarily conducive to a party-based polity – a party *system*.

All of this seems obvious enough in retrospect. It was neither obvious nor grasped while it was happening. We take it as self-evident that if a society is consulted, and the more extensively it is consulted, the more the expression and articulation of its demands require intermediary linkages and transmission belts. Yet that these linkages would take the form and nature of a party-type arrangement was not only unforeseen but largely misapprehended. All the developments just recounted occurred – let it be repeated – within the mental fog of practical experience, out of the force of facts far more than out of the foresight, let alone the design, of ideas.

Upon returning from the United States, where he had seen the first modern parties emerging and operating under democratic conditions, Tocqueville's overall comment was that "parties are an evil [*mal*] inherent to free governments."[81] This was not saying much more than Washington had said. And while Tocqueville perceived the difference between aristocratic and democratic parties, his emphasis was definitely elsewhere, namely, on the qualitative (not quantitative) distinction between "big" and "small" parties, the former based on principles and general ideas and the latter being in no way different from "dangerous factions."[82] Not only was Tocqueville's interest in parties very peripheral, but his concern was very much in the line of all his predecessors: that parties should not be factions.[83] In 1888 James Bryce provided, in his *American Commonwealth,* an extensive description of how the party machines operated in the United States; but his theoretical contribution did not go much further than asserting (in 1921) that "parties are inevitable. No free large country has been without them. No one has shown how representative government could be worked without them."[84]

Until World War I, the two major authors dealing specifically with the party topic were Ostrogorski[85] and Michels.[86] In spite of major differences, both were concerned with, and dismayed by, the undemocratic and oligarchic nature of parties, not with how parties entered – as a subsystem – the theory and practice of democracy. Their problem was democracy *without* or *within* parties, not democracy as a political system resulting *from*, and based *upon*, parties. Michels presented his book as a "sociology" of parties. Nonetheless, the founder of the sociology of parties proper was not Michels but Max Weber.[87] It was Weber who called attention – with far greater subtlety than Marx and

23

Engels – to the social bases of politics in general and of parties in particular; and his insights to this effect are as penetrating as they are innumerable. With respect to the developments reviewed here, however, Weber was largely responsible for having suggested a misleading historical perspective. His sociological thread led him to assert, for instance, that "also the parties of antiquity and of the middle ages can be designated as parties,"[88] thereby perpetuating the confusion between factions and/or former "parts" (such as the Guelfs and the Ghibellines) and modern parties. The fact that parties are such because they enter an entirely novel *political construction* and are, in turn, shaped by it escaped Weber, as it escaped his predecessors and contemporaries.

It bears repeating, therefore, that the term party becomes distinctive and acquires a positive connotation because it indicates a new entity. The name is different because the thing is different. Mansfield eloquently introduces the novelty of the case: "We must appraise the near-ubiquity of party government today in the light of its complete absence in the past." But I must take exception to his subsequent explanation: "On this evidence it seems necessary to distinguish parties from party government. . . . Because the reason for partisanship is so simple and compelling, the respectability, not the existence, of party is the distinguishing mark of party government."[89] It is very true that the reasons for partisanship are simple and compelling; but they have not generated, over the millenniums, parties: They have produced "factions." Hence it is the existence of *party*, not its respectability, that needs to be explained.

1.4 A rationalization

The question may be raised: What is the present-day relevance of antecedents? Why go back to the origins? The answer is that the past is the original map, the design of the foundations. In the course of time the building grows, and the foundations are covered up. This is why from time to time it is well to look back at the original design. Among other reasons, we become so involved with subtleties that we lose sight of fundamentals. We seldom ask: Why? What is *the* purpose of a party system? Parties came about because they were needed, because they served a purpose. Do they still serve that same purpose? And if they do not, or if they are being used in the pursuit of other purposes, it should be made clear; for it is *not* clear. We are traveling more and more through the ever-growing jungle of party politics without really knowing where we started, let alone where we are heading.

For some 150 years parties have fared and developed as a matter of practice far more than of theory. For this reason, among others, the message tends to get lost. And I submit that the message can be recaptured and the rationale of the party era reconstructed – if only in a skeletal fashion – on the basis of the following three premises:

1. Parties are *not* factions.
2. A party is *part-of-a-whole*.
3. Parties are channels of *expression*.

1. Parties are not factions; that is, unless a party is different from a faction, it is not a party (but a faction). The perception of this difference is still retained by most languages and certainly in ordinary usage.[90] Parties are often criticized, but they are *not* an evil by definition. Faction is always, at least in common parlance, a bad name, and factions *are* an evil. Parties – it is often said – are a necessity. Factions are not a necessity; they simply exist. Apparently the term faction has not lost, in common use, its original connotation, namely, that factions are nothing but the expression of *personal* conflicts, of ego-regarding and public-disregarding behavior. In the words of Burke, factional strife represents only a mean and interested struggle for place and emolument.[91]

To be sure, party members are not altruists, and the existence of parties by no means eliminates selfish and unscrupulous motivations. The power-seeking drives of politicians remain constant. What varies is the processing and the constraints that are brought to bear on such drives. Even if the party politician is motivated by crude self-interest, his behavior must depart – if the constraints of the system are operative – from the motivation. The difference is, then, that parties are instrumental to collective benefits, to an end that is not merely the private benefit of the contestants. Parties link people to a government, while factions do not. Parties enhance a set of system capabilities, while factions do not. In short, parties are *functional* agencies – they serve purposes and fulfill roles – while factions are not.[92] This is so, ultimately, because a party is a part of a whole attempting to serve the purposes of the whole, whereas a faction is only a part for itself. Of course, parties may be dysfunctional, and this is why parties too are subject to strong criticism; but not to the criticism that applies to factions – lack of functional justification.[93]

If parties are not factions, it would be wrong to forget, on the other hand, that parties have long been preceded by factions and that it is the reason for faction – not for party – that is simple and compelling. The resulting *caveat* is that parties may well relapse into something resembling faction. In this sense factionalism is the ever-present temptation of a party arrangement and its ever-possible degeneration. This helps to explain not only why party systems fail and collapse but also why the ancient theme of the horror of factionalism may from time to time be revived in the censure, or even the rejection of parties.[94] This equally goes to justify the recurrent demand for a direct, partyless democracy.[95] The actual distinction between party and faction may indeed become fine; but precisely for this reason it should be kept conceptually firm. The more parties come to behave like factions, the more it is important to realize that our rebuke is directed less against the idea of party than against its factional degeneration.

2. A party is part-of-a-whole. Semantically speaking, "party" conveys – and is meant to convey – the idea of part. This association calls our attention to the subtle link between a part and its whole. A whole can be conceived monolithically, or organically, that is, as not being composed of parts. However, this means merely that we have no reason to be concerned with parts (and parties). But if we are concerned with those parts that are parties, the implication is that we are considering a *pluralistic whole*. And if the polity is conceived as a pluralistic whole, then what is required is a whole made out of *parts* in the plural: a whole-of-parts, and indeed resulting from the interplay of its parts. This is the same as saying that the whole cannot be identified with just *one* part. In this case a part is not a part, and a whole is not a whole.

If it is wrong to neglect the association between part and party, it would also be quite wrong, on the other hand, to consider the party as a part that is unrelated to the whole. If a party is not a part capable of governing for the sake of the whole, that is, in view of a general interest, then it does not differ from a faction. Although a party only represents a part, this part must take a *non-partial* approach to the whole.

Admittedly, "serving the whole" is vague. But the vagueness of an imperative may well enhance its general applicability, as long as the imperative is meaningful or can be meaningfully specified. It can also be conceded that the general interest, the public interest, the common good, and similar normative symbols lack objective standards.[96] But the conclusion does not follow that they are mere pieces of rhetoric or that they merely indicate whatever the politician's overall design may be.[97] That standards are relative and subjective does not imply that there are none.[98] Granted that there are many publics and many public interests, each of them can be distinguished from, and is at any time opposed by, particularistic, private-regarding interests. What is in the general interest is always debatable, especially because we debate what is *more* in the general interest of which public. But it can always be demonstrated beyond doubt that some things do *not* maximize the collective welfare of any public, that they are *not* in the general interest (no matter how defined). For every issue has solutions that benefit only the few, if not a single individual, to the detriment of the many. Collective benefits do not come about gratis and on their own; but collective non-benefits, or collective damages, are always around the corner. The common weal, the public interest, and similar de-ontological symbols can be dismissed if, and only if, it can be demon-strated that they bear no weight in human motivation, that they lack behavioral reality. Meanwhile, it is well to bear in mind that the chances of a *concordia discors,* a balancing of togetherness and separa-tion, hinge on the effectiveness of the imperative that requests the winning "part" to be "impartial," to govern for all and not only for itself.

3. Parties are channels of expression. That is to say, parties belong, first and foremost, to the means of representation: They are an instru-ment, or an agency, for *representing* the people by *expressing* their demands.[99] As parties developed, they did not develop – throughout the nineteenth and well into the twentieth centuries – to convey to the people the wishes of the authorities but far more to convey to the authorities the wishes of the people. This is by no means to assert that *all* parties *always* express and represent. I am saying only that those parties that are parts (in the plural) have found their essential raison d'être and their nonreplaceable role in implementing representative and responsive government. It is important to keep in mind that this development was largely natural, or unplanned. Parties became means of expression along with the process of democratization of politics. At the same time, responsible government became "responsive" precisely because parties supplied the channels for articulating, communicating, and implementing the demands of the governed. It was, then, the cumulative, self-sustaining progression from faction to party, from re-sponsible to responsive government, and from the parliamentary to the electoral party, that established the fundamental function, functional role, and systemic placement of parties – in short, what parties *are for.*

Thus far I have spoken of parties, somewhat interchangeably, as (i) representative agencies and (ii) expressive instruments. Corre-latively, their major activities can be referred to as a representative function and an expressive function.[100] But my emphasis is on the latter.

The notion of representation confronts, with respect to parties, two major difficulties. In the first place, the concept has received a great deal of technical elaboration, and it would be out of proportion and too demanding to bring these intricacies to bear on the party topic. While there is no expression without some loosely conceived repre-sentative capacity, it is highly controversial whether parties can be said to represent their voters (rather than their members). In the second place, and still more important, representation is perfectly conceivable and possible without parties. As a matter of fact, the theory of representation does not fare well in accommodating parties.[101] On both counts, therefore, the representative function of parties can hardly be brought forward as their major and qualifying function.

Another suggestion might be to speak of "voice function" and to perceive parties as voice channels. The suggestion arises from Hirschman's brilliant analytical treatment of the term.[102] Yet "voice" is too broad for our purposes, for it can also apply, *inter alia,* to demonstrations, riots and still other ways of making oneself heard. Parties enter this focus, therefore, as *one* of very many, and very diverse, avenues and ways of "voicing."

Above all, then, parties are expressive instruments performing an *expressive function.* The suggestion is conveyed, thereby, that parties can best be conceived as means of communication – and perhaps under cybernetic auspices. However, my notion of expressive function is not intended only in the literal sense that parties are upgoing transmission belts of claims and grievances. There is more to it. If parties were doing nothing more – as instruments of expression – than "transmitting information," then it would follow that their time is bygone. Parties could well be replaced by opinion polls, surveys, and – as technology already permits – by the citizens themselves sitting at their computer terminals and typing in, for machine-processed auscultation, their political preferences and thoughts. However, parties provide for something that no poll or machine can supply: They transmit demands *backed by pressure.* The party throws its own weight into the demands it feels compelled to respond to. And my notion of expressive function should be understood with this qualification appended. As Key put it, "political parties are basic institutions for the translation of mass preferences into public policy."[103] In a similar vein a very dissimilar author, Schattschneider, declared that "the only kind of organization that can translate into fact the idea of majority rule is the political party."[104] Both had in mind, it seems to me, the expressive function. Putting it another way, my expressive function is a label – the best shorthand I have been able to find – for what they had in mind.

The objection remains that my reconstruction highlights only half of the picture. Parties do not only *express;* they also *channel.* In Neumann's wording, parties "organize the chaotic public will."[105] They aggregate, select, and, eventually, deviate and distort. This is indeed so. And the objection can be pushed further by asserting that *more* than expressing and reflecting public opinion parties shape, and indeed manipulate, opinion. This can equally be conceded, excepting for the "more." I would only concede that parties *also* form and manipulate opinion. For the two sides of the coin – expression and manipulation – can hardly be treated as equivalent. Granted that parties are a two-way communication channel, the conclusion does not follow that parties are a transmission channel downward *to the same extent* that they are a transmission belt upward. There is manipulation and manipulation; and as long as parties are parts (in the plural), a party system lends itself to expression from below far more than to manipulation from above. It may well be that the people have no opinions of their own or that their opinions are largely formed by opinion makers. However, this circumstance only confirms the extent to which a multi-centered, crosscutting manipulative impact differs from a unicentered, self-reinforcing type of manipulation, thereby indicating that real manipulation, or "repressive manipulation," takes over precisely when party pluralism subsides.

It is a disturbing paradox that our growing quest for precision and measurement should be paralleled by a growing neglect of *weighing words* and by a growing imprecision of the words chosen. This makes it all the more necessary to begin from, or revert to, what is fundamental. To say that a party system is a pluralistic system of "parts" that forcibly "express" the opinions of the governed does leave a great deal unsaid – granted. But it is the premise that gives perspective and proportion to the many things that remain to be said.

NOTES TO CHAPTER 1

1 Voltaire's article is on "Faction" (1778 Geneva ed. of the *Encyclopédie,* vol. XIII p. 765). However, the article on "Party" reads: "party is a faction, interest or power [*puissance*] which is considered opposed to another"; and one of the examples given is that "Italy has been torn for centuries between the parties of Guelphs and Ghibellines." We thus come full circle. The quotations can also be found in Voltaire's *Dictionnaire Philosophique.*

2 See, in general, Sergio Cotta, "La Nascita dell' Idea di Partito nel Secolo XVIII," in *Atti Facoltà di Giurisprudenza Università Perugia,* LXI, Cedam, 1960; Erwin Faul, "Verfemung, Duldung und Anerkennung des Parteiwesens in der Geschichte des Politischen Denkens," *Politische Vierteljahresschrift,* March 1964, pp. 60–80; Mario A. Cattaneo, *Il Partito Politico nel Pensiero dell' Illuminismo e della Rivoluzione Francese,* Giuffrè, 1964; Harvey C. Mansfield, Jr., *Statesmanship and Party Government: A Study of Burke and Bolingbroke,* The University of Chicago Press, 1965. Cotta is particularly relevant for Machiavelli, Montesquieu, and Bolingbroke; Cattaneo focuses on the protagonists of the French Revolution; Mansfield concentrates, in spite of this title, on Burke. I have also found very useful, for the overall constitutional setting of the party debate, Mario Galizia, *Carattere del Regime Parlamentare Inglese del Settecento,* Giuffrè, 1969.

3 Machiavelli, *Discorsi sopra la Prima Deca di Tito Livio,* I, 4 and 7. The difference is that the Romans handled "tempers" by "ordinary means," while factions and sects testify to the recourse to "extraordinary routes."

4 *Considerations sur les Causes de la Grandeur des Romains et de leur Décadence,* ch. 9.

5 See *L'Esprit des Lois,* XIX, 27 (in ed. Garnier, 1949, t. I, p. 16).

The significant passage to this effect is, however, in the *Lettres Persanes*, CXXXVI, where Montesquieu notes that in England "one sees freedom emerging incessantly from the flames of dissent and sedition." But no reference is made to parties.

6 Book XI, ch. 6.

7 See, e.g., *Pensées*, 1802: "Liberty giving frequently birth to two factions, the superior faction is pitiless in exploiting its advantages. A faction which dominates is no less terrible than a prince in fury." See also *Pensées* 631, 1816; and *L'Esprit des Lois*, III, 3.

8 Major author, for already in 1701 John Toland had published the *Art of Governing by Partys* (note the spelling). His position was this: "Divisions ought carefully to be avoided in all good Governments, and a King can never lessen himself more than by heading of a Party; for thereby he becomes only the King of a faction, and ceases to be the common father of his people" (p. 41). For the earlier and minor writings see Caroline Robbins, " 'Discordant Parties': A Study of the Acceptance of Party by Englishmen," *PSQ*, December 1958, pp. 505–529.

9 *The Idea of a Patriot King* (1738), in *The Works of Lord Bolingbroke* (hereinafter called *Works*), Carey and Hart, in 4 vols., Philadelphia, 1841, vol. II, p. 401. All my page references are from this edition. See also, ibid., p. 402: "Parties, even before they degenerate into absolute factions, are still numbers of men associated together for certain purposes, and certain interests, which are not . . . those of the community by others. A more private or personal interest comes but too soon . . . to be superadded, and to grow predominant in them . . . but such a party is then become a faction."

10 *A Dissertation upon Parties* (1733–1734) (hereinafter called *Dissertation*), Letter V, in *Works*, vol. II, p. 50. See also Letter XIX, p. 168, where Bolingbroke makes the point that the difference between parties is "real," not "nominal," only when it is a "difference of principles."

11 *Dissertation*, Dedication, in *Works*, vol. II, p. 11.

12 In his words, "The two parties were in truth become factions in the strict sense of the word." (*Of the State of Parties at the Accession of King George the First*, in *Works*, vol. II, p. 433).

13 *Dissertation*, Letter IV, in *Works*, vol. II, p. 48. Note also the proximity to Burke with respect to Burke's celebrated definition of representation in his Bristol Address (below, n. 75).

14 *Dissertation*, Letter XIX, in *Works*, vol. II, p. 167.

15 One is reminded of Hobbes' argument in favor of the Leviathan; but also of Marx's dictatorship of the proletariat: the proletariat seizing power to end all power and the state to end the state. In Bolingbroke's words, a country party is "the last party," the party whose interest is to "destroy every future excuse for party" (in Galizia, op. cit., p. 31). The difference is, of course, that Bolingbroke's country party was a defensive, not an offensive, instrument.

16 In *Works*, vol. II, pp. 11, 21.

17 Aside from the two major writings (*A Dissertation upon Parties* and *The Idea of a Patriot King*, which cover the period 1733–1738) and the essay *Of the State of Parties at the Accession of King George the First* (cit.), one should also see *The Craftsman* (Caleb

d'Anvers, ed., starting in 1726), esp. nos. 17 and 40 (1727), and the *Remarks on the History of England* (1730), esp. Letters VIII, XI, XIV, and XXIII.

18 Part I, Essay VIII: *Of Parties in General*, p. 58. Hume's *Essays, Moral, Political and Literary* are divided into Part I (1742) and Part II (1752). All my page references are from vol. III of *The Philosophical Works of David Hume* (hereinafter called *Works*), Edinburgh ed. of 1826, in 4 vols.

19 *Of the Coalition of Parties*, Part II, Essay XIV, in *Works*, vol. III, p. 538. The difference appears to be that Hume drops the chimera of the "patriot King," Bolingbroke's constitutional version of the enlightened despot, and lays the emphasis on a solution of "coalition," actually of coalescence among parties. The difference is, however, mostly in emphasis, for Bolingbroke also advocated a "coalition of parties" (see *Works*, vol. II, pp. 48, 438).

20 *Of the Parties of Great Britain*, Part I, Essay IX, in *Works*, vol. III, pp. 72–73.

21 This is particularly the case in *Of Parties in General* (Part I, Essay VIII) and *Of the Parties in Great Britain* (Part I, Essay IX), but also in the preceding essays of Part I, *That Politics May Be Reduced to a Science* (Essay III), *Of the First Principles of Government* (Essay IV), and *Of the Independence of Parliament* (Essay VI), where his criticism is directed against the "party men."

22 *Of Parties in General*, in *Works*, vol. III, p. 58.

23 Ibid., pp. 59–65. Emphasis in the original.

24 E.g.: "Were the British government proposed as a subject of speculation, one would immediately perceive in it a source of division and party, which it would be almost impossible for it . . . to avoid" (*Of the Parties in Great Britain*, in *Works*, p. 67, my italics).

25 As John Plamenatz rightly stresses, "As a philosopher, an epistemologist, Hume has received his due. . . . As a social and political theorist less than justice has been done to him" (*Man and Society*, McGraw-Hill, 1963, I, p. 299). In his own criticism of Hume's theory of parties, however, even Plamenatz does some injustice to his author (see esp. pp. 320–324) by failing to appreciate that Hume was actually dealing with factions, not with the parties on the basis of which Plamenatz passes his judgment.

26 *Thoughts on the Cause of the Present Discontents* (1770), in *The Works of Edmund Burke*, Boston, Little, Brown, 1839 (in 9 volumes), vol. I, pp. 425–426. My page numbers refer to this edition.

27 Ibid., p. 426.

28 Ibid., p. 430. See also p. 387: "The court party resolve the whole into faction"; and p. 421: "[The King's men are] more intent on the emoluments than on the duties of office."

29 Ibid., pp. 421–424, *passim*.

30 Ibid., p. 428.

31 Harvey Mansfield, Jr., "Party Government and the Settlement of 1688," *APSR*, December 1964, pp. 937, 945. On the eighteenth-century English parties, Lewis B. Namier is the fundamental source. See esp. *The Structure of Politics at the Accession of George III*, 2nd ed., St. Martin's Press, 1957, and also his *Monarchy and the Party System*, Oxford University Press, 1952.

32 Note that I am not implying that Burke actually conceived a gov-

ernment by party. In this respect I differ from the main thesis of Mansfield's *Statesmanship and Party Government*, op. cit.

33 As this chapter shows, there is little point, and it is very misleading, to speak seriously of Greek and Roman "parties" or to recall as such the Guelfs and Ghibellines or even the Levellers. The eighteenth-century parties were, at best, proto-parties. By retrogressing further we encounter the ancestors of the ancestors. Among the influential spokesmen for the contrary view, cf. George H. Sabine, *A History of Political Theory*, Holt, Rinehart and Winston, 1951, ch. 24, and Leslie Lipson, *The Democratic Civilization*, Oxford University Press, 1964, pp. 307, 317. See also below, 1.3, Max Weber, and n. 87.

34 This is well documented by Cattaneo, *Il Partito Politico nel Pensiero dell' Illuminismo e della Rivoluzione Francese*, op. cit. While it pursues a different problem, a wealth of documentation to this effect is also in J. B. Talmon, *The Rise of Totalitarian Democracy*, Beacon Press, 1952. See also Yves Levy, "Les Partis et la Démocratie," in *Le Contrat Social*, 1959, no. 2 (pp. 79–86), and no. 4 (pp. 217–221); and "Police and Policy," in *GO*, July–September 1966, esp. pp. 490–496. Levy, however, overstates the impact of Rousseau, who simply reasserted, in his condemnation of parties, the established view.

35 All the quotations are drawn from Cattaneo, op. cit., pp. 84, 86, 89, 95–96. Some authors speak of a "Jacobin model." E.g., C. B. Macpherson, *Democracy in Alberta*, University of Toronto Press, 1953, pp. 241–242, writes that according to the Jacobins there must be "a single mass party which, by embracing all true democrats, transcends party." This appears to be a misreading. No "mass party" was in question, and Robespierre only repeated, if unawares, Bolingbroke. Cf. this statement in *Le Défenseur de la Constitution*, no. 3, May 1792: "There are only two parties left in the Republic: those of the good and bad citizens, that is, of the French people and of ambitious and avid individuals." The notion of a Jacobin model is developed by Felix Gross, "Beginnings of Major Patterns of Political Parties," *Il Politico*, 3, 1965, pp. 586–592. But his argument is an *ex post* rationalization. During the entire nineteenth century, continental Europe looked at the British model; and if the outcome was often quite different, this fact is hardly due to the influence of alternative intellectual models.

36 See Cattaneo, op. cit., pp. 75–77.

37 *The Federalist*, no. 10.

38 For the overall context see R. A. Dahl's brilliant analysis of "Madisonian Democracy," *A Preface to Democratic Theory*, The University of Chicago Press, 1956, pp. 4–33.

39 Washington's Farewell Address is dated September 17, 1796. See in *Documents of American History*, 5th ed., Appleton, 1949, I, p. 172. The italics are mine.

40 Above, n. 19.

41 The proximity of Jefferson to Bolingbroke is noted by Mansfield, Jr., *Statesmanship and Party Government*, cit., pp. 113, 196. More generally, see William N. Chambers, *Political Parties in a New Nation: The American Experience 1776–1809*, Oxford University Press, 1963, *passim*, and with reference to Jefferson esp. pp. 6, 92–93, 106–112, 181–183.

42 *De l'Influence des Passions sur le Bonheur des Individus et des Nations,* Lausanne, 1796, ch. 7.

43 *Principes de Politique,* ch. VII, in *Oeuvres,* Pléiade, Paris, 1957, p. 1158.

44 This is not to concur with the view that toleration of opposition is the secular product of religious toleration and that parties are secularized sects and congregations. No such direct link exists, and my linkage is between toleration and pluralism.

45 See esp. *Contrat Social,* Book II, ch. 3; Book IV, ch. 1; and above, n. 34.

46 As noted above, 1.1 and n. 6, Montesquieu had no place for parties in outlining the English constitution. Bolingbroke is even more interesting in this respect, for his antiparty stand was as explicit as his emphasis on the separateness of the "parts" of the constitution. In the *Remarks on the History of England* he approvingly quoted and defended the assertion that "in a constitution like ours the safety of the whole depends on the balance of the parts, and the balance of the parts on their mutual independency on each other" (Letter VII, in *Works,* vol. I, p. 331). And Bolingbroke understood the latter to imply that "the resolutions of each part . . . be taken independently and without any influence, direct or indirect, on the others" (p. 333).

47 Even today, in most countries parties remain, juridically, private associations with no constitutional recognition. Among the few notable exceptions are the Bonn Fundamental Law and the French Constitution of 1958.

48 *The Rise of Totalitarian Democracy,* op. cit., p. 44.

49 See G. Sartori, *Democratic Theory,* Praeger, 1967, chs. 12, 13, 15, and esp. pp. 261–268, 293–298, 358–359, 377–378.

50 Therefore, Talmon's argument that the eighteenth-century fathers of democracy postulated a world that would lead to what he calls "totalitarian democracy" is a reconstructed argument. If we account for their real motivations, there was no totalitarian goal in their minds. They too were individualists revolting against the Middle Ages.

51 Implicitly, my argument is analogous to Max Weber's mental experiment on the Protestant ethics. Weber showed that the material factors that might have caused capitalism did exist also in India and China, while the *Wirtschaftsethik* did not. Likewise, it was not structural differentiation as an endogenous and material process that can account for a pluralistic belief system. For Weber, see *Gesammelte Aufsatze zur Religionssoziologie,* 3 vols., Tubingen, 1922.

52 Edward A. Shils, *The Torment of Secrecy,* Heineman, 1956, p. 153.

53 Frederic J. Fleron, Jr., makes the point very well: ". . . the connection between modernization, development, differentiation, division of labor, industrialization, democracy, and pluralism" tend to be "related definitionally rather than empirically," that is, in terms of one another rather than as "lawful connections between the processes denoted by the concepts" ("Toward a Reconceptualization of Political Change in the Soviet Union," *CP,* January 1969, p. 234).

54 An apex of this confusing extension can be found in Leo Kuper and M. G. Smith, eds., *Pluralism in Africa,* University of California

Press, 1969. This is an aspect of the boomerang effect discussed *infra*, 8.4.

55 For a general overview see John W. Chapman, "Voluntary Association and the Political Theory of Pluralism," in J. R. Pennock, J. W. Chapman, eds., *Voluntary Associations*, Atherton Press, 1969, pp. 87–118. For a historical analysis of how political pluralism struck roots and evolved in the West during the nineteenth and twentieth centuries, see Gian Paolo Prandstràller, *Valori e Libertà: Contributo ad una Sociologia del Pluralismo Politico Occidentale*, Comunità, 1966.

56 I take this to be a descriptive, not a normative, statement, in that it does not express the values of the observer but the values of those observed.

57 The first quote is from Robert A. Nisbet, *Community and Power*, Oxford University Press, 1962, p. 265; the second is from William Kornhauser, *The Politics of Mass Society*, Free Press, 1959, p. 81. Kornhauser is also very relevant on how pluralism relates to intermediate groups (esp. pp. 76–84, 131–141) – a major concern of Tocqueville and Durkheim.

58 For the emphasis on conflict see Ralph Dahrendorf, "Out of Utopia: Toward a Reorientation of Sociological Analysis," *AJS*, September 1958. See also D. A. Rustow, "Agreement, Dissent and Democratic Fundamentals," in Kurt von Beyme, ed., *Theory and Politics*, Nijhoff, 1971. In a different vein, Bernard Crick, "The Strange Death of the American Theory of Consensus," *PQ*, January–May 1972. In general, see Lewis A. Coser, *The Functions of Social Conflict*, Free Press, 1954, and *Continuities in the Study of Social Conflict*, Free Press, 1967. A massive bibliography (up to 1954) is in Jessie Bernard et al., *The Nature of Conflict*, UNESCO, 1957, pp. 225–310. It should be well understood that the text makes reference to "conflict" – period – not to "conflict of interest" and even less to "latent" conflicts.

59 Balfour's dictum is in his Introduction (1927) to Bagehot, *The English Constitution*, p. xiv. On the concept of dissent see the distinctions of Edward B. McLean, "Limits of Dissent in a Democracy," *Il Politico*, September 1970, pp. 443–456, among (i) innovation, (ii) disagreement, (iii) deviance, and (iv) disobedience.

60 The most recent confirmation to this effect is the case of Northern Ireland. See Richard Rose, *Governing Without Consensus: An Irish Perspective*, Beacon Press, 1971. Colombia's decade of *violencia* between 1948–1958 is another good instance (*infra*, ch. 6, n. 84).

61 A concrete illustration of this conception can be found, e.g., in R. A. Dahl, *Who Governs?*, Yale University Press, 1961, pp. 315–325, and, more extensively, in his *Pluralist Democracy in the United States: Conflict and Consent*, Rand McNally, 1967. Charles E. Lindblom, *The Intelligence of Democracy: Decision Making Through Mutual Adjustment*, Free Press, 1965, is also relevant in this respect, if only by implication.

62 Amitai Etzioni, *The Active Society*, Free Press, 1968, p. 470. Etzioni's analysis of consensus in ch. 17 (esp. pp. 466–484) is very insightful. For a review of definitions and approaches see, in general, Theodor M. Newcomb, "The Study of Consensus," in Robert K. Merton et al., eds., *Sociology Today*, Basic Books, 1959.

63 For the many qualifications and agonizing intricacies, which I cannot follow here, of this process, see the brilliant historical outline of Hans Daalder, "Parties, Elites and Political Development in Western Europe," in J. LaPalombara and M. Weiner, eds., *Political Parties and Political Development*, Princeton University Press, 1966. For a masterful analytical dissection see Stein Rokkan, "Nation-Building, Cleavage Formation and the Structuring of Mass Politics," in *Citizens, Elections, Parties*, McKay, 1970. In the perspective of polyarchy the sequential ordering is neatly sketched by Robert A. Dahl, *Poliarchy: Participation and Opposition*, Yale University Press, 1971, ch. 3. On the crisis of legitimacy notion in particular, see the chapter by Lucian W. Pye in Leonard Binder et al., *Crises and Sequences in Political Development*, Princeton University Press, 1971.

64 The confusion between a substantive "ruling" and a formal "rule" arises in English. For the meaning rendered as "regulatory principle" the French word is *règle*, and the Italian *regola*.

65 From a somewhat different angle the bearing of pluralism on majority rule theory is well detected by Leon B. Epstein, *Political Parties in Western Democracies*, Praeger, 1967, pp. 15–18, 357–358. The above does not detract that the majority principle also finds its limits and limitation in the unequal intensity of preferences (see G. Sartori, "Tecniche Decisionali e Sistema dei Comitati," *RISP*, 1, 1974, and "Will Democracy Kill Democracy? Decision-Making by Majorities and by Committees," *GO*, Spring 1975).

66 The importance of toleration – which I tend to consider the basis on which the rest of the edifice stands – is well highlighted by Plamenatz, *Man and Society*, op. cit., vol. I, ch. 2, "Liberty of Conscience." See also his chapter in Bryson et al., eds., *Aspects of Human Equality*, Harper, 1956.

67 See Kornhauser, *The Politics of Mass Society*, op. cit., pp. 80–81. David Truman, *The Governmental Process*, Knopf, 1951, is, in general, relevant to the point.

68 See Jean Blondel, *An Introduction to Comparative Government*, Praeger, 1969, pp. 74–75. Blondel elaborates the distinction between natural and imposed development on pp. 79–84 and, with specific references to parties, on pp. 103–111.

69 On African pluralism, above, n. 54; on the latter, as currently exemplified by India, see L. I. and Susan Rudolph, "The Political Role of India's Caste Associations," in Eric A. Nordlinger, ed., *Politics and Society*, Prentice-Hall, 1970. While the Rudolphs' focus is on how the caste "association can approximate a voluntary association" (even though birth in the caste remains a "necessary condition"), they make quite clear that appurtenance to the Indian caste is "completely ascriptive," that once born into a caste one "has no way to change social identity," and that the cultural and social homogeneity of the caste members "results in a sense of exclusiveness" (pp. 252–253).

70 Kenneth Janda (assisted by G. Rotkin and D. Sylvan), *ICPP Variables and Coding Manual*, 4th ed., March 1972, No. 3.4 of the "International Comparative Political Parties Project," Monograph Series, Northwestern University. The point is made, in general, by Karl Deutsch in noting that the "pluralism model" posits negative

(i.e., self-corrective and self-restraining) feedbacks on account of "cross-pressuring," i.e., of the fact that conflict positions are superimposed and, thereby, not reinforcing. ("Multipolar Power Systems and International Instability" [with J. D. Singer], *WP*, April 1964, pp. 393–394.) For other operational suggestions see Robert Presthus, "The Pluralist Framework," in Henry S. Kariel, ed., *Frontiers of Democratic Theory*, Random House, 1970, pp. 274–304.

71 *Experience and Its Modes*, Cambridge University Press, 1966, p. 321.

72 This is, e.g., the major focus of Mansfield, Jr., *Statesmanship and Party Government*, op. cit.

73 The full extent of party government proper is detailed by the "paradigm" of eight conditions set forth by Richard Rose, "The Variability of Party Government: A Theoretical and Empirical Critique," *PS*, IV, 1969.

74 *Thoughts on the Cause of the Present Discontents*, in *Works*, op. cit., p. 395. Emphasis in the text. See also p. 379: "It had always . . . been held the first duty of parliament to *refuse to support government, until power was in the hands of persons who were acceptable to the people, or while factions predominated in court in which the nation had no confidence.*" (Emphasis in the text.)

75 Burke's theory of representation was formulated in the *Bristol Address* of 1774 and has been as misapprehended as his idea of party. Just as Burke's party broke away from faction, his representation began the modern era by breaking away from the medieval notion of mandate. See my article "Representational Systems," in *International Encyclopedia of the Social Sciences*, Macmillan, and Free Press, 1968, XIII, esp. pp. 466–468. Cf. Heinz Eulau, et al., "The Role of the Representative: Some Empirical Observations on the Theory of E. Burke," *APSR*, December 1959, pp. 742–756.

76 *De la Démocratie en Amérique*, vol. II, I, 21 (p. 94 in Gallimard ed., 1961). The text of Tocqueville sounds very much like saying that in aristocracies the members of parliament are mostly concerned about their "part," or side, not about electors.

77 In LaPalombara and Weiner, eds., *Political Parties and Political Development*, op. cit., p. 52.

78 Suffrage extensions have been extensively analyzed by Stein Rokkan, *Citizens, Elections, Parties*, op. cit., Part II, pp. 145–247.

79 Maurice Duverger, *Les Partis Politiques*, 2nd rev. ed., Colin, 1954, p. 1. The book was first published in 1951. Reference is generally made to the original, for the English translation (Methuen, and Wiley, 1954) is not always accurate.

80 Basically, this refers to the Socialist and the Catholic parties. For the distinction between "internally created" and "externally created" party, see Duverger, *Les Partis Politiques*, op. cit., pp. 8–16. The mass party will be discussed in vol. II.

81 *Démocratie en Amérique*, op. cit., vol. I, II, 2 (p. 178).

82 Ibid., p. 79; and *Voyages en Sicile et aux Etats Unis*, 1957, pp. 196, 197–198, 260–261.

83 See in general the detailed analysis of Nicola Matteucci, "Il Problema del Partito Politico nelle Riflessioni d'Alexis de Tocqueville," *Il Pensiero Politico*, I, 1968.

84 *Modern Democracies*, Macmillan, 1921, vol. I, p. 119.

85 M. Ostrogorski, *Democracy and the Organization of Political Parties* (F. Clarke, trans.), Macmillan, 1902, 2 vols. (Vol. I is on England, Vol. II on the United States.) The best on Ostrogorski is the Introduction of Seymour Martin Lipset, "Ostrogorski and the Analytic Approach to the Comparative Study of Political Parties," to his abridged ed. (in one vol.) of the above-cited work, Quadrangle Books, 1964, pp. ix–lxv. Ostrogorski advocated, from an individualistic standpoint, the remedy of replacing parties with free-floating, i.e., non-institutionalized, leagues of voters dissolving in between elections. In the same vein he was preceded by Charles C. P. Clark, *The "Machine Abolished" and the People Restored to Power*, Putnam's, 1900.

86 Roberto Michels, *Political Parties: A Sociological Study of the Oligarchical Tendencies of Modern Democracy*, Free Press, 1962. Michels' title was, however, *Zur Sociologie des Parteiwesens in der Modernen Demokratie*, and the book first appeared in German in 1911 and in Italian in 1912. His study was focused on the German Socialist party, and his standpoint was that of a disappointed Socialist. The best on Michels is the Introduction of Juan Linz to the new Italian ed. of his above-cited work, Il Mulino, 1965. See also G. Sartori, "Democrazia, Burocrazia e Oligarchia nei Partiti," *RIS*, Luglio–Settembre 1960.

87 Max Weber's thoughts on parties are scattered in *Wirtschaft und Gesellschaft*, 4th ed., Tübingen, 1956, I, pp. 167–169 and esp. II, pp. 675–678, 845–858, 865–876. The major nucleus was written between 1917 and 1919.

88 Cit. in Giordano Sivini, ed., *Sociologia dei Partiti Politici*, Il Mulino, 1971, p. 16. But see *infra*, ch. 2, n. 8.

89 *Statesmanship and Party Government*, op. cit., p. 2.

90 This is to exclude only the recent usage of "faction" in American political science, to be discussed *infra*, 4.1. It seems to me, in fact, that English ordinary usage also retains the historical, negative connotation of the word, for one never hears an American or British politician saying "my faction."

91 *Supra*, 1.1 and n. 27 above.

92 Function is intended here in the innocent, common-sense meaning in which historians also use it. The technical complexities of the concept will be discussed in vol II.

93 This also goes to distinguish faction from interest group. Factions are not perceived as performing an "interest articulation function," as Almond would have it. But see *infra*, ch. 4.

94 In 1912 Benedetto Croce, who was to become a decade later the symbol of the liberal opposition to fascism, advocated, very much in the vein of Bolingbroke and Hume, a coalescence of parties and a party above parties. ("il Partito come Giudizio e come Pregiudizio," in *Cultura e Vita Morale*, Laterza, 1955, pp. 191–198.) In the aftermath of World War II Simone Weil wrote, very much in the spirit of Ostrogorski, that "the abolition of parties would almost represent an absolute good." ("Appunti sulla Soppressione dei Partiti Politici," in *Comunità*, gennaio–febbraio 1951, p. 5.)

95 This linkage is no longer in the forefront of the current demands for a participatory democracy. Yet one has only to read Ostrogorski and Simone Weil to realize its bearing.

96 These notions overlap but are not synonymous. E.g., the general interest can be defined distributively, i.e., as what interests each member of the collectivity under consideration; the common good has, instead, a more objective and indivisible connotation; while the public interest points to a regulative ideal. Much of the literature and of the controversy is in Carl J. Friedrich, ed., *The Public Interest*, Atherton Press, 1962, *passim*.

97 Cf., among the critics, Glendon Shubert, *The Public Interest: A Critique of the Theory of a Political Concept*, Free Press, 1961; Frank J. Sorauf, "The Public Interest Reconsidered," *JP*, November 1957 (both authors also contribute to the Friedrich vol. cited above); and Kenneth J. Arrow, "Public and Private Values," in Sidney Hook, ed., *Human Values and Economic Policy*, New York University Press, 1967. See, *contra*, Anthony Downs, "The Public Interest: Its Meaning in a Democracy," *Social Research*, Spring 1962; and esp. Felix Oppenheim, "Self-Interest and Public Interest," *PT*, August 1975. On the use of reason in elucidating the notion of public interest, see Richard E. Flathman, *The Public Interest, an Essay Concerning the Normative Discourse of Politics*, Wiley, 1966.

98 I have argued elsewhere that this is a highly unrealistic brand of "realism." (*Democratic Theory*, op. cit., ch. 3, esp. pp. 31–35.)

99 To the best of my knowledge, "expression" and "expressive function" were first used by Walter Bagehot, *The English Constitution* (1867), Oxford University Press, 1968, p. 117. Significantly, Bagehot applied the notion to the House of Commons, not to the role of parties.

100 My list does not include Almond's functions of "articulation" and "aggregation" of interests, because it is premature to enter too much detail.

101 See, again, my article "Representational Systems," in *International Encyclopedia of the Social Sciences*, loc. cit. On the role of parties in the representational process, see Austin Ranney, *The Doctrine of Responsible Party Government*, University of Illinois Press, 1956.

102 Albert O. Hirschman, *Exit, Voice, and Loyalty*, Harvard University Press, 1970.

103 V. O. Key, Jr., *Public Opinion and American Democracy*, Knopf, 1961, p. 433.

104 E. E. Schattschneider, *The Struggle for Party Government*, University of Maryland, 1948, p. 10.

105 In Sigmund Neumann, ed., *Modern Political Parties*, The University of Chicago Press, 1956, p. 397. The channeling function of parties is analyzed *infra*, 2.1 and 3.1.

2

The party as whole

2.1 No-party versus one party

Thus far party has meant *parties* – party indicated a plural. Single-party states materialized only after World War I, and until then the expression "one-party system" appeared a contradiction in terms. It made no more sense than to say "limbless quadruped." To be sure, one can take a quadruped and cut off its legs. But can we expect it to walk? Is it still a quadruped? According to the rationale of party pluralism, if a party is not a part, it is a pseudo-party; and if the whole is identified with just one party, it is a pseudo-whole. We are thus peremptorily confronted with the *sui generis* nature of the one party. So-called one-party systems exist. But do they have anything in common with the pluralistic party systems? That is, in common with the systems in which the parties are "parts" and the whole is the output of an interplay between more than one part?

To be sure, single parties differ widely, as we shall see. For the moment, however, we are dealing with the concept of the single party. This is also to say that the notion of unipartism is taken in its *strict sense*, with reference to the founders, i.e., to the first wave of single-party states of the 1920–1940 period: the Soviet, Nazi and Fascist types of unipartism.[1] Even so, the assertion that the single party identifies with the whole needs to be qualified, for it is obvious enough that the single party is *smaller* than the whole – in fact, it is often an elite party with restricted membership, a vanguard party that foreruns the whole. Yet the single party is not a "part" in any of the senses in which parties in the plural are such. Aside from the dimensional adjustment, the single party displays the characteristics of wholism, or of wholeness, in that it flatly rejects the idea of a whole resulting from a competitive interplay of parts. Even *within* the single party any kind of formalized intra-party division is banned: It is heresy, intolerable deviance. Thus communism, nazism, and (with lesser intensity) fascism testify to the existence, or resurgence, of a monochromatic belief system based on the principle of unanimity and the horror of dissent.[2]

On the other hand, and conversely, even though a whole is always *larger* than a part, whenever it is represented by only one party, it no longer can be an impartial whole, a whole above its parts. While a pluralistic whole is many sided, a monistic whole is one sided. Not only is a part without counterpart a pseudo-part, but a whole that does not contain parts (in the plural) lacks the completeness of a *real* whole – it is a "partial" whole, in both senses: It excludes and it takes sides.

These adjustments do not detract, then, from the fact that the rationale of party pluralism has no fit for the rationale of party monism. Hence what is the rationale of the one party? The issue may be usefully explored in the light of the following question: Why *one party* instead of *no parties?* Clearly, to the extent that the purpose of the one party is to eliminate "many parties," the difference would not be appreciable: The pure and simple prohibition of any part at all would do just as well.

The no-party notion comprises, however, two different cases: (i) the *partyless* and, in the main, the pre-party states (such as Saudi Arabia, Yemen, Jordan, Afghanistan, Nepal) and (ii) the *antiparty* states, that is, the regimes that have suppressed preexisting parties, take an antiparty stand, or profess an antiparty doctrine.[3] The first group is of little interest, for the partyless states are only traditional polities that have resisted or escaped, so far, modernization. Most of the antiparty states are, on the other hand, military regimes, which relate to underdeveloped or developing societies, and often claim a provisional status on emergency contingencies.[4] As Huntington puts it: "The no-party state is the natural state for a traditional society. As a society modernizes, however, the no-party state becomes increasingly the anti-party state."[5] What remains to be added is that the more modernized and/or developed the society, the more antipartism yields to unipartism – at least in the sense that the latter solution proves to be far less fragile and far more effective than the former. The one-party state is, in other words, the end solution that, when party pluralism fails, characterizes the politically developed societies. And my question bears precisely on why this should be the case.

Resuming the historical perspective, that is, the focus on the interwar founders of the one-party states *par excellence*, the first thing to note is that unipartism was born last and that this was by no means accidental. It was not merely that unipartism took over as a reaction to the failure and alleged shortcomings of party pluralism, as in Italy and Germany, or in the face of a very fragile and shaky beginning, as was the case with Kerenski in Russia. Ideally speaking, the single party can hardly be conceived unless one perceives the existence of a vacancy, of a party space, a *Parteiraum*, requiring occupancy. Practically speaking, moreover, the more complex the instrument, the more time it takes to forge it; and surely a party among others (a voluntary association bent upon seeking votes) is a simpler tool than a party replacing all the other parties (and thereby seeking total control). Something had to be learned first from the experience with parties (in the plural), and new circumstances had to emerge.

With respect to party pluralism the major circumstance was the extension of the suffrage. With respect, instead, to unipartism the decisive antecedent has been the emergence of a *politicized society*. If a distinction is drawn – as it should be – between political development of the *polity* and political development of the *society*, the latter involves the political awakening and activation of the population at large. As a result, and at the end, a politicized society is a society that both takes part in the operations of the political system and is required for the more effective performance of the system.[6] Even where parties were not permitted or were kept under tutelage, it gradually came to be realized that the population at large could no longer be side-stepped and discounted as an irrelevant entity. The pure and simple awareness of this fact represents a momentous turning point. The outs are in, or must be brought in. "The masses" not only cannot be kept out indefinitely, but it is useful to involve them. If their enmity is dangerous, their indifference is wasteful. Parties (in the plural) may be repressed, but the problems raised by politicization remain. And a partyless polity cannot cope, in the long run, with a politicized society.

When the single party was conceived and/or implanted, Western democracies had reached a state of development characterized by (i) large, if seldom universal, enfranchisement and (ii) the emergence of structured party systems pivoting on mass parties.[7] The two are closely related, for parties acquire organizational strength and consolidation in response to the extension of the suffrage. The plain fact is that the entry into politics of mass publics creates a new problem – *channelment*. And to say that a party system becomes structured amounts to saying that it has reached a stage of consolidation at which it can, and actually does, perform a channeling function. The need for a stabilized system of canalization follows, in part, from the nature of mass publics but basically stems from a pure and simple fact of magnitude. The larger the number of participants, the more the need for a regularized traffic system.

With universal suffrage, then, the party system acquires a new property. As long as the politicized society remains a relatively small elite society, the party system can remain in a state of flux. But when the society at large becomes politicized, the traffic rules that plug the society into the state, and vice versa, are established by the way in which a party system becomes structured. At this point, parties become channeling agencies, and the party system becomes the system of *political canalization* of the society.

It is now easy to see why the single-party states materialize at the moment they do and to explain why the most viable and durable alternative to "many parties" is "one party" – hardly a party void (no matter whether partyless or antiparty). No parties at all leaves a society out of reach, out of control, and no modernized regime can afford, in the long run, to settle on this unsafe and unproductive solution. A post-traditional society either can be freed or has to be seized; but the more it modernizes, the less it can be left to itself or be expected to remain dormant. For better or worse, in a politicized society the no-party solution is, in perspective, ephemeral. The party as a channel of *expression* may be short-lived; but the party as a *channel*, period, is born to remain. And whatever else the single party may be, it surely is a channeling agency. This is indeed the bridge across which the parties that are parts have paved the way to a successor, which is the party without counterpart.

The one party's reason for being appears to be, then, that a modern society cannot be left unchanneled. However, the fact is not simply that single-party states either inherit a politicized society or promote one. It is, further, that they need a pervasively politicized society far more than do the pluralistic polities. The one party claims exclusiveness and is therefore acutely confronted with a problem of self-justification and self-assertion. Whether or not the single-party states arise in a revolutionary situation and by revolutionary means, they are perceived as exceptional, "special" regimes – not merely as "new" regimes. Therefore, the monistic polities cannot expect to acquire legitimacy simply with the passing of time; they must show that they can do more, better and faster, than the pluralistic systems. If the claim cannot be sustained by deeds, it will have to be sustained all the more by words. In any case, the society must be mobilized, persuaded, and asked for trustful, if not unconditional, dedication. All these tasks require a powerful system of irrigation, so to speak, and the natural instrument for mobilizing a society is precisely the single party. Not only, then, does a modern society need to be channeled. The logic of the one-party formula leads further: to a society that must be "chained." It is only by compulsive regimentation and monopolistic indoctrination, in fact, that the single-party state succeeds to party pluralism and can succeed where a pluralistic polity may fail.

2.2 *The party-state system*

The following issues may now be fruitfully discussed: (i) in what sense a single party is a "party" and should be called such and (ii) whether it makes sense to speak of the one-party state as being a "party system."

Max Weber, despite his overly loose conception, noted that the

Guelfs ceased to be a party once they ceased to function through *freie Werbung* – free soliciting in the political market.[8] And the point was forcibly stated by, among others, Sigmund Neumann with reference to the Nazi party: "To call such a dictatorial organization a 'party' is a misnomer and often a conscious misconception," for the "dictatorial party monopoly, which prevents the free formation and expression of opinion, is the precise antithesis of the party system."[9] It should be conceded, I believe, that the logical force of the argument is difficult to challenge. It has not been challenged by elaborate counterarguments on the same plane but on the different plane that it does not fit the study (or the evidence) of the developing areas.[10]

With reference to my first question, this much can be said with reasonable assurance: It would be to the advantage of clarity if the party without counterparts was terminologically distinguished from the party that is a part. However, we apparently have no alternative labeling, and the specialist must often bow, under such circumstances, to the linguistic conventions that have received universal acceptance. Moreover, as we have seen, there is a genetic linkage between parties in the plural and party in the singular. In particular, what really and radically changes in passing from party pluralism to unipartism is the nature of the *system;* but the single party as such carries over whatever techniques and organizational structure it previously had. The one party in power kills the other parties but remains a party-like organizational weapon. Hence as long as the rationale of the two kinds is clearly distinguished, there is a sense in which it makes sense to speak of "one party."[11]

The case is very different when we pass on to say "one-party system" – for this is indeed a misnomer leading to a number of serious misconceptions. How can one party produce, alone, a *system?* A system of what? Surely not *of parties.* Hence, the one party cannot produce a party system.

The term system is important, because it brings in an important analytical tool. It is true that its technical sophistication varies considerably across disciplines[12] and that even within each discipline there is considerable oscillation between a strict, exacting sense and a loose, feeble sense.[13] In particular, it is permissible to speak of party system without abiding by all the requirements of systems analysis proper.[14] Yet, and at a minimum, the concept of system is meaningless – for purposes of scientific inquiry – unless (i) the system displays properties that do not belong to a separate consideration of its component elements and (ii) the system results from, and consists of, the patterned interactions of its component parts, thereby implying that such interactions provide the boundaries, or at least the boundedness, of the system.[15] It is immediately apparent that the so-called one-party system fulfills neither requirement. With respect to the first, the description of the unit (the single party) coincides with the description of the system. With respect to the second, the patterned interactions that do occur do so not within, but across the boundaries indicated by the term party.

Parties make for a "system," then, only when they are parts (in the plural); and a party system is precisely the *system of interactions* resulting from inter-party competition. That is, the system in question bears on the relatedness of parties to each other, on how each party is a function (in the mathematical sense) of the other parties and reacts, competitively or otherwise, to the other parties.

A major source of confusion is, possibly, that while it cannot be said that a single party produces a "system of parties," it can be said that each party can be perceived (from the inside or studied in isolation) as a "system," meaning that each party is as such a microcosm of its own and indeed a miniature political system. In the latter case, however, the object under investigation is not the party system but the *party-as-a-system*. So expressed, the difference might appear slight. Yet by confusing the two things we are the victims of a major error: the *unit jump fallacy*. We are mistaking, in fact, one level of analysis for another, specifically, the level at which the unit of analysis is system for a level at which the unit of analysis is party.

We are thus led to the correct question. If one party alone cannot produce a system of its own (i.e., a party system), where is the system? The question is, then, to which *systemic unit* does the single party belong? Given the fact that the single party does not interact with other parties, what is the area of its bounded, patterned, and self-maintaining interdependencies? Where the system resides is appropriately suggested by the authors who use the term *party-state system*. The label is usually applied to the Communist states,[16] but it is equally fitting for nazism, Italian fascism, and whatever draws on these prototypes. In the abstract language of a rationalization the argument is that while the parties that are parts cannot for this very reason identify themselves with the state, the party as a whole can only identify itself – ideally – with the state. Two wholes cannot coexist unless they tend to coincide. In this sense the single party can be said to be a duplication of the state.[17] Whether it is the party that tends to absorb the state or, vice versa, the state that tends to absorb the party, in either case a party-state system is "a system of unitarism," as Ernest Barker called it.[18]

Lest simplification result in oversimplification, some qualifications are in order. Even in the most totalitarian state "monolithic unity is only imperfectly realized."[19] In a party-state system public office is, in the main, a byproduct of party office. This does not imply, however, that all officials must be card-carrying members of the party. This depends very much, among other things, on whether the single party's membership policy is restrictive or not. In the second place, a bureaucratic merit system may well coexist alongside a party career system. And as long as the party controls the bureaucracy, this solution surely represents a gain in efficiency. In the third place, the party must draw, for the technical jobs, on technical talents. And here the monolith is exposed to its major cracks, for the relation between the party politicos and the technical intelligentsia can become a very recalcitrant matter. In the fourth place, and above all, in the apparat-state, as Ionescu calls it, there are several "apparats," and how these are keyed into each other (especially how the political police and the army relate to the party apparat) is indeed an intricate matter, ranging over a wide spectrum of possibilities and variations.[20]

All in all, the party-state amalgamation is never perfect and is obtained in many different ways to a very different extent. It should also be understood that I am not arguing that wherever there is only one party, there must be a party-state system. My argument is, rather, that we have either this kind of system or no significant system. And this is especially to say that the concepts that apply to the structured and differentiated polities cannot be carried over, as such, to diffuse and embryonic polities. Bearing the above qualifications in mind, the point remains that the party and the state are – vis-à-vis the population at large – two mutually sustaining and reciprocally reinforcing agencies. Whether it is the state that serves the party or, conversely, the party that serves the state, whatever the prevalence and the major vector of interaction, the fact remains that the (consolidated) one-party polities distinctly lack a party system precisely because they are party-state systems. And the implications are far-reaching.

When parties (in the plural) interact among themselves, we have a situation in which the parties are left to operate a system of their own, that is, an independent subsystem. More technically, inter-party interactions are both conducive to, and result from, *subsystem autonomy*. Contrariwise, the distinctive characteristic of a party-state system is that it does *not* allow subsystem autonomy. Not only does the single party not make for an independent subsystem, but the very reason for being of the arrangement is to impede subsystem autonomy. Otherwise, why have one party rather than no party? If we refuse party pluralism, its alternative with respect to encouraging other types of sub-group autonomy is the partyless, not the party-swallowing, solution.

While the notion of subsystem autonomy is crucial,[21] it appears at times too narrow and, at other times, too broad. The two usages should be distinguished; and this can be easily done, I suggest, by saying *subsystem* autonomy with reference to the strict meaning and *sub-*

group autonomy when the broader meaning is intended. There are many advantages in the relaxed, or broader, connotation.[22] For one thing, it sets aside the troublesome issue as to whether the analytic group in question is a system. Not only might the systemic issue be immaterial, but we may not be clearheaded as to whether the entity is a system *from within* (e.g., the party-as-system), or *from without* (e.g., the inter-party system). For example, in which respect is the judiciary, the bureaucracy, or the army a system? Is it with respect to the unit judiciary, army, bureaucracy, or with respect to the unit system? These questions need not trouble us if we say sub-group rather than subsystem. Furthermore, when reference is made to sub-groups in general, it should be understood that the import of this autonomy can be very different. An army that is a highly autonomous sub-group indicates, in all likelihood, that the autonomy of a civilian government is either dubious or endangered. Likewise, if the bureaucracy is a highly autonomous sub-group, the indication presumably is that we have a bureaucratic rule. On the other hand, the independence of the judiciary is a long-sought and long-fought conquest, for the autonomy of this sub-group represents the cornerstone of our civil liberties and does indicate that arbitrary rule is curbed.

It cannot be said, then, that any and all sub-group autonomy is "functional" or that it testifies to the degree of liberty-independence, poliarchy and/or pluralism of a society. This can be said, instead, with reference to the narrow connotation. If the notion of *subsystem autonomy* is used restrictively, that is, only when the unit definitely is the system – as is clearly the case with the party subsystem, the labor union subsystem, and the pressure group subsystem – then it does follow that subsystem autonomy is an excellent indicator both of poliarchy and of how free a society is with respect to the state. In particular, it can be safely asserted that the power of a society over the state largely and primarily hinges on the autonomy of the party subsystem. This is so because the autonomy of other sub-groups may well free a society *from* the state, but falls short of making a society free *to* influence the state.

The matter can be probed further by noting that, within the "'house of power,"[23] a party system represents a limiting case of subsystem independence, for party pluralism operates on the principle that parties are voluntary organizations, organizations created at will, like any other private enterprise, by private citizens. Not only is membership not compulsory and not only is the citizen offered a choice among the existing organizations, but the system allows – costs of entry notwithstanding – the voluntary creation of new political organizations. In this sense, a party system is not only an independent but also an *open* subsystem. Contrariwise, a party-state system cannot even conceive the party as being a voluntary organization; and the lack of subsystem autonomy makes the system in question a *closed* system. Whether the admission to the single party is restricted or not, in any case the system allows neither the voluntary creation of political organizations nor a choice among alternative political organizations.

Clearly, whether or not parties are left to operate an independent subsystem does make a crucial difference. Hence to say that only the political systems characterized by party interactions, and thus by a "system" of such interactions, should be called party systems is not a terminological quibble. It calls attention to the fact that in the monocentric polities the system-like properties reside in the party-state interactions and thereby to the fact that such systems are characterized by lack of subsystem autonomy. "One-party systems" do not exist and should not be called such – for in this case the actual referent is a "state system" in which the party canalization serves the purposes of the state, not the purposes of the society. A party system recognizes dissent and institutionalizes opposition; a party-state system denies the validity of dissent and impedes opposition. Parties in the plural are instruments of expression; the party in the singular is an instrument for extraction. And while we can say that the society shapes the party system, it cannot be said that the society shapes a party-state system. Quite to the contrary, it is the party-state system that shapes the society. On all counts, the logic of one system is the obverse of the logic of the other.

With respect to the word party, we are constrained by our shortage of words, and no great harm follows if the term is applied also to a non-part, to a part claiming to be the whole. With respect to the term system, however, its misuse has no justification in word shortage, and actually testifies to the waste of an important analytical tool as well as to the unnecessary violation of the golden rule that different things should be named differently.

2.3 One-party pluralism

Over the past decades we have been discussing whether a democracy is possible or conceivable without more-than-one party.[24] Until the fifties the case was approached as a matter of black or white. In the sixties, and as we proceed into the seventies, the case is being increasingly discussed as a matter of shades. Formerly the reply was definitely in the negative. Currently it tends to be in the affirmative. One of the many reasons for this switch is that the referents have changed, that we are observing a broader and very diversified world, and that – as a consequence – many authors now speak of "one party" in a very loose sense, with reference to the hegemony, dominance, or predominance of one party *over others.*

It follows that the appraisal of the concrete evidence must await a discussion of the classificatory issue.[25] As long as one author cites one-party cases that, for the next author, do not belong to the same class, nor even to unipartism, we are talking past each other, and we are likely to end up with a *petitio principii*, with proving by definition, and in this instance by misclassification, what remains to be proved. But we can still confront the theoretical issue, with the understanding that reference is made only to the political systems in which no party except one is legally permitted and actually exists. Under this clear-cut situation the point of interest resides, clearly, in the intra-party processes.

As a rule, in the monocentric polities intra-party divisions are prohibited; that is, they cannot be institutionalized or formalized. Yet the dialectics of life – not only of politics – is that any *position* engenders an *opposition,* i.e., a counterposition. Regardless of the party statute, the fact remains that larger groups split into smaller groups and that the informal intra-party processes are as they should be: riddled by disagreement, rivalry, maneuverings, and battlings.[26] The rare instances in which the single party tolerates or even permits, within its ranks, subunit organization and some kind of formalized opposition are, doubtlessly, very relevant with respect to "one-party pluralism"; but the argument need not be confined to these special instances.[27] Even when no subunit organization materializes and the intolerance or fear of dissent is well enforced all the way down the line, men do fight each other, and the more bitterly the greater the stake. And the fact that individual and/or group conflict is ubiquitous, that it exists in any and all political systems, confronts us with the issue of whether intra-party conflict and dissent can be a substitute, an ersatz, for inter-party competition.

The scholars who speak of "one-party pluralism" are evidently inclined to answer in the affirmative; and this is surely the case when we hear of "one-party democracy." The argument is formulated by Duverger as follows: "To the extent that factions develop freely inside a single party . . . pluralism is reborn within the party and there it can play the same part. . . . It is therefore conceivable that a single party may coincide with some kind of political democracy."[28] Nothing much has been changed or added to this formulation in the 25 years since it was made. However, to make sure that we are not quarreling about a word, let us set aside the term pluralism and focus on the phrase "it can play the same part." The question is: Are there sufficient similarities between a single party that allows, if only de facto, for inner subdivisions on the one hand, and a more-than-one-party system on the other hand, to warrant the thesis that there is some kind of *functional equivalence* between them?

The first caution is, as one writer nicely puts it, that even "in the most extreme forms of autocracy, there can be intense competitive rivalry, if only for the ear and favour of the autocrat"; but to widen the meaning of the terms competition and competitive "to cover the intrigue of the palace corridor and the party committee room would blunt the edge of the analytical tool."[29] And the point deserves to be pursued in detail. Competition among leaders within the single party is a struggle among power holders confronting each other *directly*. Here we have primarily, if not exclusively, a leader-to-leader relationship, a face-to-face struggle among rulers, the outcome of which does not have to pass the test of electoral competition and legitimation. In a party system, instead, intra-party competition is only one side of the coin, the other being inter-party competition. And since it matters little to gain control of a party lacking followers, the side of the coin that matters most is inter-party competition. The essence of party pluralism is, then, that party leaders confront one another *indirectly*: They vie with each other with an eye to the voters – and this entails far-reaching consequences.

In the party-state systems, state and party reinforce and duplicate each other, while in the pluralistic systems they split and are disjoined. The implication is that in the monistic case the party's outlook is the state's outlook. They are both located at the altimetric level of "who governs," and, in this sense, it is the state's point of view that absorbs the party's. In the case of party pluralism the parties instead are located at a halfway point between the governed and the governors, and it is the policy as envisaged from the altimetric level of "who is governed" that tends to become the state's policy. This is the same as saying that – by virtue of their very mechanics – a one-party polity makes power autocratic, while a plural-party system democratizes power. When there is competition between more-than-one party, a party governs so far as it is responsive to, and takes the part of, the governed; whereas the single party governs permanently, and hence its problem is who will govern the party itself.

All in all, nothing goes to show how and why intra-party rivalry can be a substitute for, or assimilated to, inter-party competition. Intra-party dissent *alone* expresses – and induces – a "private" far more than a "functional" contest. The argument that rivalry and conflict always exist in politics, no matter how they are processed, is short-legged and misses the whole sense of political engineering. It does matter how conflict is channeled – indeed, the processing makes all the difference. Historically, this is borne out by the fact that in-group conflict among politicians – indeed the predecessor and equivalent of intra-party

49

rivalry alone – has always and only produced factions (in the historical meaning). Thus, while factional plurality has existed ever since political life came into being, democratic pluralism has existed only in relatively few countries for a relatively short time. In particular, there is no evidence, over the centuries, that factionalism and group conflict as such have ever paved the way to a democracy.

More technically, Duverger's thesis fails to account for the unit difference, thereby entering the list of the "unit jump" fallacies. The monistic polities have only one unit: the party-as-system. The pluralistic polities contain two units: the parties taken one by one, plus the inter-party system. This is the same as saying that in the first case we have, at best, only one (internal) electoral-competitive process, while in the second case we have two (internal and external) electoral-competitive processes. Where, then, is the *substitution?* Even if we grant more than is due, i.e., that what goes on within the single party can meaningfully be called competition, the same occurs within each of the parties of a party system. Hence it is not that the single party provides something in exchange for what it lacks. And the single party lacks precisely what makes a polyarchy "democratic": electoral competition and free elections.

Inter-party competition has been subjected, of late, to rough handling. On the one hand the charge is that parties – especially twopartism – offer no "real choice" and that their competitive behavior results, in the final analysis, in emasculation, in collusive behavior, and in diverting attention from fundamentals to trivialities. In short, competition may comfort monopoly.[30] On the other hand parties – especially extreme multipartism – are portrayed as exasperating conflicts and divisions, as creating "artificial issues," as proposing grand choices that are wholly unrealistic. From this angle competition overheats the market, breeds overpromising and polarization, and creates unmanageable problems, problems beyond solution. In either case the collective goods or benefits resulting from the mechanisms of competition are always sub-optimal for reasons that have been well explained.[31] Much of all this criticism is, at some point or another, correct. No rosy-hued picture of competition is intended here. However, and over and over again, our problem is (awaiting the measures) *weighing.* Do the shortcomings counterweigh, or even cancel out, the benefits? In the case in point do the shortcomings of inter-party competition weigh more than its positive by-effects – as they are stated in the competitive theory of democracy outlined by Schumpeter,[32] implemented by Friedrich,[33] and developed by Dahl?[34]

The assertion that "liberal-democracy is not by definition precluded by the presence of a one-party system"[35] might well represent the current, prevalent mood of the discipline.[36] But I am unable, regretfully, to find arguments to sustain the thesis that whenever inter-party competition (among diverse parties) is repressed, it can be replaced by intra-party conflict (within the single party). We are not interested, after all, in conflict per se, but in its returns. Therefore, the thesis presumes, and leaves us with the assumption that men fighting for their own survival – and not always metaphorically – in a jungle-law type of setting, will and can provide collective benefits. The assumption is, then, that the house of power is inhabited by formidable altruists. This might well be the case for particular individuals and, in the aggregate, for the first revolutionary generation. But such circumstances are neither frequent nor durable; and no polity can be constructed, for duration and for the time of routine, on the basis of such wishful thinking. If prediction must be sustained by argument – and the notion of one-party pluralism is generally intended as a hopeful prediction – then the prediction is thin.

NOTES TO CHAPTER 2

1 This notably excludes the so-called one-party states in the United States and the volatile or largely unstructured African single parties. The reasons for these exclusions are given *infra*, 4.3 and ch. 8.

2 The major difference, in this respect, between Lenin on the one hand and Hitler and Mussolini on the other, is that the latter two openly declared themselves antidemocratic, while Lenin had never theorized unanimism. In fact, from 1917 until the Tenth Congress of the Bolshevik party of March 1921, there was free and indeed enraged debate within the party. However, Lenin put the lid on opposition in 1921, and this meant the lid on internal dissent; for opposition parties, and specifically the two Socialist parties, had been fought from the outset with whatever fraud and violence fell short of formal outlawing. See Leonard Schapiro, "Putting the Lid on Leninism," *GO*, January–April 1967, esp. pp. 181–191. In general, see L. Schapiro, *The Communist Party of the Soviet Union*, Random House, 1959; and for all the details see the monumental work of Edgar Hallett Carr, *History of Soviet Russia*, Macmillan (7 vols.), 1951–1964, vols. I–III, "The Bolshevik Revolution."

3 The distinction is drawn from Samuel P. Huntington, *Political Order in Changing Societies*, Yale University Press, 1968, esp. pp. 403–408.

4 Military regimes are currently concentrated in South America (in 1974: Bolivia, Brazil, Chile, Ecuador, Paraguay, Peru, and Uruguay) and in Africa. While I abide by Huntington's distinction between partyless and antiparty, it should be clear that most Latin American regimes are antiparty *pro tempore*, not in principle. The case might well be different, in the long run, in the new African states, for in this area the military might well develop a full-fledged antiparty doctrine, unhampered by legitimacy problems. The African military regimes are enumerated *infra*, ch. 8, esp. Tables 29 and 31.

5 Op. cit., p. 407.

6 Though my politicized society is close enough to the ordinary notion of mass society, the emphasis is laid here on only one of its many aspects. My politicized society is also close to what most authors now call a mobilized society. I shall, however, use the term mobilization in its narrower, original sense.

7 The Leninist party falls under this generalization in that Lenin conceived it in exile and in a broad Western contest. The fact that it was theorized as a "vanguard" type of party owes both to the Marxist doctrine and to the Russian situation in 1917. The notions of mass party and of structured party system will be discussed in vol. II. For a preliminary underpinning see *infra*, 8.1.

8 Max Weber, *Wirtschaft und Gesellschaft,* Winckelmann, ed. (1956), I, Part 1, III, sect. 18, "Concept and Essence of Parties."

9 *Modern Political Parties,* op. cit., p. 370, and "A one-party system is a contradiction in itself" (p. 395). In the same vein, Ernest Barker, *Reflections on Government,* Oxford University Press, 1942, wrote: "When the State . . . abolishes all parties other than the single party . . . it really abrogates the essence of party" (p. 39). Gabriel Almond puts it very concisely: "The structure we call *party* in the totalitarian system is not a party at all" ("Comparative Political Systems," *JP,* August 1956, p. 397). Leslie Lipson asserts: ". . . a party is, by definition, a part of the whole. As such, it signifies the existence of other parts, i.e., a coexistence of parties. To speak of a one-party system, therefore, is to employ a contradiction of terms" (*The Democratic Civilization,* op. cit., p. 311). See also Charles E. Merriam and Harold F. Gosnell, *The American Party System,* 4th ed., Macmillan, 1949, p. 8; and Harold D. Lasswell and Abraham Kaplan, *Power and Society,* Yale University Press, 1950, p. 171.

10 This point is well appraised by Austin Ranney, "The Concept of 'Party,'" in Oliver Garceau, ed., *Political Research and Political Theory,* Harvard University Press, 1968, esp. pp. 148–151. The counterargument is made, e.g., by T. Hodgkin, *African Political Parties,* Penguin Books, 1961, pp. 15–16; Gwendolen Carter, in Carter, ed., *African One-Party States,* Cornell University Press, 1964, pp. 1–2; and David E. Apter, *The Politics of Modernization,* The University of Chicago Press, 1965, pp. 181–185. Note, *contra,* the cautious approach of Coleman and Rosberg: "By definition a party is a "part"; both competition and the concept of system imply the existence of more than one part . . . we will not attempt to resolve these admittedly serious conceptual ambiguities. The immediate point is to note that, with few exceptions, African political parties initially emerged through electoral competition" (in James S. Coleman and Carl J. Rosberg, Jr., eds., *Political Parties and National Integration in Tropical Africa,* University of California Press, 1964, p. 3, n. 4). But see *infra,* ch. 8.

11 This concession leaves us – we shall see – with some unresolved difficulties. As Domenico Fisichella correctly points out, the one party is a "party" in structural and also in genetic (historicogenetic) terms; but the assimilation does not hold in functional terms. (*Partiti e Gruppi di Pressione,* Il Mulino, 1972, "Introduction," pp. 26–31.)

12 A major distinction, cutting across disciplinary boundaries, is the one among (i) social system, (ii) cultural system, and (iii) personality system. These systems may be distinguished by their units of analysis, respectively, (i) roles, (ii) value orientations and beliefs, (iii) motivations, drives, and need-dispositions. None of these systems is intended here.

13 In political science, e.g., the electoral system is far less a "system" than the political system or the party and pressure group subsystems.

14 For the application of systems analysis in the political science setting the prominent author is David Easton. See in particular *A Framework for Political Analysis*, Prentice-Hall, 1965, and *A Systems Analysis of Political Life*, Wiley, 1965.

15 In more detail, the foregoing implies, (i) that there must be such an interdependence of parts or variables that the resulting relationships have an "order," so that not just anything can happen; (ii) that this order must tend to self-maintenance; (iii) that the self-maintenance in question includes the maintenance both of the boundaries and of the "distinctive relationships of the parts of the system within the boundary" (Talcott Parsons and Edward A. Shils, eds., *Toward a General Theory of Action*, Harvard University Press, 1952, pp. 107–108).

16 E.g., Jan F. Triska, ed., *Communist Party-States*, Bobbs-Merrill, 1969. We can also use, to be sure, one-party polities, unipartism, and similar terms. What matters is to avoid the misleading diction.

17 This is to contradict the suggestion, which I find misleading, of Sigmund Neumann that nazism was a "dual State" (loc. cit., p. 414). The "dualism" is instrumental to a self-reinforcing system. On the other hand, my "duplication" does not imply that the single party is necessarily an "executive agency," as C. W. Cassinelli holds ("The Totalitarian Party," *JP*, February 1962, pp. 111–141).

18 *Reflections on Government*, op. cit., p. 288.

19 Merle Fainsod, *How Russia Is Ruled*, new ed., Harvard University Press, 1963, p. 387, and, for an extensive illustration, Parts III and IV. See also Frederick C. Barghoorn, *Politics in the USSR*, Little, Brown, 1966. The cracks in the monolith have been analyzed, and somewhat emphasized, by Robert C. Tucker, "The Conflict Model," *Problems of Communism*, November–December 1963; Sidney Ploss, *Conflict and Decision-Making in Soviet Russia*, Princeton University Press, 1965; Carl A. Linden, *Khrushchev and the Soviet Leadership 1957–1964*, Johns Hopkins Press, 1966.

20 See Ghita Ionescu, *The Politics of the European Communist States*, Praeger, 1967, esp. pp. 227–269.

21 See esp. Robert A. Dahl, *Modern Political Analysis*, Prentice-Hall, 1963, pp. 35 ff. Pursuing this path, Gabriel A. Almond and G. Bingham Powell combine subsystem autonomy (high, limited and low) with the cultural criterion (*Comparative Politics: A Developmental Approach*, Little Brown, 1966, esp. pp. 259–272).

22 See Samuel E. Finer, *Comparative Government*, Allen Lane Penguin Press, 1970, pp. 48–49, 575–586.

23 This is Max Weber's image.

24 The alternative question is whether democracy might be not only possible but indeed preferable without parties. This is the issue of

direct democracy and will not be discussed here. Cf. my *Democratic Theory*, op. cit., ch. 12. Granted that a direct partyless democracy is "possible" (with the qualifications stated *supra*, 2.1), what remains to be shown is that it would make a democracy work better (see *infra*, 4.3, Key's doubts on the matter).

25 This caution applies not only to the fluid, developing polities but also, and in particular, to the so-called American single-party states. Quite aside from the open question of their classification (*infra*, 4.3 and 6.5), the member states of a federal state are clearly a case by itself on account of their enfeebled autonomy with respect to the areas subject to federal control.

26 *Supra*, 2.2 and n. 19 above.

27 The interesting experiment, in this respect, is the one of Nyerere's Tanganyika African National Union, which permits two members of the party to contest each electoral seat. Tanzania became independent, however, only in 1961, Nyerere obtains 95 percent of the votes, and it is both difficult and too soon to assess the significance, let alone the prospects of duration, of the device (*infra*, 8.2 and n. 23). Madagascar is also cited with Tanzania but is subject to even greater cautions. The only strong case is, in fact, Mexico, to be discussed *infra*, 7.3.

28 *Les Partis Politiques*, op. cit., p. 310 (North trans., p. 278). While Duverger brings in, inappropriately, also the example of Southern politics (*infra*, 4.3), it is fair to note that his generalization is tentative and that the case in point is Turkey, with reference to the rivalry between Inonu and Bayar, within the People's Republican party, while Kemal Ataturk was still alive. Turkey is examined *infra*, 9.1.

29 William H. Morris-Jones, "Dominance and Dissent," *GO*, August 1966, p. 454.

30 See Hirschman, *Exit, Voice, and Loyalty*, op. cit., esp. ch. 5. This is also the underlying thesis of C. Wright Mills, *The Power Elite*, Oxford University Press, 1956; and of Henry S. Kariel, *The Decline of American Pluralism*, Stanford University Press, 1961.

31 See esp. Mancur Olson, Jr., *The Logic of Collective Action – Public Goods and the Theory of Groups*, Harvard University Press, 1965, *passim*.

32 Joseph A. Schumpeter, *Capitalism, Socialism and Democracy*, Harper and Brothers, 1942, ch. 22, esp. p. 269.

33 Specific reference is made to his "rule of anticipated reactions," which is best formulated in Carl J. Friedrich, *Constitutional Government and Politics*, 2nd ed., Ginn, 1941, ch. 25, esp. pp. 589–591. See also Friedrich's *Man and His Government: An Empirical Theory of Politics*, McGraw-Hill, 1963, ch. 11.

34 Most of Dahl's work, starting with the volume coauthored with C. E. Lindblom, *Politics, Economics and Welfare*, Harper, 1953, is centered on the working conditions of democracy, as shown by Domenico Fisichella, *Temi e Metodi in Scienza Politica*, Sansoni, 1971, ch. 6. See, most recently, Dahl's *Poliarchy*, op. cit.; also my *Democratic Theory*, op. cit., ch. 6, and esp. pp. 124–128.

35 Blondel, *An Introduction to Comparative Government*, op. cit., p. 151. Note that Blondel goes so far as to specify "liberal de-

mocracy," while most authors, and certainly Duverger, refer to some vague kind of democracy.

36 Two statements, converging from very distant vantage points, seem particularly indicative. According to Jerzy Wiatr, "political pluralism . . . need not take the form of an outer differentiation into various parties and groups, but may also develop in the inner life of the governing party," which is, in fact, the Polish United Worker's party (in *Cleavages, Ideologies and Party Systems,* op. cit., p. 286). And Fred W. Riggs concurs: "In the case of a *one-party system* . . . the elected assembly is readily dominated by the ruling party and cannot safeguard opposition rights for *minority parties.* However, a functional equivalent can be provided inside the ruling party by its own elected congress. If . . . sufficiently powerful, it might be able to protect the rights of opposition factions within the party" (*Administrative Reform and Political Responsiveness: A Theory of Dynamic Balancing,* Sage, 1970, p. 583). The italics are mine, and point to the fuzziness acquired by the one-party notion.

3
The preliminary framework

3.1 Channelment, communication, expression

In the course of the analysis, two functions, or two major systemic roles of parties, have come to the fore: expression and channelment. A third function – communication – needs to be entered for the completeness of the argument. For one thing, the expressive function implies communication and might well be considered part and parcel of the communication function. Hence I should explain why I say "expression" rather than "communication" and, at the same time, how the two are related. In the second place, it could be argued that the channeling function too involves communication. And this cannot be denied, since communication is the requisite of everything.

Given the prerequisite nature of communication, one option is to adopt an overall cybernetic approach, such as the one cogently developed by Deutsch.[1] Accordingly, the party comes to be perceived as "the communication network that functionally specializes in the aggregation of political communications (i.e. communications relating to the authoritative allocation of values) for a polity."[2] The alternative option is the one pursued by Almond, namely, to spell out a "political communication function" alongside the other systemic functions.[3] And this is how the notion is intended here.

The reason for my having left aside, so far, the communication function is that it does not have sufficient discriminating power. As will be remembered, the expressive function characterizes party pluralism, i.e., the party that belongs to a party system. The channeling function emerges at a later stage, the stage of structural consolidation of the party polities, and appears applicable not only to the party systems but also to the party-state systems.[4] At this point the political communication function can be usefully entered in the analysis – with the caution that we have a problem of fitting historically derived categories into a purely analytical class.

With respect to inclusiveness, communication is doubtless an all-inclusive category and perhaps the universal category *par excellence*. All political systems, without exception, can be said to have political communication. Channelment comes next. It is equally an all-inclusive category, but its range is not as broad, for no significant channeling occurs in the no-party polities. Thus expression is the least inclusive of the three categories, for it does not apply to all party polities but only to the ones with party subsystem autonomy. In short, all polities share the property of communication; all party polities share the property of channelment; but only party systems share the property of expression.[5] The first difference between the three functions is, therefore, that they belong to different levels of abstraction. In particular, communication is more general, expression more specific. Also, communication travels beyond the party area, while channelment and expression presuppose that parties exist. So far so good. The controversy arises when these concepts are employed for assessing the closeness or distance among political systems. As a rule, the more general, i.e., the more abstract, a category, the more it cancels differences and makes things appear similar. In climbing a ladder of abstraction there is, then, a point at which minor similarities may cancel out major differences.[6] It is here that the issue is joined. For instance, a man and an ostrich are the same – i.e., belong to the same class – in that they are both two-legged animals. However, is this a significant assimilation?

In the case in point it is correct to say that both party systems and party-state systems perform a "channeling function" and that an important aspect of this canalization resides in the fact that both systems provide channels of communication. But the argument cannot be left at such a high-flown level of abstraction. If it were, then surface, and indeed superficial, similarities would outweigh profound differences. Communication per se consists of a two-directional flow, that is, includes both messages from below (demands) and messages from above (orders, or authoritative allocations). The question is: Who speaks and who listens? Who controls the input side of the funnel? Some feedback is always involved, to be sure, but political communication is not a dialogue among equal partners for the sake of entertainment. The conduit has a direction, and the direction of the conduit establishes how the circulation is maneuvered. This is the same as saying that a *sufficient* definition of political communication must specify what kind – communication *from whom to whom.* And failure to separate "expressive" from "authoritative" communication beclouds the crucial point.

A subsystem of parties (in the plural) allows expressive communication, that is, enables the citizens to communicate *to* the state. Conversely, a party-state system provides a communication network devised for communicating *to* the society. It is not simply that a party system allows a choice among channels while a party-state system offers a channel without choice. The critical element lies – we know – in the autonomy of the subsystem. In and by itself, a choice among channels could approximate a choice among chains. The point is whether the political communication network is shaped at the sub-system level, independently from the state system. If this is the case, then a party subsystem links a people to a government by providing an expressive system of communication that keeps the state under control. Conversely, the party-state identification links a government to the people by creating a system of authoritative communication that keeps the citizens under control. Hence a party system can be defined as a system of free (autonomous) canalization in which *expression prevails,* throughout the political system, over repression; whereas a party-state system can be defined as a system of compulsory (monopolistic) canalization in which *repression prevails,* all along the line, over expression.

My preference for *expressive function* largely bears, then, on the level of abstraction at which generalizations retain sufficient specificity. Thus, in my approach, "communication" is brought down and subsumed under "expression" rather than vice versa. Another difference should be stressed, however. My definition of the expressive function overlaps the notion of communication only in part. In the main, the expressive function is plugged into the power flow. This is why the antonym of expression is – in my usage – *repression* and near-synonyms: coercion, extraction, and, more loosely, orders, commands, and authoritative allocations. Expression is not intended merely as a transmission of messages. If the problem was that of having the authorities informed about the feelings of the citizens, then it could be solved by institutionalizing opinion surveys. The problem is, instead, to have the citizens' "voices" ingrained into a mechanism of retaliation and enforcement. To pursue the imagery of Hirschman, voices must have the option of exit – of switching to another firm.[7] If no party market, and thereby no party exit, is available, then "voice" is either powerless or can easily be silenced. And all of this is easily blurred or missed under the communication focus.

In conclusion, both party systems and party-state systems appear to be a requirement of modern political systems in that they provide a channeling system for the society. But beyond this point of similarity the two systems fall wide apart. If the argument is left at this level of abstraction, or generality, it leaves us with too much of a *vacuum.*

3.2 The minimal definition

Interestingly enough, in Duverger's standard work the question, "What do we mean when we use the term party?" is never raised.[8] Yet political groups engaged in a struggle for power have always existed. They were formerly called factions; they are now called parties. What is the difference? Purely nominal? Only a difference in magnitude? Unless we are prepared to reply that a party is merely a macrofaction, we are logically required to begin by defining party vis-à-vis faction. As Friedrich succinctly puts it: "If a definition does not distinguish a party from a faction, we must either hold the two to be identical in fact, or alter the definition so as to distinguish them."[9] This was, in effect, Burke's problem: The intent of his definition was precisely to draw the line between factions and honorable connections.[10] Currently Burke is in disrepute. Most present-day writers regard his definition as normative (which it is) and unrealistic (which is a different matter). The crudely realistic view is well exemplified by Schattschneider: "A political party is first of all an organized attempt to get power. . . . Burke obscured the issue . . . but it is equally just to say that parties are held together by the 'cohesive power of public plunder.' "[11] The pace was set, however, by Schumpeter: "A party is not . . . a group of men who intend to promote public welfare 'upon some principle on which they are all agreed. . . .' A party is a group whose members propose to act in concert in the competitive struggle for political power."[12]

While both Schattschneider and Schumpeter made it a point to present their definitions in contradiction to Burke, one wonders whether this is a necessary antithesis. Take, for instance, the following definition: "Political parties . . . are social organizations that attempt to influence (1) the selection and tenure of the personnel of government by putting forward candidates for elective office, (2) the policies of government according to some general principles or proclivities upon which most of their members agree. . . ."[13] Reading between the lines, and without too much stretching of the imagination, one can detect here, under (1), a soft-pedaled merger of Schattschneider and Schumpeter and, under (2), an echo of Burke. In effect, the relation between the stances of Burke and Schumpeter could well be interpreted as follows: Both principles and mechanisms are required, in conjunction, to make a party a part of a whole. It is unsafe to leave the matter – as Burke had to do – to noble intentions; but it is insufficient to leave it only to the feedbacks of party competition. If the intent is to identify party in opposition to factions, and thereby to counteract factional degeneration, then Burke is not superseded. If the intent is to bring out the mechanics by which parties are turned into instruments of democracy, or popular power, then Schumpeter gives the clue. On the other hand, if both Burke and Schumpeter are set aside, then Schattschneider's "realism" – and much of our current cynicism – makes parties indistinguishable not only from factions but also, across the world, from a bewildering maze of power-seeking groups.[14]

Before pursuing the theme further, two questions are in order: First, what is the purpose of definitions, and, second, what is their importance? Definitions serve many purposes, and their nature varies accordingly. Simple definitions simply declare – and make clear – the meaning of a term. Complex definitions are a far more complex affair, for they are supposed to enumerate the attributes or properties of a concept, and this presupposes, in turn, a composition rule. Only simple definitions are intended here. Even so, for the purposes of an inquiry on parties the simple definition cannot be too simple. It cannot consist merely of declaring what the author's stipulation is; it must confront the problem of making the notion *distinctive*. Therefore, it must confront, first and foremost, the question: Parties are different *from what?* There are many varieties of political groups and groupings. A definition of party must be such that it excludes *non-parties*. But this is more easily said than done. It turns out, in fact, that "party" is bounded by many borders and that most definitions draw some borders while neglecting others.

In any event, how important is the definition? Does it really matter? Duverger does not provide one. Epstein, in his somewhat narrower but still comparable volume, is not sanguine about definitions either, for he observes: "Almost everything that is called a party in any Western democratic nation can be so regarded."[15] However, this holds only under the clause: "Western democratic nations." If this qualification and delimitation are not provided, then we run into trouble unless we state what it is that our universe includes and excludes. In effect, even Epstein ends up with a synthetic and yet discriminating definition of party: "any group seeking votes under a recognizable label."[16] And the fact is that definitions are reentering – after some 20 years of disgrace – present-day political science.

In no small part this happens because the global comparative expansion of the discipline confronts us with a very fuzzy world. Further, and concurrently, the more we proceed along the operational path, the more we must reckon with very precise definitions – if only of the operational variety. I would add an even more compelling reason: the computer revolution. Whether or not the behavioral persuasion in politics has changed its outlook with respect to defining, the fact remains that computers cannot be fed, and data banks turn out to be a crazy enterprise, under the extant assumption that personal knowledge and intuitive understanding make up for what inadequate or missing definitions leave undefined. I would predict, therefore, that definitional accuracy will become all the more important the more we realize that the computer is already entering its fourth generation and, thereby, that we are already lagging far behind the constraints and requirements of the technological revolution in learning. At any rate, and whatever the reason, it is a fact that the most recent literature on parties does labor, in greater detail and awareness than ever before, with the definitional problem.[17]

A number of authors propose definitions that are quite lengthy – though short of being a synopsis of a description.[18] And it goes without saying that complex definitions are lengthy by definition. It should be understood that classifications and typologies also go to define the class "party" with respect to one or more of its properties. (This is particularly the case with historical typologies.) In general, parties are defined in terms of (i) actors, (ii) actions (activities), (iii) consequences (purposes), and (iv) domain.[19] But parties can also be defined with exclusive respect to their function, to their structure, or to both; or in the light of the input–output scheme; and in still other ways.

To reduce the maze two restrictions can be entered. First, some authors are more definition conscious than others, and it suits my present purposes to focus on those who clearly address themselves to the question: *From what*, and on the basis of which discriminating elements, do parties need to be distinguished? This is not the only question to which a definition responds. For instance, one might also ask: *In relation to what* do parties perform their role? But the latter is a complementary question in that it presupposes that parties have been identified with respect to some discriminating characteristic or other. Hence the first, if non-exhaustive, task of the definer is to *delimit*.[20] A party not only differs from a faction; it also differs from a "political movement," and even more from a mere "political association." Political movements and associations may become parties: But qua mere movements and associations they are not yet parties.[21] On the other hand, parties need to be distinguished from pressure or interest groups. Nor is this all. Suppose we settled for this definition: Parties are political groups intent upon gaining and maintaining control of the instrumentalities of government. Under this definition there are labor unions, armies (whether public or private ones), and churches that would doubtless qualify as parties. Nor can it be said that such a lumping is counterintuitive, among other reasons because a computer is not sensitive to intuition.

The second restriction, which is particularly attuned to empirical research, is the *minimal definition* restriction.[22] A definition is minimal when all the properties or characteristics of an entity that are not indispensable for its identification are set forth as variable, hypothetical properties – not as definitional properties. This is the same as saying that whatever falls beyond a minimal characterization is left to verification – not declared true by definition. The rule as such is simplicity itself. It is worthwhile to dwell, nonetheless, on how it works. And the minimal definitions proposed by Lasswell and Kaplan, Riggs, and Janda, provide to this effect an excellent illustration.

In the classic *Framework for Political Enquiry* by Lasswell and Kaplan we read: "D.F. A *party* (political) is a group formulating comprehensive issues and submitting candidates in elections." According to the authors, this definition makes a party distinguishable from non-organized and inactive segments of public opinion in that – they say – a group "involves organization." Likewise, the definition excludes the groups that seek to affect decisions by the use of violence, as well as pressure groups. For parties only "secure and exercise power through the formal coordination of votes." Further, the authors indicate that the definition distinguishes parties from factions (which do not submit comprehensive issues) and stress that it equally excludes the uniparty systems (which they refuse to call such).[23]

The definition by Riggs is "any organization which nominates candidates for election to an elected assembly."[24] Riggs emphasizes that his definition is purely structural (not functional), because of the important methodological point that we should make "structural criteria the basis for classification" and then use "functional variables in hypotheses." He concedes that the definition may not, nor does it pretend to, bring out the most important characteristic of parties, for "it only specifies a way of deciding what to include and what to exclude from the category under consideration." Prima facie it might seem that the definition excludes the single, or at least the totalitarian, party; but Riggs indicates that this exclusion is not intended and is obtained – if one so wishes – by inserting the clause that the candidates have to meet "competition."[25] It is noteworthy that Riggs, as opposed to Lasswell and Kaplan, drops the "comprehensive issues," presumably because this is not a structural criterion – at the cost, however, of enfeebling the *discrimen* between parties and factions, which remains a concern for Lasswell and Kaplan.[26] On the other hand, their assumption that group involves organization is somewhat gratuitous, and Riggs clarifies this point by replacing "group" with "organization." The most interesting aspect of the comparison emerges, however, from the term "election." On the basis of the argument by Riggs, the definition by Lasswell and Kaplan affords no criterion for excluding – as they intend – the single party. Conversely, Lasswell and Kaplan would probably read Riggs' definition as implying that the single party is not included, while Riggs specifies that it is.[27]

The definition by Janda reads as follows: Parties are "organizations that pursue the goal of placing their avowed representatives in government positions."[28] The novelty is that, here, elections no longer are the crucial distinguishing criterion. Janda explains that his formulation is expressly designed to include both the electoral process (which he understands to imply, as do Lasswell and Kaplan, inter-party competition) and the placing in government positions "by a direct act of designation," that is, when no electoral competition occurs. Janda's logic could be interpreted as follows: If we wish to make clear that both parties in the plural and parties in the singular are included in the definition, then it is unclear, or ambiguous, to bring in the electoral clause. It can be argued, therefore, that Janda's definition has the merit of dispelling the ambiguity detected in the previous definitions. On the other hand, by dropping the electoral clause we lose its powerful, and multiple, discriminating power. Thus Janda's definition verges on being subminimal. In particular, it might well fail to distinguish parties from pressure groups, or even from military and religious organizations.[29]

Clearly, all the authors cited pursue a minimal definition strategy. As many attributes or properties as possible are dropped from the definition, with the understanding that attributes that formerly appeared as *definitional properties* are restated as *hypothetical or variable properties*. The gains in definitional simplicity, and in respect to a correct separation between matters of fact to be ascertained empirically and matters of definition, are of no small import.[30] Yet a rule is always simpler than its application. Not only do our authors diverge, as one would expect, but each definition apparently has its weak spots. Drawing on the previous discussion, let me thus propose the following:

A party is any political group identified by an official label that presents at elections, and is capable of placing through elections (free or nonfree), candidates for public office.[31]

This definition retains the property that cannot be dropped – the electoral criterion of discrimination – without paying toll to ambiguity. The single party is explicitly included, and this on two counts. In the first place, if single parties are compared, discretely, to parties that have counterparts, the two classes need not be considered heterogeneous, if for no other reason than that a dictatorially ordained party can also perform in a pluralistic setting. Unipartism and party pluralism fall apart not at the party-unit level but at the systemic-unit level – and the *definiendum* here is the party, not the system. In the second place, also the single party "channels" – whether for façade or deeper reasons – the population at the polls. True enough, under unipartism elections are unfree. They can be, furthermore, a sham, given the ease with which the ballots can be stuffed and the returns rigged. Yet unfree elections are elections insofar as it matters here, namely, that an electoral occurrence (regardless of its substance) suffices to distinguish the single party from those political groups that do not make recourse to electoral rituals (or legitimation, manipulation, coercion, fraud, or whatever the appropriate word might be).[32]

Free elections, on the other hand, seem to require the clause "is capable of placing through elections." The visible reason for this clause is that it permits the exclusion – a very necessary one – of the parties that are nothing but "labels."[33] Also, it helps restore the distinction between parties and their factional sub-groups, in that whereas factions may propose the candidates, it is the party that obtains their election. My major intent, however, is to replace the organizational requirement – which is either saying too much or making "organization" evanescent – with the requirement that the group in question be effective and cohesive enough (if only on a spontaneous, election-by-election, organizationless basis) to have some of its candidates elected. And the cohesive side of the picture is hinted at by the qualification "identified by an official label." Within the format of a minimal definition this qualification is perhaps redundant. By the same token, however, parsimony might militate against specifying that both free and unfree elections are intended. If this were so, the abridged definition would be as follows: *A party is any political group that presents at elections, and is capable of placing through elections, candidates for public office.*

The minimal definition fulfills its purpose when it suffices to identify the object. Beyond this purpose, however, it is by no means a sufficient definition; that is, it cannot satisfy other purposes. The minimal definition is required only to dispel *indefiniteness* by indicating what is to be included in, or excluded from, a given class. Thus minimal definitions of parties have neither explanatory nor predictive power. It is by no means certain that they hit on what matters most (surely the one I propose does not); and it is quite certain that they do not convey the significance and reason of being of the entities thus defined. For this latter purpose we need a framework, a conceptual scheme, to which I now return for some final comments.

3.3 An overview

The argument has been that we cannot build a theory of parties and of party systems unless we establish what is *not* a party, and unless we are clearheaded about the essential *what for* of parties. It could even be that parties and party systems exist only because they exist, that is, for no purpose other than self-perpetuation. But we should not postulate a Parkinson's law of parties simply by not asking – in a hyperfactual mood – what parties are for. It is proper, therefore, to start from the foundations, that is, from the question of why parties were born and what it is that was born under that name.

Party, we know, is a new name for a new thing: And the name is new because the thing is new. The term was not used in a political sense until the sixteenth century, and it was only with Bolingbroke

64

that the issue came into visibility. In the main, during the entire eighteenth century parties were still regarded with great suspicion, not only because parties and factions were still mingled conceptually but also because they were difficult to differentiate in actual practice. It was during the nineteenth century that the distinction was clearly affirmed and that parties became widely accepted as legitimate and necessary instruments of free government. Conceivably, there are a number of ways of looking at the rationale of the party era. Throughout the political vicissitudes of mankind, however, one underlying theme has been recurrent: how to reconcile private existence and public coexistence, anarchy and order, differences and harmony. Whether the initial unit is the individual, primary or secondary group, or a national community, at each level the ultimate problem is: How does the smaller unit relate to, and integrate with, the larger unit? When parties were born – that is, when political divisions and differences became institutionalized – the question was again and even more pressingly and explicitly: How can it be made that a part does not endanger unity, and how can a part be put to use for the benefit of the whole?

The part-whole framework brings out very clearly the rationale of party pluralism, which is as follows: If a party is a part, it follows that the whole cannot be represented or constituted by just one party, although it does not follow from this that each party should behave as a part for itself, as a part unrelated to the whole. And the part-whole framework equally applies, in the reverse, to the rationale of the single party, or of the party-state system, as follows: If a party is a part, it is a "bad" party; and if the whole does not coincide with its good part, it is a "false" whole.

The part-whole framework also provides an understanding of how fragile and precarious a party system experiment can be. Parties can go off course on two sides. On the one side their course is menaced by excessive partisanship and/or a relapse into factionalism: The parts overwhelm the whole. On the opposite side their course is menaced by monopoly and/or unitarism: The whole overwhelms the parts. Through time, then, the course of a system of parties results in a difficult *via media* between the Scylla of disintegration (the whole falls apart) and the Charybdis of unanimism (the parts are englutted by the whole). Parties stay safely on course only when they manage to balance partisanship and impartial governing, loyalty to the party and loyalty to the state, party interest and general interest.

Furthermore, the part-whole framework neatly splits the question of what parties *are for*, that is, what is their primary purpose and/or function. When parties are "parts" (in the plural), then it stands as a fact that they are expressive agencies, i.e., that they serve the primary purpose of forcefully conveying to the authorities the demands of the public as a whole. It stands as a fact because the coercive party cannot materialize under the mechanics of a system of party pluralism. Conversely, when the "good party" represents the "real whole," then it stands as a mystery how the single-party arrangement could or would serve the same purpose. All the chances, let alone the evidence, are that the monopolistic party will extract from the "whole" (the public as a whole) what is desired by the "part" (the party without counterparts). In short, the parties that are parts are instruments for running a pluralistic whole: They presuppose diversity and institutionalize dissent. The non-part party denies, instead, the very principle of diversity and institutionalizes the repression of dissent.

Admittedly, the foregoing is highly abstract and amounts only to a mapping of fundamentals. It is for this reason, and within this ambit, that the opposition between party systems, on the one side, and party-state systems, on the other, has clear-cut features. In terms of rationale, it is *either-or*. The *more-or-less* will come in terms of empirical evidence. Thus far my focus has been on the pylons, on the hinges. But, clearly, we must also search for the joints.

In principle, the starting point should not make much difference. Whether we go from the hinges to the joints or, vice versa, from the joints to the pylons, the procedural order of the inquiry should be immaterial. If both elements are surveyed, at the end the two procedural routes should meet. In practice, however, it does make a difference whether one starts from the fundamentals or, instead, from the data end. If we are to judge by the development of the party literature over the past 20 years on the basis of the impulse that the study of parties received from Duverger's pioneering general theory, the most striking thing is how few progeny have followed from Duverger; that is, how little has followed in terms of broad theory building. By now the bibliography is, to say the least, massive.[34] But the more we know about parties, the more we are faced with a proliferation of threads, and the less we seem capable of pulling them together. Perhaps this happens in no small part because we have so much empirical evidence to reckon with. Whatever the reason, the fact remains that the shades obscure the colors, the details and the secondary take precedence over the primary. Hence the task of pulling the threads together inferentially, that is, starting from the empirical evidence, appears by now unmanageable. We are thus left to hope that the task of theory building can be managed the other way around, from the fundamentals down to the particulars. At least, to go back to the initial metaphor, the present work is predicated upon the assumption that from the hinges we can arrive at the joints.

A final comment is in order. Not only does the preliminary framework summarized in this section lack completeness – as is obvious – but it also lacks – admittedly – adequate proof, for the burden of proof has been largely laid, so far, on the force of logic; and logic is no substitute for evidence. Whether the evidence fits, as well as whether the empirical argument is actually furthered by our preliminary framework, remains to be seen. Nonetheless, there is a force in logic that should not be dismissed too lightly. Rational argument does affect human behavior, and men do respond to a "logic" of things. The empirical study of politics does not require that logical sloppiness should be praised.

NOTES TO CHAPTER 3

1 See specifically Deutsch, *The Nerves of Government*, op. cit. In general Richard R. Fagen, *Politics and Communication*, Little, Brown, 1966.
2 Samuel H. Barnes, *Party Democracy: The Internal Politics of an Italian Socialist Federation*, Yale University Press, 1967, p. 241. While Almond and Easton are also put to use, the definition by Barnes brings to the fore how the communication focus applies to parties.
3 See esp. Almond and Bingham Powell, *Comparative Politics: A Developmental Approach*, op. cit., ch. 7.
4 *Supra*, 1.4 and 2.1.
5 It should be clear that these three functions are selected for the preliminary outline because, and to the extent that, they touch upon essentials. They will be detailed in vol. II, where the entire list of the functions imputed to parties is introduced.
6 This methodological point is probed in my "Concept Misformation in Comparative Politics," *APSR*, December 1970.
7 Hirschman, *Exit, Voice, and Loyalty*, op. cit., and *supra*, 1.4.
8 At best, an incidental definition can be found on p. 218 of *Les Partis Politiques*, cit. Duverger in confronting the problem in his 1953–1954 lectures points out that the definition changes over time (that is, as parties change) and indicates that 50 years ago the appropriate definition was ideological; that the current, prevalent definition is based on social class; and that the organizational definition of parties is important only for certain types, especially the Communist parties. See M. Duverger, "Classe Sociale, Ideologia e Organizzazione Partitica," in Sivini, ed., *Sociologia dei Partiti Politici*, op. cit., pp. 109–114.
9 *Constitutional Government and Democracy*, Ginn, 1950, p. 420.
10 *Supra*, 1.1.
11 E. E. Schattschneider, *Party Government*, Holt, Rinehart and Winston, 1942, pp. 35–37.
12 *Capitalism, Socialism and Democracy*, op. cit., p. 283.
13 Bernard Hennessy, "On the Study of Party Organization," in William J. Crotty, ed., *Approaches to the Study of Party Organization*, Allyn and Bacon, 1968, p. 1.
14 True enough, Schattschneider qualifies his statement that "parties are defined in terms of the bid for power" (*Party Government*, cit.,

p. 36) by adding that "the party method . . . is a peaceable method" (p. 37). This is not implied, however, by his definition (while it is implied by the definitions which make reference to electoral competition).

15 L. Epstein, *Political Parties in Western Democracies*, op. cit., p. 9.

16 Ibid., p. 11. See, in more detail, on p. 9: ". . . any group, however loosely organized, seeking to elect governmental officeholders under a given label . . . rather than an organization is the crucial defining element."

17 This is testified by the overview and valuable analysis of William J. Crotty, "Political Parties Research," in Michael Haas and Henry S. Kariel, eds., *Approaches to the Study of Political Science*, Chandler, 1970, *passim*, but esp. pp. 290–295. See also the chapter by Austin Ranney, in Garceau, ed., *Political Research and Political Theory*, op. cit., and Fred W. Riggs, cit. below, nn. 19 and 24.

18 The following is an illustration: "A political party is a formally organized group that performs the functions of *educating* the public . . . that *recruits* and promotes individuals for public office, and that provides a comprehensive *linkage* function between the public and governmental decision-makers. It is distinguished from other groups by its dedication to *influencing policy making* on a broad scale, preferably by controlling government and by its acceptance of institutionalized rules of *electoral conduct* – more specifically, capturing public office through peaceful means." (Crotty, "Political Parties Research," loc. cit., p. 294. The italics are mine.)

19 See Fred W. Riggs, *Parties and Legislatures: Some Definitional Exercises* (mimeo), paper presented at the IPSA Montreal Congress, 1973, pp. 3–9.

20 The theoretical importance of the problem of "delimitation" is well stressed by, among others, Harry Eckstein in his Introduction to *Internal War*, Free Press, 1964, pp. 8–16. As he notes, "one can define a concept in terms of its delimitation . . . [and] at the beginning of enquiry one may have little more than a definition to serve as a delimitation of a subject" (p. 9).

21 For the distinction between political associations, movements, and parties, see David E. Apter, "A Comparative Method for the Study of Politics," *AJS*, November 1958, p. 227. If movements become parties, they usually develop into "external" (externally created) parties, while political associations, or clubs, have often been the birthplace of the "internal" parties. Specifically on the notion of association see Robin Williams, *American Society*, Knopf, 1951, pp. 450–455. For movements in general (including sect formation, religious and political revolutions, nationalistic and charismatic movements) see Neil J. Smelser, *Theory of Collective Behavior*, Free Press, 1962, ch. 10, "The Value-Oriented Movement."

22 On minimal, as well as on simple and complex definitions, see G. Sartori, F. W. Riggs, Henry Teune, *Tower of Babel: On the Definition and Analysis of Concepts in the Social Sciences*, Occasional Paper of the International Studies Association, Pittsburgh, 1975, pp. 32–35 and *passim*.

23 *Power and Society: A Framework for Political Enquiry*, op. cit., pp. 169, 170–171.

24 F. W. Riggs. *Administrative Reform and Political Responsiveness:*

A Theory of Dynamic Balancing, op. cit., p. 580. This is the most recent formulation. For a variant, see below, n. 27.

25 The quotations are from "Comparative Politics and the Study of Political Parties," in Crotty, ed., *Approaches to the Study of Party Organization*, cit., pp. 50–51. This is in fact Riggs' major text on the topic; and see his entire review and very valuable discussion, pp. 46–72.

26 After all, factions can be powerfully organized and do nominate candidates for elections in the very real sense that the party is only the passive recipient of the nominations decided within, and by, the factional sub-groups. The point is pursued *infra*, ch. 4.

27 The impression is reinforced by this variant of Riggs' definition: ". . . any organization which nominates candidates for election to a *legislature*" ("Comparative Politics and the Study of Political Parties," loc. cit., p. 51; the italics are mine). That is, the word legislature has strong associations with constitutional government based on party pluralism.

28 Kenneth Janda, *A Conceptual Framework for the Comparative Analysis of Political Parties*, Sage, 1970, p. 83. This Sage paper abridges Janda's *ICPP Variables and Coding Manual*, op. cit., which is the source to consult for a better understanding and a full appreciation. It is important to add that Janda's definition is constrained by his research assignment, which covers also the "illegal parties." One wonders, however, whether this inclusion should not be sought via a specification clause.

29 In general, the drawback seems to be that while the first part of Janda's definition is too loose and open ended, the final clause is unnecessarily restrictive. What if a party does not pursue the goal – because it is too small, or because it is an anarchic/revolutionary party whose declared goal is to restore direct democracy, or for still other reasons – of placing its representatives in "government positions"? Should it not be considered a party, in spite of the fact that it competes at elections identified by a party label?

30 The fruits can be seen best in the various works of Riggs, who has pursued the minimal definition strategy more consciously and systematically than most other authors.

31 One may note, with reason, that the foregoing applies nicely to the post-1945 world, but not historically. While the Italian Fascist regime did hold two single list elections in 1924 and 1934, the Nazi regime felt no need of electoral legitimation. Hence under my minimal definition, the Nazi party would not be a "party." This goes to explain why earlier writers refused to call party the single party (*supra*, ch. 2, n. 9) and points to the unresolved difficulties of this assimilation (*supra*, ch. 2, n. 11).

32 Note that the proposed definition equally permits (in spite of the electoral characterization) the inclusion of the revolutionary parties to the extent that they do enter electoral contests – whatever their ultimate goals or ideology.

33 This is the characterization stressed by Epstein (above, n. 16). If taken seriously a mere "façade definition" implies that all the labels should be counted: And this leads to something like a quadruplication of the numbers involved. Label counting alone would confront us, in many countries, with 15 to 30 parties.

34 See, as of 1964, the selected and analytically arranged bibliography in LaPalombara and Weiner, eds., *Political Parties and Political Development*, op. cit., pp. 439–464; and, subsequently, Jean Charlot, "Nouvelles Études de Partis Politiques," *RFSP*, Août 1970, pp. 818–821. The pace of the publications since 1964 has been, if anything, accelerating. See also the two valuable articles by Joseph A. Schlesinger (on "Party Units") and by Harry Eckstein (on "Party Systems") in the *International Encyclopedia of the Social Sciences*, cit., vol. XI. A recent overview is Crotty, "Political Parties Research," in the Haas, Kariel vol. cit.; but see also the judicious appraisal of the state of the art by Derek W. Urwin, "Political Parties, Societies and Regimes in Europe: Some Reflections on the Literature," *EJPR*, I, 1973.

4

The party from within

4.1 Fractions, factions, and tendencies

By studying parties we imply that the party is a meaningful unit of analysis. Yet we go above the party as a unit, for we also study the party system. By the same token we can go below the party as a unit and study, thereby, the party subunits. Even if the party is the major unit of analysis, the analysis is incomplete unless it probes how these subunits enter – and alter – the party. As Eldersveld well puts it, in and by itself the party is "a miniature political system. It has an authority structure. . . . It has a representative process, an electoral system, and subprocesses for recruiting leaders, defining goals, and resolving internal system conflicts. Above all, the party is a decision-making system. . . ."[1] As the foregoing suggests, there are many ways of studying parties from within – as many, almost, as there are of studying political systems themselves. Two lines of inquiry, however, have received most of the attention: The issue of intra-party democracy, and the organizational approach.

The first goes back to Michels' "iron law of oligarchy" and has been, in effect, the major focus and concern in the study of intra-party processes.[2] Even though one would not expect totalitarian and authoritarian parties to practice democracy within their ranks any more than they practice democracy in the management of the polity, nevertheless the single party often claims, today, to be internally democratic. Hence one must decide, first, whether a given form is democratic and, second, whether the form corresponds to the substance of democracy. Given the variety of yardsticks by which "democracy" can be assessed, the problem posed by Michels is likely to remain an endlessly debated issue. But whether intra-party processes are really democratic is not my concern here.

The organizational approach is more recent: It was prompted by Duverger and leads the study of parties into the general area of organization theory. To be sure, the study of the organizational structure has a bearing on the democracy issue, for a democratic process requires certain structures and not others. On the other hand, organization theory is concerned with organizational problems, not with democracy – let alone that a structure may be democratic and the actual processes oligarchic or pseudodemocratic. The organizational focus pursues, then, its own issues. And, again, this is not the inquiry intended at this point.[3]

My reason for saying party *sub-units* is precisely that the focus is on the *next unit,* that is, on the major and most significant breakdown immediately below the party-unit level. Whatever the organizational – formal and informal – arrangement, a party is an aggregate of individuals forming constellations of rival groups. A party may even be, when observed from the inside, a loose confederation of sub-parties. At the other extreme, the totalitarian party also contains an informal group structure often characterized by intense group struggle. And these inner-party divisions, along with the kind of interactions thus resulting, are in themselves a distinct and crucial area of concern. The issue is, then, how the unit "party" is articulated, or disarticulated, by its sub-units. As noted previously, the party itself is – from within – a system. Hence it is proper to say that we are now focusing on the party-as-system – on a system whose parts are the party subunits.

The first difficulty on our way is that we lack an established terminology for designating the party subunits. Italians call them "currents" (*correnti*); Germans generally speak of wing and tendency (*Richtung* and/or *Flügel*); and French and English writers are equally loose and metaphorical on the matter. On the other hand, American political scientists have settled for "faction" – in my opinion unfelicitously. Historically, factions are what parties are *not;* currently, they are made to appear the inner, intrinsic *stuff* of parties. In ordinary usage, faction is evaluative; in political science, we are told, it is neutral. It is dubious whether the latter is an appropriate way of handling the *Wertfreiheit* issue.[4] And it is even more dubious whether there is any reason, or wisdom, in dismissing the historical connotation. To be sure, we do give new meanings to old terms all the time; and the more we bring back to new life obsolete words and connotations, the better for the richness of language. The point is, then, whether the classic meaning of faction is obsolete. And this does not seem to be the case.

In the first place, it appears that those investigating the new states are inevitably brought to use "faction" in the traditional associations of the term. Thus Huntington speaks of factionalism with reference to groupings that have

little durability and no structure. They are typically the projections of individual ambitions. . . . Reports that 42 parties exist in Korea or 29 in South Vietnam or 18 in Pakistan are false on their face. Such groupings are, in fact, factions, and they closely resemble the political cliques, juntos, factions, and family groupings which dominated eighteenth-century politics in Europe and America.[5]

It is appropriate to add that this applies not only to much of the Third World – thereby including a majority of the African states – but also, and equally well, to most Latin American countries. If there is one word that recurs over and over again in the description of South American politics, it is *personalismo,* personalism; and this is a good Spanish equivalent of faction as understood from Roman times to Machiavelli and up to Tocqueville. In the first place, then, it is a sure fact that old-time or old-type factions are still very much alive and in good health in most of today's world. In the second place, and reverting to the developed polities, it is one thing to say – as I have said – that parties supersede factions as a new and broader unit, and quite another to imply that factions do not survive, or may not be revived, as *parts-of-parties,* that is, as party subunits. And I have implied all along that traditional-type factions are not superseded in fact, nor obsolete in meaning, in the Western party polities either.

I thus have at least three misgivings as to the current, "special" political science usage of faction. First, if we need a broad, neutral term for the party subunits in general, faction is a bad choice, a word highly unsuited for this purpose; for on valid life-experience grounds the word retains in most countries a deep-rooted evaluative meaning. The suggestion is thereby conveyed, at least to the general public, that the stuff of politics is inherently dirty and wicked. My second misgiving is that the "special" meaning runs counter to the rule that the vocabulary of science should lessen, not increase or indeed create, ambiguity; whereas the factions spoken of by Key or Richard Rose,[6] for example, are clearly not the factions spoken of by Huntington. The net result is that we have injected a very confusing comparative equivocation into the discipline and that we are mixing up parochial with worldwide yardsticks. My third misgiving relates to the dismissal of the historical connotation. This dismissal tends, among other things, to remove from visibility the crucial lesson and concern of the past, as if modernity had exorcised, once and for all, factional degeneration, the risks and costs arising from groups that are only projections of individual ambitions. And if this is so, then we are missing much, though by no means all, of what politics is still about. In summary, we need a broad, neutral label that has yet to be found; we have created unnecessary ambiguity; and we have lost, or weakened, a specification that we need.

Having given my reasons for keeping in use "faction" to designate a specific type of political group, it behooves me to suggest another designation for the whole class of party subunits. For instance, if "nucleus" was available, it might suit this purpose. But party nuclei are generally understood as being grass roots, minimal and local units. With reference to the party nuclei we tend to investigate the intra-party processes from the bottom upward and in their countrywide, peripheral diffusion. My focus is, instead, on the major party subunits – major both in the sense that they are the first encountered as we descend below the party as a unit and in the sense that they aggregate the lower units, such as the nuclei, in and around the central party headquarters. Differently put, the nucleus level of analysis includes the party militants and participants; whereas I am interested in the higher levels, in the upper strata of the party.

All things considered, I have settled for the term *fraction*. There are, no doubt, some drawbacks to this choice as well. First, "fraction" has a special meaning in the Marxist vocabulary, particularly in the Leninist tradition. Secondly, the German *Fraktion* is the parliamentary party (indeed a pre-Marxist denomination, for it goes back to the 1848 Frankfurt parliament). Despite these inconveniences, I have been unable to find anything better; and the drawbacks appear smaller than the advantages. By entering a new general term, the first gain is that faction can be used again without ambiguity in its specific meaning. In the second place, "fraction" is surely more neutral and uncommitted than "faction" – at least insofar as the former term has a far shorter history and far less eminent ancestors than the latter. Furthermore, one can easily get accustomed to saying fraction, given the fact that we already speak of fractionism and fractionalization. In this connection "fraction" conveys the suggestion that an index of fractionalization need not be confined to party systems[7] and that it may work equally well for party systems *and* party fractions.

The major problem remains, namely, that the within-party anatomy cannot be adequately explored without the help of a more articulate framework. Rose suggests that we should distinguish between faction and tendency. As he defines them, a faction is a "self-consciously organized body, with a measure of cohesion and discipline thus resulting," while a tendency "is a stable set of attitudes rather than a stable group of politicians."[8] While the distinction is valuable, an organizational variable may not be an appropriate distinguishing mark. It would follow that if a tendency organizes itself, it becomes a faction; and, conversely, that there can be no factionalism unless a political group is cohesively organized. It seems to me, instead, that individual factionalism is perfectly conceivable and that a tendency can organize itself without losing its nature, that is, remaining as Rose defines it, "a stable set of attitudes." I would thus retain *tendency* to indicate the more diffuse, as against the more bounded and more visible, party subunits – such as the left and right party tendencies.

Having gone as far as the vocabulary at hand permits, we still need a more analytic slicing. Fractions are of many sorts, that is, the world of party subunits is a very diversified world. This variety is of utmost importance, for different subunits produce different units. More fully stated, different kinds of fractions impinge on (i) the degree of co-hesiveness and, conversely, of fragmentation of a party and (ii) the ways and means of intra-party interactions and dynamics. On both counts it is very meaningful to say that the nature of a party is in the nature of its fractions. Parties that are similar in ideology and organi-zational structure – e.g., the Catholic or the Socialist parties – can each be very different across the world in that their fractions are different. But here we enter a no-man's land. Hume probed into the nature of factions. We operate, instead, on the assumption that they are all alike or, at any rate, that their differences are not worth pursuing in any detail: All fractions are fractions, period. Contrariwise, my feeling is that unless we come to grips with the anatomy of parties, our under-standing of politics will always be handicapped by an important miss-ing variable.

4.2 A scheme of analysis

Thus far we have a threefold terminological articulation: *fraction* (the general, unspecified category), *faction* (a specific power group), and *tendency* (a patterned set of attitudes). In this mapping a pure faction and a pure tendency represent opposite ends of the sub-party con-tinuum. A party composed of pure factions would be a highly frac-tionated party, or at least a party whose inner divisions are highly visible and highly salient. At the other end, a party that is composed only of tendencies would be a party whose inner divisions obtain low visibility and low salience and thereby, according to our definition, a party with little fractionism.

Two additional, and residual, possibilities must be envisaged: The first is the *non-aligned partisans*, the independent members who iden-tify themselves with the party platform, with "positions supported by the whole of the electoral party, rather than with factions or tenden-cies."[9] The second is the *atomized party*, the party which is fragmented leader by leader, with very small groups revolving around each leader – generally members of parliament. Fractions are often "personalized," but the situation envisaged here is of atomized personalization. Both patterns – non-aligned or atomized – delimit the periphery of our topic. That is to say that the sub-party level of analysis is, in either case, of little significance. A party that is entirely composed of "independents," or is fully "atomized," has no significant fractional articulation beyond the face value of these characterizations.

It should be clear, on the other hand, that most parties are – at the subunit level – amalgams, combinations of differing proportions of fac-tions, tendencies, independents, and/or atomized groupings. From this angle, therefore, the residual groupings also must be taken into account, if for no other reason than that their presence alters the mix, i.e., the relative weight of each element of the amalgam. Moreover, the non-aligned partisan and/or the atomized area may function as support groups and indeed may become the most courted cards in the game, for they may well strike the balance between the party's majority and minority.

On the basis of the foregoing preliminary mapping, the sub-party anatomy can be fruitfully explored along four dimensions: (i) organizational, (ii) motivational, (iii) ideological, (iv) left-and-right. Clearly, these dimensions overlap and hang together; but it is unclear how. While we wait for adequate research to establish their correlations and interdependencies, it is useful to abide by a scheme which is as analytical as possible.

1. The *organizational dimension* comes first for a number of reasons. To begin with, the distinction between party and faction has often been drawn, in the past, along organizational lines, under the assumption that the party is the organized and the faction the organizationless body.[10] By now we know not only that the party subunits can be powerfully organized, but that the party might even compare with its subunits as the lesser organized entity.[11] This rectification makes, if anything, the organizational variable more important. Fractions range all the way from maximal to minimal sub-group autonomy vis-à-vis the party unit. This immediately provides an indicator as to which level of analysis – the party's or the sub-party's – is more relevant. And, clearly, it does make a wealth of difference whether, and to what degree, a party is made up of subunits that operate their own network of loyalties, hold their congresses, seek money for themselves (not for the party), have their press and their press spokesmen, and – all in all – relate to the party as quasi-sovereign groups. Finally, the organizational variable has priority in that it provides, in all likelihood, the hardest indicator for assessing within-party fractionalization. On the other hand, the organizational dimension must be allowed to vary independently. The main reason for this is contagion: Organization elicits organization. If some fractions become organized, other formerly organizationless fractions may have to follow suit, if for no other reason than to be able to compete effectively against the organized groups. By becoming organized, however, a fraction need not lose its nature as qualified by the other dimensions.

2. The *motivational dimension* is the one that probes more directly into "factionalism" proper. Hume drew to this effect the distinction between factions from interest and factions from principle. In more than two centuries we have not come up with anything better. Hume's "interest" might be rendered by advantage and near-synonyms: "util-

ity," "convenience," "opportunism," and "expediency." But "interest" is
clear enough. I shall follow, therefore, the wording of Hume with the
understanding that factions of interest subsume two distinguishable
referents: Naked *power factions* (power for power's sake), on the one
hand, and *spoils factions* (side payment more than power oriented),
on the other. Hume's factions from principle present a similar problem,
albeit a more serious one. The term principle is easily associated today
with ideology and ideological principledness. It should be understood,
therefore, that my fractions of principle include two varieties: *ideological groups,* but also pure and simple *idea groups,* or opinion groups,
i.e., groups whose ideas and ideals do not share the other characteristics of the ideological groups. In some respects this distinction is unnecessary. In other respects it is as important as the one – on which
the European literature has long dwelled – between parties of ideology
and parties of opinion.

Unscrupulous power and/or spoils groups point to what is generally
understood by "faction": They are *the* factions *par excellence.* The
opinion and/or ideological groups are, instead, disinterested; that is,
their major interest resides in promoting ideas and ideals (leading, to
be sure, to a corresponding policy). The extreme form of the fraction
of principle is the witness group that testifies to a value and goal
message. Thus while factions of interest are motivated by immediate
and tangible rewards, fractions of principle are, above all, *promotional
groups.*

The major difficulty along the motivational dimension is camouflage.
A faction of interest does not declare to be such, to be nothing but a
power or spoils group maneuvering for place and emolument. It can
seek cover under the banner of efficiency and technical realism; but it
can equally disguise itself under ideological garments. On the other
hand, ideology can be a very effective camouflage both in the sense
that it legitimizes a power-seeking group in the perception of its very
actors and in the sense that it cannot be easily uncovered by the observer. There are many recipes for obfuscating the real motivations.
This is, then, a tricky dimension. A first indicator might be whether or
not a fraction is clientele based. Spoils are very important to the factions of interest, both because they confer power and because they attract followers. Therefore, the factions of interest tend to be *clientele
groups,* to have a clientelar mode of operation and a clientelar-type
network.[12] Contrariwise, fractions of principle can best be detected, at
least prima facie, by their lack of a clientele base, by the fact that their
self-maintaining and recruiting force derives, more than from any other
single factor, from their intellectual appeal or belief proselytism. But
this is only a first, and by no means decisive, indication. For instance, the
presence or absence of a clientele structure might depend on whether

a group is in or out of power. It also relates to broad cultural styles. The exploration of the motivational dimension requires a battery of indicators, observations over time, and the reputational method.

3. The *ideological dimension* doubtlessly overlaps with the motivational dimension. Among other things, ideology is a powerful motivating force. On the other hand, a whole range of motivations has nothing to do with ideology. Therefore, the two continua should be disentangled. The motivational continuum goes from pure disinterest (the witness fraction) to sheer selfishness (the spoils faction). The ideological continuum goes from the extreme of ideological fanaticism and future-oriented principledness to the opposite extreme of sheer practicalism and pragmatism.[13] And if the two continua are so construed, it follows that the two dimensions vary independently. An ideological fraction may well be a witness group but can equally be a spoils group. Likewise, a pragmatic fraction can be either spoils motivated or wholly disinterested (e.g., testifying to honesty in politics or to technical competence).

To be sure, the foregoing raises some intriguing problems. As noted, ideology turns out to be – in the present-day world – a very useful and effective camouflage. And we do encounter, frequently enough, fractions that qualify, at the same time, as ideological and spoils seeking. Now, the causal factor and whether such fractions are more spoils oriented than ideologically motivated, or vice versa, are a matter of empirical research; and only research can throw light on whether the ideology is nothing but a legitimizing smoke screen. These intricacies testify, therefore, to the importance of keeping the ideology-pragmatism dimension separated from the disinterest-selfishness dimension. It is only too easy, otherwise, to be deceived by appearances and/or to establish one-to-one aprioristic correspondences among the elements of the sub-party puzzle.

The ideological dimension is distinctive, and should be distinguished, for still another reason. When speaking of more-or-less ideology and, conversely, of more-or-less pragmatism, the implication need not be motivational but might well be cultural. That is, the ideological dimension differs from all the others in that it points to a cultural factor, to the overall temper (and temperature) of politics in a given cultural setting.

4. The *left-right dimension* comes last, in my enumeration, because I trust it least. What compels us to utilize the left-right identification and ordering is a formidable reason, namely, that this appears to be the most detectable and constant way in which not only mass publics but also elites perceive politics. An additional reason is that the left-right positioning is, often enough, the one that does least violence to the identification of tendencies, non-aligned positions, and atomized

configurations. Indeed, the most appropriate example of what we mean by "tendency" is provided in left-right terms.

Yet the drawbacks remain. When we come to analyze left-and-right, we soon discover that it is a hopelessly multidimensional dimension: the layman's "index" of politics, so to speak. Being a layman's index, it turns out to be a grand oversimplification resulting from a compound of fuzzy criteria.[14] The scholar might be tempted, therefore, to allocate this dimension to the *rhetoric*, thereby excluding it from a *science*, of politics. But this is, perhaps, a too drastic solution. The approach suggested here is that the left-right continuum can be handled best if we see first how far we can go without it. The suggestion is, then, that much of what is lumped together under the left-right interpretation of politics can be reallocated under the motivational and the ideological dimensions. This alerts us, in the first place, to the complexity of the bundle, for the reallocation brings out how often the fit is inexact and disconcerting. And the end result might well consist of a cleaned up, less emotionally loaded, or more disenchanted notion of left-and-right. We may well end up, that is, with transforming the common man's index of politics into something that the specialist can trustfully use as an index.

However that may be, if the left-right dimension is kept to the last, the first advantage is that it can be used *residually*, that is, to mean the only sure thing it does mean: a perception. Under the clause "left-right as perceived," it is useful and correct to identify both parties and party subunits as being leftist, center placed, or rightist. It is useful because it is a ready-made, simple ordering (even though it is, in effect, both a spatial and an evaluative ordering). It is correct because we are simply allowing that parties and party subunits are so perceived. Therefore, under the "as perceived" clause the left-right identification can be safely taken at its face value – and is not intended to explain more than it can explain.

The second advantage resulting from the residual use is that we are now clearly required to allow this dimension to vary in conjunction with, but independently of, the others. In spite of deep-rooted value taboos, "leftness" can combine with a pure power-seeking and/or spoils-oriented motivation, just as "rightness" can coincide with a candid idea-motivated group. Furthermore, leftness can be highly pragmatic, and rightness highly ideological. These associations may have become infrequent; but this is not something than can be settled a priori or by definition.

As anyone can see, the foregoing scheme of analysis is tentative, embryonic, and far from being exhaustive. Among the criteria that would have to be added in pursuing a more analytical underpinning, game theory and coalition theory would seem to afford, albeit loosely, the most promising suggestions. In this connection a relevant preliminary distinction is that between the personalistic or *personalist fraction* serving and following the fortunes of one undisputed boss,[15] and what might be called the confederative or *coalitional fraction,* that is, the alliance-type group that contains no single general but many colonels and majors. Also, and on the basis of a complementary approach, fractions are different in that their role, and role playing, is different. In this respect one finds *support groups,* that is, fractions of the bandwagon type, eager to join the winner and satisfied by side payments; *veto groups,* fractions whose major purpose and strategy is to obstruct; and *policy groups,* i.e., the fractions seeking to govern and impose policy. As coalition theory indicates, these types can be quite fluid, for a blocking coalition (of veto groups) can find its ways to becoming a winning coalition (of the policy type), just as a winning coalition may lose, thereby taking on the role of a blocking coalition.[16] On the other hand, these patterns may become crystallized and persist over time. And the purpose of these distinctions is precisely to pin down the extent of intra-party role fluidity and differentiation.

Finally, classic distinctions such as that between strategy and tactics apply to fractions just as much, or as well, as they apply to politics in general. Thus Janda codes the party subunits as being either *strategic* or *tactical.*[17] It equally goes without saying that other relevant variables are the *size* of each fraction (as expressed by the percentage of votes and/or seats controlled in each body: within the party, in parliament, and in the cabinet); and especially the time *duration.* Unfortunately, the latter indicator can be very insidious, for a fraction might simply change name or recombine (through mergers and splits) diverse groups while maintaining its name. What matters is, therefore, whether there is substantial stability and continuity – and this is very much a matter of impressionistic, albeit informed, judgment. At least for broad comparative purposes I would rather speak, then, of *stability-durability,* loosely divided into low (i.e., volatile type of fractions), medium, and high. If the chronological duration alone points to high stability, so much the better. But if the time count indicates, instead, volatility, then it is wise to look into the degree of organization, the degree of ideological cohesiveness, the type of motivation, and, more than anything else, the significance of the unit of measure, that is, the permanence of the label.

The major breakdowns of the scheme outlined in this section, and the resulting typology, can be summarized in a checklist form as in Table 2.

The table has the merit of requiring the scholar to check, independently, all the items. While more items could be added – whether a fraction is strategic or tactical, vision or issue oriented, etc. – the danger

Table 2. *Breakdowns and typology of party fractions (checklist)** *

Structure	Organized	___
	Organizationless	
	Half and half**	___
Motivation	Spoils-power group	___
	Idea-promotional group	___
	Both (+) Neither (−)**	___
Attitude	Ideological	___
	Pragmatic	___
	Both (+) Neither (−)**	___
Positioning	Leftist	___
	Centrist	___
	Rightist	___
	Vague**	___
Composition	Personalist	___
	Coalitional	___
	Half and half**	___
Role	Policy	___
	Support	___
	Veto	___
	Fluid or other (−)	___

*Unless otherwise indicated, use plus signs.
**If unknown or unascertainable, use question marks.

is that a longer list of as yet rough categories might be checked by implication rather than on the basis of information. Size is not entered (maxi-, medium, and mini-fractions) so as to avoid stating the obvious. The stability-durability and the relative importance of each fraction are not entered, on the other hand, because they raise problems of assessment and coding that require separate consideration; but they are, obviously, important items. If strong intensity or prevalences are detected, these can be indicated by two (or even three) plus signs. If the minuses are too frequent – over a number of fractions in a number of countries – then the scheme is a poor one. A high number of question marks would testify, instead, to the poverty of our information. The table only provides, to be sure, a first working tool – fraction by fraction, at one single point in time. If the checking is repeated over time, however, the sequence of the stills is likely to give interesting dynamic information, especially along the dimensions of motivation, positioning, and role. Moreover, if a sufficient number of countries are covered, then one might draw from the foregoing a table of significant and patterned clusters. For instance, we might find a strong correlation between organization and only the extreme ends of the left-right spectrum; or between personalist factions and unstable positioning; or between centrism and policy role – and so forth. But it is too soon to say.

4.3 *Southern politics: "factions" without parties?*

The conjecture that in most countries party subdivisions are likely to exist, to be significant, and to affect the operational code of the party is merely a conjecture because only three countries have been studied with a deliberate focus on the sub-party units: the so-called one-party states in the United States, Italy, and Japan.[18] To be sure, the literature on Latin American parties incessantly speaks of factionalism, *personalism,* and the like. But this literature has little bearing on our discussion in that it refers to the pre-mass party. The United States, Italy, and Japan belong, instead, to the phase of party consolidation in which the party as a unit becomes meaningful. The three investigations have not been carried out, however, under the assumption that party subdivisions are a normal occurrence, to be studied because the subunit level is a significant level of analysis. They have been prompted, rather, by the assumption that the cases in point represented pathological patterns, if not instances of political teratology. On the other hand, no attempt has been made to ask similar questions, to treat at least two of these cases in some parallel form, and even less to do so under a common conceptual framework; nor has there been any attempt at matching the respective findings.

To be sure, this strictly contextual treatment is not without justification. American "factionalism" – as American scholars want to have it – is studied because the party system is atrophied. With respect to what – since Key wrote his classic book on the subject – is known as Southern politics, the question is: What happens without turnover, that is, when one and the same party remains permanently in office? With respect to Italy the question, instead, is: How is it that, and what happens when, a structured system of six to seven parties duplicates, and indeed multiplies, this multiplicity at the sub-party level? Hence Italian "currents" – as they are euphemistically called – are studied because they contribute to the hypertrophy of partisanship. As for Japan, the literature appears to take note of its "multifactionalism" as a matter of course, with little speculation or interrogation about it.

One could hardly stumble, then, into more recalcitrant evidence, at least for comparative and theoretical purposes. Nonetheless, and in spite of the fact that different questions about entirely different systems leave us to skate on very thin ice, I shall attempt to bring the discussion under a converging focus. This requires, in the first place, a reassessment of the theoretical context in which the American findings have been placed.

Whatever the worth of the "one-party democracy" class,[19] it is strange that the United States should have been involved in such a matter. With respect to "democracy" – understood as a constitutional rule that protects the inalienable rights of the citizens – the states of the Union are not sovereign. Their deviations from the patterns established by the Federal Constitution, the U.S. Supreme Court, and the presidency may be significant and, at close range, disturbing. But this does not detract from the fact that – with respect to the principles and fundamentals of American democracy – the single states are granted only a subordinate and limited autonomy. Hence Florida or Louisiana or Mississippi, or any of the other one-party states of the United States, are not states in the sense in which Mexico and Tanzania are such.[20] We encounter, again, the unit jump fallacy: A sub-state, i.e., a member of a federal state, is made equal to a sovereign state. The first point is, then, that Southern politics has little to do with establishing or disestablishing a democracy.[21]

The question that immediately follows is in what sense, if any, roughly one-half of the American states can be called "one-party states." Key and much of the ensuing literature are remarkably loose on the matter. On the one hand, and despite some complaints,[22] the Solid South (plus Republican Vermont) is, or has long been, spoken of as a one-party area. On the other hand, Key's major point was that "the South really has no parties."[23] The two stands are, in principle, inconsistent.[24] Are we confronted with a one-party or with a no-party situation?[25] Presumably, the reply might be that the alternative is not applicable. Even so, the reply would have to be neither – not both. The complication or, better, the complexity of the matter stems from the fact that the United States owe to their federal structure a *two-tier party system*, one state-narrow and one nationwide. It follows from this that each level is of itself incomplete and/or reflective of the other level. With respect to "democracy," for instance, the state level has a wholly subordinate jurisdiction (a clear case of incompleteness). With respect to the point at issue the consequence of a two-tier party system is that two parties exist almost everywhere – that is, also at the state level – even though in the so-called one-party states the minor party owes its existence and characteristics to the nationwide system, thereby acquiring relevance mainly with respect to the presidential elections and to dispensation of the patronage flowing from the federal center. One might say, therefore, that the existence of two parties – which is by no means the same as a twoparty *system*[26] – remains the standing pattern throughout the United States, if only in exogenous and incomplete terms, that is, on account of the superimposition of the national twoparty system.

The foregoing implies that when American scholars speak of the "one-party" areas of their country, the label is inappropriate and misleading. What they are really describing is a situation in which two parties (as identified by the numerical criterion of classification) fail to produce the *mechanics* of twopartism, that is, in which two parties are not competitive enough to produce alternation in power. This pattern is entirely different from the one-party pattern. It belongs – as we shall see in detail later – to the *predominant-party* type of party system,[27] which is, in turn, one of the possible, normal outcomes of a twoparty *format*. And the point that American so-called unipartism is not such – but a deceptive misclassification – must be forcibly reiterated on comparative, transnational grounds.

If we wish a science of politics to exist, we must bow to the obvious necessity of dismissing a two-yardstick vocabulary, one for internal and one for worldwide consumption. Even for a dismal science it is absurdly antiscientific to enter dissimilar facts under a same class with the cryptic understanding that while the category is identical, its animals are different. To be sure, in case studies things are seen close up and thus magnified, whereas in comparative studies things are seen at a distance and thus minified. This is inevitable, and intuitive adjustments that cannot be expressed by our vocabulary are always necessary when we switch from the near and concrete to the distant and abstract. Yet any decent classification must be able to accommodate both the monographic, or nation-by-nation, findings on the one hand and the transnational evidence on the other. In the case in point, moreover, this is not a problem, for the world scene already suggests a category for accommodating the American pattern: the class of the predominant-party systems – defined as those systems in which the same party wins, over time, the absolute majority. Thus the persistence, over the decades, of the error-inducing error of saying "one-party" South, testifies to a most surprising parochialism. But let us now look, if sweepingly, into the facts of the matter.

Drawing from the criteria (not from the terminology) of Schlesinger, the states of the Union have displayed over the period 1870–1950 two fundamental patterns: (i) twoparty competitive (9 states) or cyclically competitive (12 states); (ii) one-party predominant (27 states).[28]

Both groups are, to be sure, a somewhat mixed bag. The first group of 21 states assimilates the competitiveness that leads to recurrent alternation in office and what might be called credible competitiveness, that is, the ability of the minority party to mount a substantial and consistent competitive threat.[29] Schlesinger's measure, here, is the ability of the minority party to win, if only cyclically, at least two consecutive victories. The second pattern – one-party predominant – includes both a group of 16 near-competitive states (the minority party occasionally wins a single victory, but by default of the predominant party, not on its own strength), and a definitely subcompetitive group of 11 States (the Solid South, Oklahoma, and Vermont) in which the minority party has never won a governorship and makes a poor showing, if any, at all elections.[30] The distribution changes, to be sure, as the time period and/or the criteria change. Thus Ranney and Kendall find, from 1914 to 1952, 26 twoparty states and 22 one-party and "modified one-party" states.[31] But distributive discrepancies are immaterial to my argument.[32] As I said, roughly half of the American state party systems did not qualify, at least up until the sixties, as displaying twoparty mechanics, even though they had, as a rule, a twoparty format. Hence we are left with some 22 to 27 states of the predominant-party system type.

The estimate can be challenged on still other grounds. In Mississippi and South Carolina, for instance, most elections are not even contested. Hence the argument can be made that these two states belong – together with some Swiss cantons – to what Girod calls the "lonely party" pattern.[33] Also, Minnesota and Nebraska elect their state legislatures on a nonpartisan basis, that is, without party labels. Here the argument could be that these are genuine cases of politics *sans* parties.[34] Despite these additional complexities, what matters most – within the general pattern of one-party predominance – is that some 11 states fall, by all criteria, below any standard of even potential competitiveness: They definitely are *subcompetitive*. This is, across the world, a rather unique case. And this is why Southern politics requires a separate special consideration of, and at, the sub-party level. Here "factions" (in the American meaning of the term) appear to matter more than parties.

Key found a wide and scattered variety of arrangements. Yet two distinct patterns clearly emerge from his account: (i) multifactionalism (Florida being the extreme case) and (ii) bifactionalism (Georgia, Louisiana, North Carolina, Tennessee, Virginia). The bifactional situation can be, in turn, either balanced (the two factions are not too uneven) or unbalanced (Virginia, North Carolina, and Tennessee each have a strong, cohesive majority faction faced by a relatively weak minority faction).[35] These findings suggest a number of interesting queries.

It is frequently assumed that "party cohesion is a direct function of the degree of competition between political parties."[36] Hence the lesser the competition, the higher the intra-party fractionism. The hypothesis may be reformulated, in a broader context, as follows: Parties are cohesive, and remain the significant unit of analysis, with respect to their vote-getting preoccupation. This is the same as saying that the electoral party (not the nominating or candidate-proposing party) provides the optimal standpoint for considering the party as a non-divisible unit. If, however, a party finds for itself – for whatever reason – an electorally safe situation, the party unit and unity will tend to give way to sub-party disunity. Under this condition, then, the real units are the fractions; and the more subcompetitive the inter-party situation, the higher the intra-party fractionalization.

If this conclusion is tested against the 11 Southern states, one would expect to find (i) that the near-competitive group tends to be bi-factional, while (ii) the subcompetitive group gives way to multi-factionalism. The first subhypothesis is borne out by the evidence. The two Southern states that are near-competitive – North Carolina and Tennessee – are also bifactional.[37] The second subhypothesis fares less well. A majority of the subcompetitive states are multifactional (Alabama, Arkansas, Florida, Mississippi, South Carolina, Texas), but three states (Georgia, Louisiana, and Virginia) are bifactional. Key's explanations were, for Virginia, that "Republican opposition contributes to the creation of one tightly organized Democratic faction," and, for Georgia and Louisiana, the importance of "personalities" (plus Louisiana's ticket system).[38] These considerations suggest that a different measure of competitiveness might fit the case of Virginia, which clearly was – in Key's assessment – as near-competitive as North Carolina and Tennessee. As for the other two exceptions, the personality argument points to the importance of a taxonomy of fractions – such as the one outlined in the preceding section – and to the necessity of accounting for the electoral arrangement (in the case of Louisiana, the ticket linkage among candidates). All in all, both the first grand hypothesis and the two subhypotheses are not disconfirmed, and they might well be confirmed if better qualified by some additional conditions. Yet none of the foregoing seems to hold if one turns to the Italian pattern. By most standards the Italian party system is adequately competitive. It is also highly structured, and many would take this to imply that the Italian parties are cohesive. Nonetheless, the system is characterized by "multifactionalism," that is, in my terminology, by a very high degree of intra-party fractionism.

There is little point, at this stage of our ignorance, in trying to re-state the relation between competitiveness of the party system and sub-party fractionalization. The *caveat* clearly is that the students of Southern politics are the victims of excessive self-tailoring. As for the remedies, a first suggestion is that our generalizations must be qualified by the type of party system to which they apply (or do not apply). This implies, in turn, that sloppy categorizing represents one of our major weaknesses. In the second place, the electoral system – in all its many aspects – might well be an important, neglected variable. For instance, is competitiveness the same (or is it perceived in the same way) in plurality and in proportional electoral systems? A third possibility is that ideology is also relevant, in the sense that the generalizations that hold for pragmatic politics may not hold for ideological politics, and vice versa. Finally, and surely, we need to improve "condition analysis," for the suspicion is very strong that our failures in generalizing relate in no small part to unstated and as yet unidentified conditions. Among these, the constitutional pathways are only too often glossed over.

Another set of queries relates to whether, and in what sense, bifractionalism is a rough substitute for twopartism and, by the same token, multifractionalism an ersatz of multipartism. The answers depend very much on the setting in which these queries are raised. If the setting is unipartism (and, still worse, one-party democracy), the problem is misstated. Was Key right, then, in asserting that the South "really has no parties"? Yes and no, I dare say: Yes in the sense that it brought him to the point; no in the sense that the South is not really a case of politics without parties, but rather – in a comparative perspective – of party system atrophy. This atrophy results from historical conditions; but it results also from the two-tier structuring of American party politics, which allows for the deficiencies of one level to be compensated (and in some respects projected) at the other level. Hence to say that the South has no parties is true only in the sense that the units that matter are the sub-party units. And in this perspective the conclusions of Key and of much of the following literature can be, I feel, safely generalized. Key found that "political disorganization" – which is equal to "chaotic" and "discontinuous" factionalism – works to the advantage of the haves and to the detriment of the have-nots, that it "confuses the electorate," that it makes a government "especially susceptible to individual pressures and especially disposed toward favoritism," and such that it "lacks the power to carry out sustained programs of action."[39] If the critics of parties – along the Ostrogorski line – and the advocates of a partyless direct democracy really wish to probe their arguments, they should reckon with these findings and conclusions.

Viewed overall, the American evidence does not bear on fractions *without* parties but, rather, on fractions *above* parties. Likewise, it does not testify to a variant of *unipartism* but to a major group of *predominant-party systems*. These two rectifications suggest that the American evidence has yet to be properly exploited on comparative and theoretical grounds. The major comparative risk, or limitation, inherent in the American experience results from the fact that the Republican and Democratic parties are among the few Western mass parties which do not have card-carrying members, and thereby from the fact that the nomination of party candidates for office is not a closed, impenetrable within-party affair but is often a first-election affair.[40] A pre-election that is – in most respects – the *real* election does represent a unique feature that requires careful comparative handling. On the other hand, it would be reckless to say, in general, that the primary arrangements defy transnational comparability. In the appropriate perspective the case of Southern politics does provide – as I have attempted to show – a major, comparative testing ground. I shall now attempt to see whether the Italian and Japanese patterns of fractionism can also be put to comparative use, that is, whether the loose ends of arguments coming from far-removed experiences can be somehow brought together.

4.4 Italy and Japan: fractions within parties

The Italian situation represents an extreme case of partisan hypertrophy. At the party level Italy belongs – in my taxonomy – to the systems of extreme and polarized multipartism.[41] Since the late forties the students of Italian politics have been counting, and accounting for, the interplay of some six to seven "relevant" parties.[42] Since the late fifties, moreover, they have had to reckon with a crescendo of intraparty fractionism.[43] In the early seventies there was a moment at which a fine counting pointed to the active existence, below the surface of the overall party spectrum, of as many as 25 "currents," alias fractions and factions.[44] But to avoid excessive complication we may settle here for the two more relevant and interesting cases: the Christian Democratic party (*Democrazia Cristiana,* or DC) and the major Socialist party.

The Christian Democratic party being the dominant Italian party, it has understandably attracted the most attention. By the end of 1971 its anatomy displayed nine "currents" – eight of which without doubt relevant – all of them sharing the various spoils, all of them officially organized, and most of them expressing their independent, dissonant viewpoints on whatever daily issue.[45] That is to say that the DC fractions are semi-sovereign, represent by and large the primary loyalty of their members (splintering the party from the top all the way down to the rank and file), and invest most of their time and ingenuity in relentlessly maneuvering for a larger share.

In a number of respects the fractional development of the major Socialist party, the PSI (*Partito Socialista Italiano*), is even more interesting.[46] In 1961 the then undisputed Socialist leader Pietro Nenni put it very explicitly at the party's congress: "Fractionism has been in the last four years, at first covertly (from the Venice to the Naples congresses) and since then openly, the internal malady of the party. From Naples onwards, the most impressive and frightening fact has been the rigidity of the currents, which has turned them into fractions."[47] Nenni was prophetic. Ten years later, in 1971, the PSI had little to envy, or to learn, in terms of fractional strife, from the Christian Democratic party. The Socialist party was deeply split, in 1971, into four to five fractions. If one adds to this that two other Socialist parties were in existence at the time and that both derived from a secession (thus representing, with respect to an ideally united party, another set of four fractions, two reformist and two strongly leftist), the overall Socialist area turns out to be as fragmented – at the sub-party level – as the denominational area.

The Socialist development is particularly interesting not only because one would expect a denominational, interclass party such as the DC to be more heterogeneous and exposed to inner fragmentation than a Socialist platform, but also because the DC has been "corrupted" by the temptations of power uninterruptedly since 1948, while the PSI has long waged against the DC the accusation of colonizing the country and the banner of working-class "purity"; let alone the fact that it was only in 1963 that the Socialists gained access, with some subsequent interruptions, to governmental power.

How can this development be explained? In principle, or on logical grounds, it was not to be expected, and indeed took most observers by surprise. The rational argument would seem to be that multipartism allows ample room for accommodating qua parties the differences and divergencies that twoparty systems can accommodate only at the sub-party level. It would seem to follow that the more numerous the parties, the greater the homogeneity of each party and the lesser the need for intra-party fractionism. Conversely, the fewer the parties, the greater the likelihood of party heterogeneity and, thereby, of sub-party fractionism. Given the circumstances, this rationalization only helps explain why the observers were slow in catching up with what was boiling in the Italian pot.

Another assumption – though a far less plausible one from the outset – was that

in contrast to parties in the United States, the problem of factions seems to have been solved in Europe (1) because of the more streamlined and hierarchical organization of European mass parties, (2) because of their apparently higher degree of programmatic homogeneity, and (3) because of the greater institutional centralization of European political systems.[48]

This assumption testifies, more than to anything else, to the distorted or inadequate comparative perspective resulting from a single-country yardstick. A third, more plausible and less parochial assumption hinges on the size principle. Here the explanation is that party subdivisions are the inevitable consequence of the mass membership of mass parties: The larger a party, the less it can be controlled, or the more it is bound to reorganize itself, informally, on the basis of minor and more manageable units.[49] While it can hardly be denied that size is always meaningful in these matters, it is a very frustrating variable when we attempt to underpin its thresholds. As it stands, the argument appears far too abstract, and the size principle alone appears to be an insufficient principle of explanation. For one thing, equal bigness does not seem to produce equal fractionism. Furthermore, it is not clear why the internal slicing of oversized parties should take one form – the fractional type of structuring – rather than any other. For instance, why should it be a fractional instead of a "stratarchical" arrangement?

Rather than attempting to refine the foregoing speculations, let us revert to the evidence at hand. As we already know, the explanations given for the case of Southern politics do not hold well – at least vis-à-vis the Italian case. The Italian party system is, in the main, well structured; its minor parties are not, in spite of their smallness, ghost parties; and the electoral contests are competitive. Let it be recalled, in this latter connection, that the Italian Communist party controls, in 1975, more than 33 percent of the total vote, and that the governing-oriented democratic majorities have been very thin ones all along. Therefore, it cannot be said of Italian electoral contests that it makes little difference who wins. Not only are Italian parties competitive, but their competition has a vital, survival aspect to it.

If Italian fractionism cannot be explained in the light of the American experience, our search for explanatory clues should turn to a more similar case, such as the one of Japan.[50] As a matter of fact, with respect to "factional politics" the similarity between Italy and Japan appears impressive: It is a similarity verging on twinship. The two major Japanese parties – the predominant Liberal Democratic party and the Socialist party – are each described as a "federation" or a "coalition" of sub-parties. The very same words are used by most observers of the Italian scene. The question put by Scalapino and Masumi is: "Do the Liberal Democrats represent a party, or are they a federation of parties?" And their reply is that Japanese politics is characterized by a constitutive "primacy of faction over party."[51] In a strikingly similar vein, the question put by an Italian observer (who was, at the time, also a member of parliament) is whether the DC is a party "*with* currents, or *of* currents."[52]

A closer inspection indicates, as one would expect, that similar statements can fit dissimilar phenomena. If we focus, for instance, on the electoral party, Italy has not proceeded along the path of fractionism as far as Japan. At election time the Italian parties do perform as parties: The electoral party is cohesive, and the candidates do owe their election – and know it – to the party slate.[53] Hence, at least for electoral purposes, the party is, in Italy, the real unit. Contrariwise, in Japan elections are not fought by the local party branches but essentially by the local fractional associations. To be sure, in both cases (and one can safely add in most, if not all, cases) the party candidates bitterly fight each other. But in Japan the electoral party is outflanked by the out-party organizations of the candidates (which may not be card-carrying members and which may well impose themselves upon the party), whereas in Italy the candidates fight for their election via the local party branches and fight each other, in between elections, precisely for control of the party branches.

On the other hand, if the focus shifts from the electoral party – the vote-catching unit – to the policy-making party, and especially to how the fractions strive for the control of their party, then the argument could well be reversed; that is, the Italian DC might well appear far more fissured than the Japanese Liberal Democrats. In Japan there is no crossing of party lines. The Italian fractions instead influence the policy orientation of the party and even blackmail their own party in transparent syntonization with the fractions of other parties. This has been particularly the case, in the past ten years, with the DC's left-wing fractions, whose weight with, and influence over, their party hinges, more than on anything else, on Socialist fractional support. In like manner, the Socialist party slid to the left of Nenni and ousted him, very much with the indirect help of the DC's leftist fractions. This is not to say that Italian politics proceeds at two levels – the party's and the sub-party's – and that in some major respects the governmental coalitions count less than the cross-party fractional alliances.[54] This would be going too far because, *inter alia*, the cross-party fractional alliances are not full grown and fully concerted alliances: They result from tacit understanding, and are indeed all the more effective the more covertly and indirectly the factions obtain external reinforcements. Thus the coalitional game cannot be given the same weight at each of the two levels. But, surely, the Italian cross-party inter-factional alliances are part of the overall coalition game.

On balance, therefore, it appears that the aggregate degree of fractionalism in Italy and Japan remains, in spite of the differences, strikingly close and that the two countries provide – at the sub-party level – a good comparative match. In striking contrast to the American pattern, in both countries a solidly entrenched fractional subsystem operates *within* the parties. Whichever unit or level counts for more, it cannot be said that the fractions replace the party, for the party units are far from being atrophied or irrelevant.

The major difference between Italy and Japan is at the systemic level. Given a similar hypertrophy of fractionism, its consequences may be different in different party systems. The Italian party system requires coalition governments. Furthermore, given the extension of the overall ideological spectrum, the Italian governmental coalitions are very heterogeneous and result, on this account, in inefficient and ineffective government. For the past 20 years Japan has been, instead, a predominant-party system characterized by liberal-democratic single-party governments. This major systemic difference entails that while the Italian fractions cross the party lines, the Japanese ones operate within their party. In both cases governments are short-lived; but the efficiency of government is far less impaired in Japan than in Italy. This is so, among other reasons, because the Italian fractional game largely undermines the division of roles between government and opposition, whereas Japanese fractionism does not (as long as the system remains of the predominant type).

With all of this, if we come to the causal question – how the Italian and Japanese fractional hypertrophy can be explained – the comparability of the two cases is of little help. The current Japanese pattern results from the 1955 "fusion" of formerly distinct parties. Moreover, and still more important, the prior and primordial units of Japanese politics were what are today its fractions. Hence the genesis of the current party system can be described as a double layer of superimpositions, or as a two-step confederative process, originating from the units that remain – despite their coalescence – the real protagonists of the game. Conversely, the current Italian pattern results from a process of "fission." The Italian genetics of the case is that the parties came first, and their fractionism grew and consolidated itself later. It turns out, then, that the Italian case is by far the more perplexing of the two, and that the experience of one does not suggest what causal factors might explain the development of the other.

Presumably, if the available evidence allowed more countries to be collated, some clues might emerge from broader and more detailed comparisons. For the time being, however, we can only acknowledge defeat. That is, our three cases – the United States, Japan, and Italy – do not indicate, as far as I am able to detect, any common, fundamental "deep reason" for their unusual and somewhat extreme standing in fractional and factional performance. We seem to be left, therefore, with the usual type of unique historical explanation – with the impact of the past over the present. There is, most certainly, ample evidence to this effect. Yet how can it be that the present has no impact upon the past? With due respect to what history can and does explain, there is still a way of pursuing the scientific type of explanation. This is to suggest that we turn to the *applied science* and, specifically, to what I call political engineering.[55]

4.5 The structure of opportunities

In regard to the approach of any applied science, medicine is the obvious analogy. Doctors do not know the cause of many dysfunctions and diseases, and yet they cure them. Granted that the safest cure is the one that removes the cause, the therapy need not reconstruct and follow the path of the genesis. Whatever causes a headache, we take an aspirin. Whatever the reason for appendicitis, we have recourse to an appendectomy. In this perspective – actually the perspective of an applied science at its inception – we may neglect the ultimate causal factors and concentrate on *how* we can intervene, *where*, with sufficient success. By so doing, we are likely to hit only on intervening or more superficial causal factors. Yet not only in practice but also in theory this would be no negligible accomplishment. In the case in point my suggestion is, then, that we turn to the *structure of opportunities*, that is, to the overall context of rewards and deprivations, of payoffs and sanctions, in which party men live and operate.

4.5 The structure of opportunities

The structure of opportunities is important, to begin with, for the shaping of the party system itself. As we have just seen, the Japanese "electoral parties" are far more fractured than the Italian ones. This should not come as a surprise if one looks into the respective electoral and financing arrangements. The Japanese electoral system is neither a single-member district system nor a list system of proportional representation; it is (since 1947) a multimember district system characterized by small constituencies electing from three to five representatives.[56] The Italian electoral system for the Chamber of Deputies is, instead, a list system of highly proportional representation (given the very large size of the constituencies) in which the voter expresses both a party preference and, within the party list, a candidate preference. Hence the vote for the party list takes precedence and must not be imperiled by intra-list battlings for the highest number of preferences.[57] Conceivably, the fight for the preference vote could be pursued in Italy as the fight for election is carried out in Japan, that is, via collateral organizations of the candidates. But here we come to a second element: the resource factor, and specifically the political money variable.

The Japanese Liberal Democratic party results from successive fusions; but the allocation of the resources has not been "fused": The funds still go to the original component units rather than to the party as a whole. This is even more the case with the Japanese Socialist party, which receives its major support from labor unions that are highly fragmented and decentralized, that is, gravitating at the enterprise and plant level. In sum, Japanese political money flows very much along the channels of the general pattern of the Japanese social structure: a structure based on familistic, occupational, and organizational "personal connections" (*kankei*) that create strongly compartmentalized ensembles.[58]

The Italian party finance pattern is altogether different. Probably the discontinuity between the Italian pre-Fascist and post-Fascist parties has been far greater than the discontinuity between prewar and postwar Japanese parties. Whatever the reason, the Italian parties are the major recipients and collectors of political money. Some of it, doubtlessly, goes directly to the fractions;[59] but not enough to pay for out-party electoral organizations of the candidates. Nor would the Italian electoral arrangements justify this kind of investment policy.

Be that as it may, my theme is not how the structure of opportunities shapes the party system but how it shapes the sub-party processes. And a prior clarification is in order with respect to how the structure of opportunities relates to the resource base. Despite the fact that opportunities and resources already are, in themselves, very broad categories pointing to large clusters of variables, I propose to reduce the first cluster to just one "opportunity variable": the intra-party electoral system. Furthermore – as my subtitle suggests – I shall submit the resources (specifically, political money) to the opportunities and actually assume that such resources are given, albeit in unknown amounts. The first reduction, or *tour de force,* will be explained throughout this section. But I should explain now why I subsume the resources into the opportunities.

The development of politics makes politics a full-time profession (with salaries) operating on the basis of specialized, large-scale agencies (with costs). Prima facie it would seem to follow that political money – which is not the money for "corruption" but simply the money required to cover the cost of politics – must reign today more than it ever reigned in the past. Yet large resources are invested in political entrepreneurs and enterprises which go afoul, and meager means propel major political events. While political money is a well-kept secret, there is one standing conclusion resulting from all the interest group studies across the Western world, namely, that economic and financial power has to accommodate itself, willy nilly, to the polity it finds. Political money has to reckon with "givens" – the sites that happen to be influential (e.g., parliament, bureaucracy, parties) – and to seek "access." In short, money feeds, and thereby influences, a given structure of opportunities; but money hardly makes it what it is. A closer look at the matter suggests, therefore, that the growth of mass politics and democracy brings about a decrease, not an increase, of the power of money. Let it be added that the Western politician seldom is, nowadays, someone who uses politics as a means for gaining wealth. Not only is he far more power driven than profit driven, but he well perceives that property is not power and, more precisely, that his power does not hinge on his wealth. Furthermore, the money the politician needs often has a low cost (to him), for money has lost its preindustrial rarity. It no longer is the sovereign that searches for the money, but the money that searches for the sovereign.

Coming to the point, the party finances do not explain why party systems are as they are, nor their variance across the world. And I can think of only one good reason for political money to be given to the party subunits instead of to the party as a unit, namely, that the latter is a more profitable investment than the former. If the fractions are under party control, then there is little to be gained by bypassing the comptroller. The question hinges, therefore, on how the party loses or, conversely, gains control over its fractions.[60] And this brings me back to the structure of opportunities and specifically to the intra-party electoral arrangements. That electoral systems have an impact has been forcefully stated by Duverger. The gist of his well-known "laws" is that a single-member district system reduces the number of parties, whereas proportional representation multiplies them. Duverger's laws have been widely challenged.[61] Granted that his laws, as they stand, do not hold for the party system and the electorate at large, nobody has ever wondered whether they might hold, instead, for small electorates (such as the party members) operating in simpler and less "disturbed" arenas. Presumably, this question has not been raised because we have not paid much attention to how different the party and the sub-party levels of politics are.

At the party level – as expressed by inter-party electoral competition – we have *visible politics*. At the sub-party level we have *invisible politics* – relatively speaking, of course. It follows that a number of factors that condition the visible, public behavior of politicians are no longer operative when we come to their intra-party behavior.

In the first place, the visible sphere of politics is characterized, if to a different degree, by overpromising: And this confronts the politician with serious, acrobatic problems of face saving and consistency. Visible politics is deeply conditioned, furthermore, by the anticipated reactions of the electorate. But invisible politics can proceed without paying much toll to these preoccupations. In the second place, statutes and legal constraints carry, in the visible sphere of politics, a weight that gets lost when politics becomes invisible. Since parties enact rules for themselves under which the rule maker and the rule addressee largely coincide, party statutes are seldom complied with beyond the extent that suits the interests of the interested parties. If the constitution of a country says, "Parties are not permitted," it is difficult to go around such a provision. But if the statute of a party says, "Factions are prohibited," the provision can well remain a *flatus vocis* – words with no consequence. In the third place, the rationality assumption does not fare well with mass publics, that is, in the visible arena of politics; but it is not unrealistic to assume that politicians are "rational," or rational enough, in playing their own, invisible game of politics.

Compared with visible politics, then, intra-party politics is *pure politics* – in two respects: It is more simple, and it is more genuine. It is more simple in the sense that many exogenous factors and disturbing variables can be set aside: Pure politics is made of, and explained by, fewer variables. It is more genuine in the sense in which Machiavelli described politics: Politics is only politics. And these premises pave the way to my conclusion, namely, that the opportunity structure bearing on fractionism can be reduced to two variables – organizational structure and electoral system – and ultimately to the latter.

Party statutes contain, roughly, three major elements: a set of prohibitions, the organizational structure, and the electoral arrangements. The prohibitions can be tacitly unheeded on the basis of reciprocal whitewashing, and their effectiveness is highly uncertain. The organizational structure is a firm element, but it deals effectively with fractionism in one case only, and an extreme case at that: "democratic centralism," as Lenin pleasantly called it. The Communist-type organization is, in fact, a structure of *vertical centralism*. Its secret is to sever horizontal communications, to have only up-and-down communication lines, and especially descending ones. No democratic party has been able, or shown as yet the desire, to go that far.[62] On the other hand, other organizational remedies against fractional proliferation are not easily found. In the final analysis we are thus left with the electoral system. Prima facie we are not left with much. However, if invisible politics is made of fewer variables than visible politics, the implication is that a same variable need not have – and indeed is unlikely to have – the same import at the party and at the sub-party levels. And this is particularly true for the voting and electoral arrangements.

Let us first assess what voting means and how elections are perceived by the average citizen of a democratic polity. Under normal, routine circumstances the average citizen gives neither much time nor much attention to the polls. He can hardly be blamed, for the normal voter has only an *electoral,* not a *decisional,* vote. His voting choice only enters – and this in a near-infinitesimal portion – the decision of who will actually make the decisions for him or in his name. For the average citizen, therefore, the act of voting, and the manner in which he is made to vote, is a very marginal circumstance. If his candidate is elected and his party is successful, his major gratification is symbolic. No doubt he may also expect, from politics, material advantages. But only a very naïve voter expects politics to "pay" quickly and personally, i.e., directly into his pockets. On the other hand, and in any case, if his vote comes to nothing or his party has a poor showing, this will hardly be a tragedy for the average citizen, and will hardly affect his daily life problems.

If we now turn to the intense partisan for whom a political career is his life choice, the case is clearly very different. To begin with, he has at his disposal two kinds of votes: an electoral vote *plus* a decisional vote – a vote that actually goes to determining the policy decisions. Furthermore, his electoral and decisional votes reinforce each other and can be traded off vis-à-vis one another. In the second place, in party life voting is very frequent. Better stated, the voting atmosphere – which includes bargains about future vote exchanges – is very much part of the daily life of a ranking politician. In the third place, and finally, the gratifications resulting from this continuous voting process are by no means only symbolic: They are, for the winner, very substantial. All these differences – with respect to the voting experience of the ordinary citizen – converge in pointing out that for the career-seeking partisan the electoral system, i.e., the way in which he is made to vote and in which the votes are counted, is part and parcel of his *career system:* His career depends, above all, on how many party votes he can muster and control. The votes he receives rank his power; the higher the ranking, the more his vote has a market and a decision-making value; and all of this culminates, for the winner, in very concrete and immediate rewards.

There is no exaggeration, therefore, in asserting that the intra-party electoral arrangements are, for the career-seeking politician, his *routes to incumbency,* or his pathways to success. After all, the way in which the votes are counted and weighed decides who wins over whom. This implies, in the first place, that the electoral system variable is far more powerful in intra-party matters than elsewhere. It also implies that the electoral system is the most living part of the party's "living constitution": When it comes to voting, the chips are down, and all the actors have a vital interest in having the rules respected. All of this adds up to saying that the electoral system is indeed central to the structure of opportunities – as perceived by the partisan – for it carries powerful rewards (if well exploited) and severe deprivations (if mishandled or disregarded).

Fully stated the thesis is as follows. Whenever the party is important, that is, whenever political careers must go through the party career system, then the crucial variable – across all the democratic parties and regardless of the particular country – is the internal electoral arrangement; and this is so because electioneering represents, from the standpoint of the incumbents, the central element of their structure of opportunities. Two predictions or expectations are thereby implied: (i) that the behavior of the party's elites will reflect a strategy of maximal exploitation of the electoral system and (ii) that the rewarding tactics of vote maximization will change as the electoral system changes.

With reference to what is already known about the effects (and noneffects) of electoral systems on the number of parties, the sub-party level of analysis leads to the following modification: that while the electoral system fails to explain, of itself, the variance between 2 and, say, among 10 parties and is not, in particular, a sufficient cause of the multiplication of parties, the electoral system does become a *sufficient cause* of the multiplication of fractions. It should be stressed that I do not say sufficient *and* necessary. Nor do I say *the* sufficient cause. This allows that other causal factors may be equally important. I shall, in fact, point out that ideology too can be a sufficient cause. Likewise, I have already indicated that the intra-party electoral arrangements are a decisive variable only when the politician cannot bypass, as a rule, the party career system. It follows that other causal explanations are required for the less party-structured polities. The obvious illustration is, here, American "factionalism," which stands out as a case by itself precisely because it hinges on the primaries far more than on a within-party *cursus honorum*.[63] Let me restate, therefore, my general hypothesis in a more complete form: While electoral systems are, per se, a sufficient cause of intra-party fractionism, they are neither the sole nor a necessary causal factor. Simply and practically put, the laws of Duverger may well be wrong for parties and correct for fractions. But this requires an ad hoc reformulation, to which I now turn.

Hypothesis 1. A winner-take-all type of electoral system, i.e., a plurality system, will contain and/or reduce the number of fractions, that is, will maintain or encourage fusion. Assuming an ideological context, maxi-fractions are likely. Assuming a nonideological (pragmatic) context, a dual majority-minority interplay is likely.

Hypothesis 2. A highly proportional type of electoral system (hereinafter called pure PR) will allow a high degree of fractionism, that is, will encourage and produce fission. Regardless of context – whether ideological or pragmatic – maxi-fractions are unlikely, and both medium-sized and mini-fractions are likely.

Hypotheses 1 and 2 are largely self-explanatory, at least at this stage of the argument. They envisage extreme cases, and this places them on winning grounds. But many real world situations are likely to be found somewhere in between plurality and pure PR systems. How many of these in-between possibilities should we take up? The question is not rhetorical, for the possibilities of the case easily add up to impressive numbers.[64] If we recall, however, that we are observing pure politics, and specifically the kind of "genuine politics" immortalized by Machiavelli's description of the cunningness of the politician, then our exploration does not require much detail. On the advice of Machiavelli we might even close the issue by saying that any system falling short of the winner-takes-all solution can be neutralized and outmaneuvered – in the sub-party jungle – without too much difficulty. But this would be a too sweeping foreclosing. I shall envisage, therefore, the two intermediate arrangements – the majority premium and the clause of exclusion – which stand out for their brutality, i.e., for promising effectiveness.

The majority premium consists of giving a premium in seats to the list (in this case the fraction) having obtained the highest vote. In intra-party matters, however, this device displays a major weakness: It encourages neutralizing, viz., counterbalancing, alliances. That is, if the majority premium aims at penalizing, and thereby reducing, the proliferation of fractions, its purpose can be defeated by overnight inter-fractional alliances that leave the fragmentation – as soon as the party's congress election is over – exactly as it was. It is equally easy to understand why this device encourages a concerted alliance strategy. This is so because an electoral aggregation larger than the premium would in fact penalize the winner. For instance, if the 51-percent majority of votes is entitled to 65 percent of the seats, a list turnout of 70 percent would give a premium to the minorities. On the other hand, fractions are in a position to estimate their forces: The information is, to this effect, quasi-perfect. It is not difficult, therefore, to work out well-calculated alliances that see to it that the premium keeps everybody alive and in decent shape. To be sure, the device can be made more stringent. For example, two-thirds of the seats go to the list having obtained the relative majority, and the remaining one-third to the second winner.[65] But under such strictures a plurality system is preferable on all counts. Hence with regard to the majority premium device no hypothesis (prediction) is warranted.

The clause of exclusion, or *Sperrklausel*, consists of establishing a threshold for admission to representation. Thus while the majority premium aims at encouraging maxi-fractions and at rewarding the larger fraction, the clause of exclusion aims at eliminating the mini-fractions. In spite of this difference, one could argue that if the premium device can be easily outflanked, so can the threshold device. In the first case it is a matter of working out the electoral alliances in such a way that the winning alliance obtains only a minimal premium. In the second case all that is required is that the mini-fractions join forces, if only overnight, to the extent required for passing the threshold. But the parallelism is deceiving. For one thing, the penalty is very different. Under the premium arrangements, the price paid by the losers (and for miscalculations) is underrepresentation. Under the exclusion clause, the penalty is non-representation – something very close to extinction. And this entails other differences.

The exclusion clause creates *ipso facto* two classes of fractions: the mini-fractions (defined by the level of exclusion, i.e., standing below it) and the sufficient fractions, defined as the ones that are not imperiled by the threshold. These two classes are strongly unequal. The mini-fractions can survive only by finding allies that are willing to save them. The sufficient fractions have no such need. They may be willing to save the mini-fractions, but the bargain must be struck on their grounds, and there is no "rational" reason for a sufficient fraction to save a mini-fraction unless the latter pays a price and/or reduces its demands. In the end, therefore, mini-fractions no longer pay off: Their size is unrewarding. Conceivably, the fractionalization may be such that no unequal alliances are necessary, in the sense that the mini-fractions can pass the threshold simply by joining their own forces. However, this is only one of the many possible distributions. And the difference in stakes may also make, in this respect, a difference. If we take a highly fractional pattern that is, or pretends to be, ideologically motivated, then the alliance game must reckon with the arithmetics of ideology, i.e., with ideological contiguity and consonance. If the stake is over- or underrepresentation – as in the case of the majority premium – even unholy alliances can be digested in the name of mutual interest. But if what is at stake is the extinction of the ideological enemy, then unholy alliances smack of stupidity. Let the example be a 15-percent threshold of exclusion, 8 fractions, and the following distribution (from left to right): 4, 8, 22, 20, 30, 6, 5, 5. In arithmetics the two mini-fractions on the left could ally themselves with the mini-fractions on the right. In ideological arithmetics this is difficult to accomplish even at the sub-party level, and it is more likely that the three right-wing fractions will take the risk of making the threshold on their own, i.e., on a minimal winning coalition basis. Hence I will not bow, in this case, to the Machiavelli-inspired *caveat* and will take the risk of submitting a hypothesis.

Hypothesis 3. If PR is corrected by an exclusion clause, the fractional subsystem is likely to stabilize itself into medium-sized fractions, their size being established by the threshold sufficiency. On the other hand, it is unlikely that the exclusion clause will be effective with thresholds below the 20-percent level.[66]

The question might be – since three of my hypotheses bear on the containment or the reduction of fractionism – whether the number of fractions really makes a difference. Without entering a debate to be taken up when the same question is raised with respect to the number of parties,[67] let me simply point out that the "veto game" requires multifractionism, whereas bifractionism is generally conducive to a leadership system and eventually to the alternation of leadership. This is no small difference, especially if one considers that, once started, the veto game tends to go beyond brinkmanship. Still it is reasonable to wonder whether it is worthwhile to hamper a process of fission that is bound to find, at some point, a physiological halt. The interesting question is, then, how far party fractionism can go on its own, unfettered wings.

The assumption that fractionism must come to a natural end presupposes a constant-sum game. But the game appears to be variable sum. If the pie consisted of cabinet positions only, then a ceiling could be assumed to exist – albeit a stretchable one.[68] The big pie consists, however, of the areas under party "colonization"; and since there is no visible frontier to the colonizing process or to the fertile imagination of man in inventing ulterior spoils for conquest, the sum is indeed variable. The distributive criterion is also very relevant in the matter. A distributive system can be proportional; that is, the spoils are divided in proportion to the size and strength (thereby including the position value) of the fractions. But this limit can be overruled by a per capita distributive criterion: The spoils are to be divided not only in proportion but also per head (in this case, per fraction). In practice this means that, regardless of its strength, no fraction can be denied access to the spoils. The appetite grows with the eating, and new pies must be incessantly seized or created. There is no foreseeable end, then, along the route of fractional proliferation and voracity once the process attains momentum.

The problem exists. But have we really found an adequate therapy? Clearly, my explanatory clue – that fractionism responds to, and is caused by, the structure of opportunities – has an inherent, fundamental limitation: It does not apply by definition to Hume's factions from principle, that is, neither to the idea groups nor, even less, to the ideological fractions. Since these groups are not motivated by interest, it follows that they are largely insensitive to inducements and disincentives. On the other hand, this hiatus represents a severe stricture only vis-à-vis the fractions that are *pure* fractions of principle. The purity is very important, for any eventual "impurity" falls under the jurisdiction of my approach (as implicitly suggested in Hypothesis 1). It follows that the extent to which the structure of opportunities analysis happens to fit with the evidence is a good indicator of the extent to which principles and ideology are a camouflage, or are highly mixed with expediency and interests. Let it be pointed out, in this connection, that we are not far removed from the conditions of small group experimentation. Party leaders are a small group; and they are, as a rule, stable enough. It is not altogether uncommon, therefore, to find the same core of party leaders operating at different points in time under different electoral arrangements. And this suggests that the hypotheses set forth in this chapter are amenable to adequate, if imperfect, testing. However that may be, the limitation of my explanatory clue must be acknowledged. One way of acknowledging it – but also of testing it – is suggested in Hypothesis 4.

Hypothesis 4. The number of ideological fractions is inversely related to the number of parties; the number of fractions of interest bears no relation to the number of parties.

The rationale of the foregoing hypothesis is as follows. Given that the fractions of principle, and especially of ideology, are – if pure – largely insensitive to material rewards and deprivations, their number is likely to be, in a given ideological spectrum, relatively constant. Therefore, if there are enough parties to accommodate them, the fractional division will tend to coincide with the party division: At the limit, each fraction becomes a party. Conversely, the larger the discrepancy between numerous ideological fractions and few parties, the more we shall have parties divided by fractions. Let us now assume that no evidence supports the first part of the hypothesis. This given, it is the second half of the hypothesis that applies. The inference is as follows: Whenever a pattern of extreme multipartism is supplemented, at the sub-party level, by extreme fractionalization, the credibility of ideological fractionism decreases as the number of the fractions increases. For example, the Italian figures have been, at some point, of 8 parties incorporating some 25 fractions. It is difficult to believe, and even more difficult to demonstrate, that there are enough ideologies to sustain such a total. Furthermore, if one looks into the actual distribution, some 14 fractions were located in only 2 parties, which happen to be the post-1964 major governing parties: 9 in the Christian Democratic party and 5 in the Socialist party. Still more revealing, the Socialist fractional crescendo coincides very much with the party's access to the spoils of government – as predicted by the rule that applies to the fractions of interest.

At least one conclusion thus seems reasonably warranted: Not all the fractions in question owe their existence to a "creed." If this is their claim, it cannot be believed. On the other hand, this does not warrant the conclusion that all the fractions in question have been "corrupted" and thereby that they should all be reclassified as fractions of interest.

4.5 The structure of opportunities

This problem can be avoided if Hypothesis 4 is developed and transformed into Hypothesis 5.

Hypothesis 5. If the structure of opportunities rewards minifractions, the degree of fractionism is likely to be high, regardless of whether the fractions are ideological or not.

There is no hidden malice in this hypothesis. Its rationale simply is that – given a constant number of ideological fractions – a structure of opportunities that rewards even very small fractions will increase, or produce, a surplus of fractions of interest. On the other hand, if no ideological fractionism exists, the rule, i.e., the hypothesized incentivation, applies equally well. This brings us, it will be noted, very close to Hypothesis 2. The difference is mainly of generality. That is to say that while Hypothesis 2 specifies the structure of opportunity (PR), Hypothesis 5 leaves the system of incentives open to eventual, further specifications.

Yet the distinction between fractions of principle and of interest deserves to be pursued. Theoretically, the distinction is clear enough, but we are left with the problem of its operationalization. Especially when we come to the mixed cases, the question is precisely whether some fractions are *equally*, 50–50, principled and interested, or *more* on the side of principledness than on the side of self-interestedness – and vice versa. It would be overly ambitious to raise – with respect to things as poorly defined as ideology – a direct "how much" question, that is, to ask for a measure. If, however, we are content with *prevalences*, then the inquiry can be pursued, beyond the symptoms mentioned so far, with the help of indicators.

A first indicator could be called the index of fickleness. Over time we can count how many times the leader of a fraction has changed positioning along the internal ideological spectrum of his party. To be sure, a politician can change principles and be much the wiser for that. But how often, and with what coherence? A high rate of maneuvering and outmaneuvering from right to left, and subsequently from left to right, testifies to the prevalence of tactics over ideology and principles. This test can be repeated on the membership of each fraction. In this case we would obtain an index of longevity – as opposed to friability – of the sub-party groupings. Furthermore, a satisfactory distinction between strategy and tactics applied, over time, to an adequate selection of issues could also yield significant results.[69] Finally, we should look at the spread, whether nationwide or concentrated in few pockets (basically where the fraction boss resides), of each fraction. The indication is, here, that single-area fractions can hardly be credited with an ideological nature. And while the findings

103

of any single indicator could be challenged, a battery of indicators pointing to the same conclusion would provide adequate evidence.

Let me recapitulate. First, I am not putting forward a unicausal explanation. Since my argument applies to the fractions of interest or sufficiently tainted by interests, it is clear that at least another causal factor – principles and ideology – is assumed. Thus my problem is, implicitly, to what extent the fractionalization of parties belongs to the process of ideologization of politics, and to what extent it remains a very old thing – the factions of the classics – and thereby belongs, at least in part, to the failings of political engineering.

Second, my argument does not pretend to be genetic, in the sense that it does not pretend to reach, or to remove, the ultimate causes or the deep determinants of fractionism. It is frequently assumed that deep determinants are discovered by a sociological understanding and exploration of politics. With respect to party fractionism, however, the socioeconomic approach has failed, so far, to detect any relevant, significant correlation between social origin, economic and environmental conditions, on the one hand, and the actual configuration of the sub-party world, on the other.[70] This is hardly surprising if one takes the view that intra-party politics verges on being "pure" politics.[71] At any event, the problem is approached here – as stated in premise – from the standpoint of application, and precisely of political engineering. It may well be that this approach leaves us with proximal and even, perhaps, superficial causation. It shuns, however, the egg-and-chicken type of vicious regression. Furthermore, it affords a clear test: whether or not an intervention yields the predicted behavioral response.

Third, while I narrow the structure of opportunities to the electoral (career) system, this reduction is compensated, hopefully, by a corresponding enlargement. The one variable I have is a powerful variable. The underlying assumption is that visible politics and invisible politics are quite different things and therefore that our understanding has much to gain if the party and the sub-party levels are analyzed separately. The argument that intra-party politics is no longer conditioned and complicated by the factors brought into play by visibility might be suspected of being too well tailored to my purpose, which is – admittedly – to end up with a well identifiable, reliable variable admirably suited for cross-party comparisons throughout the world. If this should be the case, the sin is unintended and I would have to confess guilt. For I do not subscribe to the view that our problems should be defined by, and thus confined to, the data base.

4.6 From party to faction

We are back where we began. Starting from the pre-party factions we have arrived, after a long journey, at the within-party fractions and factions. It is appropriate, at this point, to assess the importance of the problem. Most evaluations of intra-party fractionism – at least in the three countries in which it is more visible and better studied – are highly critical, especially when the observer is a participant one. Key's judgment of factional politics was harsh. The same is true for most Japanese and Italian observers. The actors themselves, the politicians, often subscribe to the condemnation of their internecine battlings, as is confirmed by the fact that both the Italian and the Japanese major parties are under strong pressure, from their own respective ranks, for reforms intended to lessen factional virulence.[72] On the other hand, it is not unusual to find scholars dismissing the problem in the "this is as should be" vein. But there is a path between outrage and acquiescence – I mean, between two blindnesses.

Throughout the record of history, factions emerge as the despair of politics – at least, of "republican" politics. It is strange, therefore, that the more we demand of politics to provide the good life, the less we seem to confront its perennial stumbling block. Parties, I said at the beginning, supersede factions and are parties precisely to the extent they differ from factions. As I might put it now, parties owe to their competitive visibility the constraints that make them different from factions. Yet parties are units made of subunits; and the subunits are largely invisible. However, if Western civilization has managed to come up with a satisfactory constitutional solution for curbing the arbitrary rule of man over man, political engineering can also cope, I believe, with the problems arising from the dark insides of politics – under one, essential condition: that this is a concern, and that we keep a keen eye on the endless cycle of extinction and revival of factions proper.

To be sure, parties cannot be, nor should they be, monoliths. It can also be conceded that fractionism might have a positive value. But the vindication of fractionism must be, when appropriate, well justified. This is hardly the case with the argument that fractionism testifies to the vitality and authenticity of intra-party "democracy."[73] Democracy has a dim future if the word is stretched and abused to this extent. Intra-party democracy bears on how the rank and file relates to the party elites; and the magic of a word can hardly regenerate the harsh reality of factionalism – if it can be shown that this is all it is.

Leaving aside the rhetoric of democracy and its abuses, there is one justification that, at least in the Italian case, appears plausible. Its gist is that, given an immobilist type of party system leading to immobile

105

coalition governments, "change" is sought and can be obtained only via sub-party and fractional cross-party dynamics.[74] On the other hand the argument can be reversed, without any loss of plausibility, as follows: Italian cabinets are paralyzed not only by the ideological dissonance, or distance, among their coalition partners, but also by the aggravating fact that each party is paralyzed from within by the veto game played by its factions. Clearly, the issue depends on whether the evidence testifies more to a "factional" veto game, or to a "fractional" innovative dynamics. Awaiting such a scrutiny, I would go back to the preliminary point that there is little we can understand and discuss as long as the assumption remains that the party underworld is all alike, all made of one and the same stuff. The first step is, then, to identify the diverse nature of fractions in relation to their "connatural" styles of behavior.

As with icebergs, it is only a small part of politics that stands above the water line. My case rests, admittedly, on much darkness and few icebergs. It is quite possible, among other things, that my case is overstated, and this because my generalizations are drawn from extreme instances and, above all, from the Italian experience. On the other hand, it is well known that Latin American politics is largely factional; and there are good grounds for assuming that this is equally the case with most of the new states. As other icebergs are exposed or explored, we might well discover that factions are more relevant than we have hitherto suspected in many unsuspected countries as well.[75] When Duverger launched the study of parties, the first words of his preface acknowledged "a basic contradiction" and indeed a somewhat vicious circle: A general theory of parties requires preliminary information which, in turn, is not forthcoming "so long as there exists no general theory."[76] The sub-party level of analysis must confront, and muddle through, the same vicious circle.

NOTES TO CHAPTER 4

1 Samuel J. Eldersveld, *Political Parties: A Behavioral Analysis,* Rand McNally, 1964, p. 1. While this is a case study of the Detroit metropolitan area, it is of high theoretical value.
2 Eldersveld himself dwells at length on a reformulation of the Michels' issue.
3 The organizational approach is reviewed in vol. II.
4 For my views on "freedom from value," G. Sartori, "Philosophy, Theory and Science of Politics," *Political Theory,* II, 1974, pp. 151–154. In the case in point, "faction" can hardly be made neutral by definitional *fiat.*
5 Huntington, *Political Order in Changing Societies,* op. cit., pp. 412–413.
6 See below, nn. 8 and 23, and *infra,* 4.3.
7 Reference is made, in particular, to the index of fractionalization

developed by Douglas Rae, to be discussed *infra,* 9.5.

8 Richard Rose, "Parties, Factions and Tendencies in Britain," *PS,* February 1964, p. 37.

9 Ibid., p. 38.

10 E.g., and to stand for all, C. J. Friedrich, *Constitutional Government and Democracy,* op. cit., p. 421, where he finds the distinguishing feature of a party in "the requirement of stable organization."

11 The extreme case appears to be Uruguay, whose (dubious) two-party system is (or was, up until June 1972) only an electoral façade with respect to the real actors, i.e., the *lemas* and *sub-lemas* of the Blanco and Colorado parties. In this instance the party actually is a confederation more than a federation of its fractions. But see *infra,* 4.4, Italy and Japan.

12 The notion of clientele group and structure has been underpinned by a number of studies. Specific applications to individual countries are Joseph LaPalombara, *Interest Groups in Italian Politics,* Princeton University Press, 1964 (the Italian title is far more revealing: *Clientela e Parentela,* Comunità, 1967); Sidney Tarrow, *Peasant Communism in Southern Italy,* Yale University Press, 1967, esp. pp. 68–81 and *passim;* Keith R. Legg, *Politics in Modern Greece,* Stanford University Press, 1969; and Nobutaka Ike, *Japanese Politics, Patron-Client Democracy,* Knopf, 1972. There is no particular reason for confining clientelar politics to a transitional stage of the modernization process. Patron-client ties are found, if under a different name, in the U.S. "machines" and in the Spanish and Latin American *caciquismo.* In general see Eric Wolf, "Kinship, Friendship and Patron-Client Relations in Complex Societies," in *The Social Anthropology of Complex Societies,* A.S.A. Monographs 4, Tavistock, 1966, pp. 1–22; Alex Weingrod, "Patrons, Patronage and Political Parties," *Comparative Studies in Society and History,* July 1968; James C. Scott, "Corruption, Machine Politics, and Political Change," *APSR,* December 1969; John D. Powell, "Peasant Society and Clientelist Politics," *APSR,* June 1970; James C. Scott, "Patron-Client Politics and Political Change in Southeast Asia," *APSR,* March 1972; R. Lemarchand, K. Legg, "Political Clientelism and Development," *CP,* January 1972; Carl H. Landé, "Networks and Groups in Southeast Asia: Some Observations on the Group Theory of Politics," *APSR,* March 1973; Robert Kern, ed., *The Caciques,* University of New Mexico Press, 1973; Luigi Graziano, "Patron-Client Relationships in Southern Italy," *EJPR,* April 1973, and L. Graziano, ed., *Clientelismo e Mutamento Politico,* Angeli, 1974. This growing body of literature is very promising but difficult to unravel for my purposes. In particular, "clientele" and "patronage" – especially with reference to the patronage type of party – should be distinguished.

13 My reasons for construing an ideology-to-pragmatism continuum are given in "Ideology, Politics and Belief Systems," *APSR,* June 1969. See also *infra,* 5.3. This dimension is operationally construed by Kenneth Janda as "ideological factionalism" versus "issue factionalism" (*ICPP Variables and Coding Manual,* op. cit., pp. 159–161a). While my notion of pragmatism implies an issue orientation

– and thereby rejoins the operational definition of Janda – I prefer, conceptually, to approach this dimension with reference to its cultural background.

14 See G. Sartori, "From the Sociology of Politics to Political Sociology," in S. M. Lipset, ed., *Politics and the Social Sciences,* Oxford University Press, 1969, pp. 78–79. See also the analysis pursued *infra,* 10.3.

15 My "personalist factionalism" is very close to Janda's "leadership factionalism" (loc. cit., pp. 161–163). The more traditional labeling does not imply that leadership capabilities are actually involved.

16 How bargaining turns a blocking coalition into a winning coalition is shown by Brian Barry, *Political Argument,* Routledge & Kegan Paul, 1965, pp. 245–249. For the notions of blocking and winning coalitions see William H. Riker, *The Theory of Political Coalitions,* Yale University Press, 1962, pp. 103–104 and *passim.* Riker considers also the "losing coalition," which can be assimilated to support groups.

17 *ICPP Coding Manual,* cit., p. 163.

18 The order of the entries reflects the magnitude of the available evidence. Actually, the documentation on the third country, Japan, is insufficient (at least for the non-Japanese-speaking), and I shall have to refer to this case very tentatively (below, n. 50). Following Japan, India would be the next promising candidate on my agenda, except that only the inception of the Indian party system has been systematically explained at the fractional level of analysis (Myron Weiner, *Party Politics in India – The Development of a Multi-Party System,* Princeton University Press, 1957). The rest of the evidence is too fragmentary (see, e.g., Paul Brass, "Factionalism and the Congress Party in Uttar Pradesh," *Asian Survey,* September 1964; and Mary C. Carras, "Congress Factionalism in Maharashtra: A Case Study," *Asian Survey,* May 1970). In the European context, aside from Italy, only the literature on England permits, if indirectly, exploring the sub-party level in sufficient detail. See (in addition to Rose, "Parties, Factions and Tendencies in Britain," loc. cit.) S. E. Finer, H. B. Berrington, D. J. Bartholomew, *Backbench Opinion in the House of Commons 1955–1959,* Pergamon, 1961; P. G. Richards, *Honorable Members – A Study of British Backbenchers,* Faber, 1963, esp. pp. 145–160; Robert J. Jackson, *Rebels and Whips: An Analysis – Dissension Discipline and Cohesion in British Political Parties,* St. Martin's, 1968; P. Seyd, "Factionalism Within the Conservative Party: The Monday Club," *GO,* Autumn 1972.

19 *Supra,* 2.3.

20 The more recent addition to this misclassification is Michael Leiserson, "Factions and Coalitions in One-Party Japan: An Interpretation Based on the Theory of Games," *ASPR,* September 1968. While the article actually deals with game theory, its title is an ulterior, significant instance of the insignificance acquired by the class of unipartism.

21 This applies, to be sure, to constitutional democracy – a prior condition, however, of whatever else a "substantive democracy" is required to be. For this view see my article "Democracy," in

International Encyclopedia of the Social Sciences, op. cit. The point can be underpinned in cultural terms. According to Daniel J. Elazar, *American Federalism: A View from the States,* Crowell, 1966, pp. 79–140, even though the subcultural tendency of the South is, among the whites, "traditionalist," this is a subculture that belongs to a common Lockean-liberal political culture.

22 E.g., A. Ranney and W. Kendall note that the "Mississippi party system is not the same kind as the Soviet party system" and complain that using the same term – one-party – for both "unavoidably tends . . . to identify these things in the minds of students" ("The American Party System," *APSR,* June 1964, p. 479). The argument is even more compelling nowadays, with data banks and computer processing. We shall never make sense out of the one-party class if we have some 25 states of the Union mixed up, under this category, in our software. On the other hand, even Ranney and Kendall do not push their complaint to its logical conclusion: for they too end up with leaving ten states under the one-party rubric (p. 484).

23 *Southern Politics in State and Nation,* Knopf, 1960, p. 299. Key's analysis was concisely restated in *American State Politics: An Introduction,* Knopf, 1956.

24 It does not detract from Key's stature to note that his theoretical grasp is inferior to his other talents. His major comparative problem – comparing the American one-party and twoparty systems – is dismissed in two lines: "The problem thus phrased presupposes that one-party systems are alike, but they are not: that two-party systems are alike, but they are not" (ibid.). The retort could be that bad classifications need to be improved.

25 The difference is underpinned *supra,* 2.1. The issue is generally eschewed throughout the literature, beginning (very much along the same lines as those of Key) with Alexander Heard, *A Two-Party South?* University of North Carolina Press, 1952.

26 This is the difference between "format" and "mechanics" of twopartism spelled out *infra,* 6.4.

27 *Infra,* 6.5.

28 See Joseph A. Schlesinger, "A Two-Dimensional Scheme for Classifying States According to Degree of Inter-Party Competition," *APSR,* December 1955. This distribution is based on the control of governorships.

29 The reason for broadening the twoparty class so as to comprise credible competitiveness will be clear on comparative grounds (*infra,* 6.4). A too narrow definition of competitiveness (such as the one provided by Schlesinger's first class) would rule out, to begin with, the United States (at the federal level) as a twoparty polity.

30 This distribution is drawn from Schlesinger's classification, loc. cit. His breakdowns are as follows: (i) competitive states (9), (ii) cyclically competitive (4), (iii) one-party cyclical (8), (iv) one-party predominant (16), (v) one-party (11). I have aggregated the first three and the latter two classes. Another conceivable aggregation would give the following three patterns: (i) competitive (13 states), (ii) cyclically or near-competitive (24 states), (iii)

one-party predominant (11 states). The reason for the aggregation adopted in the text is that it fits the general definition of the predominant-party systems.

31 "The American Party System," loc. cit., esp. pp. 482–484. The authors combine the electoral returns for the presidency, the governorships, and the Senate, which inevitably makes their assessment different from Schlesinger's. Other differences are due, however, to the classificatory schemes and related definitions. With respect to the 11 subcompetitive states, the only discrepancy is Oklahoma, which is "one party modified" for Ranney and Kendall, while definitely "one party" for Schlesinger. California, Illinois, Michigan, Wisconsin, Montana, Missouri, and Maryland are twoparty according to the criteria of Ranney and Kendall, and one-party predominant in Schlesinger. Since the latter admits that his one-party predominant and one-party cyclical classes are "similar" in terms of "the overall dimension of competition" (loc. cit., p. 1125), even here the substantive discrepancy is really a minor one. The differences are very substantial, instead, with respect to the taxonomy proposed by R. T. Golombiewski, "A Taxonomic Approach to State Political Party Strength," *WPQ*, September 1958, which gives 19 twoparty states, 13 "weak minority-party states," and 14 one-party states (p. 501). On the other hand, Avery Leiserson obtains exactly the same distribution as Ranney and Kendall for the period 1933–1952: 26 twoparty competitive or cyclically competitive, and 22 one-party predominant states (*Parties and Politics*, Knopf, 1958, Appendix IV, p. 377). Leiserson's breakdowns are as follows: 10 competitive, 16 cyclically competitive (8 for each party), 14 dominant Democratic, and 8 dominant Republican. With respect to Ranney and Kendall, the main difference is that Leiserson combines the modified one-party and one-party classes into what he calls dominant pattern.

32 For a discussion of the various measures of party competition see R. E. Dawson, J. A. Robinson, "Inter-Party Competition: Economic Variables and Welfare Policies in the American States," *JP*, II, 1963, esp. pp. 270–278. But see, more fully, *infra*, ch. 7, n. 3.

33 The lonely party differs from unipartism as a spontaneous development does from an imposed development. *Infra*, ch. 6, n. 131.

34 The caution is that a nonpartisan showing may only disguise an underlying, de facto partisan alignment. At any rate, nonpartisan politics is real, and on the increase, at the municipal level; and here it surely deserves special attention. See esp. Charles R. Adrian, "Some General Characteristics of Nonpartisan Elections," in O. P. Williams and C. Press, eds., *Democracy in Urban America – Readings*, Rand McNally, 1961. See also C. R. Adrian, "A Typology for Nonpartisan Elections," *WPQ*, June 1959; and Eugene C. Lee, *The Politics of Nonpartisanship*, University of California Press, 1960. On the specific case of Nebraska see Richard D. Marvel, "The Nonpartisan Nebraska Unicameral," in Samuel C. Patterson, ed., *Midwest Legislative Politics*, Institute of Public Affairs, University of Iowa, 1967.

35 See esp. Key's summation in ch. 14: "Nature and Consequences of One-Party Factionalism," pp. 293–311. See also the monographic study by Allan P. Sindler, "Bifactional Rivalry as an Alternative to

Two-Party Competition in Louisiana," *APSR*, September 1955. It should be stressed that all my accounts apply from the time of Key's writing up to the middle sixties. New patterns have emerged since. By now it is pretty clear that the South no longer is a safe Democratic party reservoir: Competitiveness is emerging, especially at the presidential elections (in 1968 and in 1972 one may well speak of a Southern "presidential republicanism").

36 Golombiewski, loc. cit., p. 501.

37 Let it be recalled that my "near-competitive" class corresponds to Ranney and Kendall's "modified one-party," and to Schlesinger's "one-party predominant." Key attempts no generalization but does point out that "in both North Carolina and Tennessee the majority Democratic factions derive unity from the opposition of Republicans" and that "the cohesiveness of the majority faction in these states points to the extraordinary influence of even a small opposition party" (op. cit., p. 300).

38 *Southern Politics*, op. cit., pp. 300–301.

39 Ibid., pp. 302–310. A summary of the findings to this effect is in Fred I. Greenstein, *The American Party System and the American People*, Prentice-Hall, 1963, pp. 57–60. Dawson and Robinson point out that the degree of inter-party competition does not possess an "important intervening influence between socioeconomic factors and liberal welfare programs" (loc. cit., p. 289, n. 32); but this was not the real thrust of Key's argument. The same applies to the findings of Thomas R. Dye, *Politics, Economics, and the Public*, Rand McNally, 1966, which are in themselves extremely interesting but do not measure Key's central point. The argument is appraised in general *infra*, 6.1.

40 For an overall analysis of the various primary arrangements and their impact, see Sara Volterra, *Sistemi Elettorali e Partiti in America*, Giuffrè, 1963, pp. 157–219.

41 *Infra*, 6.1, 6.2.

42 For an introductory account see my chapter, "European Political Parties: The Case of Polarized Pluralism," in LaPalombara and Weiner, eds., *Political Parties and Political Development*, op. cit., esp. pp. 140–153; and, more broadly, Dante Germino, Stefano Passigli, *Government and Politics of Contemporary Italy*, Harper & Row, 1968, ch. 4. But see *infra* ch. 6, n. 45.

43 The first major English account of this development is in the two articles of Raphael Zariski, "The Italian Socialist Party: A Case Study in Factional Conflict," *APSR*, June 1962, and "Intra-Party Conflict in a Dominant Party: The Experience of Italian Christian Democracy," *JP*, I, 1965. Among the more recent studies in English, see A. J. Stern, S. Tarrow, M. F. Williams, "Factions and Opinion Groups in European Mass Parties," *CP*, July 1971, which is, in spite of its title, exclusively on Italy. See also Alan Zuckerman, "Social Structure and Political Competition: The Italian Case," *WP*, April 1972, esp. pp. 429–432.

44 This count excludes only the Italian Communist party (PCI), whose intra-party dynamics is largely invisible and cannot be assimilated to the patterns of the non-Communist parties. For how the organizational structure of the PCI impinges on its cohesiveness, see Giacomo Sani, "Le Strutture Organizzative del PCI," in VV.

AA. *L'Organizzazione Partitica del PCI e della DC,* Il Mulino,
1968, esp. pp. 167–196. It should also be clear that the Italian
correnti is used with the same lack of discrimination as is "faction"
by American scholars. Italian politicians speak of their fractions as
"currents" precisely to eschew the negative associations, which are
very strong in Italian, of the term faction.

45 The date 1971 is significant, for at that time the DC reformed its
statute with the declared purpose of reducing internal fractionism.
The nine fractions in question were: (i) *Iniziativa Popolare* (Ru-
mor, Piccoli), 20%; (ii) *Impegno Democratico* (Colombo, Andre-
otti), 15%; (iii) *Nuove Cronache* (Fanfani, Forlani), 17%; (iv)
Tavianei (Taviani), 10%; (v) *Morotei* (Moro), 13%; (vi) *Base*
(De Mita, Misasi), 11%; (vii) *Forze Nuove* (Donat Cattin), 7%;
(viii) *Forze Libere* (Scalfaro) 4%; (ix) *Nuova Sinistra* (Sullo),
2%. The percentages refer to the DC congress. All the foregoing
"currents" were represented in the party directorate, and all (except
the last one) had cabinet posts under the Colombo government.
Since 1971 the number of DC fractions has decreased, but a "personalist" disintegration (and multiplication) has been on the
increase.

46 Over the years, Italian socialism has undergone many splits and
mergers, which makes the various denominations difficult to follow.
The overall pattern has been, in substance, of two Socialist parties:
the PSI, whose eminent leader has been Nenni and which speaks
very much a Marxist language, represents the bulk of the Italian
Socialist tradition and polls nearly twice as many votes as the
Social Democratic party; and the Social Democratic party (currently relabeled PSDI), which represents the reformist tendency.
However, it can equally be said that Italian socialism has three
souls: reformist, "maximalist," and revolutionary. During the period
1964–1972 these three souls have been actually represented by
three parties, the third being the pro-Communist PSIUP (Italian
Socialist Party of Proletarian Unity), which reached in 1968 a peak
of almost 5 percent of the total vote but collapsed (and shortly
after dissolved) at the 1972 general elections. The major data
source on the PSI is Antonio Landolfi, "Partito Socialista Italiano:
Strutture, Organi Dirigenti, Correnti," *Tempi Moderni,* V, 1968.

47 Quoted from Antonio Landolfi, *Il Socialismo Italiano,* Lerici, 1968,
p. 119. Since Nenni's use of "fraction" is Marxist, this statement
means that the former currents had transformed themselves into
something unacceptable. On the growth of fractionism in the PSI
see esp. Franco Cazzola, *Carisma e Democrazia nel Socialismo
Italiano,* Istituto Sturzo, 1967. Also the Stern, Tarrow, Williams
article (above, n. 43) is mainly on the Socialist party.

48 Stern et al., "Factions and Opinion Groups in European Mass
Parties," loc. cit., p. 529. It should be clear that the authors report
an assumption they do not share.

49 See Michele Sernini, *Le Correnti nel Partito,* Ist. Ed. Cisalpino,
1966, p. 47; and Luigi D'Amato, *Correnti di Partito o Partito di
Correnti,* Giuffrè, 1964, p. 19.

50 My sources on Japan's fractionism are: Robert A. Scalapino and
J. Masumi, *Parties and Politics in Contemporary Japan,* University
of California Press, 1962, pp. 79–101, 169–174; Hans H. Baer-

wald, "Factional Politics in Japan," *Current History,* April 1964; Lee W. Farnsworth, "Challenges to Factionalism on Japan's Liberal Democratic Party," *Asian Survey,* September 1966; G. O. Totten, T. Kawakami, "The Functions of Factionalism in Japanese Politics," *Pacific Affairs,* 1966, pp. 109–122; L. W. Farnsworth, "Social and Political Sources of Political Fragmentation in Japan," *JP,* II, 1967; S. D. Johnston, "A Comparative Study of Intra-Party Factionalism in Israel and Japan," *WPQ,* II, 1967; A. J. Heidenheimer, F. C. Langdon, *Business Associations and the Financing of Political Parties: A Comparative Study of the Evolution of Practices in Germany, Norway and Japan,* Nijhoff, 1968; Nathaniel B. Thayer, *How the Conservatives Rule Japan,* Princeton University Press, 1969, and his article "The Election of a Japanese Prime Minister," *Asian Survey,* July 1969; Chae-Jin Lee, "Factional Politics in the Japan Socialist Party: The Chinese Cultural Revolution Case," *Asian Survey,* March 1970; Michael Leiserson, *Coalition Government in Japan,* in S. Groennings, E. W. Kelley, M. Leiserson, eds., *The Study of Coalition Behavior,* Holt, 1970. On the cultural factor, which is very relevant, see R. E. Ward, "Japan: The Continuity of Modernization," in Lucien W. Pye, Sidney Verba, eds., *Political Culture and Political Development,* Princeton University Press, 1965; Scott C. Flanagan, "The Japanese Party System in Transition," *CP,* January 1971, pp. 238–247 (the *kankei* theory); and B. M. Richardson, *The Political Culture of Japan,* University of California Press, 1973. See also *infra,* ch. 6, n. 134.

51 *Parties and Politics in Contemporary Japan,* op. cit., pp. 94, 85. M. Leiserson pushes this conclusion even further, if we are to judge by the fact that he makes Japanese multifactionalism equal to a multiparty system (as if no unit jump was involved).

52 Luigi D'Amato, *Correnti di Partito o Partito di Correnti,* op. cit., *passim.* In a subsequent work, *L'Equilibrio di un Sistema di 'Partiti di Correnti,'* Scienze Sociali, 1966, D'Amato makes it quite clear that the party is "made of" currents, and draws very harsh conclusions from the primacy of the fractions over the party.

53 This is confirmed by the experience with party splitting, which (aside from the physiological dualism between a social-Marxist and a social-democratic party) has a long and persistent record of failures. The electoral importance of the party is well understood by the DC members, if we are to judge by the fact that the DC has never had a secession, in spite of its very broad left-right stretch and heterogeneity.

54 This more extreme interpretation has been plausibly put forward, however, by Antonio Lombardo, "Dal Proporzionalismo Intra-Partitico al Fazionismo Eterodiretto," *RISP,* II, 1972.

55 See, e.g., my "Political Development and Political Engineering," in John D. Montgomery, Albert O. Hirschman, eds., *Public Policy,* XVIII, Harvard University Press, 1968, esp. pp. 262–276.

56 Japan shares with Ireland the characteristic of having the smallest multimember constituencies with the smallest variance. The Irish average size is 3.7 members per constituency; Japan's average size is 4.

57 The importance of the size of the constituency is demonstrated by Douglas Rae, *The Political Consequences of Electoral Laws,* Yale

University Press, 1967 (and 1971). The Italian average is 20 members per constituency, with high variance across the electoral districts. It should also be noted that only 30 percent of the voters give the preference vote (mostly in the South, with the Northern percentage ranging from 10 to 20 percent). See Luigi D'Amato, *Il Voto di Preferenza degli Italiani* (*1946–1963*), Giuffrè, 1964.

58 See Scalapino and Masumi, *Parties and Politics in Japan*, op. cit., pp. 86–101, and particularly the *kankei* theory of Flanagan (above, n. 50).

59 Interestingly enough, this has been especially the case with the left-wing DC "base" fraction, financed by Mattei's state petrol agency as a means for obtaining a pro-Arab foreign policy. Some of the details are in Giorgio Galli, Paolo Facchi, *La Sinistra Democristiana*, Feltrinelli, 1962.

60 See, *contra*, Giovanna Zincone, "Accesso Autonomo alle Risore: Le Determinanti del Frazionismo," *RISP*, I, 1972, whose conclusion is that the financing avenues and facilities are the major single factor. While my perspective is different, it can hardly be denied that money is a necessary condition.

61 The laws of Duverger and the overall issue are discussed in detail in vol. II.

62 It is noteworthy, in this connection, that the Italian neo-Fascist party, the MSI, settled its internal strifes by imitating, in a number of respects, the Communist-type organization. Things have changed since Duverger theorized (correctly, at the time of his writing) a distinct Fascist-type organizational structure.

63 This goes to qualify my statement (*supra,* 4.3) that the Southern "factions" stand above party: above because they bypass the party career constraints; and yet not outside nor without party, because the electorate at large does identify with the party label.

64 This can be easily gathered from any account of the wealth of existing (let alone imagined and proposed) electoral systems. A good general overview is: W. J. M. Mackenzie, *Free Elections*, Allen & Unwin, 1958.

65 This is known in Argentina, where it remained in force until 1963, as the Saenz Peña system and is generally classified as an "incomplete list system." In substance it is a double-premium system that beheads, in a multiparty pattern, all the third parties.

66 The discussion in the text is not purely speculative. The Italian DC used first the premium device, then PR (introduced in September 1964), then (in September 1971) the *Sperrklausel* (with only a 10/15-percent threshold, however), which was swiftly abandoned a year later. For some of the concrete details see G. Sartori, "Proporzionalismo, Frazionismo e Crisi dei Partiti," *RISP*, III, 1971, esp. pp. 646–651.

67 *Infra,* ch. 5. While the issue is not the same at the two levels, nonetheless the terms of the party-number debate can be adapted to the fractional level as well.

68 The Italian governments have reached the respectable size of some 25 ministers plus about 60 undersecretaries of state. Significantly, and despite efforts to the contrary, the Italian one-party cabinets remain equally plethoric.

69 This suggestion relates to Janda's coding, above, n. 13.

70 See Alberto Spreafico, Franco Cazzola, "Correnti di Partito e Processi di Identificazione," *Il Politico*, IV, 1970; and especially the follow-up of Stern, Tarrow, Williams, "Factions and Opinion Groups in European Mass Parties," loc. cit., which is basically a research on the PSI designed to explain its fractions along socioeconomic lines. While this research evidence cannot be considered sufficient – it bears on one party in one country only – nonetheless it is highly indicative, for the Italian Socialist party represents, from the standpoint of a sociology of politics, an optimal case.

71 This is not to imply that the sociology of politics obtains a high explanatory power at the party level of analysis. I argue the contrary in "From the Sociology of Politics to Political Sociology," in Lipset, ed., *Politics and the Social Sciences*, cit.

72 In 1963 a report of the Japanese Liberal Democratic party recommended a set of provisions for abolishing fractions (see Baerwald, "Factional Politics in Japan," loc. cit., pp. 226–227; and Farnsworth, "Challenges to Factionalism on Japan's Liberal Democratic Party," loc. cit., pp. 502–505). Nothing much followed. In Italy, however, the DC adopted in 1971 a clause of exclusion, even though the vested interests obtained, in 1972, its dismissal (above, n. 66).

73 This is a very frequent justification, and Samuel H. Barnes (*Party Democracy: Politics in an Italian Socialist Federation*, op. cit., p. 181) reports that over 90 percent of his group of PSI members agreed with the statement that currents are an "instrument of democracy." The finding testifies, more than to anything else, to the fact that the party is fractured all the way down the line. Clearly, those who practice fractionism are bound to justify it.

74 Stefano Passigli, "Proporzionalismo, Frazionismo e Crisi dei Partiti: Quid Prior?" *RISP*, I, 1972, p. 132. But see esp. Germino and Passigli, *Government and Politics of Contemporary Italy*, op. cit., pp. 127–132.

75 Other possible extensions of fractional analysis are suggested by Ralph W. Nicholas, "Factions: A Comparative Analysis," in *Political Systems and the Distribution of Power*, A.S.A. Monographs 2, Tavistock, 1965. The author approaches the issue, however, from the standpoint of social anthropology. Norman K. Nicholson, "The Factional Model and the Study of Politics," *CPS*, October 1972, confirms, in my reading, that while a general theory is very much in demand, it can hardly emerge from a conceptual morass reinforced by a multidisciplinary eclecticism. It is noteworthy that Nicholson identifies three structural models (village, polycommunal, and hierarchical factionalism), none of which accounts for "factions" as treated in the historical literature (*supra*, 1.1.) and as a specific sub-unit of any party in any and all polities.

76 *Political Parties*, op. cit. (North trans.), p. xiii.

PART TWO

Party systems

5

The numerical criterion[*]

5.1. *The issue*

There are more than 100 states that display, at least on paper, some kind of party arrangement.[1] The variety of these arrangements is as impressive as the number. How are we to order the maze? For a long time party systems have been classified by counting the number of parties – whether one, two, or more than two. By now, however, there is a near-unanimous agreement that the distinction among one-party, twoparty, and multiparty systems is highly inadequate. And we are even told that "a judgment as to the number of major parties . . . obscures more than it illuminates."[2]

One reaction to the party-counting approach is simply to drop the numerical base, precisely "on the assumption that the traditional distinction between two-party and multiparty patterns has not led to sufficiently meaningful insights." Thus LaPalombara and Weiner propose – for the competitive party systems – the following fourfold typology: (i) hegemonic ideological, (ii) hegemonic pragmatic, (iii) turnover ideological, (iv) turnover pragmatic.[3] The scheme is highly suggestive; but it is too sweeping. Another reaction is to let the data – especially the electoral turnouts – determine the classes, i.e., different clusters of party systems. This is the suggestion, for example, of Blondel.[4] A third reaction is to wonder whether we need classes at all, i.e., whether there is any point in classifying party systems. The argument is, here, that our universe is continuous and therefore that all we need is an index of fragmentation, or of fractionalization, or of linear dispersion, and the like. These suggestions will be taken up and discussed in due course.[5] For the time being, let us simply note that almost every writer comes up with his own scheme.[6] By now classifications and typologies of party systems are a plethora, and "confusion and profusion of terms seems to be the rule."[7]

[*] Parts of Chapters 5, 6, and 7 appeared with the title "Typology of Party Systems – Proposals for Improvement," in Stein Rokkan, Erik Allardt, eds., *Mass Politics: Studies in Political Sociology*, Free Press, 1970. The difference between the earlier, abridged draft and the present one is also of substance. Throughout Chapters 5 and 6 I have greatly benefited from the advice of Hans Daalder. While responsible for my own errors, I owe him many improvements.

We are seemingly entering, then, a vicious circle. On the one hand, we are on the verge of drowning in an *embarras de richesse*. On the other hand, this very proliferation attests that the universe of party systems badly and increasingly needs to be charted. But this appears to require further additions to the "profusion and confusion." The lesser evil is, perhaps, to backtrack and to review the case from the beginning. Was there something fundamentally wrong in the initial start, or have we gone astray somewhere along the way? It is not clear, in effect, where we stand on the issue. Do we mean that the number of parties is of little consequence? Or do we mean, instead, that our classifications fail to sort out these numbers?

To the first question I would reply that it does matter how many are the parties. For one thing, the number of parties immediately indicates, albeit roughly, an important feature of the political system: the extent to which political power is fragmented or non-fragmented, dispersed or concentrated. Likewise, simply by knowing how many parties there are, we are alerted to the number of possible "interaction streams" that are involved. As Gunnar Sjöblom points out, 2 parties allow for only 1 stream of reciprocal interaction, 3 parties allow for 3 streams of interaction, 4 parties for 6, 5 parties for 10, 6 parties for 15, and 7 parties for 21.[8] Since these possible interaction streams occur at multiple levels – electoral, parliamentary, and governmental – the indication clearly is that the greater the number of parties (that have a say), the greater the complexity and probably the intricacy of the system. For instance, from the vantage point of the electors a pairwise comparison between the programs entails, for 8 parties, 28 comparisons, for 9 parties 36, and for 10 parties 45 comparisons. Furthermore, and in particular, the tactics of party competition and opposition appear related to the number of parties; and this has, in turn, an important bearing on how governmental coalitions are formed and are able to perform.

All in all, the real issue is not whether the number of parties matters – it does – but whether a numerical criterion of classification enables us to get a hold of what matters. So far the answer is clearly no. And the preliminary reason is equally clear: No accounting system can work without counting rules. If we resort to counting, we should know how to count. But we are even incapable of deciding when one is one and when two is two – whether a system is, or is not, a twoparty system. Thereupon we leap to infinity; that is, we give up counting altogether: Having failed to establish when two is two, we cover all the rest, in an exhausted mood, simply by saying more-than-two. It is no wonder, therefore, that the number-of-parties approach leads to frustration. Not only are three classes insufficient, but, as they stand, they do not sort out the cases.

5.2 Rules for counting

The current state of the art is, plainly, that we have dismissed the numerical criterion of classification before having learned how to use it. And there are many reasons, I believe, for giving this criterion another try. For one thing, the number of parties is a highly visible element that provides "natural" cutting points and reflects the real world terms of politics. Thus – regardless of our indexes – politicians and voters alike will continue to fight for, and argue about, more or fewer parties, whether the number of parties should be increased or reduced. On the other hand, let us not forget that parties are the coagulant, or the coagulation units, of all our measures. After all, the number of votes and seats that each party wins at elections is our best and safest data base.

In the light of the foregoing I propose to begin with the counting rules and to explore, with the aid of these rules, the mileage afforded by a classification based on the number of parties. As will be seen, the numerical criterion can be put to efficient use. On the other hand, it will be equally seen that this efficient use is not unaided. At the beginning and for quite a long stretch it is fair to say that while not alone, the numerical criterion remains the primary variable. But a point is reached at which the pure and simple counting fails us.

5.2 Rules for counting

In a nutshell, the problem is: Which parties are *relevant?* We cannot count all the parties at face value. Nor can we settle the problem by counting them in an order of decreasing strength. True enough, *how many* relates to *how strong*. The question remains: How much strength makes a party relevant, and how much feebleness makes a party irrelevant? For want of a better solution we generally establish a threshold below which a party is discounted. But this is no solution at all, for there is no absolute yardstick for assessing the relevance of size. If this threshold is established – as is often done – at the 5-percent level, it leads to serious omissions.[9] On the other hand, the more the threshold is lowered, the greater the chances of including irrelevant parties. The relevance of a party is a function not only of the relative distribution of power – as is obvious – but also, and especially, of its position value, that is, of its positioning along the left-right dimension. Thus a party that ranges at the 10-percent level may well count far less than a party that obtains only a 3-percent level. A limiting, but eloquent case, is that of the Italian Republican party, whose average return over some 25 years has been around 2 percent: Nevertheless it is surely relevant, for it has tipped the balance, over the whole period, of a number of governmental majorities.

Clearly, if the problem has a solution, it lies in stating rules according to which a party is to be counted or discounted. In substance we are required to establish a *criterion of irrelevance* vis-à-vis the smaller parties. However, since the bigness or smallness of a party is measured by its strength, let us first underpin this notion.

The strength of a party is, first of all, its electoral strength. There is more to it; but as long as we proceed with the numerical criterion, the base is given by this measure. However, votes are translated into seats, and this leads us to the strength of the parliamentary party. To avoid unnecessary complication we may thus settle for the "strength in seats" – which is, in the final analysis, what really counts once the elections are over. Again for the sake of simplicity – but also of comparability – it is often sufficient to refer, in the bicameral systems, to the seats in the lower chamber – provided the other chamber does not have different majorities. It is permissible, then, to start with this measure: The strength of the parliamentary party as indicated by its percentage of seats in the lower chamber.

The next step is to shift the focus to the party as an instrument of government. This shift is of little interest with respect to twoparty systems; but the more numerous the parties, the more we must inquire as to the *governing potential*, or the coalition potential, of each party. What really weighs in the balance of multipartism is the extent to which a party may be needed as a coalition partner for one or more of the possible governmental majorities. A party may be small but have a strong coalition-bargaining potential. Conversely, a party may be strong and yet lack coalition-bargaining power. The question now is whether a realistic estimate of the *coalition potential* of each party can be made on the sole basis of its strength. Clearly, the reply is no, for this criterion would lead us to consider all the possible numerical majorities, whereas we are interested in the *feasible coalitions*, which means only the ones that are ideologically consonant and permissible.[10] Hence the rule for deciding – in a multiparty situation – when a party should, or should not, be counted, is the following:

Rule 1. A minor party can be *discounted as irrelevant* whenever it remains over time superfluous, in the sense that it is never needed or put to use for any feasible coalition majority. Conversely, a minor party must be counted, no matter how small it is, if it finds itself in a position to determine over time, and at some point in time, at least one of the possible governmental majorities.

This rule has a limitation, for it applies only to the parties that are governing oriented and, furthermore, ideologically acceptable to the other coalition partners. This may leave out some relatively large parties of permanent opposition – such as the anti-system parties. Therefore, our criterion of irrelevance needs to be supplemented –

122

residually, or under special circumstances – by a "criterion of relevance." The question may be reformulated as follows: What size, or bigness, makes a party relevant regardless of its coalition potential? In Italy and France one finds, for instance, Communist parties that poll one-fourth, and even as much as one-third of the total vote but whose governmental coalition potential has been, for the past 25 years, virtually zero. Yet it would be absurd to discount them. We are thus led to formulate a second, subsidiary counting rule based on the power of intimidation, or, more exactly, the *blackmail potential*[11] of the opposition-oriented parties.

Rule 2. A party *qualifies for relevance* whenever its existence, or appearance, affects the tactics of party competition and particularly when it alters the *direction* of the competition – by determining a switch from centripetal to centrifugal competition either leftward, rightward, or in both directions – of the governing-oriented parties.

In summary, we can discount the parties that have neither (i) *coalition potential* nor (ii) *blackmail potential.* Conversely, we must count all the parties that have either a governmental relevance in the coalition-forming arena, or a competitive relevance in the oppositional arena.

These rules may appear unduly complicated and, in any case, difficult to operationalize. Their operational underpinning will be discussed later.[12] At the moment let us note, to begin with, that both criteria are postdictive, for there is no point in using them predictively. With respect to Rule 1 this means that the "feasible coalitions," and thereby the parties having a coalition potential, coincide, in practice, with the parties that have in fact entered, at some point in time, coalition governments and/or have given governments the support they needed for taking office or for staying in office. In most cases, therefore, the rule is easily applicable – provided, of course, that we dispose of the very simple information it requires.

Turning to Rule 2, the objection could be that the direction of competition is no easy thing to assess. In theory this may be true – and will be seen at the end. But in practice the notion of blackmail party is mainly connected to the notion of anti-system party – and both the relevance and the anti-system nature of a party can be established, in turn, by a battery of ulterior indicators. If my rule brings to the fore the blackmail party of Anthony Downs, this is because party competition is very central to my overall argument. Nonetheless, since the blackmail party generally coincides with an anti-system party (otherwise it would be comprehended, in all likelihood, under Rule 1) the assessment can well be pursued in the parliamentary arena. That is, the blackmail potential of the electoral party finds its equivalent in the veto potential, or indeed the *veto power,* of the parliamentary party with respect to the enactment of legislation. If there is any doubt as to whether a blackmail party should be counted or discounted, the matter can be pursued and checked on these grounds.

All in all, I submit that the difficulty of my rules either resides in the fact that scholars find it easier to deal with comparative politics without any substantive knowledge of the countries they cover, or in the fact that my rules demand data that are seldom systematically assembled. I have no remedy, I am afraid, for the first difficulty. As for the second difficulty, if my rules are more easily stated than applied, this is so because we never have the information we need until we ask for it. Let it be added that there is nothing "softer" in the information required by my rules than in many of the data in which the social scientist currently places his unreserved confidence. On the other hand, it is simply not true – as we shall see[13] – that we dispose of better measures for the same thing: counting the number of "relevant" parties with respect to their "position value." We do dispose of better measures – but for something else.

Thus far we know when three is three, four is four, and so forth; that is, we can sort out the *cases.* The next question is: Does the numerical criterion also allow the sorting out of new *classes?* Until now we have been concerned with counting (according to rules). The new question raises, so to speak, a problem of intelligent counting. As a rule of thumb, few parties denote low fragmentation, whereas many parties indicate high fragmentation. However, as we count the parties we can also account for their strength. And there is one distribution that ostensibly stands out as a case by itself: When one party commands, alone and over time, the absolute majority (of seats). That is, intelligent counting is all we need for sorting out – just by looking – that distribution in which one party "counts more" than all the other parties together: the class of the predominant-party systems. The advantage of sorting out this system is not only that four classes are better than three (unipartism, twopartism, and multipartism) but also that we now have a clean notion of fragmentation. Clearly, a predominant-party system can result from an excess of fragmentation of all the other parties – as in India. If we decide, however, that the salient property of the Indian party system is that the Congress party rules alone, then "fragmentation" obtains a clear definition: A party system is declared fragmented only when it has many parties, none of which approaches the absolute majority point.

There is still another class that intelligent counting can sort out. If we leave the area of the competitive party systems and pass to the noncompetitive, we may still find polities (e.g., Poland and, better still, Mexico) with more than one party in which the "secondary parties" cannot be entirely dismissed as pure and simple façades. On the other hand, these secondary, peripheral parties do count less: They are, so to speak, licensed and permitted to exist only as subordinate parties. These are the systems I call hegemonic. And they can be detected by intelligent counting, which means, in this case, counting the hegemonic party first and the subordinate parties separately.

At this point the possibilities of the numerical criterion seem pretty much exhausted. I will enter shortly the distinction between limited (moderate) and extreme (polarized) pluralism. But these classes cannot be identified and sustained on numerical grounds only. This is the point at which the number-of-parties variable becomes secondary and the ideology variable takes precedence.

5.3 A two-dimensional mapping

A classification is an ordering based on mutually exclusive classes that are established by the principle, or criterion, chosen for that classification. A typology is a more complex matter: It is an ordering of "attribute compounds," i.e., an ordering resulting from more than one criterion.[14] According to this distinction, up to now we have discussed a classification, not a typology; i.e., we have identified *classes*, not *types*, of party systems. And the numerical criterion can yield, I am suggesting, seven classes, indicated as follows:

1. one party
2. hegemonic party
3. predominant party
4. twoparty
5. limited pluralism
6. extreme pluralism
7. atomized

With respect to the traditional threefold classification, two innovations are self-evident. First, I break down into three categories the traditional "one-party lump" that brings together the most incongruent variety of heterogeneous phenomena, thereby allowing the reclassification of a number of polities erroneously identified as one-party into either the hegemonic or the predominant-party class. Second, I break down the traditional "multiparty lump," under the assumption that the single-package treatment of the more-than-two party systems testifies only to the poverty of our counting rules.

As for my last category, the "atomized" pattern requires little explanation: It enters the classification as a residual class to indicate a point at which we no longer need an accurate counting, that is, a threshold beyond which the number of parties – whether 10, 20, or more – makes little difference. The atomized party systems can be defined in the same way as atomistic competition in economics, that is, as "the situation where no one firm [has] any noticeable effect on any other firm." [15] This points up as well that the numerical criterion applies only to party systems that have entered the stage of structural consolidation.[16]

Despite the overall analytical improvement, the first category is, very visibly, inadequate. One is just one, and under the numerical criterion the varieties and differences among the one-party polities totally escape recognition. At the other end, and still worse, it is unclear how the classes of limited and extreme pluralism are to be divided. The common-sense assumption underlying this distinction is that three-to-five parties, viz., limited pluralism, have very different interactions than six-to-eight parties, viz., extreme pluralism. But neither our counting rules nor intelligent counting can really sort out the two patterns. The reason is that when we enter the area of fragmentation – let us say from five parties onward – this fragmentation may result from a multiplicity of causal factors, and it can be underpinned only in the light of such factors. Briefly put, the fragmentation of the party system can reflect either a situation of *segmentation* or a situation of *polarization*, i.e., of ideological distance. It is evident, therefore, that there is something that counting cannot detect and yet is essential. This adds up to saying that we are peremptorily required to pass from the classification to the typology and, thereby, to implementing the numerical criterion with ideology as a criterion.

It will be recalled that I have already spoken of an ideology-to-pragmatism continuum.[17] In this reference the meaning of the word ideology is specified by its opposite, viz., pragmatism. But the connotation intended in the present context is more analytic. The term is used here first to denote an *ideological distance*, that is, the overall spread of the ideological spectrum of any given polity, and second to denote *ideological intensity*, that is, the temperature or the affect of a given ideological setting. More precisely, the notion of ideological *distance* enters the apprehension of the more-than-one party systems, whereas the notion of ideological *intensity* is essential to the apprehension of the one-party polities.

Awaiting the full-fledged taxonomy that will emerge at the end of the inquiry, the foregoing considerations lead to a two-dimensional, preliminary mapping that might be called the modified classification. The modified classification is intended to settle the problem that the numerical classification leaves unsettled: how to dispose of "segmentation."[18] The solution lies in having the segmented polities checked by the ideology variable. If they are fragmented but not polarized, they will be attributed to the type of (ideologically) *moderate* pluralism. If

5.3 A two-dimensional mapping

Table 3. *Patterns, classes, and types of multipartism*

Pattern	Class	Type
Low fragmentation ⟶ (up to 5 parties)	Limited pluralism ⟶	Moderate pluralism
Segmentation ⟶	. . . .	
High fragmentation ⟶ (above 5 parties)	Extreme pluralism ⟶	Polarized pluralism

they are fragmented and polarized, they clearly belong to the type of (ideologically) *polarized* pluralism. The modified classification differs, then, from the numerical one only with respect to the classes of limited and extreme pluralism, which are replaced by the types that I call moderate and polarized pluralism. The expected correspondences are illustrated in the conversion scheme of Table 3.

Having labored on the mapping, we might wonder whether the exercise is worthwhile. Does the modified classification yield insights? The contention could be, for instance, that the numerical criterion provides an indication, if only a very imperfect one, of the *distribution* of political power. The distribution is, however, a very tricky thing to assess. I would rather say, therefore, that what the mapping provides is a fairly good indication of the *dispersion* – either a segmented or a polarized dispersion – of power.

To begin with, as it now stands the one-party case is clear: Political power is monopolized by one party only, in the precise sense that no other party is permitted to exist. Then there is the case in which one party "counts more" than all the others – but in two very different ways. On the one hand we find a hegemonic party that permits the existence of other parties only as "satellite" or, at any rate, as subordinate parties; that is, the hegemony of the party in power cannot be challenged. On the other hand we find the predominant-party system, that is, a power configuration in which one party governs alone, without being subjected to alternation, as long as it continues to win, electorally, an absolute majority. Twoparty systems pose no problem, inasmuch as their power configuration is straightforward: Two parties compete for an absolute majority that is within the reach of either. This leaves us with the power configuration of multipartism in general, which can be spelled out as follows: (i) No party is likely to approach, or at least to maintain, an absolute majority, and (ii) the relative

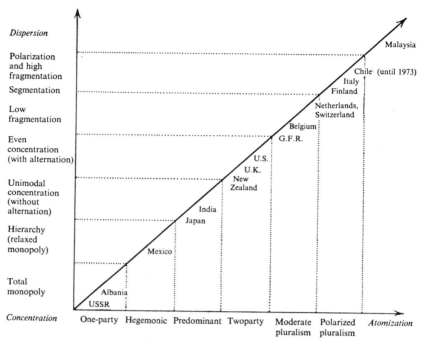

Figure 4. Countries plotted by power dispersion of party systems

strength (or weakness) of the parties can be ranked according to their respective coalition indispensability (or dispensability) and/or (iii) their eventual potential of intimidation (blackmail).

The foregoing power structures can be identified as follows: (i) *monopoly*, (ii) *hierarchy* (or relaxed monopoly), (iii) *unimodal concentration* (i.e., prevalence without alternation), (iv) *even concentration* (or bipolar concentration), (v) *low fragmentation* and/or *depolarized segmentation*, (vi) *high fragmentation with polarization*. If these power configurations and their corresponding party systems are plotted with respect to how the various polities are sorted out, we obtain the arrangement illustrated in Figure 4.

The number of parties, I have argued, matters. What remains to be explained is: Precisely with respect to what does it matter? When party systems are classified according to the numerical criterion, they are classified on the basis of their *format* – how many parties they contain. But the format is interesting only to the extent that it affects the *mechanics* – how the system works. In other words, the format is interesting to the extent that it contains *mechanical predispositions*, that it goes to determine a set of functional properties of the party system first, and of the overall political system as a consequence. Hence my subsequent inquiry will hinge on the distinction and relation between format and mechanics. This is tantamount to saying – in the light of my distinction between the classification and the typology of party systems – that we shall be exploring how the *class*, which denotes the format, relates to the *type*, which connotes the properties.

NOTES TO CHAPTER 5

1 The "International Comparative Political Parties Project" enumerates about 90 countries and 250 political parties, a figure that includes only the parties that pass the 5-percent threshold of seats. See Janda, "Retrieving Information for a Comparative Study of Political Parties," in Crotty, ed., *Approaches to the Study of Party Organization*, op. cit., Appendix B. On the other hand, Blondel counts 107 one-party and more-than-one party systems (*An Introduction to Comparative Government*, op. cit., p. 140).

2 Crotty, "Political Parties Research," in *Approaches to the Study of Political Science*, cit., p. 282.

3 *Political Parties and Political Development*, op. cit., pp. 34, 36.

4 See esp. Jean Blondel, "Party Systems and Patterns of Government in Western Democracies," *CJPS*, June 1968; and his *Introduction to Comparative Government*, cit., pp. 155–160. But see also Kenneth Janda, *Information Retrieval, Applications to Political Science*, Bobbs-Merrill, 1968, pp. 147–148.

5 But especially *infra*, 9.3, 9.5, and 9.6.

6 A recent instance is James Jupp, *Political Parties*, Routledge & Kegal Paul, 1968, whose classes are: (i) indistinct bi-partisan (e.g., the United States, Brazil, Turkey, South Korea, Iran); (ii) distinct bi-partisan (e.g., Britain, Japan, Denmark, Norway); (iii) multi-party (e.g., Italy, Belgium, Iceland); (iv) dominant-party (e.g., India, Mexico); (v) broad one-party (e.g., Spain, Poland, Yugoslavia, Kenya); (vi) narrow one-party (e.g., Egypt, Portugal); (vii) totalitarian; (viii) non-party. (See ch. 1 and Appendix, pp. 111–112.) As the examples show, most classes contain weird companies.

7 Roy C. Macridis, "Introduction" to his reader, *Political Parties – Contemporary Trends and Ideas*, Harper & Row, 1967, p. 20. But then Macridis proposes his own typology (p. 22). For the bibliography in general, *supra*, ch. 3, n. 34.

8 *Party Strategies in a Multiparty System*, Lund, Studentlitteratur, 1968, pp. 174–175.

9 This is the case, for example, with Janda's international comparative parties project (above, n. 1). A 5-percent threshold having been established, Italy turns out as having three parties: Christian Democrat, Communist, and Socialist. It so happens that during the period covered by Janda's survey three other parties, which pass unnoticed, were needed for establishing coalition majorities (whereas the Communist party had no governmental relevance after 1947). A more flexible solution is the one adopted by Richard Rose and Derek Urwin, namely, to include the parties that have participated in at least three elections and have attained the 5-percent mark at least once (*PS*, September 1970, p. 290). Even this solution, how-

ever, would fail to detect the case of the Italian Republican party recalled in the text and many others (e.g., Norway and Sweden, *infra*, ch. 6, n. 62). Alternatively, Rose makes the following suggestion: "Survey techniques provide one way to establish the number of parties in a system" (*Governing Without Consensus*, op. cit., p. 221). This is fair enough for Northern Ireland, but in more complex polities the general public misses, among other things, the subtleties of the position value of the parties. Abram de Swaan, *Coalition Theories and Cabinet Formations*, Elsevier, 1973, lowers the cutoff threshold to 2.5 percent (but lifts it, for Denmark, to 3.5); even so he misses, in the case of Italy, not only the Republicans but also the Liberals when they actually held cabinet positions.

10 The gulf separating the mathematically possible from the ideologically feasible coalitions is underpinned by the principle that governmental coalitions must be "connected." See Robert Axelrod, *Conflict of Interest*, Markham, 1970, ch. 8. Connected, or adjacent, coalitions are called "closed" by de Swaan, *Coalition Theories and Cabinet Formations*, op. cit.

11 The label is not only drawn from but related to the blackmail party of Anthony Downs, *An Economic Theory of Democracy*, Harper & Row, 1957, pp. 131–132. See *infra*, ch. 10.

12 *Infra*, 9.4.

13 *Infra*, 9.5 and 9.6.

14 This is the definition of P. A. Lazarsfeld and Allen H. Barton: ". . . by 'type' one means a specific attribute compound" ("Qualitative Measurement in the Social Sciences," in D. Lerner, H. D. Lasswell, eds., *The Policy Sciences*, Stanford University Press, 1951, p. 169). Whenever it is unnecessary to distinguish the classification from the typology, I shall use the term taxonomy. Strictly speaking, a taxonomy is an intermediate ordering between the classificatory and the typological (matrix-type) orderings. But this amount of detail is unnecessary for my purposes.

15 M. Olson, *The Logic of Collective Action*, op. cit., p. 49.

16 For the notion of structural consolidation, *infra*, 8.1.

17 *Supra*, 4.2 and ch. 4, n. 13.

18 The concept of segmentation is analyzed *infra*, 6.3.

6

Competitive systems

6.1 Polarized pluralism

Our apprehension of party systems is very uneven. By and large, the systems that have been more adequately explored are the "bipolar systems," the twoparty systems and the systems that follow a similar dualistic logic, i.e., the systems that I call moderate pluralism. Extreme and polarized pluralism confronts us, instead, with a category whose distinctiveness has escaped attention. There are two reasons for this. One is the use of dualistic blinders, that is, the tendency to explain any and all party systems by extrapolating from the twoparty model. These dualistic blinders have been proposed by Duverger as an almost "natural law" of politics:

We do not always find a duality of parties, but we do find almost always a dualism of tendencies. . . . This is tantamount to saying that the center does not exist in politics: We may have a center party, but not a center tendency. . . . There are no true centers other than as a crosscutting of dualisms.[1]

I will argue, contrariwise, that when we do not have a center party, we are likely to have a center tendency. For the moment let it just be pointed out that Duverger's dualistic blinders lead him – as subsequent developments have abundantly confirmed – to astonishing misperceptions, as when he finds that Germany and Italy are the two European countries that "display a rather marked tendency" toward "bipartism."[2]

The second reason we already know well, namely, that the case of extreme pluralism can hardly be singled out unless we know how parties are to be counted. To this day, after having counted as far as two, what follows is "polypartism." But as soon as we establish an accounting system we can do better.

Since we need an operational demarcation, let us establish that the turning point is *between five and six* parties.[3] It is well to repeat that the parties in question must be *relevant*, i.e., result from discarding the parties that lack "coalition use," unless their "power of intimidation" affects the tactics of inter-party competition. Admittedly, my counting rules still leave room for arguing whether a small, marginal party should be counted or not and may still confront the classifier with some troublesome borderline cases. But this is hardly a tragedy. In the first place there is no magic in the numbers five and six; that is, their magic is an operational artifact only. In terms of substantive knowledge the threshold can – and indeed should – be expressed more loosely by saying that the interactions among more-than-five parties tend to produce a different mechanics than the interactions among five-or-less parties.[4] In short, the border line is not *at* five (or at six), but *around* five (or six).[5] In the second place, and in any event, we have a control variable: ideological distance. Therefore, while accounting discrepancies may disturb the classification, they will not affect the typology.

I propose to discuss in the next section which countries actually enter the class, and especially the type, of extreme and polarized pluralism. For a preliminary orientation it will suffice to say that the analysis in this section basically draws on the experience of the German Weimar Republic in the twenties, of the French Fourth Republic, of Chile (until September 1973), and on the current case of Italy. In any event, with respect to a party system that has remained largely unidentified, the preliminary task is to analyze *in vitro* its distinctive features and systemic properties. In what follows these features will be presented in an order of visibility rather than of importance.

1. The first distinctive feature of polarized pluralism resides in the presence of relevant *anti-system parties.* The system is characterized by an anti-system opposition – especially of the Communist or of the Fascist variety, but also of other varieties. However, since the notion of anti-system party has been subjected to debate and also to considerable misunderstanding, a number of points deserve to be reassessed.

It is useful to distinguish, to begin with, between a broad and a strict definition of "anti-system." Over time the degree and the intensity of an "anti-attitude" are bound to vary. Furthermore, not all the anti-system parties are such in a same sense: The negation covers, or may cover, a wide span of different attitudes ranging from "alienation" and total refusal to "protest." Now, clearly, alienation and protest are different in kind, not merely in degree.[6] Yet the distinction cannot be easily applied on empirical grounds, because large electorates cover all these sentiments, or attitudes. Voters can be protesters, while the party activists can be alienated. Likewise, the party leadership can be ideologically motivated, whereas the rank and file may simply lack bread. On the other hand, at the level of the political system the consequences of alienation and/or of protest are not markedly different: Whatever the nature, at the source, of the anti-attitude, a government faces the same daily difficulties.

There are, then, at least two reasons for conceiving "anti-system" broadly: variations over time and varieties in nature. These variations and varieties find their minimal denominator in a common *delegitimiz-*

ing impact. That is, all the refusal-to-protest parties – ranging as it were from an extraparliamentary to a Poujade or Common Man type of opposition – share the property of questioning a regime and of undermining its base of support. Accordingly, a party can be defined as being anti-system whenever it *undermines the legitimacy* of the *regime* it opposes. To be sure, protest parties can indeed be flash parties and surely are less anti, and less durable, than the parties expressing an alien or alienated ideology. This difference notwithstanding, at each point in time the political system faces a "crisis of legitimacy." And as long as the protest attitude, or feedback, persists – no matter whether under changing flags – the polity faces a lack of support which joins forces with the ideological enmity.

On the other hand, the difference between ideological and protest opposition must be duly accounted for – over time, if not at particular points in time. That is tantamount to saying that the broad definition contains a narrower, more specific connotation. A first approximation to this more specific connotation points to the fact that an anti-system party would not change – if it could – the government but the very system of government. Its opposition is not an "opposition on issues" (so little so that it can afford to bargain on issues) but an "opposition of principle." Thus the hard core of the concept is singled out by noting that an anti-system opposition abides by a belief system that does not share the values of the political order within which it operates. According to the strict definition, then, anti-system parties represent an *extraneous ideology* – thereby indicating a polity confronted with a maximal ideological distance.

The foregoing implies, in the first place, that anti-system is by no means the same as, or equivalent to, "revolutionary." If a party is actually dedicated to revolutionary preparation and activities, then it should be called a revolutionary party. Such a party is surely anti-system, but the obverse is not true: An anti-system party need not be, in any concrete sense and even less in actual practice, revolutionary. If the distinction is often blurred, this is because "revolutionary" may apply to long-run goals (with little short-run implementation) and particularly to verbal goals. However, since the verbal element is entered under my "delegitimizing impact," we are left with a neat demarcation between anti-system party and revolutionary party.

It should also be clear that variations of tactics and strategy are immaterial to my concept. In particular, I have never equated anti-system with "outside the system."[7] An anti-system party may operate from within no less than from without, by smooth infiltration no less than by conspicuous obstruction. The fact that the major Western Communist parties are currently playing their game within the system, and according to most of its rules, does not alter the test: whether or not they pursue and obtain a delegitimizing impact.[8] And this is the perspective in which the so-called integration of Western communism can best be assessed and measured – as we shall see.

2. The second distinctive feature of polarized pluralism resides in the existence of *bilateral oppositions*. When the opposition is unilateral, i.e., all located on one side vis-à-vis the government, no matter how many parties oppose it, they can join forces and propose themselves as an alternative government. In the polarized polities we find instead two oppositions that are mutually exclusive: They cannot join forces. In fact, the two opposing groups are closer, if anything, to the governing parties than to one another. The system has two oppositions, then, in the sense that they are *counter-oppositions* that are, in constructive terms, incompatible.

The two foregoing characteristics are the most visible ones and already suffice to identify the category. If there are more than five parties, if the system displays bilateral counter-oppositions (in the plural) which include parties that oppose the very political system, then this type is definitely far removed from the type of multipartism characterized by a unilateral opposition and the absence of relevant anti-system parties. Actually, these distinguishing traits are so easily detectable that it is astonishing they should have escaped attention – indeed a proof of the extent to which we have been victims of a dualistic blinding. A number of additional characteristics are less visible, though not less important, and can be explained as consequences or ramifications – though it should be clear that we are analyzing a syndrome.

3. If one wonders how we pass from unilateral to bilateral oppositions, one is immediately alerted to the third feature: The systems of polarized pluralism are characterized by the center placement of one party (Italy) or of a group of parties (France, Weimar). Granted that whether it is a unified or a fragmented center makes a difference, all our cases have or had – until falling apart – a fundamental trait in common: Along the left-to-right dimension *the metrical center of the system is occupied.* This implies that we are no longer confronted with bipolar interactions, but at the very least with triangular interactions. The system is multipolar in that its competitive mechanics hinges on a center that must face *both* a left and a right. While the mechanics of moderate pluralism is bipolar precisely because the system is not center based, the mechanics of polarized pluralism is multipolar and cannot be explained, therefore, by a dualistic model.

It is important to stress that when one speaks of a center-based system, one is concerned only with a *center positioning*, not with center doctrines, ideologies, and opinions – whatever these may be.[9] The physical occupation of the center is, in and by itself, of great consequence, for it implies that the central area of the political system is *out of competition* (in the dimension in which competition occurs). In other terms, the very existence of a center party (or parties) discourages "centrality," i.e., the centripetal drives of the political system. And the centripetal drives are precisely the moderating drives. This is why this type is center-fleeing, or centrifugal, and thereby conducive to immoderate or extremist politics.

The existence of center-located parties also raises a number of intriguing questions with respect to their policy capabilities. Years ago I suggested that the center is basically constituted by retroactions, thereby implying that the center parties tend to be passive far more than initiating and instigating agencies. I was thus led to emphasize the "immobilism" of a center positioning. I still believe in this diagnosis, but the recent Chilean experience – which was characterized by a chronic fickleness of the in-between parties – vindicates a more positive interpretation. I would put it thus: Even though the center parties tend to be immobilistic, they remain an equilibrating force that performs a "mediating role" – and mediation, or brokerage, is not the same as immobilism. This having been conceded, I hasten to add that a center positioning seemingly condemns to a policy of mediation, in the sense that a different role backfires on the party's positioning without paying off in performance or accomplishment. A center party that attempts to outdo the parties located on its left or right will contribute, more than to anything else, to a crescendo of escalation and extremization.

4. If a political system obtains anti-system, bilateral oppositions and discourages – by the very fact that its center is physically occupied – centripetal competition, these traits add up to a polarized system. *Polarization* can thus be revisited in more detail as a fourth, synthetic characteristic. In the Italian and Chilean cases the "pull" is (was) mostly at the left; in the Weimar case it became stronger, in the thirties, on the right; in the case of the Fourth Republic it was more evenly distributed at both ends. The fact remains that in all cases the spectrum of political opinion is highly polarized: Its lateral poles are literally *two poles apart,* and the distance between them covers a maximum spread of opinion.[10] This is tantamount to saying that cleavages are likely to be very deep, that consensus is surely low, and that the legitimacy of the political system is widely questioned. Briefly put, we have polarization when we have *ideological distance* (in contradistinction to ideological proximity).

To be sure, the system is center based precisely because it is polarized. Otherwise there would neither be a central area large enough to provide space for occupancy, nor would a center placement be rewarding – for the center parties capitalize on the fear of extremism.

Nonetheless, it should not escape our attention that we are confronted here with a vicious whirl. In the long run a center positioning is not only a consequence but also a *cause* of polarization, for the very fact that the central area is occupied feeds the system with center-fleeing drives and discourages centripetal competition.

5. The fifth feature of polarized pluralism has already been touched upon. It is the likely prevalence of the *centrifugal drives* over the centripetal ones. The characteristic trend of the system is the enfeeblement of the center, a persistent loss of *votes* to one of the extreme ends (or even to both).[11] Perhaps the center-fleeing hemorrhage can be stopped; still the centrifugal strains appear to counteract successfully any decisive reversal of the trend. The most eloquent cases to this effect have been the Weimar Republic and Chile; but the French Fourth Republic also displayed a center-fleeing trend. Until October 1947 the Communists entered the various postwar governments, and at the other extreme no adversary movement had emerged in the electoral arena. By 1951, however, the Gaullist reaction (tellingly labeled RPF, *Rassemblement du Peuple Français*) swept the country, the four "constitutional parties" located between the Communist and Gaullist extremes, which had polled in June 1946 as much as 73.5 percent of the total vote, had fallen to a bare 51.0 percent, and the major losses (from 28.1 down to 12.5) were of the Christian Democrats, one of the two pivotal parties of the center area. At the subsequent and last election of 1956 the centrifugal tendency appeared lessened in terms of electoral returns, but the Gaullist surge was replaced, if only in part, by the Poujade surge, by all standards a right-wing anti-system protest.

The Italian trend is, albeit with a slower pace, similarly centrifugal. In 1948 the Christian Democratic party came very close to the 50-percent mark, but has averaged since then less than 40 percent. Likewise, and more significantly, in 1948 the Italian center coalition parties (DC, Social Democrats, Republicans, and Liberals) totaled 62 percent; in 1953 the total vote of the four parties had already dropped below the 50-percent mark. The fate of the center-left group, i.e., of the "opening to the left" experiment, has been no different. In 1963 the new center-left majority represented 60 percent of the total vote; at the 1968 elections it had gone down to 56 percent; and by 1974 this majority had fallen wide apart, with the Socialist party declaring that no center-left alliance was any longer possible with the Social Democrats. The extremes have, instead, done well. From 1946 to 1972 the Italian Communist party rose steadily from 19 to 27 percent of the total vote; and at the 1972 elections the neo-Fascist MSI doubled its previous vote (from a 5-percent average over time to almost 9 percent). And the more recent evidence at hand, the regional elections of June 1975, conclusively testify to the predictive power of the model. The Communists have gained five percentage points, leaping to the unprecedented peak, in a Western democracy, of 33.4 percent; the Christian Democrats are down to 35.3; and while the Liberals have almost disappeared (2.5), the extreme neo-Fascist right remains, with 6.4, above its average turnout. The centrifugation has seemingly reached its ultimate frontier.[12]

6. The sixth feature of polarized pluralism is its congenital *ideological patterning*. When one finds a large ideological space, it follows that the polity contains parties that disagree not only on policies but also, and more importantly, on principles and fundamentals. We are thus referred to a more substantive meaning of ideology. As noted earlier, "ideology" may signify, (i) a highly emotive involvement in politics and (ii) a particular mentality, a *forma mentis*. In monistic polities the emphasis will be on the first element, on "ideological heating." But in pluralistic systems the emphasis should be laid on the second, on the "mentality," that is, on ideology understood as a way of perceiving and conceiving politics, and defined, therefore, as a distinctly doctrinaire, principled, and high-flown way of focusing political issues. This ideological *approach,* and indeed *forma mentis,* springs from the very roots of a culture (not merely of the political culture) and typically reflects the mentality of rationalism as opposed to the empirical and pragmatic mentality.[13] This is not to say that given a rationalistic culture, ideologism necessarily follows. I simply mean that a rationalistic culture is the most favorable soil for the cultivation of ideological politics, whereas an empirical culture makes it difficult for an ideological approach to take root.

Be that as it may, in the systems under consideration parties of "true believers" stand side by side with parties of "cool believers"; i.e., the ideological temperature of the various parties can be very different. The common characteristic is, then, that all the parties fight one another with ideological arguments and vie with one another in terms of ideological mentality. The congenital ideological patterning of the polarized polities should not be confused, therefore, with *ideological fever.* The temperature of politics may cool down, but a lessening of ideological passion does not transform, per se, an ideological mentality into a pragmatic mentality.

Of course, a polity is ideological because the society is ideologized. Even Doctor Pangloss would have known that. However, if we are to enter a post-Panglossian age of political sociology, due attention should be paid to the fact that the very configuration of the party system maintains and upholds the ideological patterning of the society. Objective socioeconomic cleavages may no longer justify ideological compartmentalization, and yet denominational, Marxist, and nationalistic

137

parties are able to maintain their appeal and to shape the society according to their ideological creeds. When a party system becomes established – passing beyond the stage of atomization – parties become built-ins, they become the "natural" system of channelment of the political society. And when there are several built-in, established parties, the system acquires a vested interest in fostering an ideological type of canalization – for at least two reasons. The first is that if so many parties are to be perceived and justified in their separateness, they cannot afford a pragmatic lack of distinctiveness. The second reason is that in a situation of extreme pluralism most parties are relatively small groups whose survival is best assured if their followers are indoctrinated as "believers"; and a law of contagion goes to explain why the largest party (or parties) is likely to follow suit.

The latter may appear a debatable inference. While the interest of the small parties in ideological canalization is clear, it is far less clear why the largest, or the two largest parties, should not abide by "catch-all" tactics, as Otto Kirchheimer put it.[14] The notion of catch-all parties has been drawn from the twoparty, three-party, and predominant-party systems. Yet it can be plausibly extended to the poly-party polities. It can well be argued, e.g., that the Italian Christian Democratic party is nothing but a catch-all party. Yes and no, however. For one thing, the DC (*Democrazia Cristiana*) had a more pragmatic platform under the De Gasperi leadership, in the early fifties, than when the subsequent generation took over.[15] Moreover, the left-wing DC fractions that have largely conditioned the party in the past 15 years play, very definitely, an ideological game.[16] Likewise, the long-held doctrine of the "non-reversibility" of the center-left coalition sounds absurd on pragmatic grounds. Finally, the fierce engagement of the DC, in 1974, in the referendum on the divorce law can hardly be interpreted as a catch-all performance. All in all, if the parochial, country by country, yardstick is replaced by a comparative, common yardstick, then one cannot fail to perceive the extent to which the ideological patterning of a polarized polity does restrict the catch-all game.

7. The seventh feature of polarized pluralism is the presence of *irresponsible oppositions*. This feature is closely related to the peculiar mechanics of governmental turnover of the center-based polities. On the one hand, the center party (or the leading party of the center) is not exposed to alternation: Being the pivot and the very backbone of any possible governmental majority, its destiny is to govern indefinitely. On the other hand, the extreme parties, the parties that oppose the system, are excluded almost by definition from alternation in office: Under normal circumstances they are not destined to govern. Under these conditions we cannot have, therefore, *alternative coalitions*, the swing of the pendulum from one group to another group of

parties. We find, instead, a *peripheral turnover* – peripheral in that the access to government is limited to the center-left and/or the center-right parties only. Differently put, alternative coalitions presuppose a system in which *all* the relevant parties are governing oriented and acceptable as governing parties. Contrariwise, peripheral turnover consists of permanently governing parties that merely change partners in their neighborhood.

Peripheral and restricted access to government helps to explain, then, why polarized pluralism lacks a significant responsible opposition and is characterized by both a semi-responsible and a typically irresponsible opposition. An opposition is likely to behave responsibly if it expects that it may have to "respond," that is, to give execution to what it has promised. Conversely, an opposition is likely to be the less responsible the less it expects to govern. Now, in the polarized polities the turnover of the possible allies of the center leading party is mostly imposed by ideological constraints. Furthermore, the center-left and center-right parties are likely to share only a secondary governmental responsibility. Finally, governmental instability and shifting or quarrelsome coalitions obscure the very perception of who is responsible for what.

On all these counts, even the governing-oriented parties of the system are not motivated to play the role of a responsible opposition; they can afford to be *semi-responsible*. And the anti-system parties are, if anything, motivated to be *irresponsible;* they are a permanent opposition, refusing to be identified with the political system, whose promises are not expected to fall due. Hence polarized pluralism is characterized by semi-responsible opposition with reference to the parties located at the periphery of the center, and by irresponsible opposition with reference to the extreme parties that oppose the system. And the role played by an irresponsible opposition leads us to the final characteristic.[17]

8. The final feature of polarized pluralism is the extent to which the polity displays a pattern that I call *politics of outbidding,* or of over-promising, which is very different from what is meaningfully called competitive politics. Competitive politics consists not only of competitiveness, that is, of how close the competitions are to each other; it consists also of *rules of competition.* The notion of competitive politics comes from economics, and when we have recourse to analogies, we should see to it that the analogy does not get lost along the way. Economic competition is made possible by two conditions: first, that the market escapes monopolistic control; second, and no less important, that the goods are what they are said to be. In the field of economics this latter condition is satisfied by legal control. If fraud were not punished and if producers could easily get away with selling

something as something else – glass as diamonds, yellow paint as gold, water as medicine – a competitive market would immediately founder.

Similar, if less stringent, conditions apply to political competition. Competitive politics is conditioned not only by the presence of more than one party but also by a minimum of fair competition (and of mutual trust) below which a political market can hardly perform as a competitive market. Admittedly, in politics we must be less exacting, and political fraud is more difficult both to detect and to control than economic fraud. Yet the distinction between responsible and irresponsible opposition allows an equivalent distinction between fair and unfair political competition. If a party can always lightheartedly promise heaven on earth without ever having to "respond" to what it promises, this behavior surely falls below any standard of fair competition. And I submit that under these conditions "competitive politics" is both an inappropriate choice of vocabulary and a misunderstanding of the facts. Actually, the political game is played in terms of unfair competition characterized by incessant escalation. And the politics of outbidding results – to revert to the economic analogy – in something very similar to *inflationary disequilibrium:* a situation in which competitors "strive to bid support away from each other by stronger appeals and promises," so that the competition for the available supply increases while the supply does not.[18]

The foregoing is, then, the syndrome of extreme and polarized pluralism. A tentative explanation of its etiology would be out of order in this context. The point is to show that the traditional multiparty category grievously muddled two radically different cases and that the more-than-two party systems cannot be lumped together in a single package. It is important to ask, nonetheless, what are the chances of survival of the polarized polities. Surely, this variety of multipartism is an unhealthy state of affairs for a body politic. A political system characterized by centrifugal drives, irresponsible opposition, and unfair competition is hardly a viable system. Immoderate and ideological politics is conducive either to sheer paralysis or to a disorderly sequence of ill-calculated reforms that end in failure. This does not necessarily imply that the polarized polities are doomed to impotence and, ultimately, to self-destruction. They are, however, hardly in a position to cope with explosive or exogenous crises.

The chances of survival of the polarized polities brings us to reconsider the anti-system parties. The question is whether the system will manage to survive long enough to absorb such parties into the existing political order. The historian will inevitably discover that, in the long run, revolutionary parties lose their original impetus and accommodate themselves to the regimes they have been unable to overthrow. But the political scientist may well have to discover that the "long run" was too long for the living actors – and for the political system. By and large, it took one-half century for the Marxist Socialists to integrate – and their integration has not been without losses, in many countries, to the Communist parties. Meanwhile, while the Socialists were hesitating, democracy collapsed in the interwar period in Italy, Germany, and Spain. Moreover, the problem of absorbing communism is of another order. If we are reminded of the conditions of the working classes during the nineteenth century and the early decades of the twentieth, revolutionary socialism was indeed a "politics of despair." But present-day Communist parties in France, Italy, or even Finland hardly reflect conditions of despair – by comparison, they reflect welfare. On the other hand, whereas socialism was and has remained, internationally, a fairly loose and, nationally, a fairly spontaneous movement often characterized by an anti-apparat attitude, communism enters the arena backed by a concrete "father figure" and as a powerfully regimented movement firmly entrenched through a formidable organizational network.[19]

If the analogies between socialism and communism do not bear serious scrutiny, let us confront the so-called integration of the major Western Communist parties on its peculiar, *sui generis* grounds.

The thesis of the "integration" of communism has been expounded in many versions. Its boldest version is that, by now, the major European Communist parties are "positively integrated," meaning by this that they are the truly reformist parties and/or that they are, at least in Italy, the real bulwarks for maintaining the constitutional system. With respect to the latter contention history may soon tell. Meanwhile, it is well to review the general argument, namely, that Western Communist parties have entered bourgeois coalition governments and that no dire outcome has in fact followed.

In the late thirties Chile and in the immediate aftermath of World War II many European countries (plus, again, Chile from 1946 to 1948) have known all-inclusive "national front" coalitions with Communist participation. More significantly, since the late sixties Communist parties have entered Western coalition governments in three countries: Finland (between 1966 and 1971), Chile (from 1970 to 1973), and Iceland (from 1971 to 1974). But Iceland – with a voting population of just about 100,000 – hardly is, in this as well as in other respects, a telling case. In Chile the Communists had a relatively weak parliamentary strength (6 out of 50 senators and 22 out of 150 deputies), Allende did not have a majority in the congress, and the natural course of the experiment was brutally interrupted by military seizure. We are thus left with one relevant case only: Finland. However, so far the Finnish Communist party has entered three coalition governments largely as a concession to Soviet pressure – not as a needed partner on the basis of parliamentary arithmetics. Its major post has been, in 1971, the ministry of justice; and this is to point out that it has never been given controlling positions, such as the ministries of interior or of defense. On the other hand, its ascent to government has resulted in a serious decline of turnout. Possibly for this reason, but also because of fierce internal battlings between a "liberal" and a Stalinist tendency, the Finnish Communist party has not reentered, from 1971 to 1975, any coalition government.

It turns out, then, that the extant evidence is largely immaterial to the crux of the matter. For the matter hinges on the very crucial difference between (i) a coalition government with *Communist participation* and (ii) a *Communist-controlled* coalition government, i.e., a coalition in which the Communist party takes one or more of the key portfolios. And the facts of the matter are that we have as yet no instance of a Communist party that holds the levers, or controlling positions, of the central government and submits, when the time falls due, to a free electoral verdict resulting from unfettered, pluralistic competition. We only have, across the world, abundant evidence to the contrary.

There is a very great difference between "positive integration" and "negative integration." This difference is best pursued with reference to the concrete instance of the Italian PCI.[20] As described by its propounders, the positive integration of the PCI amounts to a "constructive opposition": It follows, logically, that the PCI behaves just about as any normal, loyal opposition.[21] This interpretation finds its best supporting evidence[22] in the unquestioned fact that "almost three quarters of the Italian legislation between 1948 and 1968 has been consented to by the communists" and that, since then, no bill is even submitted to parliament without the *nihil obstat* and without being previously bargained with the PCI.[23] However, it is an equally unquestioned fact that most of this legislation deals with trivial minutiae and that the crucial issues are very seldom, if ever, decided.[24] That is, positive integration quickly appears "negative" as soon as *decisions* are weighed against *nondecisions*. In this latter perspective the sober interpretation is that the Italian governments and parliaments have been increasingly paralyzed by the veto power of the PCI and, moreover, that the side payments of whatever decision has been enacted have been, in the aggregate, too costly to bear.

Since I cannot pursue the matter in any detail, the general and decisive point seems to be that the "positive integration" thesis founders when it is asked to explain why Italy turns out to be, politically, the sick man of Western Europe. If the reply is – as it generally is – that the deterioration should be imputed to the Christian Democratic party, that is, to the party that has dominated all the coalition governments for almost 30 years, then the unavoidable ulterior question becomes why is it that the DC has not been ousted from office. And this question leads us back to the systemic properties of polarized pluralism and, above all, to the fact that the DC owes its power and its permanence in office precisely to the presence of the anti-system parties. In short, the wishful interpretation fails us precisely in failing to account for the overall systemic performance of the Italian polity. Systemically speaking, its explanatory power is almost nil.

Having established the difference between a positive and a negative integration and also, I submit, the far greater plausibility of the sober interpretation, we may now attempt to look forward at the future prospects. The crucial test resides – in light of our definition of anti-system parties – in the processes of *delegitimization* and, conversely, of *relegitimization*. It cannot be doubted, I believe, that up until the seventies the former processes prevailed in Italy over the latter ones.[25] But it can be argued that the trend is now reversed. However, this issue quickly becomes unmanageable unless we appraise first the difference, and then the interplay, between *visible politics* and *invisible politics*.

In a first and uninteresting sense, a large slice of the political process escapes visibility because it is too minute and because we cannot keep our searchlights on everything. In a second sense, invisible politics is deliberately hidden and consists of its unpleasant and corrupt part: political money, spoils, clienteles, and dirty deals. This is surely a crucial component of invisible politics, but its variance is hardly correlated wth the variables under consideration. We are thus referred to a third way of dividing the visible from the invisible part of politics, according to which the former corresponds to the words and promises destined for the mass media, while the latter corresponds to the deals and words for mouth-to-ear consumption. This is the distinction that bears on our discussion.

As a rule of thumb, the lesser the ideological bent, the less irresponsible the opposition, and the lesser the outbidding, the greater the (relative) proximity and convertibility between rhetoric and feasibility, between image selling and deeds. Conversely, the more a polity abandons itself to outbidding, to irresponsible opposition, and to ideological goal setting, the greater the inconvertibility and the gulf between visible politics, i.e., what is said in public, and invisible politics, i.e., what is done in private.

The distinction between visible and invisible politics helps redress, in the first place, the erroneous contention that no Western polity no longer is "really" ideological.[26] I would say, instead, that – given a wide ideological spread – pragmatic bargaining is feasible only under the cover of invisibility, whereas the visible game of politics must continue to be played, and indeed to be overplayed, ideologically. And the inconvertibility between invisible and visible politics that characterizes the polarized polities goes to explain, in the second place, why my focus is on the vote-seeking party, not on the parliamentary party, and even less on its power elites. If the center-fleeing tendencies of polarized pluralism are assessed at the electoral level and with respect to the electoral party, this is hardly because at this level I have a measure of centrifugation, while at the invisible, or least visible, levels measures yield to impressionistic speculations. My reason is, rather, that when visible and invisible politics fall wide apart, we end up in a vicious circle: Leaders entangle themselves in their own ideological nets to the point of becoming, in the long run, prisoners of their own image selling. And this last remark brings me back to the issue at hand.

The question, "How does an anti-system party integrate in the system?" hinges – in the final analysis – on whether reciprocal processes of *relegitimization* replace the earlier process of *delegitimization*. I say reciprocal, because integration posits that a policy of relegitimization is pursued by, and from, both camps (if pursued from one end only, the outcome is not integration but takeover). And the precise question is: How fast, and at which level, can decades of reciprocal delegitimization be offset by a policy of relegitimization? Intellectuals and elites are relatively easy switchers compared with mass publics. And the distinction between invisible and visible politics entails that a relegitimization that remains confined to the low-visibility areas may well leave the *expectations* of the anti-system electorates pretty much as they were.[27] The test is, here, whether the elites do in fact pursue their relegitimizing intents all the way down to the masses and the mass-media level. And while surveys could well detect and measure the pace and extent to which a *reciprocal* relegitimization is taking place at the mass level, current research designs are unimaginative, and the more important matters are the ones that are investigated least. Thus the chances of survival of the polarized polities cannot be appropriately assessed. Their "external" fragility and exposure to exogenous crises – such as inflation for Weimar, and Algeria for France – cannot be doubted and remain a constant. But the overcoming of their "internal" weakness with respect to the anti-system parties (and attitudes) remains, to date, a non-calculated risk largely entrusted to wishful thinking. For the time being, all we know for sure is that more votes mean *more power*. It is as simple as that – and this is what my measure of centrifugation detects.

In the summing up, the analogy on the basis of which it is predicted that Communist parties will follow the evolution of the Socialist parties disregards crucial differences. For one thing, parties are shaped by their history, that is, by the socialization processes of their leaders and cadres. Furthermore, and in particular, what remains to be seen is – in terms of the Communist integration or coalescence – the level at which it occurs. The thing we know for sure is that if a polity is centrifugal at all levels – electoral, parliamentary, and party leadership level – then it is doomed: It can only, and quickly, end in deflagration. This is what happened during the last three years of the Weimar Republic and during the course of the Allende presidency in Chile. That is equally to say, therefore, that a system of polarized pluralism can endure only if the centrifugal tactics of electoral competition are lessened, or eventually counteracted, in the other arenas. This is doubtlessly the case with Italy. Thus the centripetal convergence that may be said to exist among Communist and bourgeois party leaders at the invisible levels goes to explain how the Italian polity enjoys the longest record of survival of the type; but leaves, to date, its systemic characteristics as they have been described.

6.2 Testing the cases

The preceding represents the full range of possibilities and properties afforded by a system of polarized pluralism. While I have made passing reference to countries that substantiate the analysis, I have deliberately dealt with a type. This implies that no concrete system should be expected to display, at least with equal salience, *all* the features of the type. But the preliminary question is: To what kind of "type" does my type belong? Is it an ideal type, a prototype, a pure type, an extreme type, a polar type, or something else besides? Given the methodological fuzziness underlying the typology of types – and especially the notion of *Idealtypus* – let the distinction simply be between (i) polar or pure types and (ii) empirical or extracted types.[28]

Polar types are such in that they represent the extreme ends of a continuum or of a serial order. Not only do they mark the outer boundaries within which the actual cases vary, but they also define the dimension along which a continuum is drawn. In turn, pure types are such in that they represent the standards, parameters, or models against which the concrete instances can be compared in terms of greater or lesser proximity. The two kinds – polar and pure – are very close in that they are both constructed on the basis of the conceivability, not of the frequency or probability, of empirical occurrence. One can also say that polar-pure types are essentially heuristic constructs. Conversely, the empirical or extracted types are geared to the frequency or likelihood of empirical occurrence and serve a nesting more than a heuristic function. To be sure, an empirical type is also "ideal," in some sense of the word, and may be as abstract as a pure type. The difference is that the empirical type tends to be "extracted" from the morphological or idiographic evidence on the basis of occurrence or of averages. In particular, while polar types are construed dichotomously (as opposites), empirical types represent any number of distinguishable contiguities.

The reply to the preliminary question, thus, clearly is that polarized pluralism is a polar and/or a pure type. This characterization does not lessen in the least the importance of such a type. Indeed, empirical types presuppose, and are helped by, the ideation of polar types. Concrete societies have been better analyzed and understood after Tönnies' establishment of his *Gemeinschaft–Gesellschaft* dichotomy. Weber's *Idealtypen* may will be ambiguous; yet we endlessly revert to Weber. The same is true, to cite another instance, in the case of Durkheim's mechanical as opposed to organic solidarity. And the study of parties is handicapped precisely by our having to deal with an "endless" continuum, i.e., a continuum bounded at one end only – its totalitarian end.[29] The notion that party systems can go from one to an infinite number of parties only reveals a lack of theoretical grasp. True enough, in a pulverized or atomized pattern the number of parties can be very high – this being so precisely because such parties are pre- or embryo-parties (and in this sense irrelevant). But in a structured pattern there is an end to how many the relevant parties can be – this end being "ended" precisely by the terminal nature of my type. It should be clearly understood, therefore, that the analysis of the competitive systems developed in this chapter starts with a polar type, which is subsequently implemented and followed by three extracted or empirical types. Bearing this methodological premise in mind, let us come to the acid test: the sorting out and testing of the concrete cases.

According to my counting rules, the following is a comprehensive, if not exhaustive, list of the "fragmented" countries which either are in the vicinity or enter the area of extreme and polarized multipartism:

Chile (1961–1973)	5–7 parties
Denmark (1947–1971)	4–5 parties
Finland (1951–1972)	6 parties
France (Fourth Republic)	6 parties
France (Fifth Republic)	4–5 parties
Israel (1949–1973)	5–7 parties
Italy (1948–1972)	6–7 parties
Netherlands (until 1967)	5 parties
Norway (1945–1969)	5 parties
Switzerland (1947–1971)	5 parties
Weimar Republic (1920–1933)	5–6 parties

It is immediately apparent that the five-to-six parties area is a crowded area. This is tantamount to saying that we have a number of borderline cases hovering across the *classes* of moderate and extreme pluralism. The finding is not particularly disturbing, since we know from the outset[30] that at the ends of the spectrum the numerical criterion cannot perform unaided, that is, without the aid of the ideology variable. But before we enter this control variable, two cases – the Netherlands and Denmark – are of particular interest and deserve an appraisal on their own merits (Tables 5 and 6).

Counting all the parties represented in parliament, Denmark exhibited in 1973 as many as 10 parties[31]; and the Netherlands was, in 1971, up to no fewer than 14 parties – indeed a remarkable feat for a country having a voting population of about 8 million.[32] Nonetheless, I have indicated that the actual format of the Danish party system has been – over the period 1947–1971 – of four to five parties.[33] Likewise, at least until 1967 the Dutch party system has been a five-party system, with two major parties (Socialists and Catholics), two Protestant parties (Anti-Revolutionaries and Christian Historical), and a growing conservative (Liberal) party.[34] But this no longer appears to be the case. The recent developments seemingly point – in both countries – to a "defreezing" of their party systems.

This defreezing is less evident, or more dubious, in the Netherlands, for here we already have a ten-year trend which suggests that the growing fragmentation of the party system largely coincides with the rise and wane of flash parties. In a parliament of 150 members, the Peasants reached a peak of 7 seats in 1967 but were 3 in 1972; the Democrats '66 were 11 in 1971 but 6 in 1972; the Democratic Socialists '70 were equally back, in 1972, to 6 seats; and the earlier "Provo" and "Kabouters" never gained national representation and are extinguished. Only the Radicals did well between 1971 and 1972; but so did the other new parties that have since declined; and the Liberals, a traditional party, did better. And the latest evidence at hand, the provincial elections of March 1974, shows that while the Liberals are still progressing, the Socialists are recouping their original strength. Instead the Democrats '66 have collapsed, and the decline of the Democratic Socialists '70 is confirmed.

The Dutch developments highlight the controversial relation of classifications to change. A classification of party systems based on party numbers detects their degree of fragmentation. But if this were all, we would not really need "classes." While the cases can be moved from one class to another, nonetheless a classification imputes permanence and boundedness. If no such imputation is justified, then ever-changeable rank orderings and more sensitive indexes would be more attuned to the real world. On the other hand, the Dutch parabola goes to confirm the extraordinary resilience, over time, of party formats. Thus an endless counting and recounting of the Dutch parties overstresses or would have overstressed, a spurious dynamics.[35] The Dutch parabola

Table 5. *Netherlands: electoral returns 1946–1972*

	1946	1948	1952	1956	1959	1963	1967	1971	1972
Communist	10.6	7.7	6.1	4.8	2.4	2.8	3.6	3.9	4.5
Pacifist Socialist	—	—	—	—	1.8	3.0	2.9	1.4	1.5
Democrats '66	—	—	—	—	—	—	4.5	6.8	4.2
Socialist (PvdA) *	28.3	25.6	29.0	32.7	30.4	28.0	23.6	24.6	27.4
Democratic Socialists '70	—	—	—	—	—	—	—	5.3	4.1
Radical (PPR)	—	—	—	—	—	—	—	1.8	4.8
Catholic People's (KVP) *	30.8	31.0	28.7	31.7	31.6	31.9	26.5	21.9	17.7
Anti-Revolutionary (ARP) *	12.9	13.2	11.3	9.9	9.4	8.7	9.9	8.6	8.8
Christian Historical (CHU) *	7.8	9.2	8.9	8.4	8.1	8.6	8.1	6.3	4.8
Political Reform Party (SGP)	2.1	2.4	2.4	2.3	2.2	2.3	2.0	2.4	2.2
Liberal (VVD) *	6.4	7.9	8.8	8.8	12.2	10.3	10.7	10.3	14.4
Peasant (Poujade type)	—	—	—	—	—	2.1	4.8	1.1	1.9
Other	1.0	2.9	4.7	1.5	1.9	2.3	3.4	5.6	3.7

* Relevant parties over the whole period.

Table 6. *Denmark: electoral returns 1945–1975*

	1945	1947	1950	1953	1953	1957	1960	1964	1966	1968	1971	1973	1975
Danish Communist Party	12.4	6.7	4.6	4.7	4.3	3.1	1.1	1.2	0.8	1.0	1.4	3.6	4.2
Left Socialists	—	—	—	—	—	—	—	—	—	2.0	1.6	1.5	2.1
Socialist People's Party	—	—	—	—	—	—	6.1	5.8	10.9	6.1	9.1	6.0	4.9
Social Democrats*	32.8	40.0	39.6	40.4	41.3	39.4	42.1	41.9	38.2	34.2	37.3	25.7	30.0
Center Social Democrats	—	—	—	—	—	—	—	—	—	—	—	7.8	2.2
Radical Liberals*	8.2	6.9	8.2	8.6	7.8	7.8	5.8	5.3	7.3	15.0	14.4	11.2	7.1
Justice (Single Tax) Party	1.9	4.5	8.2	5.6	3.5	5.3	2.2	1.3	0.7	0.7	1.7	2.9	1.8
Agrarian Liberals (Venstre)*	23.4	27.6	21.3	22.0	23.0	25.1	21.1	20.8	19.3	18.6	15.6	12.3	23.3
Conservatives*	18.2	12.4	17.8	17.3	16.8	16.6	17.9	20.1	18.7	20.4	16.7	9.1	5.5
Christian People's Party	—	—	—	—	—	—	—	—	—	—	2.0	4.0	5.3
Independents	—	—	—	—	2.7	2.3	3.3	2.5	1.6	0.5	—	—	—
Progress Party (Poujade type)	—	—	—	—	—	—	—	—	—	—	—	15.9	13.6
Other	3.1	1.9	0.3	1.4	0.6	0.4	0.4	1.1	2.5	1.5	0.2	—	—

* Relevant parties over the whole period.

seemingly supports, therefore, the contention that classifications are not merely mapping devices but also seize, when felicitous, systemic properties. Of course, the format may remain stable precisely because the party behavior changes. In the Dutch case, the new flash parties have received a disproportionate support from the new age cohorts (which are also radicalizing many of the established parties in most Western countries). But the freezing of Western party systems pointed out by Lipset and Rokkan does not entail that the parties are unchanging.

Denmark is interesting, instead, for the unprecedented suddenness and magnitude of its 1973 electoral earthquake. In 1971 only five parties passed the 2-percent threshold and were represented in the *Folketing;* in 1973 five more parties entered, carrying more than one-third of the total vote. In particular, two new parties barely founded before election day polled almost one-fourth of the vote. The 1973 landslide was unprecedented by all standards: A count of how many votes were lost or gained by each party gives a 60-percent switching. The 1975 election has been, however, somewhat reinstating, with one major exception: The sustained strength of the Progress party. For the rest, what seems to be emerging, or reemerging, is a two-bloc system centered, respectively, on the Social Democrats and the Agrarian Liberals. The difference is (as in the case of the Netherlands) a greater radicalization, with two recent parties – not only the Progress but also the Christian People's party – seemingly taking hold. In any event, if Denmark were to be reclassified as a system of extreme pluralism, the question would become whether Denmark is also transforming itself into a system of polarized pluralism. Naturally, the two events need not be synchronous. On the other hand, as the examination of Finland will show, a system can be extreme in terms of party numbers and yet remain semi-polarized. And similar problems, or queries, arise – albeit to a lesser extent – with respect to Norway. At the 1973 elections the Norwegian Labor party suffered its worst defeat in 25 years – down to 35 percent of the vote, with only 40 percent of the seats – so that Norway seemingly has ceased to be a predominant party system.[36] Furthermore, the 1973 elections have brought to the fore a sixth, unquestionably relevant unit in the standing parliament: the Socialist Election Alliance, resulting from the joined forces of the Communist and the Socialist People's parties (both unrepresented in the 1969 parliament), plus a leftist splinter group of the Labor party. Finally, even in Norway a new protest party – the Anders Lange's party (claiming drastic reduction in taxation and public intervention) has polled 5 percent of the vote.[37]

While it is premature, as we learn from the Dutch experience, to reclassify and to draw conclusions from one election only, the preliminary inspection of our list of countries does reveal that the freezed party systems are under serious challenge – for the Nordic countries are, presumably, only the forerunners of a more general trend. However that may be, for the time being the major problem is to decide whether the borderline countries (for the classification) belong, or do not belong, to the *type* of polarized pluralism.

Let us immediately apply the control variable: ideological distance. Under this criterion it immediately appears that Switzerland definitely belongs to the type of moderate pluralism. The same is true, if to a diminishing extent, for the Netherlands. The party fragmentation of the two countries reflects *segmentation,* not polarization. In particular, Switzerland appears the most depoliticized country of the entire group, presumably because the cantons remain the center of gravity of Swiss politics. From a national standpoint, the Swiss party system is extremely loose and decentralized: the federal center "administers," leaving the stuff of politics to be debated and decided at the periphery.[38] As for Denmark and Norway, the two countries may well be approaching a phase of semi-polarization, but it is too soon to say; and the standing fact remains that until 1975 neither has displayed relevant anti-system parties nor centrifugal competition. The Danish extreme left (Communist, Left Socialist, and Socialist People's party) has never surpassed the 12-percent level. The Norwegian extreme left, which emerged at the 1973 elections under the label "Socialist Electoral Alliance," has totaled 10 percent of the votes and obtained 16 seats: 1 to the Communists, 9 to the Socialist People's party, and 6 to Labor dissidents. All things considered, Switzerland, the Netherlands, Denmark, and Norway do not belong to the polarized type. The dubious cases under the numerical criterion are no longer dubious under the ideological criterion. The control indicators dispel any doubt about Switzerland and point only to a beginning of polarization in the other three countries.

There is still another country that deserves preliminary and, indeed, special attention: Israel. Israel is a most baffling case – and this quite aside from the fact that it is a microcosm of all the conceivable complexities. On surface – that is, if one follows the endless splintering, renaming, and recombining of its parties – the Israeli party system may appear, to date, very fluid. On the other hand, if one disregards the party names and aggregates the returns into three major clusters – left, center-to-right, and religious – one finds, over the period 1949–1973, a remarkable stability. The left group of parties (whose major components are *Mapai,* now *Avodah,* i.e., the dominant Labor party, and *Mapam,* closer to Marxist socialism) has displayed, before the 1973 election, variations in the order of 2 percentage points above or below the 50-percent threshold. The center-to-right group of parties – whose pivotal element is *Herut,* a right-wing party – has been somewhat more unstable but oscillating (before 1973) around the 25-percent mark.

Table 7. Israel: aggregate electoral returns 1949–1973

	1949	1951	1955	1959	1961	1965	1969	1973
United Workers' Party: *Mapan* Labor Party: *Mapai* (*Avodah* since 1968) Unity of Labor: *Achdut Avodah* (1955–1961) Workers' List: *Rafi* (1965)[1] Aligment-*Maarah* Coalition (1969 and 1973)[2] Affiliated Arab Lists	50.4	49.8	47.6	51.3	48.8	51.2	46.2	39.6
Independent Liberals (from 1965)[3]	—	—	—	—	—	3.8	3.2	3.6
Progressive Party (to 1959) General Zionists (to 1959) Liberal Party (1961)[4] State List (1969)[5] Free Center (1969)[6] Freedom Party: *Herut* (1949–1961) *Gahal* Coalition (1965 and 1969)[7] Front Coalition: *Likud* (1973)[8]	20.8	26.0	27.2	24.2	27.4	21.3	26.0	30.2
National Religious Party: *Mizrachi*[9] Orthodox Religion: *Agudat Israel* (since 1961) Orthodox Workers: *Poalei Agudat* (since 1961) *Torah* Front (until 1959)[10]	12.2	11.9	13.8	13.6	15.4	14.0	14.7	12.5
Communist[11]	3.5	4.0	4.5	2.8	4.2	3.4	3.9	4.8
Other	13.1	8.3	6.9	8.1	4.2	6.3	6.0	9.3

[1] *Mapai* split of Ben Gurion. [2] *Mapam, Mapai, Achdut Avodah, Rafi.* [3] Center party which neither entered *Gahal* nor *Likud,* a successor of the Progressive party. [4] Merger of the Progressives and General Zionists. [5] *Rafi* split, i.e., second split of the Ben Gurion followers. [6] *Herut* split. [7] *Herut* and Liberal bloc. [8] *Gahal,* Free Center, State List. [9] Since 1951, currently *Mafdal,* it receives two-thirds of the religious turnout and includes a labor segment,

And the stability of the turnout of the religious group of parties is amazing, especially if one considers that the voters have more than tripled (440,000 in 1949 and over 1.5 million in 1973).

However, the aggregations largely oversimplify the matter. The aggregated returns result from an extremely fragmented, proliferating and splitting-prone collection of parties that are not only highly heterogeneous among themselves, but also highly fractionalized at the sub-party level (with a strong patronage and clientelar entrenchment). Take the religious camp. Within a same religion the major religious party (*Mizrachi*) enters most coalitions (and has become, after the 1973 elections, the most courted coalition partner between the Alignment and *Likud*), while *Agudat Israel* has an anti-Zionist origin and has refused, since 1952, to share governmental responsibilities (even in the 1967 national unity government that launched the Six Day War). As a first approximation, one could say that Israel combines the fragmentation and multiconfessionalism of the Netherlands with the poly-ethnicity of Switzerland. But this is only a first approximation. The Protestant and Catholic parties of the Netherlands can be entered into the left-right continuum, whereas the Jewish religious parties represent one of the few cases of irreducible multidimensionality – for their over-arching purpose is to extend the sphere of religious controls. Let it be added that religion plays, in Israeli politics, a contradictory or, at least, an ambiguous role. On the one hand, throughout 2000 years of Diaspora the Jews have maintained their identity on religious grounds. On the other hand, the presence of truly confessional parties is at odds with the modernizing nature of the new state and represents, at least potentially, the most divisive cleavage in Israeli society.[39]

If we turn to the other comparison, it quickly appears that Israel is, in effect, more deeply polyethnic than Switzerland. To be sure, the Swiss speak three languages, whereas Israel has adopted Hebrew (though respecting Arabic) as its unifying national language. Yet, by now the Swiss "nations" are more accommodated to each other than the Jewish "tribes." This is so, understandably, because Israel is a new state of immigrants. But the Israeli melting pot has not been as effective as hoped. The Israeli population is composed of two major ethnic and cultural groups: the *Ashkenazim* (originally, the Germans), which comprise the Jews of European, Russian, and American origin, and the *Sephardim* (originally, the Spanish), largely merged with the *Orientals*, originating from the Mediterranean countries, Iraq and Iran. These

Source to Table 7 (*cont.*)

Ha Poel HaMizrachi. [10] In 1949 *Torah* comprehended all the religious parties and for the subsequent three elections the two Orthodox parties. [11] Since 1965 split in two: *Maki* (*Moked* in 1973), which is pro-Israel, and *Rakach*, the pro-Arab new Communist party.

"tribes" not only belong, then, to different cultures but also to a different historical time: They are, so to speak, asynchronous. And they are not fusing. If anything, a Sephardi-Oriental subculture is consolidating itself in opposition, or at least in contradistinction, to the Westernizing culture.[40]

On the foregoing grounds it would be quite surprising not to find a fissured society and a highly fragmented party system. Unquestionably, then, Israel belongs to the class of extreme pluralism. But it does not display the properties of the type: It is not polarized, even though the tensions and conditions of a polarized development are well in the picture. However, there is another side to the coin: Israel is a small, encircled country fighting for survival and exposed to overriding external threats. In this respect Israel can be approached to Finland – except that the Finns perceive themselves as having established a *modus vivendi* with the Soviet Union, whereas the Israeli are still, and indeed increasingly, aware of their vulnerability. On these grounds solidarity and coalescence become a must. And this may suffice to explain why Israel is, in spite of its fragmentation, a "moderate" (i.e., non-polarized or only semi-polarized) type of polity. Yet Israel is more *sui generis* than that.

The argument that the number of parties affects the mechanics of the party system assumes an endogenous game of politics, that is, a sufficient degree of international autonomy in internal affairs. This is not the case of Israel; and this is why we should not expect my "mechanical predispositions" to apply. The fact remains that Israel hardly belongs to any type. If it is not polarized, one can equally point out that it does not display the alternative coalitions that characterize the moderate polities; nor is Israel a predominant-party system (*Mapai* has never surpassed the 40-percent mark). Thus the most intriguing aspect of the Israeli pattern is that, despite its numerous parties, it lacks a center pole in contradistinction to a left pole.[41] Currently, only the Independent Liberals qualify as having a center positioning; but, mustering less than 5 percent of the total vote, they can hardly be perceived as a center pole. One explanation for this strange void is that the real, if only potential, switchers of the system – the parties that can shift from a left-oriented to a right-oriented coalition, thereby playing a "center role" – are the religious parties (especially *Mizrachi*). But this is hardly a sufficient explanation.

Up until 1973, the Israeli turnouts did not suggest any definite trend: The political system appeared, despite its nominal fickleness and maneuverings, quite frozen in its unique state of equilibrium. The Kippur war came as a shock and doubtless reinforced the reasons for coalescing over the pulls of segmentation. However, in the face of the surprise and delusions of October, the most significant aspect of the December

1973 election was not the enfeeblement of the Alignment led by the prime minister Golda Meir, but that the *Likud* opposition bloc went up only from 26 to 30.2 percent. One could still say that the 1973 returns point to the emergence of a sizable, unified opposition and, therefore, to a possible trend toward a system based on alternative coalitions. Yet my guess is that such a trend would have to await new and even more traumatic events. Not even the Kippur war can release Israel from being a prisoner both of its distant and recent Jewish past. The paradox of Israel is that it is a new state (i) founded on immemorial memories and (ii) preestablished to its 1948 formal establishment. The World Zionist Organization and the Jewish Agency for Palestine shaped the future state of Israel during the British mandate from the 1920s onward. *Mapai* is the dominant party of Israel because it was dominant in the Zionist organization; and it is no mystery that the flow of financial and manpower resources from the Diaspora to Palestine was highly selective and actually discriminated against dissenting political groups.[42] The major key to the understanding of the case of Israel is, therefore, in the exogenous forces that first created the new state and subsequently influenced the self-steering of the polity. If Israel is a most baffling case, this is because Israel cannot be explained *within* Israel. The new state results from, and is shaped by, a fantastically intricate convergence of historical and external cross-pressures. When the new state was born, the "proportions" had already been allocated; and very elaborate *proporz* mechanisms ensure their maintenance (as the stability of the returns confirms). Furthermore, Israel depends, even more than ever before, on outer resources and support; and it is the external menace that counterweighs not only its internal, enduring Diaspora, but also the seeds of a confessional-secular *Kulturkampf*. And if this is so, there is little point in trying to bring Israel into one of the patterns that develop in the self-monitoring polities. Israel is very definitely a case by itself to be understood as such.[43]

We are thus left with six cases, that is, with six countries to be investigated as polarized polities. These countries are arranged according to their greater-to-lesser proximity to the "pure" type. Thus Weimar, Italy, and France (with specific reference to the Fourth Republic) are entered first. Chile is fourth on account of its peculiarities. Finland comes next as the least proximal case. As for Spain (1931–1936), it is included only as an additional illustration, under the caution that the Spanish experiment was chaotic and far too brief.

The Weimar experience (Table 8) displays two major characteristics: First, and during its whole course, an extraordinary degree of fluctuation of the party votes (with the sole exception of the Catholic *Zentrum*); and, second, an overwhelming leftward orientation in 1919–1920 that was upturned in a rightist surge in 1932–1933. The center-

Table 8. *Weimar Republic: electoral returns (Reichstag)*

	1919	1920	May 1924	Dec. 1924	1928	1930	July 1932	Nov. 1932	1933
Ind. Socialists	7.6	18.0	—	—	—	—	—	—	—
Communist	—	2.0	12.6	9.0	10.6	13.1	14.6	16.9	12.3
Social Democrat[1]	37.9	21.6	20.5	26.0	29.8	24.5	21.6	20.4	18.3
Democratic Party[2]	18.6	8.4	5.7	6.3	4.9	3.8	1.0	1.0	0.9
Center (Catholic)	19.7	13.6	13.4	13.6	12.1	11.8	12.5	11.9	11.2
People's Party[3]	4.4	14.0	9.2	10.1	8.7	4.5	1.2	1.9	1.1
National People's[4]	10.3	15.1	19.5	20.5	14.2	7.0	5.9	8.8	8.0
National-Socialist[5]	—	—	6.6	3.0	2.6	18.3	37.4	33.1	43.9
Other	1.5	7.3	12.1	11.5	17.1	17.0	5.8	6.0	4.3

[1] SPD; [2] DDP; [3] DVP; [4] DNVP; [5] Nazi party

fleeing tendencies are very evident throughout the whole period, in the downsliding of the center-left progressives (DDP) and of their center-right counterpart, the People's party (DVP), both of which end in disappearance.[44]

Italy (Table 9) has already been discussed at length.[45] Here only two points seem worthy of remark. First, in contrast to Weimar the Italian electoral fluctuations are quite small, while the trend is steadfast. Until 1975 the Italian pace has been slow, but its course fixed. Second, Italy is characterized by a much more consistent center party than the ones displayed by the Weimar Republic, France, and particularly Chile – as we shall soon see. And if a unified and towering center party is an indicator of systemic solidity and stability, then it can be said that the Italian Christian Democrats represent, or have represented for almost 30 years, the most successful "feedback" among the polarized systems.

With respect to France (Table 10) the intriguing question is how much variance is explained by the constitutional intervening variable that separates the Fourth from the Fifth Republic and especially by the transformation of an assemblear system into a presidential one. Another preliminary caution is that the French double-ballot runoff makes the polity less sensitive to the electoral distributions, in the sense that the electoral system invariably underrepresents the extremes and particularly the Communist party.[46] This does not imply that the returns are not indicative. But they are very difficult to compare over the entire 1945–1973 period on two counts: the constitutional variations, and the endless shifting and recombination of its electoral units.[47]

The problem is especially posed by the Gaullists. In my analysis the

Table 9. *Italy: electoral returns 1946–1972 (low chamber) and regional elections of 1975*

	1946	1948	1953	1958	1963	1968	1972	1975
Communist (PCI)	18.9	31.0	22.6	22.7	25.3	26.9	27.2	33.4
Socialists	20.7	31.0	12.7	14.2	13.8	14.5	9.6	12.0
Social Democrats	—	7.1	4.5	4.5	6.1	14.5	5.1	5.6
Republican	4.4	2.5	1.6	1.4	1.4	2.0	2.9	3.2
Christian Dem. (DC)	35.2	48.5	40.1	42.4	38.3	39.1	38.8	35.3
Liberals	6.8	3.8	3.0	3.5	7.0	5.8	3.9	2.5
Monarchists	2.8	2.8	6.9	4.8	1.8	1.3	—	—
Neo-Fascists (MSI)	—	2.0	5.8	4.8	5.1	4.5	8.7	6.4
Other	11.2	2.3	2.8	1.7	1.2	5.9	3.8	1.6

The 1975 regional elections are added since they are quite comparable to the general elections and, in 1975, very indicative.

Gaullist movement is considered anti-system because the left-right space (ordering) implied by my concept is based not on socioeconomic but on "constitutional" policy positions; and De Gaulle did unwaveringly oppose and delegitimize the Fourth Republic as an unworkable assemblear regime. Even so the objection could be that in June 1953 the RPF (*Rassemblement du Peuple Français*) was incorporated into the system, for it entered the Laniel coalition government and again, in 1954, the Mendes-France grand national coalition (which was voted also by the Communists) called to end the Indochina war. However, in May 1953 De Gaulle had released the RPF deputies from their loyalty to him; and the RPF participated in the Laniel, Mayer, and Mendes-France coalitions with the preeminent intent of torpedoing the European Defense Community and, with it, the pro-Europe "third force" parties that identified themselves with the Fourth Republic. It is fair to say, therefore, that the Gaullists betrayed De Gaulle and were actually incorporated into the system only when they entered (under the new label RS, i.e., *Républicains Sociaux*) the Faure cabinet in February 1955. Be that as it may, I have emphasized all along that my argument hinges on the electoral party and on the electoral returns, and that the distinction between the electoral (visible) and parliamentary (often invisible) party is of major importance. If so, the "Gaullist muddle" reinforces my point. In my understanding, Gaullism had an identity and played its relevant role, throughout the Fourth Republic,

Table 10. *France: electoral returns 1945–1973 (low chamber)*

	Fourth Republic					Fifth Republic				
	1945	1946	1946	1951	1956	1958	1962	1967	1968	1973
Left Socialist and Extreme Left						1.8	2.3	2.2	3.9	3.3
Communists	26.1	26.2	28.6	25.9	25.9	18.9	21.8	22.5	20.0	21.4
Socialists	23.8	21.1	17.9	14.5	15.0	15.5	12.5			
Radicals (and UDSR) / Radicals/Center-Left	11.1	11.5	14.0	10.0	13.5	8.3	7.8	19.0[1]	16.5[1]	19.0[1]
Christian Democrats (MRP)	24.9	28.1	26.3	12.5	11.1	11.7	9.1	12.6[3]	10.3[4]	12.4[5]
Conservatives	13.3	12.8	11.2	14.0	14.6	13.9[2]	7.7[2]			
Pro-Gaullist Conservatives						6.2[6]	5.9[6]	3.7[6]	4.1[6]	6.9[6]
Gaullists (RPF in 1951)	—	—	1.6	21.7	4.3	17.5[7]	31.9[7]	37.7[8]	43.6[9]	30.1[10]
Poujadists	—	—	—	—	12.3					
Other	0.8	0.3	0.4	1.4	3.3	6.2	1.0	2.3	1.6	6.9

[1] Federation of Democratic and Socialist Left. [2] National Center of Independents (Pinay, Reynaud). [3] Democratic Center (Lecanuet). [4] Center (Lecanuet), Progress and Democracy (Duhamel), National Center of Independents (unified as Centre-PDM). [5] Social democratic reformers. [6] Independent Republicans (Giscard d'Estaing, Marcellin). [7] Union Nouvelle Republique (UNR). [8] Fifth Republic (formerly UNR) plus some Independent Republicans. [9] UDR (formerly Fifth Republic). [10] UDR plus minor Gaullist groups. (Numbers 7 to 10 represent Gaullist labels).

only as an electoral party that was perceived by the electorate as De Gaulle conceived it. Hence the fact that the RPF deputies gradually reverted (first with the ARS secession in 1952, but finally under the RS banner in 1955) in parliament to their traditional practices and allegiances, does not alter the fact that the Gaullist vote was intended as an anti-system vote – as is well confirmed by what happened to the RPF-ARS-URAS-RS members of parliament at the 1956 elections: a drastic decimation (from 21.7 to 4.3 percent).

Under the above qualifications the major reason that makes the Fourth and Fifth Republics hard to compare is that the Gaullists were anti-system under the Fourth Republic but impersonated the new system, i.e., the Fifth Republic – at least, until the 1974 presidential elections. However, the case under examination is the Fourth Republic. And in this reference Table 10 indicates, in 1951, a very evident centrifugal trend and, in 1956, the consolidation of a polarized pattern. True enough, the Fourth Republic collapsed under the menace of a praetorian army and the impact of an exogenous crisis of decolonization. Nonetheless, in 1951 and 1956 the protest and alienated oppositions had cumulatively polled 48 percent and 42.5 percent of the total vote – indeed an eloquent pointer of a widespread, lingering crisis of legitimacy.

Chile, whose electoral returns are presented in Table 11, poses to an even greater extent the same problem as France: How much is explained by the constitutional factor? Allende was put in office by the conventions of the constitution, not by an absolute electoral majority.[48] Also, the election of the president by universal suffrage imposes alliances that – in a polarized system – generate strong tensions within the center group of parties and induce acrobatic ideological leaps along the left-right dimension. Thus the radicals (PR) stood with the conservatives (i.e., at the right of the Christian Democrats, or PDC) at the beginning of the 1964 electoral campaign for the presidency won by Frei; helped the Allende vote and entered his government in 1970; and joined the anti-Allende alliance (CODE) in 1973. That is, throughout this period the radicals and the demochristians have been endlessly inverting their positioning and outflanking each other. Note that these maneuverings were not novel. The limiting case was the presidential election of Videla (PR) in 1946, which resulted from an unholy alliance spreading all the way from the Marxist left to the liberals. The implication is that if a center positioning calls for a "mediating role," such a role has never been adequately performed either by the radicals or, subsequently, by the PDC. The center that kept the Chilean polity together was provided, in effect, by the presidency. Since 1938 only one president (Alessandri in 1958) was elected by the right and only one (Allende in 1970) from the left; and on both occasions their elections resulted from a miscalculation of the other groups. The difference was that Alessandri was able to move toward the center, while Allende could not. The course of Allende's presidency was increasingly characterized, therefore, by the "center void" which is a prelude, in a polarized system, to its breakdown.

Under these conditions one wonders whether the Chilean variant of polarized pluralism really had – in party terms – a center, or whether its center amounted, in substance, to a "transit" from left to right and vice versa. To be sure, if the notion of center is purely relative and contingent upon the existence of outer parties (more to the left and right), then it is true by definition that Chile and any system of polarized pluralism have a center. However, the relativity of the notion does not impede a weighing of its substantive compactness. And in this latter perspective the major lesson to be learned from the Chilean experience is that the combination of a direct presidential election with a pattern of polarization and centrifugation precludes the solidification of a center pole, thereby creating the feeblest and most defenseless variant of an inherently fragile system. Chile was particularly exposed precisely because it was never able to stabilize and solidify – in its party structuring – a center feedback.

An ulterior variable, on which I need not dwell, is the military variable. The tradition (since 1931) of nonintervention had established the image of an army standing in the background as the guardian of the constitution – an idea that facilitated, psychologically, the congressional election of Allende. On the other hand, the existence of a military guardian subsequently conditioned his performance. This is by no means to suggest that Allende's "legalism" was imposed but to note, instead, that the MIR (the Quevarist-inspired Movement of Revolutionary Left) and his own party were posing impossible demands upon Allende. The point is, however, that one cannot generalize about the "constitutional route" to a Marxist state from the Chilean experience. Quite aside from how it ended, the whole course of the experiment was "disturbed" by an army to whom both sides appealed, according to the circumstances and with opposed interpretations, as the constitutional arbiter, trustee, or saver.[49]

In spite of all the preceding intervening variables, the electoral returns are, in themselves, very revealing. Table 11 is subdivided into four slices that account for the different equilibriums of the periods so divided, and also attempts to account – albeit very roughly – for the exchanges in ideological positioning between radicals and demochristians, and between Communists and Socialists. The table also conveys that the ideological spectrum underwent, at the end of the process, considerable stretching. Not only had the Socialists definitely moved, just before Allende's victory and under the leadership of Altamirano,

Table 11. *Chile: electoral returns 1945–1973 (Congress)*

	(PCCh) Communist	Socialist (PS)	Radical (PR)	Christian Dem. (PDC)	Liberal (PL)	Conservative (PCU)
1945	10.3	12.8	20.0	2.6	18.0	23.6
1949	—	9.3	21.7	3.9	18.0	22.7
1953	—	14.1	13.3	2.8	11.0	10.1
1957	—	10.7	21.5	9.4	15.4	13.8
	PCCh	PS	PDC	PR	PL	PCU
1961	11.8	11.1	15.9	22.2	16.6	14.8
1965	12.8	10.6	43.6	13.7	7.5	5.3
	PS	PCCh	PR	PDC	PN	
1969	15.1	16.6	13.4	31.1	20.9	
	PS MAPU Izq. Chr.	PCCh API	PR	PDC	Rad. Dem. Izq. Rad.	PN
March 1973	18.7 1.3 0.7	16.7 1.3	3.3	33.3	1.3 0.7	22.7

Source (until 1969): R. H. McDonald, *Party Systems and Elections in Latin America*, Markham, 1971, p. 134. In 1973 the Popular Unity front – PS, MAPU, PCCh, API – obtained 42.1 percent (an increase of 6 seats in the House and of 2 seats in the Senate), and the opposition (CODE) 56.2 percent of the vote. The 1973 percentages are computed from the allocation of the seats. The returns of 1949, 1953, and 1957 are highly incomplete (in 1953 as much as 48.7 percent of the vote is considered residual), but I follow McDonald for purposes of longitudinal comparability (the 1953 election produced a disturbing and ephemeral Ibanista majority). The major, unaccounted parties of the 1949–1957 period are PAL (*Partido Agrario Laborista*) and PSP (*Partido Socialista Popular*).

PS: Socialist Party; MAPU: Movement of United Popular Action (PDC split); Izq. Chr.: Christian Left; PCCh: Chilean Communist Party; API: Popular Independent Action; PR: Radical Party; PDC: Christian Democratic Party (since 1957; formerly National Falange); Izq. Rad.: Radical Left; Rad. Dem.: Radical Democrats; PN: National Party (merger of PL/PCU); PL: Liberal Party; PCU: Conservative Party.

to the left of the Communist party (loyal to the USSR and insensitive to the charm of Castro), but the Communists were equally outflanked at their left by MAPU and the Izquierda Christians, two extremist splinter groups of the PDC. True enough, these groups (and also API, the left split of the radicals) performed very poorly at the polls; but they held cabinet positions and were doubtlessly relevant. Even though it did not perform as an electoral party, MIR was even more relevant. And the same applies, later, to its counterpart at the extreme right, the paramilitary organization *Patria y Libertad.*

Reverting to the slices of Table 11, the period 1945–1961 is not very significant on three counts: (i) the outlawing between 1948 and 1958 of the Communist party; (ii) the surge in 1952 of a weird antiparty Ibanista majority; (iii) the fact that the Socialists were divided, until 1959, into two major parties, the PS and the PSP (*Partido Socialista Popular*). On all these counts the endogenous dynamics of the system was largely blocked. It is in 1961, then, that the premises that had been maturing since the popular front of 1938 became operative at a very fast pace. The first shock was, in 1961, the PDC menace to the radicals, followed in 1965 by its crushing victory over the hitherto (since 1938) pivotal party of the system. In 1965 it was equally clear that the whole spectrum had slid massively leftward: Not only was President Frei pushing his "revolution in freedom" reforms beyond the point ever reached by the radicals, but the vote for the right dropped precipitously from 31 to a mere 13 percent. Structurally speaking, however, the emergence of a towering center-left party – the PDC – pointed to the healthiest possible distribution for a system of polarized pluralism. But the 1969 elections demonstrated that this distribution was only transitional. By 1969 it was very evident that the pulls of the system were overwhelmingly centrifugal, with the extreme left going up to 32 percent and the right (now united in the PN) regaining 21 percent, both at the expense of the PDC's short-lived dream. And the 1973 elections confirmed that the polarization had destroyed whatever might formerly have been considered a center area, with the PR reduced to a mere 3 percent and the PDC regaining some strength (but not the losses of the radicals) qua leader of the anti-Allende front.

This rapid succession of dramatic swings cannot be imputed to an as yet unsolidified party system. Not only did Chile have the best record of constitutional government and free elections of any major Latin American country, but it also displayed the most highly structured party system of the continent. Over the longer period, that is, starting from the thirties, Chile can best be compared to the Third and Fourth French Republics. In the sixties, however, Chile had become more similar to Italy. First, the two countries found their respective pivotal party in a center-leaning-to-left Christian Democracy with similar doctrines and intellectual inspiration. Second, the Chilean Communist Party had nothing to learn from Togliatti's "Italian road to socialism": Both the PCCh and the PCI had long been inspired by the electoral conquest of power doctrine and by the resulting strategy of unity of action with the Socialists and of middle-class incorporation. Third, the Chilean Socialists represented an extreme version of the "maximalist rhetoric" that has also endlessly plagued Italian socialism. While socialism throughout the West has often been schismatic and torn between many souls, both the Chilean and the Italian traditional Socialist parties shared a characteristic impermeability to the social-democratic "corruption."

We shall long debate the many reasons that brought Chile to the 1973 coup. According to the foregoing analysis, one of the reasons, and by no means a minor one, was that the political system had reached a stage of nonworkability. On the sole ground of the acceleration of its center-fleeing polarization, it was an easy prediction that all the conditions of a democratic governance were rapidly dwindling.[50] And the fact that this very obvious point escaped not only the actors but also the observers represents an ominous symptom.[51] Not only is the Chilean tragedy a tragedy in itself; it also points to a colossal failure in political analysis.[52] We are seemingly living – political scientists well included – far above our political *intelligere*, i.e., our ability to understand and control the impossibles and the inevitables of politics.

While Chile is characterized by the unleashing of the dynamics of polarized pluralism, Finland (Table 12) represents the best instance of how the mechanical propensities of the type can be successfully counteracted. In spite of having the third largest Western Communist party, and despite the fact that Finland's low degree of international autonomy vis-à-vis the USSR may impose the Communists as governmental partners.[53] Finland stands out as the most hopeful and successful instance of controlled polarization. Yet a perusal of Table 12 indicates that centrifugal strains are operative. While the Communists have suffered severe losses in 1970 and 1972 and while the Social Democrats have reverted – after their 1962 low – to their average strength of one-fourth of the total turnout, nonetheless the *pro tempore* emergence of a new, protest Rural party, the lesser strength of the center Agrarian party, and the increase of the conservatives, all of this conforms to what the model predicts. Finland does represent the least proximal, or more distant, case from the pure type. But Finland becomes a most interesting case precisely because its political system performs along the cobweb of semi-polarization.[54]

Table 13, on Spain, can only show, as Linz puts it, that "in the 1933

Table 12. *Finland: electoral returns 1945–1975*

	1945	1948	1951	1954	1958	1962	1966	1970	1972	1975
Communist	23.5	20.0	21.6	21.6	23.2	22.0	21.2	16.6	17.0	19.0
Social Democrats	25.0	26.3	26.5	26.2	23.2	19.5	27.2	23.4	25.8	25.0
Rural Party	—	—	—	—	—	—	—	10.5	9.2	3.6
Center Party[1]	21.4	24.2	23.3	24.1	23.0	23.0	21.2	17.1	16.4	17.7
Liberal People's Party	—	—	5.6	7.9	5.9	5.9	6.5	6.0	5.2	4.4
Swedish Party	7.9	7.7	7.6	7.0	6.7	6.4	6.0	5.7	5.3	4.7
National Coalition[2]	15.0	17.0	14.6	12.8	15.3	15.1	13.8	18.0	17.6	18.4
Other	7.2	4.8	0.8	0.4	2.7	8.1	4.1	2.7	3.5	7.2

[1] Agrarian; [2] Conservatives.

Table 13. *Spanish Republic, 1931–1936*
(left-to-right aggregations in seats)

	Constituent Assembly 1931–33	1st Legislature 1933–36	2nd Legislature 1936
Extreme Left[1]	—	1	68
Socialists[2]	114	61	50
Bourgeois Left[3]	162	38	162
Center[4]	126	129	40
Center-Right	10	95	—
Right[5]	43	105	116
Extreme Right[6]	17	40	22
Other	3	5	5
Total	474	474	463

Source: Juan Linz, "The Party System in Spain," in Lipset and Rokkan, eds., *Party Systems and Voter Alignments*, Free Press, 1967, pp. 260–263, Table 22. The figures for the Constituent Assembly have been supplied by Linz.
[1] Communist and Maximalists; [2] PSOE; [3] Republican Action, Esquerra Catalana, Izq. Republicana, Union Republicana; [4] Radical party; [5] Opposing the 1931 constitution; [6] Pro monarchy.

Table 14. *Linear trends (regression coefficients) of aggregate returns in seven polarized polities*

	Weimar	Italy	France IV	France V	Chile	Finland	Spain
EL[1]	+2,93	+1,31	−0,22	+0,78	+3,11	+0,53	+ 7,3
CL[2]	−2,50	−0,84	−1,49	−1,34	+3,85	−0,18	− 8,9
C[3]	−3,65	−0,34	−3,32	−3,29	—	−0,47	− 7,3
CR[4]	−1,15	+0,01	+0,67	+3,65	−2,82	+0,28	—
ER[5]	+6,56	+0,51	+4,04	—	—	—	+ 8,1
Left	−1,06	+0,33	−1,70	−0,56	+6,96	+0,21	+ 1,5
Center	−3,65	−0,34	−3,32	−3,29	—	−0,47	− 7,3
Right	+4,71	+0,48	+4,49	+3,65	−2,82	+0,28	+ 8,6
Extremes[6]	+6,16	+1,85	+3,82	+0,78	+3,11	+0,53	+15,9

[1] Extreme left; [2] Center-Left; [3] Center; [4] Center-Right; [5] Extreme Right; [6] Sum of coefficients of Extreme Left and Extreme Right.

elections Spain became one more example of . . . polarized, centrifugal multiparty system."[55] An additional reason for entering the case of the Spanish Republic is, however, that Spain may well revert, in the not too distant future, to the pattern, or path, it had entered in the thirties.

There are many ways of representing trends in party strengths. A safe way is to draw a regression line on a per annum basis, with the cumulative trend simply being the multiplication of the per annum rate of change by the electoral duration of the party.[56] However, in Table 14 and in the figures thus resulting (Figures 15 through 20) a different technique is employed – whenever possible. Table 14 calculates the regression coefficients or, more exactly, the linear trends of the polities under scrutiny with respect to three sets of aggregations: (i) extreme left, center-left, center, center-right, extreme right, in the upper part of the table; (ii) left, center, right, in the midportion and (iii) the sum of the coefficients of the two extremes, at the bottom.

The measures are based on the returns carried in the country by country figures, Tables 8 through 13; they cover the same time span (up until 1973), and their explanation is as follows. The central year of the distribution (1928 for Weimar, 1958 for Italy, 1967 for the Fifth Republic, 1957 for Chile, 1958 for Finland) obtains a value o, on the basis of which the measures of Table 14 represent the angular coefficients of each aggregation, to be understood as the average *quantum* (not average *rate*) of increase, or decrease, with respect to the total turnout.[57] Only the Fourth Republic was not amenable to this treatment, for the obvious reason that with three elections condensed in one year the assumption that the intervals between elections are equal founders. Hence in the case of the Fourth Republic time has been considered a continuous variable (even though the face value of the regression coefficient has been adapted in order to make it comparable). It is unnecessary to dwell on the imperfections of the measure, and especially on the inevitable arbitrariness of the aggregations. Of course, on a single country basis the coefficients can be calculated party by party, and the aggregations can be more ad hoc.[58] For com-

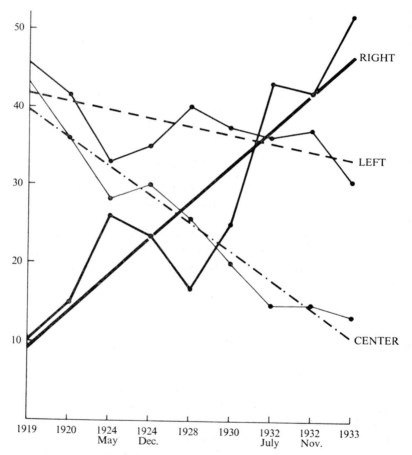

Figure 15. Trends in the Weimar Republic.

LEFT (− 1.06): Communists, Independent Socialists, Social Democrats; CENTER (− 3.65): Democrats, Center, People's party; RIGHT (+ 4.71): National People's party, National Socialists.

parative purposes, however, the aggregates must pay heed to comparability. Thus in the figures the data are manipulated in the Procustean
bed of the left-center-right tripartition – except for Chile and France.[59]
Three countries require some brief comments. First, Italy is represented by three figures to show the extent to which different aggregations produce different pictures. Thus in Figure 16*a* the trends are
unimpressive. But if the left group is disaggregated (Figure 16*b*), one
immediately perceives the reason, namely, that the Communist advance is neutralized by the losses of the other left parties. Likewise,
if the right group is disaggregated (Figure 16*c*), we find that the
losses of the moderate right obscure the gains of the extreme right.

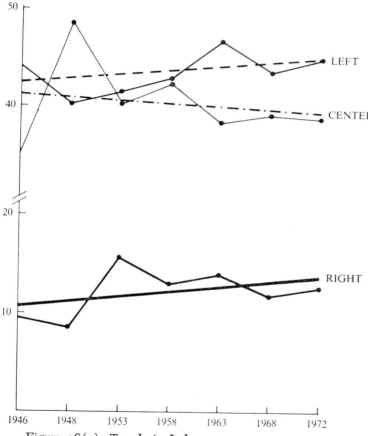

Figure 16(*a*). Trends in Italy.

LEFT (+ 0.33): Communists, Socialists (PSI and PSDI),
Republicans; CENTER (− 0.34): Christian Democrats; RIGHT
(+ 0.48): Liberals, Monarchists, and MSI (neo-Fascists).

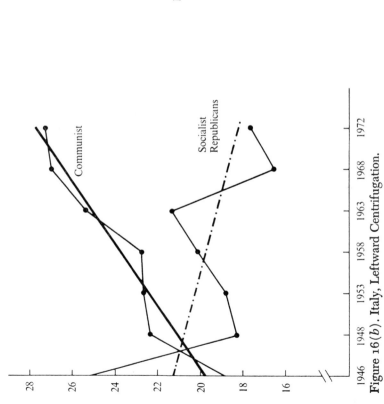

Figure 16(b). Italy, Leftward Centrifugation.

Figure 16(c). Italy, Rightward Centrifugation.

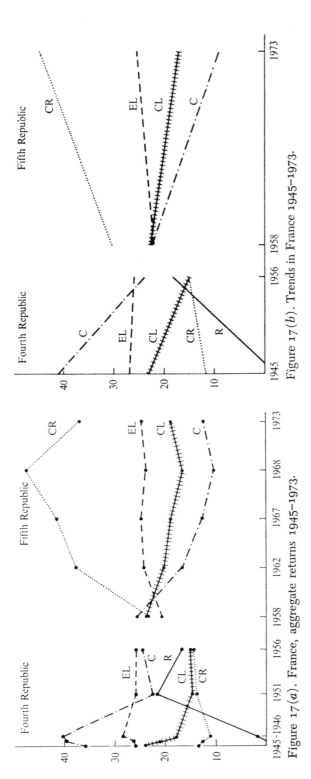

Figure 17(a). France, aggregate returns 1945–1973.

Figure 17(b). Trends in France 1945–1973.

FOURTH REPUBLIC: EL (EXTREME LEFT): Communist; CL (CENTER-LEFT): Socialist; C (CENTER): Chris-tian Democrats (Mrp), Radicals; CR (CENTER-RIGHT): Conservatives; R (EXTREME RIGHT): Gaullists, Pouja-dists. FIFTH REPUBLIC: EL (EXTREME LEFT): Communist, Left Socialist (Psu); CL (CENTER-LEFT): Social-ist, Left Radicals; C (CENTER): Christian Democrats (Mrp), Conservatives (Reynaud, Pinay, Monnerville); CR (CENTER-RIGHT): Gaullist, Pro-Gaullist, Conservatives (Ri).

In Figures 17a and 17b the time dimension is continuous with reference to the Fourth Republic, while the elections are treated as equally spaced in the Fifth Republic. The coefficients are those of Table 14.

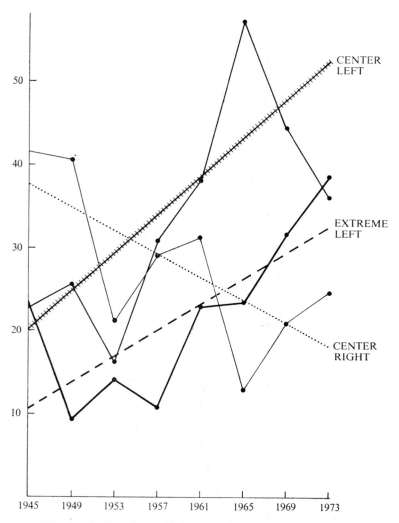

Figure 18. Trends in Chile.

EXTREME LEFT (+ 3.11): Communists, Socialists, MAPU, API; CENTER-LEFT (+ 3.85): Radicals, Demochristians; CENTER-RIGHT (− 2.82): Liberals, Conservatives, PN.

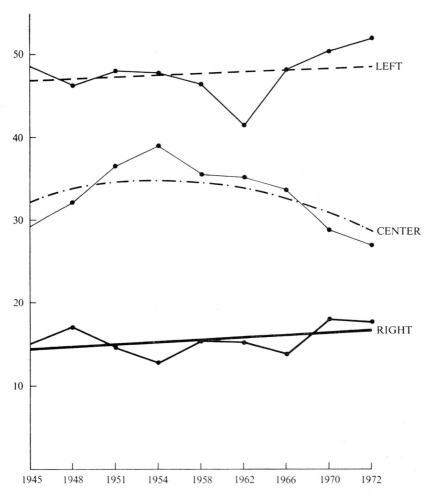

Figure 19. Trends in Finland.

LEFT (+ 0.21): Communists, Rural party, Social Democrats; CENTER (− 0.47): Agrarians, Liberals, Swedish party; RIGHT (+ 0.28): Conservatives. (Despite the parabola of the Center aggregate, the coefficient remains as calculated, i.e., an angular coefficient.)

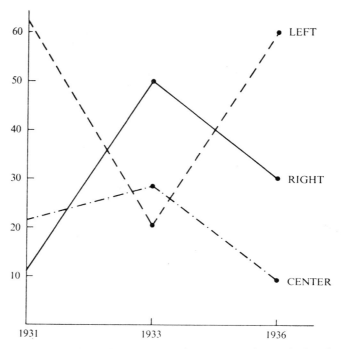

Figure 20. Spain 1931–1936 (aggregate electoral distributions).

LEFT: Communist, Socialist, Bourgeois Left; RIGHT: Center-Right to Extreme Right. (The coefficients are calculated but are not utilized in the figure.)

Second, France is intractable to a threefold aggregation, especially because the transition from the Fourth to the Fifth Republic entails that the Gaullists switch from being anti-regime to being the new regime. It follows that the Fifth Republic – to be discussed in the last section – no longer has an extreme right. Thus Figures 17a and 17b follow the fivefold aggregation, i.e., the first set of coefficients of Table 14, and the representation is divided in two – electoral returns and trends – for purposes of visual clarity.

Third, Finland. Two things are noteworthy: the almost even interval in the turnout of the three clusters (as contrasted with Italy, where the left and center are very close and the right outdistanced) and the very revealing fact that a second-degree parabola provides, for the center aggregate, a far better fit than the straight line.

The visual eloquence of the figures contains – as all eloquence – some distortion. But the distortions can be redressed by looking back at the party-by-party electoral returns. Let it also be stressed that what really matters is how the parties located at the extremes of the ideological spectrum perform vis-à-vis the in-between, centrally located, parties. What really matters is, then, a measure of centrifugation – such as the one suggested at the bottom of Table 14: the sum of the co-efficients of the two extremes. Here is the clue.

The objection might be that the type obtains a sufficient number of cases only longitudinally, over time. But this is as it should be, since we are dealing, after all, with the "deadly" end of the spectrum. Moreover, the number of cases must be related to their importance; and it turns out that the experience of extreme and polarized pluralism has affected – during the past 50 years – all the 4 major European continental countries: Weimar Germany, Spain, France, and Italy. On the other hand, if Chile is not one of the largest Latin American countries in population, it was the most significant one in terms of democratic tradition and structural consolidation of the party system.

The crucial point remains, thus, whether the electoral evidence suffices to sustain all the systemic implications outlined in the previous section. But this depends, in the first place, on whether the reading of the electoral data is banal or theoretically oriented. And my stand remains, in principle, that we have gone much too far in downgrading the import of "visible" vis-à-vis "invisible" politics.[60] Ironically, the more we find our way in the dark, the more we become forgetful of, and blind to, the sunlight. This deformation can be justified in the context of the pragmatic, or least ideological, polities. In particular, twoparty systems are hardly exciting unless one probes them behind the scenes. But the case is very different when we come to the ideological polities. Here words are weapons, and inflationary wordings play a major role in shaping the course of the polarized systems. When a society is nurtured by ideological creeds, invisible politics may well become the countervailing factor of visible politics. But even in this case the weight of what is promised visibly delimits and powerfully conditions what can be done invisibly.

6.3 Moderate pluralism and segmented societies

Limited and moderate pluralism is demarcated, at one boundary, by the twoparty systems and, at the other, by extreme and polarized pluralism. The *class* basically encompasses, then, from three to five relevant parties – and this is why I call it "limited" (in contradistinction to extreme) pluralism.

Confining the examples to the Western countries, those that fall into this class are the German Federal Republic, Belgium, Ireland (three-party format), Sweden, Iceland, and Luxembourg (four-party format), Denmark (four until the 1950s and four-five during the 1960s), Switzerland, the Netherlands, and Norway (five-party format). Those formats are not steadfast. As we know, the Danish and the Norwegian party systems are currently above the five-party size; and if the Netherlands may be reverting to its more traditional format, Sweden may well be moving, with the unicameral *Riksdag* inaugurated in 1971 and the shift to a highly proportional electoral system, from four to five parties. However, the formats just indicated have been the standing or largely prevalent ones for a quarter-century – and the remarkable thing has been, over the sixties, their resilience. We have ten countries, then, that enter the class of limited pluralism.

If the list does not appear entirely convincing, this is not because we may disagree on the relevance/irrelevance of a minor party, but rather because one may well doubt that the countries in question really share similar systemic properties. The perplexity relates to three countries: on the one hand, Belgium, to which we shall come at the end; and, on the other, Sweden and Norway, the two Scandinavian countries that have long been governed – with relatively small interruptions – by their respective Social Democratic parties. It is only banal to say that both are multiparty systems. The question is, instead, whether Norway and Sweden should not be assigned to the predominant-party systems. Consequently, Tables 21 and 22 indicate the percentages of both electoral returns and seats.

As Table 21 shows, the Norwegian Labor party held the absolute majority of *seats* until 1961, lost it only by a hair's breadth in 1961 and 1969, and therefore has suffered, until 1973, only one clear defeat in 1965. Furthermore, it should be recalled that the Norwegian Labor party started governing alone in 1935 (until the 1940 German invasion). If one discounts, therefore, the London National Coalition government of 1940–1945, the overall record is of continuous Labor single party government from 1935 to 1965 (except for a four weeks' odd interruption in 1963), with the Labor party returning to office in 1971, losing it again, and forming a minority government, supported externally by the Socialist Alliance, in 1973.[61] However, the predominance of the Labor party has been increasingly undermined since 1961. In the 1961 *Storting* the absolute majority hinged on the two seats of the Socialist People's party[62]; between 1969 and 1973 a non-socialist coalition and a Labor government alternated in office; and while the 1973 elections have reinstated Labor in power, it can govern only with the support of the Socialist Election Alliance, and the turnouts do suggest that the Labor predominance is in the wane.[63]

As we turn to Sweden[64] (Table 22) it is interesting to note that while its record of Social Democratic predominance is longer than that of Norway – it started in 1932 – nonetheless, it is largely based on minority governments – sustained, however, by a continuous Social Democratic majority in the First Chamber, which means, in substance,

Table 21. *Norway: returns and seats 1945-1973 (Storting)*

	1945		1949		1953		1957		1961		1965		1969		1973	
	Votes	Seats	Votes	Seats	Votes	Seats	Votes	Seats	Votes	Seats	Votes	Seats	Votes	Seats	Votes	Seats
Communists	11.9	7.3	5.8	—	5.1	2.0	3.4	0.7	2.9	—	1.4	—	1.0	—	—	—
Socialist Election Alliance[1]															11.2	10.3
Socialist People's Party									2.4	1.3	6.0	1.3	3.4	—	—	—
Labor Party*	41.0	50.7	45.7	56.7	46.7	51.3	48.3	52.0	46.8	49.3	43.2	45.3	46.5	49.4	35.3	40.0
Left (*Venstre*) Liberals*	13.8	13.2	12.4	14.0	10.0	10.0	9.6	10.0	7.2	9.3	10.2	12.0	9.4	8.7	2.3	1.3
Christian People's Party*	7.9	5.3	8.4	6.0	10.5	9.3	10.2	8.0	9.3	10.0	7.8	8.7	7.8	9.3	11.9	12.9
Agrarians-Center Party* (since 1959)	8.0	6.6	4.9	8.0	8.8	9.3	8.6	10.0	6.8	10.7	9.4	12.0	9.0	13.3	11.0	13.5
Conservative Party*	17.0	16.6	15.9	15.3	18.4	18.0	16.8	19.3	19.3	19.3	20.2	20.7	18.8	19.3	17.2	18.7
Anders Lange's Party (1973)[2]															5.0	2.7
Other	0.3	—	6.8	—	0.5	—	3.1	—	5.3	—	1.8	—	4.0	—	6.1	—

* Relevant parties. [1] Alliance among Communist, Socialist People's party, and labor split. [2] Protest party. Returns and seats are in percentages; the number of seats in the *Storting* was 150 until 1969, and was increased to 155 in 1973. The electoral system was changed from d'Hont to Sainte-Laguë in 1952, thus reducing the overrepresentation of the Labor party. The *Storting* is, in practice, a unicameral system.

Table 22. Sweden: returns and seats 1948–1973

	1948		1952		1956		1958		1960		1964		1968		1970		1973	
	Votes	Seats	Votes	Seats	Votes	Seats	Votes	Seats	Votes	Seats	Votes	Seats	Votes	Seats	Votes	Seats	Votes	Seats
Communists	6.3	3.5	4.3	2.2	5.0	2.6	3.4	2.2	4.5	2.2	5.2	3.4	3.0	1.3	4.8	4.9	5.3	5.4
Social Democratic Party	46.1	48.7	46.1	47.8	44.6	45.9	46.2	48.0	47.8	49.1	47.3	48.5	50.1	53.7	45.3	46.6	43.6	44.6
Agrarians-Center Party (since 1957)	12.4	13.0	10.7	11.3	9.4	8.2	12.7	13.9	13.6	14.7	13.2	14.2	15.7	15.8	19.9	20.3	25.2	25.7
People's Party–Liberals	22.8	24.8	24.4	25.2	23.8	25.1	18.2	16.4	17.5	17.2	17.0	18.0	14.3	13.7	16.2	16.6	9.4	9.7
Conservative Party	12.3	10.0	14.4	13.4	17.1	18.2	19.5	19.5	16.5	16.8	13.7	13.7	12.9	12.4	11.5	11.6	14.3	14.6
Other	0.1	—	0.1	—	0.1	—	—	—	0.1	—	3.6	—	4.1	—	2.3	—	2.2	—

From 1948 to 1968 the returns and seats are in the Second Chamber; since 1970 the Riksdag is unicameral.

majority government in financial matters. The Swedish record is also more discontinuous. While the Norwegian Labor party has been ousted but has never governed (except in exile) in coalition, the Swedish Social Democrats have joined forces with the Agrarians in 1936–1939 and again in 1951–1957.[65] Moreover, when the Social Democrats reverted to single party government in 1958, their majority hinged on the Communist party (five seats). And this has increasingly been the case (except for the 1968 legislature) to date. Indeed, in the 1970 and 1973 *Riksdag* the Social Democrats (with 163 and 156 seats against 170 and 175 seats of the non-socialist opposition) implicitly relied on the seats held by the Communist party.[66]

The question was whether our list would not be cleaner if Norway and Sweden were assigned to the predominant-party systems. This is permissible if, in turn, the 51-percent threshold established by the operational definition of the predominant-party system is relaxed on account of the principle and practice of minority governments.[67] And this is, in effect, my option; not only because "governing alone" is a very distinctive and far-reaching systemic characteristic, but also because this categorization provides a significant gain in perspective. Over the longer period, say, since World War I, Norway and Sweden broadly qualify as cases of moderate pluralism (albeit with strong tensions, during the twenties and early thirties, and with recurrent inklings of polarization) characterized by alternative two-bloc coalitions. For some 30 years, however, a predominant party has monitored, deradicalized, and stabilized the polity on an advanced social-welfare basis. This pattern is seemingly reaching its point of exhaustion. If so, the predicament facing Norway and Sweden is either to pursue the predominant formula on centrifugal grounds (i.e., leaning more and more on the extreme left) at the cost of reentering a path of polarization, or to revert to a bipolar system of alternative coalitions which would help reinstate centripetal competition.

However that may be, the general point is that the analysis of Finland and Denmark (in the previous section) and now of Norway and Sweden shatters the superficial image of a Scandinavian homogeneous group of countries sharing the property of being working multiparty systems. They may well be "working," but hardly on similar grounds and mechanisms. Finland, in spite of having to bow to occasional *bon voisinage* inclusions of the Communist party in its coalitions, basically performs as a center-based system with high governmental instability; Denmark has long been, quite to the contrary, a bipolar, two-bloc system of coalitions, whereas Norway and Sweden have long performed as predominant systems of stable single party government.[68]

Having reduced the countries that enter the *class* of limited pluralism to the German Federal Republic, Belgium, Ireland, Iceland, Luxembourg, Denmark, Switzerland, and the Netherlands, the question turns on the mechanics of the *type*. Clearly, moderate pluralism is entitled to separate recognition to the extent that its systemic properties are neither the ones of twopartism nor the ones of polarized pluralism.

Vis-à-vis the properties of twopartism, the major distinguishing trait of moderate pluralism is coalition government. This feature follows from the fact that the relevant parties are at least three, that no party generally attains the absolute majority, and that it appears irrational to allow the major or dominant party to govern alone when it can be obliged to share its power. Thus minority single party governments do materialize, but they do so either as a result of miscalculated Indian wrestlings, or on the basis of a precise calculus (such as shedding unpopular, if necessary, policies), and otherwise as disguised coalitions and transitional caretaker governments. In any case, minority single party governments are – in the context of limited and moderate pluralism – "feeble" governments, even though they may not be short-lived.[69]

It is generally, if implicitly, assumed that the German Federal Republic does not perform like Sweden. Yet on the face of the returns the difference remains inexplicable. From 1953 to 1972 the percentage strength of the Christian Democratic party (CDU and CSU) in the *Bundestag* has been 49.9 (1953), 54.3 (1957), 48.5 (1961), 49.4 (1965), 48.8 (1969), and 45.4 (1972) – indeed a better record than the corresponding one of the Swedish Social Democrats. Nonetheless, coalition governments were started in Bonn as soon as the CDU lost its absolute majority: CDU and Liberals (FDP) in 1961, CDU and Social Democrats (SPD) in the "grand coalition" of 1966–1969; and Social Democrats and Liberals after 1969. Note – always in comparison with Sweden – that the Christian Democrats maintained the relative majority in the *Bundestag* even in the 1969 elections (48.8 against 45.2 percent of the SPD) and lost it only by a hair's breadth in 1972 (45.4 to the CDU against 46.4 percent to the SPD).[70] Why then does Sweden operate so differently from Germany? The best reply appears to be that only the mechanics of the latter is bipolar – in short, that the systems are different.

Thus the formula of moderate pluralism is not alternative government but governing in coalition within the perspective of *alternative coalitions* (which does not necessarily mean actually alternating coalitions). Aside from this major difference, in most other respects the mechanics of moderate pluralism tends to resemble and to imitate – albeit with a higher degree of complexity – the mechanics of twopartism. In particular the structure of moderate pluralism remains

bipolar. Instead of only two parties we generally find bipolar alignments of alternative coalitions. But this difference does not detract
from the fact that competition remains centripetal and thereby from
the fact that the mechanics of moderate pluralism is still conducive to
moderate politics.

While the distinguishing characteristics of moderate pluralism may
not appear impressive vis-à-vis the twoparty systems, they stand out
neatly with respect to the systems of polarized pluralism. First,
moderate pluralism lacks relevant and/or sizable anti-system parties.[71]
Second, and correlatively, it lacks bilateral oppositions. To put it in the
affirmative, in a system of moderate pluralism all the parties are
governing oriented, that is, available for cabinet coalitions. Hence all
the non-governing parties can coalesce qua oppositions, and this means
that the opposition will be "unilateral" – all on one side, either on the
left or on the right. Basically, then, moderate pluralism is *non-
polarized.* That is to say that if we abide by the same yardstick, the
comparison between moderate and polarized pluralism reveals that
their respective ideological spreads are significantly, and indeed criti-
cally, different.

In synthesis, a system of moderate pluralism is characterized by
(i) a relatively small ideological distance among its relevant parties,
(ii) a bipolar coalitional configuration, and (iii) centripetal competition.[72]

It would be redundant to specify how many consequences do *not*
follow – this is simply a matter of putting the minus sign wherever
polarized pluralism obtains the plus sign. It is worthwhile recalling,
instead, that the characteristics of the type can also be used as control
indicators, that is, for controlling whether a growing fragmentation of
the party system corresponds to a growing ideological distance. Whenever the question is whether the numerical criterion is a reliable
indicator, one can swiftly check by ascertaining whether or not a more-
than-two party system contains anti-system parties and bilateral oppositions. If the system does not, we are definitely confronted with a
case of moderate pluralism. The point may be generalized as follows.
If the number of parties grows and yet all the parties still belong to
the "same world" – i.e., accept the legitimacy of the political system
and abide by its rules – then the fragmentation of the system cannot
be attributed to ideological polarization. In this case the fragmentation
is presumably related to a multidimensional configuration: a *segmented,* polyethnic and/or multiconfessional society. Conversely, when
the number of parties exceeds the critical threshold and we do find
anti-system parties and bilateral oppositions, then it can be safely
assumed that more-than-five parties reflect a degree of ideological
distance that makes a bipolar mechanics impossible.

If the question is whether moderate pluralism is a distinct type and whether it can sort out the cases, I would answer yes. The ulterior question might be, however, whether it is convenient to distinguish, within this type, a "segmented" sub-group. And the ultimate problem arising from the literature on the segmented and "consociational" democracies is whether all the countries so qualified should not be gathered into a category of their own.[73]

So far the countries brought under the rubric of *segmented pluralism* – to follow Val Lorwin – are especially the Netherlands, Belgium, Luxembourg, Switzerland, Austria, plus Lebanon. However, the list could be easily extended to include most, if not all, of the societies otherwise identified as polyethnic, multiconfessional, and/or multidimensional. Surely, Israel would qualify, and India is also a highly plausible candidate. Furthermore, if Belgium is entered, under the segmentation criterion it is difficult to exclude Canada. In the end, should the suggestion become fashionable, it will quickly be found that it is difficult to draw a line between the segmented societies and those already characterized as "culturally heterogeneous." But even if we are content with the Netherlands and Switzerland, Israel and India, Belgium, Canada and Austria, we have in the act pooled together all the conceivable competitive systems. Whatever else it may sort out, the criterion of Lorwin, Lijphart, and Lembruch does not sort out the party system. Nor – let me hasten to make clear – is this their claim. We are thus referred to my initial question, namely, whether the segmented polities should be subsumed, under my typology, as a distinct subgroup. Clearly, the question relates to all my types. It can be discussed best, however, under the case of moderate pluralism, among other reasons because multidimensionality and/or segmentation tend to be canceled out by strong ideological tensions – viz., in the polarized polities – whereas they acquire prominence precisely in the non-polarized systems.

Let us begin with the definition. In the wording of Lorwin, segmented pluralism is "the organization of social movements, educational and communication systems, voluntary associations and political parties along the lines of religious and ideological cleavages." Thus segmented pluralism is "pluralist in its recognition of diversity . . . ; it is 'segmented' in its institutionalization."[74] It is immediately apparent that the notion points first to a state of society, and only derivatively to the state of the polity. In other words, segmented pluralism is primarily a structural construct of the sociocultural variety. Fair enough – and I shall arrive also at the sociology of politics.[75] However, if we do not identify first the political structures – and particularly the party structuring – we are likely to miss this crucial question: *How is it that similar socioeconomic structures are not translated into similar party systems?* In the case in point – the segmented societies covered by Lorwin – Austria definitely has a twoparty format and has recently displayed also a twoparty mechanics[76]; Belgium has unquestionably had a three-party format (and mechanics) for some 80 years; Switzerland and the Netherlands have, instead, a polyparty system. It appears, therefore, that the segmentation of these countries is either a word with multiple meanings, or a structure without necessary consequence on the party system.

Two notes of caution should be added. The consociational diagnosis is a telling one only if it is not overly extended and diluted. Much of the current writings on consociational democracy simply enter a new, fashionable word in place of what was formerly called bargaining, pragmatic compromise, adjustment, and incremental decision making. And to the extent that this is so, we are simply blunting the sharpness of the analytic tool. In the second place, and correlatively, "segmentation" is, or should be, narrower and more precise than "cultural heterogeneity." Only under this condition can one avoid the undue or wasteful extension of the concept of segmentation to all the countries described as being polyethnic and multiconfessional. In particular, since segmentation is, at base, a sociocultural construct representing a *sui generis* state of society, it follows that the construct is helpful and meaningful to the extent that "segmented" is not mixed up with "differentiated." A difference well pinpointed by Talcott Parsons, as follows: Two differentiated subsystems do not do the same things, i.e., they have different functions which are complementary; whereas "two subsystems are segments when they are structurally distinct units both performing essentially the same functions."[77] A concurrent sharpening of the notion of segmentation is suggested by Di Palma, namely, that the societies engaged in consociational practices are characterized by "preindustrial" and "communal" cleavages, and therefore by the survival of parties of the preindustrial variety which limit, in turn, the encroachment of industrial and ideological cleavages.[78]

As the foregoing implies, consideration of the segmented societies does implement but does not justify a modification of the typology outlined so far. On the other hand, there are many lessons to be learned especially from Lijphart's analysis. Lijphart brings to the fore the decisive importance, in a segmented society, of leadership and of elite attitudes and orientations. Lest my emphasis on the *mechanical propensities* of party formats be misunderstood, let me say that if "consociational democracy" results from "overarching cooperation at the elite level with the deliberate aim of counteracting disintegrative tendencies in the system,"[79] and if the Netherlands in particular is a system created by, and dependent on, elite counteraction to its "disintegrative tendencies," then my contention that five-or-six parties

Table 23. *Belgium: electoral returns 1894–1974 (low chamber)*

	Catholic	Socialist	Liberal	Flemish National- ists	Franco- phone Parties	Others[1]
1894	51.6	17.4	28.5			1.3
1896–8	50.7	23.6	22.2			1.6
1900	48.5	20.5	24.3			1.7
1902–4	49.8	20.6	25.3			2.1
1906–8	48.6	21.5	26.7			1.9
1912	51.0	22.0	25.1			0.3
1919	36.0	36.6	17.6	2.6		6.5
1921	37.0	34.8	18.8	3.0		7.4
1925	36.1	39.3	14.6	3.9		5.9
1929	35.4	36.0	16.6	6.3		5.7
1932	38.6	37.1	14.3	5.9		4.1
1936	27.7	32.1	12.4	7.1		20.8
1939	32.7	30.2	17.2	8.3		11.6
1946	42.5	32.4	9.6	—		15.4
1949	43.6	29.8	15.3	2.1		9.4
1950	47.7	35.5	12.1	—		4.8
1954	41.1	38.5	13.1	2.2		5.1
1958	46.5	37.0	12.0	2.0		2.6
1961	41.5	36.7	11.1	3.5		6.0
1965	34.5	28.3	21.6	6.8	2.4	6.4
1968	31.8	28.0	20.9	9.8	6.0	5.5
1971	30.0	27.3	15.1	11.1	13.0	3.5
1974	32.3	26.7	15.2	10.2	11.0	4.6

Source: Keith Hill, "Belgium," in R. Rose, ed., *Electoral Behavior,* Free Press, 1974, p. 101. For 1971 and 1974 *Keesing's Archives.*
[1] In 1936: Communist 6.1, Rexist 11.5; in 1946: Communist 12.7 (they have since declined to a 3–4-percent level).

represent a critical format is mightily reinforced. In my frame of reference, if the moderate pluralism of the Netherlands depends on the conditions stated by Lijphart,[80] then the mechanical predispositions of party formats are indeed strong; for a country has recourse to con-sociational practices precisely when, and because, it approaches a dangerous format.

Before concluding, let us revert to our list of countries. The German Federal Republic has been discussed; and so have the Nether-lands, Denmark, and, if only in passing, Switzerland and Iceland. We are left with Ireland and Luxembourg, which hardly lend themselves to dispute as cases of limited and moderate pluralism, and, finally, with Belgium. And Belgium can no longer be included in the group as a matter of course.

For at least 70 years, i.e., until 1965, there can be no doubt as to the classification of the Belgian party system: As Table 23 shows, it is the most durable and clear-cut instance of a three-party format. From 1894 until the 1914 World War the Catholics dominated the scene, with the Liberals in second place and the Socialists (a constitutional, pro-system party from the outset) as a close third. From 1919 onward the Liberals are the third party. However, during the interwar period (1919–1939) the Catholics and the Socialists displayed a near-even strength (about a 36-percent average each); whereas since 1946 the Catholics (rebaptized Christian Social Party in 1945) are again the dominant party, albeit with strong oscillations: the absolute majority of seats in 1950 (almost regained in 1958), and all the way down to 30 percent in 1971. As for the Liberals, they have remained – between 1950 and 1965 – at the 12-percent level; have greatly progressed in 1965 and 1968; and are currently back to their interwar 16-percent average.

The pattern becomes more complicated, however, since 1965. It is true that the Flemish, Dutch-speaking group had already well emerged in 1939; but it was only in the second half of the sixties that the ethnic cleavage and the linguistic crisis shattered the political arena. In 1971 and 1974 not only did the Flemist Nationalist (*Volksunie*) emerge as a sizable party, but a Francophone feedback (Walloons and Brussels) entered the picture with equal strength. Are we witnessing, then, a transition from a three- to a five-party format? Furthermore, in the face of the linguistic-ethnic crisis and of the separatist tensions thus resulting, can Belgium be maintained in a type called moderate pluralism? The wording may well sound ironical. But the fact of the matter remains, to date, that the Catholics, Socialists, and Liberals continue to play the governmental game among themselves, exactly as they have done in the past. From 1919 to the present writing, Belgium has been governed almost exclusively by twoparty alternative coalitions. Table 24 supplies the details for the post–World War II period. The table is interesting not only with respect to Belgium, but also as an illustration of the formula that characterizes the three-to-five party systems (in contradistinction to both twopartism and the peripheral turnover of the center-based polities).

As shown in Table 24, in the typical mechanics of moderate pluralism minority governments are permitted only as caretaker and short-lived governments (4½ months in all in 1946 and in 1958), and single party government can exist only when sustained by an absolute majority (at least, in one chamber), as has been the case, in Belgium, in

Table 24. *Belgium: governmental coalitions 1946–1974*

Legislatures	Major-ity Low House	Composition	Majority Minority	Duration (months, rounded)
1946–1949	34.2	Socialist	min.	½
	54.0	Soc. + Lib. + Com.	maj.	4
	same	Soc. + Lib. + Com.	maj.	7½
	80.0	Soc. + Catholic	maj.	29
1949	63.2	Cath. + Liberal	maj.	10
1950–1954	51.0	Catholic	maj.	2
	same	Catholic	maj.	16
	same	Catholic	maj.	27
1954–1958	52.4	Soc. + Liberal	maj.	51
1958–1961	49.1	Catholic	near maj.	4
	59.0	Cath. + Liberal	maj.	30
1961–1965	84.9	Cath. + Socialist	maj.	51
1965–1968	66.5	Cath. + Socialist	maj.	8
	58.9	Cath. + Liberal	maj.	23
1968–1971	59.8	Cath. + Socialist	maj.	41
1971–1974	57.3	Cath. + Socialist	maj.	10
	74.0	Cath. + Soc. + Lib.	maj.	12
1974–	47.5	Cath. + Liberal	min.	

1950–1954. Otherwise, the standing rule is to switch partners. With three parties, three alternative coalitions are feasible and actually alternate: Catholic and Socialist, Catholic and Liberal, Socialist and Liberal. It is noteworthy, in this connection, that the only grand coalition of all the three parties to which Belgium has made recourse (in 1973) was prompted by constitutional reform needs and has been short-lived. As for the 1946 tripartite coalition with the Communists (11½ months in all), it simply reflects the postwar climate, common, at the time, to most of Europe.

With this I am not forecasting that the Belgian polity will or can endure as it stands. The 1974 minority Liberal-Catholic coalition represents, in effect, an anomaly that testifies to a somewhat desperate rearguard resistance. Just as the Swedish Social Democrats are clinging to their predominance on increasingly thin ice, so are the Belgian traditional parties clinging to the systemic rules they have practiced for so long. Thus far, the language conflict – and the growing, inevitable ascendance of the Flemish population – has brought about a bicephalous restructuring of the three traditional parties and produced an accommodation of the divisive pulls within the existing political structure on the basis of a *proporz* system, of dividing in two (or multiplying by two) what was hitherto undivided. It is difficult to foresee whether these arrangements will hold, whether a federal solution will turn out to be inevitable, and/or whether a more fragmented party system will end up with breaking down the tripartite pattern. Nevertheless, the most significant fact is – from the vantage point of the political scientist – the extent to which the Belgian party system has managed, to date, to perpetuate itself in the face of the increasing tensions arising from an increasingly compartmentalized society.[81] Whatever else one might want to add, the "moderating pressure" of the polity over the society is a standing fact. This is so much so that Belgium may well be considered, currently, more involved in a consociational elite effort than the Netherlands.[82]

6.4 Twoparty systems

The twoparty system is by far the best known category. This is because it is a relatively simple system, because the countries that practice twopartism are important countries, and because they represent a paradigmatic case. Even so, we are immediately blocked by this simple question: How many twoparty systems are there in existence? According to Banks and Textor, 11 of the 115 countries covered by their survey fall under the twoparty rubric.[83] But the figure is surely exaggerated, for it includes a country such as Colombia, which has what can hardly be considered a party system at all.[84] Dahl reduces the figure to 8, a number that includes Panama, the Philippines, and Uruguay.[85] Blondel indicates – albeit with various cautions appended – no fewer than 21 twoparty states.[86] Since every specialist provides a different list, let us say that popular opinion generally considers England, the United States, New Zealand, Australia, and Canada as the "classic" twoparty systems. If we enter Austria – a recent accession – we have six countries. However, Austria practiced, until 1966, "grand coalitions"; hence its twoparty system of government can hardly be considered, as yet, well established. On the other hand, Australia actually has three relevant parties; and Canada might appear even more anomalous than Australia. By a strict standard (thereby including a sufficient duration) we are thus left with three countries only: England, the United States, and New Zealand. And the final blow comes with the argument that English and American twopartism are so far apart that it makes little sense to classify them together.[87]

We are seemingly approaching the paradox of having the most celebrated type of party system running out of cases. The paradox arises because – here as elsewhere – we confront two distinct problems that we generally attempt to solve in one blow. One is to decide when a

country belongs to the twoparty *class,* and this depends on the counting rules. The other problem is to decide whether we have a twoparty
type of system.

To the first question – when is it that a third party, or even third
parties, should be discounted – the reply can be straightforward: We
have a twoparty *format* whenever the existence of third parties does
not prevent the two major parties from governing alone, i.e., whenever
coalitions are unnecessary.[88] The reply implies that the format of twopartism must be assessed in terms of *seats,* not of electoral returns. The
very obvious reason for this "must" is that governments are formed,
and perform, on the basis of their strength in parliament. The additional reason is that nearly all the polities under consideration (except
Austria, which is a PR country) abide by a single-member district
system which – as is well known – turns relative into absolute majorities, and even upturns an electoral majority into a parliamentary
minority.[89]

The argument is more complex, however, as soon as we ask: What
are the *properties* that characterize the twoparty type of system? If the
major characteristic of twopartism is that one party governs alone, we
must immediately add: alone, but not indefinitely. If it is always the
same party that remains in office election after election, we have a
predominant, not a twoparty, system. This is the same as saying that
alternation in power is *the* distinguishing mark of the mechanics of
twopartism. One may also say that "two" differs from "three" whenever
third parties do not affect, in the long run and at the national level, the
alternation in power of the two major parties. However, to avoid running out of cases neither the "alternation" nor the "governing alone"
clause is rigidly applicable.

Alternation should be loosely understood as implying the *expectation* rather than the actual occurrence of governmental turnover.
Alternation only means, then, that the margin between the two major
parties is close enough, or that there is sufficient credibility to the
expectation that the party in opposition has a chance to oust the
governing party. In other words, the notion of alternation shades into
the notion of competitiveness. Under a different, more strict interpretation the United States – which happens to be, by far, the oldest
and most continuous twoparty polity – would show feeble credentials,
for the U.S. pattern has been, since 1861, cyclical with long periods of
one-party superiority. If one looks at the presidential contests, from
Lincoln (1861) until Franklin D. Roosevelt the Republicans have won
14 presidencies and the Democrats only 5. Subsequently, from 1933 to
1953 the presidency has been Democratic; and if one attributes the two
victories (in 1952 and 1956) of Eisenhower to an above-party candida-
ture, then on their own forces the Republicans would have lost all the

presidential races from 1933 until Nixon's victory in 1968. The congressional picture is somewhat more varied. However, since the beginning of the century until the Great Depression a majority of the American people has voted Republican (except for a 1910–1914 deviation); and a majority has voted Democratic (with two deviating elections in 1942 and 1946, and two even splits in 1950 and 1952) from 1932 to date. The generalization could be, therefore, that in our century most American federal elections have been "maintaining" (or deviating and reinstating), with only one major realignment affecting Congress and the presidency: the realignment brought about by the great crash of 1929 and by Roosevelt's New Deal.[90]

With respect to alternation Australia does not fare much better. Out of ten elections Australia has, from 1946 until 1972, given only one clear victory (in 1946) and one even split (in 1961) to the Labour party. Thus the Australian Labour party was reinstated in office in 1972 after 23 years of opposition – not much of an alternation.[91] As for New Zealand, its turnover is saved by the Labour victory in 1957 amid a sequel of seven defeats. More precisely, out of ten elections the New Zealand Labour party won the first (in 1946), the fifth (in 1957), and then had to wait, like its Australian companion, until 1972; while the National party has governed for 20 years with only a single interruption. Since Canada is a debatable case, we are left to conclude that only one country – England – has performed remarkably well, since 1945, with the swing of the pendulum: Labour in 1945 and 1950; Conservatives in 1951, 1955, and 1959; Labour in 1964 and 1966; Conservatives in 1970; Labour in February and October 1974.

Turning to the *governing alone* clause, the matter is subject even more to flexibility in interpretation. That is, we must be very lenient with regard to the requirement that *both* parties should be in a position to win for themselves an absolute majority and hence to govern alone. The problem is especially posed by Australia, where the alternation in government occurs between the Labour party on the one side, and the alliance of the Liberal and Country parties on the other. *Prima facie* this is a three-party format, and the straightforward solution would seem to be to reclassify Australia as a three-party system, placing it with Belgium and West Germany.[92] But no sooner do we bring these three countries together than we are alerted to their different mechanics. For one thing, the Germans have done something that is unthinkable in the logic of twopartism: They settled, in 1965, for a grand coalition between the two major parties. Moreover, and more important, the German and Belgian Liberals are free to change, and do change, coalition partners.[93] Nothing of the kind happens in Australia. In particular, the permanent alliance between the Liberal and Country party is such that the two parties do not compete, in the constituencies, against each other: The two parties are, so to speak, symbiotic. Clearly, Germany and Belgium do not function according to the rules of twopartism, whereas Australia does.[94] Therefore, we are justified in relaxing the "governing alone" clause as follows: The turn-over may be of one versus two, provided that "two" is not a mere coalition but a coalescence.[95]

The lenient conditions for a system that functions according to the rules of twopartism would thus be the following: (i) two parties are in a position to compete for the absolute majority of seats; (ii) one of the two parties actually succeeds in winning a sufficient parliamentary majority; (iii) this party is willing to govern alone; (iv) alternation or rotation in power remains a credible expectation.

Now we understand why each writer can produce a different list of the existing twoparty countries. With reference to the twoparty *format*, the requirement of alternation in power is immaterial. Hence one can also include in the list those predominant-party systems wherein the opposition is, or was, represented by only one party (e.g., Uruguay and even the Philippines). Moreover, it is irrelevant that a party that could govern alone chooses not to do so (thus Austria qualifies for inclusion since 1946). On the other hand, in terms of format Australia should, and Canada might, be excluded. If we refer instead to the *mechanics* of twopartism, we see that the essential properties of two-partiness can be adjusted to a three-party format. Hence if we agree that the requirement of one-party government may apply to only one of the parties (the other party being a coalescence of two into one) Australia reenters; and if one-party government need not be a majority government, Canada also passes the test.

This last point cannot pass, however, without explanation. Notwith-standing the landslide Canadian election of 1958 – which rocketed the Conservative party up to 53.6 percent of the total vote, with the Liberals down to a low of 33.6 – the strongest party is clearly the latter, with 8 electoral victories out of 11 contests (1945–1974). But the peculiarity of the Canadian system lies in the cyclical revival and per-sistence over time of two minor parties: (i) the CCF, now (since 1962) NPD, New Democratic party, at the left of the Liberals, and (ii) the Social Credit party. The existence of two third parties can be explained, succinctly, by noting that "the two-party system has been weakest in those areas where the proportions of British origin have been lowest."[96] And the anomaly resides in the fact that the two minor parties often succeed in preventing either of the major ones from obtaining an absolute majority in the House of Commons.[97] Thus Canada fails to comply to the requirement of single party *majority* government: It is often ruled (after only one, traumatic and brief experience of coalition in 1917) by single party *minority* governments.

But this pattern attests, more than to anything else, to the force of the inner, systemic logic of twopartism. One could also say – with respect to the "conventions" of the constitution – that the Canadians are more British than the British themselves.[98]

The distinction between format and mechanics also affords a ranking of the countries claiming twoparty status according to whether, and to what extent, they satisfy both or only one of the aforesaid criteria. With respect to the post–World War II period, England lives up to its reputation: It is the "perfect" twoparty system in that it displays – in spite of the Liberals and other emerging third parties – both the format and the full set of properties of twopartism. No doubt, the British Liberal party menacingly looms over the horizon. At the February 1974 election the Liberals entered 14 members in the House of Commons and – much more important – held the balance of the majority.[99] However, the Liberals did not accept a coalition with the Conservatives, and the minority Labour government was confirmed in office in October 1974, if only with a bare majority of seats. To be sure, the United Kingdom *is* facing – also on account of the growing nationalism in Scotland and Wales – the dilemma of either following the Canadian pattern of minority single-party governments (in both the February and October 1974 elections each of the major parties failed to win as much as 40 percent of the vote), or of resorting to coalitions. In the latter hypothesis, not only would Britain cease to be the "perfect" twoparty system it has been between 1945 and 1974, but it would cease to be a twoparty system altogether. And this will be even more the case if the divisive pulls taking hold in Scotland and Wales are accommodated by resorting to PR.[100]

After England, the United States and New Zealand take second place: The twoparty format is as neat as it can be,[101] but the swing of the pendulum is not as it should be. The third position goes to Canada, with a dubious format but a satisfactory mechanics. Australia comes fourth: Its format is questionable and its alternation unsatisfactory. Finally, we have Austria from 1945 to 1966: a perfect twoparty format but exhibiting 20 years of grand coalition and *proporz*, the very negation of the "spirit" of twopartism.[102]

Of late, a number of writers have seemingly found a shortcut through the foregoing complexities by speaking of one-and-one-half, two, and two-and-one-half party systems. Accordingly, Japan would be one-and-one-half[103]; Australia one-and-two-halves (and the United States could be added to this category if the Southern Democrats are separated from the Northern ones); Germany two-and-one-half[104]; and Canada, presumably, two-and-two-halves. It so happens that Japan is also classified as one-party, twoparty, and multiparty[105]; that Germany becomes, on the basis of halves, like England (which is wrong); and

189

that the latest word on Australia turns it into "stable 4-party"[106] (like Denmark and/or the United States as interpreted by Burns). As for Canada, two-plus-two-halves sounds very much like making it multiparty (but the 1935–1957 period is also described as one of "one-party predominance"). As the illustrations suggest, the fraction device does not diminish but mightily adds to the confusion resulting from the lack of counting rules. What we miss when playing with halves and fractions is the very nature of the issue: whether the so-called two-party systems deserve separate recognition, that is, whether they display unique twoparty *properties*. And these properties have very little to do with the existence, or nonexistence, of impressionistically assessed "half parties."

Two failings are implicit in the current treatment – or mistreatment – of twopartism. One is our inability and/or unwillingness to confront the problem of the relevance of parties. The other is that we often confuse the constituency level with the national or systemic level. To be sure, "if a two-party system is defined as one in which only candidates from two parties contest elections, then Britain has never had a two-party system."[107] Yes – nor Britain, nor the quasi-totality of the countries generally recognized as twoparty. Instead, Colombia, Uruguay, Iran, and the Philippines would display, or displayed, almost perfect credentials. The point is, at any event, that what we detect and measure at the constituency level is the inter-party competitiveness.[108] Nobody denies that the structure and the degree of competitiveness are of great consequence in a number of respects. But I would indeed deny that the systemic performance that makes twopartism so different from the predominant systems and from multipartism in general can be in any way derived from whether the constituency contests are uncontested, two cornered, or three cornered, and from how close the contestants happen to be among themselves. More precisely, the conditions under which the incumbents enter a parliament are indeed very different from constituency to constituency and, in the aggregate, among the twoparty polities[109]; but these differences do not affect the systemic properties sorted out by my analysis.

I have conceded from the outset that the four conditions from which my definition of twopartism are contrived are lenient ones; and I have applied them as flexibly as possible. Even so, it turns out that twoparty systems are rare. This is particularly evident in a longitudinal perspective: Austria is, so far, the only new Western entry in the category, and it is still somewhat soon to say whether the pattern inaugurated in 1966 will strike durable roots. It should also be recalled, in this connection, that the longevity of English twopartism is largely a myth. Only since 1885 is it appropriate to speak of a nationwide British party system; and since then the United Kingdom has displayed three different patterns.[110] Between 1885 and 1910 – when the major parties were the Conservatives and the Liberals – six out of eight general elections did not produce real single party government: The Conservatives needed the support of the Liberal Unionists (the Liberal split of Joseph Chamberlain), while the Liberals relied on the Irish Nationalists. During the interwar period (between 1918 and 1935) Labour became the second largest party, but the Liberals survived as a relevant third party, and the whole period was characterized by instability and coalitions. It turns out, therefore, that the British have abided by the classic rules of twopartism only for some 30 years.

The rarity of the case suggests that twoparty systems are "difficult." But the emphasis is mostly on the view that twoparty systems represent a paradigmatic case, an optimal solution. The claim has generally been – until recent discontents – that twoparty systems obtain beneficial returns for the polity as a whole. More precisely, twoparty systems always "work," whereas the more parties there are, the more we find "less working" solutions and, ultimately, nonviable systems. The claim is not unwarranted; but it cannot be warranted by pointing to the countries in which twopartism happens to work. Indeed, these countries are so few that one may well argue that all of the more-than-two party systems are such precisely because the twoparty solution either did not endure, or did or would prove to be unworkable. The retort could be, then, that twopartism generally fails or would fail if attempted.

By and large, twoparty systems are explained along the lines formalized by the Downs model of party competition. The issue is simply: Under what conditions does twopartism work as predicted by the model? The model predicts that in a twoparty system the parties will compete centripetally, soft-pedaling cleavages and playing the game of politics with responsible moderation. This happens, however, because centripetal competition is rewarding. Why is it rewarding? Presumably because the floating voters themselves are moderates, i.e., located between the two parties, somewhere around the center of the spectrum of opinions. If the major group of floating voters were non-identified extremists, that is, extremists prepared to defect from an extreme left to an extreme right and vice versa, centripetal competition would no longer be rewarding. In short, twopartism "works" when the spread of opinion is small and its distribution single peaked.

This is not to say that twopartism presupposes consensus, for it is equally true that the centripetal mechanics of twopartism *creates* consensus. Making the claim more modest, let us say that the competitive mechanics of the system paves the way to consensus in that it has a conflict-minimizing bent. The macroscopic example of this is the United States. The potentiality for conflict in American society is enormous. Yet it is not reflected at the level of the party system. The fact that the United States is the only industrial society that has not produced a working-class party is largely due to a set of peculiar historical circumstances but also to the nature of American twopartism.[111] And the extent to which the party system is conflict minimizing is patently revealed not only by the very high percentage of American nonvoters, but especially by their being low-strata nonvoters. The registration requirement would hardly be an impediment if politics had a salience for the nonvoting strata – a salience it obviously does not have.[112]

There is a systemic logic to all of this. Twopartism hinges, if not on actual turnover, on the expectation of alternation in government. Now the fact that two parties are nearly equal in strength can hardly be considered "natural" or accidental. Clearly, the twoparty type of balance and oscillation is obtained and maintained via the tactics of party competition. In twopartism, parties *must* be aggregative agencies that maintain their competitive near-evenness by amalgamating as many groups, interests, and demands as possible. It should not be taken for granted, therefore, that twopartism *presupposes* a set of favorable conditions – cultural homogeneity, consensus on fundamentals, and the like. If one reviews the development of the twoparty countries historically, it appears that twopartism has largely *nurtured* and molded such favorable conditions.

At any given point in time, however, it is clear that the smaller the spread of opinion, the smoother the functioning of twopartism. Conversely, the greater the ideological distance, the more a twoparty format is dysfunctional. Therefore, it is misleading to assert that twoparty systems always work. Rather, these systems represent an optimal solution only when they work, that is, whenever they presuppose and/ or produce a highly consensual political society characterized by minimal ideological spread. Hence whenever a twoparty format does not perform as required by the Downs model, we should expect the parties to become more than two and another type of party system.[113]

6.5 Predominant-party systems

It bears repetition that my *predominant-party system* does not coincide, and indeed has very little in common, with the *dominant party* spoken of by a number of authors. The dominant party category was suggested more or less at the same time by Duverger and by Almond. Duverger's examples were the French radicals, the Scandinavian Social Democratic parties, and the Indian Congress party.[114] Probably in the wake of Almond's usage, Blanksten mentions a "dominant nondictatorial party" and offers, as clear-cut examples of the category, the

Table 25. *Countries with dominant parties* (percentages of electoral returns)

Countries	1st Party	2nd Party	Interval (% points)
Iran (1971)[1]	86	13	73
Mexico (1970)	83	14	69
Philippines (1969)[1]	82	14	68
Bolivia (1966) °[1]	80	19	61
Paraguay (1968)	71	22	49
El Salvador (1970)	60	27	33
India (1967)	41	9	32
Chile (1965) °[3]	44	14	38
Japan (1969)	49	21	28
Norway (1969)	46	20	26
France (1968) °[1-2-3]	46	21	25
Sweden (1970)	45	20	25
Israel (1969)	46	22	24
South Africa (1966) °	59	37	22
Denmark (1971)	37	17	20
Turkey (1969)	46	27	19
South Korea (1967)	51	33	18
Ireland (1965)	48	34	14
Italy (1972)	39	27	12
Iceland (1971)	37	26	11
Uruguay (1966)	49	40	9

° *Keesing's* figures. [1] Seats translated into vote percentages. [2] Second ballot. [3] Not indicative, strong electoral elasticity. Unless specified by ° the source is the *State Department Annual Reports* ("World Strength of the Communist Party Organization"), which is preferred to *Keesing's Archives* because the latter are less consistent in providing the vote percentages. Every source provides different figures; but such discrepancies are immaterial to my purpose. Whenever the election chosen is not the more recent one, this is because another election appears more representative.

Solid South in the United States, Mexico, and, as possible additional examples, Uruguay and Paraguay.[115] Over the years the list has grown, and so has the confusion.[116]

The criterion by which a party is declared dominant is seldom operationalized, but the general idea is clear enough: Whenever we find, in a polity, a party that outdistances all the others, this party is dominant in that it is significantly stronger than the others.[117] Let us draw up, therefore, a list of countries that meet this general idea. Assuming that about 10 percentage points of difference between the stronger and the other parties suffices to qualify a dominant party, some 20 countries can be rank-ordered on the basis of the interval between their dominant party and the one that comes next – as in Table 25.

At about the end of the sixties and the beginning of the seventies there was, then, a considerable number of countries that displayed, under the above specified criterion, a dominant party.[118] But a swift glance suffices to show that our odd 20 countries are, to say the least, strange bedfellows. One may immediately want, therefore, to purify the list. And there is, in principle, a very good reason for doing so. Electoral returns are trustworthy (on intuitive grounds) when they produce coalitions and alternative governments; but they can hardly be taken at their face value when they produce "dominance." For instance, Iran, Mexico, the Philippines, Bolivia, and Paraguay rank very high in the table: Each displays, so to speak, a hyper-dominant party. Is this a true verdict of the polls? How free are the elections? How do we know that the ballot boxes are not stuffed? Unfortunately most students of the suspect countries are either naïve or overcautious on the matter. True enough, electoral fraud is difficult to prove. But one essential element of information is both easy to obtain and easy to interpret, namely, whether or not the vote count is controlled or, at any rate, controllable. But even this elemental piece of information is seldom made clear; and this leaves us, again and again, with allegedly hard evidence of highly suspect validity.[119]

In the case in point let us say, *faute de mieux*, that all the countries listed in Table 25 below El Salvador are either beyond suspicion or, if suspect (this being clearly the case, e.g., of South Korea), admissible on the grounds that they do not affect the substance of the argument. One may want, however, to reduce the list to the major and most significant cases. We are left, accordingly, with the following 13 countries: India, Chile (until 1973), Japan, Norway, France (Fifth Republic), Sweden, Israel, Denmark, Turkey, Ireland, Italy, Iceland, and Uruguay (until 1973). Even so, our bedfellows remain a strange lot. They remain bedfellows because under the criterion of how much the first party outdistances the other parties Table 25 does not suggest any cutting point. One may argue that the table should be constructed on averages rather than on one "normal" election. But averages are distressingly misleading whenever a country undergoes strong electoral fluctuations – this being the case not only with Chile and France, but also with India, Turkey, and Ireland.[120] At any rate, even the averages that I have tried out leave us without cutting points. This means that if the category ("dominance" or dominant party) is significant, it should tell us what our 20 to 13 countries have in common. The question is: Does the existence of a dominant party characterize in any (common) way the party systems, or the political systems, in question?

194

As far as I am able to see, the question is bound to remain – as it has remained up to this day – unanswered. As it stands, the category only obfuscates the systemic properties of the countries it sorts out. And the reason for this is not far to seek: Dominant party is a category that confuses *party* (in isolation) with party *system*. The shift is, with most authors, verbal. Their focus is, in effect, on the major party; but they then slip in the word system; and unwarranted inferences are thus made from the major party to the nature of the system. To be sure, the Italian DC, the Israeli *Mapai*, or the Danish Social Democrats are dominant parties: But it does not follow that Italy, Israel, and Denmark have dominant party "systems." In short, the notion of dominant party establishes neither a *class* nor a *type* of party system. It is correct, and telling, to say that certain parties are "dominant." But it has not been shown that this qualifier deserves the status of a category. What remains to be seen is whether the notion of dominant party can be utilized as a taxonomic category in conjunction with other criteria and, specifically, whether it belongs in the definition of the predominant-party systems.

We have first encountered the *type* of party *system* that I call *predominant* in discussing the case of the so-called one-party states within the United States.[121] And, by now, one reason for speaking of predominance is self-evident, namely, that dominance was not a vacant term and that it had been largely misused. I also feel, however, that "predominance" – which is less strong, semantically, than "domination" – is the most fitting term for the type of party system in question; and this is also so for the additional reason that "predominance" is used, here, in contradistinction to "hegemony."

The first point to be made with respect to the predominant-party systems is that they unquestionably belong to the area of party pluralism. Parties other than the major one not only are permitted to exist, but do exist as legal and legitimate – if not necessarily effective – competitors of the predominant party. That is to say that the minor parties are truly independent antagonists of the predominant party. Therefore, the predominant-party system actually is a more-than-one party system in which rotation does not occur in fact. It simply happens that the same party manages to win, over time, an *absolute majority of seats* (not necessarily of votes) in parliament.

Clearly, the crucial condition is the authenticity of such victories. Awaiting a more critical attitude toward, and inspection of, electoral statistics, let us state this condition as follows: The monopolistic permanence in office of the same party, election after election, cannot reasonably be imputed to conspicous unfair play or ballot stuffing. In other words, we can close an eye to electoral irregularities as long as it can be reasonably assumed that in a situation of fair competition the

195

predominant party would still attain the absolute majority of seats.[122] The definition is, then, as follows: A predominant-party system is such to the extent that, and as long as, its major party is consistently supported by a winning majority (the absolute majority of seats) of the voters. It follows that a predominant party can cease, at any moment, to be predominant. When this happens, either the pattern is soon re-established or the system changes its nature, i.e., ceases to be a predominant-party system.

The foregoing definition has a virtue that weakens it and a feebleness that accrues to its virtue: It is too precise with respect to the threshold, and too vague about the duration. As the definition stands, a majority that is near-absolute but falls short of the 50-percent mark is not a sufficient condition of "predominance" as far as the qualification of the party system is concerned. This is correct in operational terms; but, at the same time, it is the feeble point of most, if not all, operational definitions related to precise thresholds and measures.[123] My threshold is established at the 50-percent mark under the assumption that constitutional government generally operates on the basis of the absolute majority principle. The facts of the matter are, however, that in Norway, Sweden, and Denmark, for instance, the "conventions" of the constitution are different, as is testified by the longstanding performances, in these countries, of minority governments.[124] Under this circumstance, my option is to sacrifice the neatness of operational precision.[125] Hence the 50-percent majority clause will be relaxed as follows: A predominant-party system is generally qualified by its major party obtaining the absolute majority of seats, with the exception of countries that unquestionably abide by a less-than-absolute majority principle.[126] In these cases the threshold can be lowered to the point at which minority single-party governments remain a standing and efficient practice.

The first amendment to the definition is supposed to obviate its excess of precision. We are left, however, with an excess of imprecision, namely: For how long must a party be predominant for the system to exhibit this characteristic? Presumably a sensible reply would be: for four consecutive legislatures at least. This answer might endanger the status of a number of twoparty systems – but this is hardly a drawback. After all, the more a typology is sensitive to variations, and the less it imprisons its cases, the more it has a dynamic value (in addition to its static one). What is disturbing about this way of handling the problem is, however, its gratuitous arbitrariness. Why four and not three or five legislatures? And this is the point at which the notion of dominant party – and more exactly its interval measure – can be put to some positive use.

Let us revert to Table 25 and to the more significant countries having "dominant parties" picked out under the definition of dominance:

India, Chile, Japan, Norway, Sweden, France, Israel, Denmark, Turkey, Ireland, Italy, Iceland, Uruguay. Now, of course, the criterion is different: how far above or below the 50-percent mark the dominant parties stand. Table 26 carries additional information: whether the countries in question have recourse to coalition governments (which include, to be sure, the dominant party), and the time period of single party government, i.e., of predominance – if any. It should be noted that now the percentages of the two first parties are given in *seats,* as required by the definition of a predominant system. Thus a comparison between the two tables also indicates how the votes are translated into seats, that is, the influence of the electoral system – if any.

Table 26 speaks aloud in one respect: It clearly shows that the "dominant party" group is not a group. India, Japan, Uruguay, and Turkey have, or surely have had, predominant-party systems.[127] Norway and Sweden are on the border line, but their longitudinal record is one of predominance. Ireland does less well than the two Scandinavian countries in terms of continuity – the Irish system has been predominant between 1933–1948 and 1957–1973, with a major interruption of ten years – but fares better in terms of nearing or surpassing the absolute majority threshold.[128]

As for the French Fifth Republic, the three "stills" in the table suggest the persistence and coexistence of opposite pulls: the traditional voting distributions of the Fourth Republic, as against the constraints of the Gaullist constitution. If one adds that the label "Gaullists" generally includes a variety of allies, it turns out that their own sole overwhelming majority in the National Assembly was the one of 1968 (after the Paris May "revolution"). In 1958 the UNR obtained a mere 40 percent; in 1962 the Gaullists owed their majority of 56.6 percent to the Independent Republicans of Giscard d'Estaing (which ran separate lists and won 33 seats); and in 1973 they were back to their 1958 level. Thus while the five elections (1958–1973) held under the constitution of the Fifth Republic afford an adequate time span, nevertheless the features of a predominant-party system have not emerged – and the 1974 presidential elections point to a completely different direction.

On the other hand, Chile, Israel, Denmark, Italy, and Iceland definitely do not qualify as predominant-party systems: The dominant party in each must govern in coalition with others, the coalition members change, and – let it be added – the governments are generally short-lived. Moreover, as we know, Denmark displays the systemic properties of moderate pluralism, while Chile was and Italy is a system of polarized pluralism. It is abundantly confirmed, then, that the notion of dominant party adds up neither to a class nor to a type.

One question remains, namely, whether the measure expressed by the percentage points of interval between the first and second party

Table 26. *Dominant parties and predominant systems* (1st and 2nd parties: percentages of seats low chamber)

	1st party	2nd party	Above/below 50%	Interval (% points)	Coalitions	Period of predominance
India (1967)	55	8	+5	47	no	since 1952
India (1971)	69	5	+19	64	no	since 1955
Japan (1969)	59	19	+9	40	no	from 1868 to 1959
Uruguay (1966)	51	42	+1	9	no	(interruption 1959–1966)
Turkey (1950)	84	14	+34	70	one imposed	from 1950–1960 and 1965–1973
Turkey (1969)	56	32	+6	24	by army	(interrupted 1960 by coup)
Norway (1957)	52	19	+2	33	rare	from 1935 to 1965
Norway (1969)	49	19	−1	30		(then interruptions)
Sweden (1968)	54	17	+4	37		from 1932
Sweden (1970)	47	20	−3	27	rare	(interruption 1951–1957)
Ireland (1957)	53	27	+3	26		from 1932 to 1973
Ireland (1965)	50	32	0	17	no	(interruption 1948–1957)
France (1967)	41	25	−9	16		
France (1968)	60	12	+10	48	yes	1968–1973
France (1973)	37	18	−13	19		
Chile (1965)	55	13	+5	42	yes	—
Chile (1969)	37	23	−13	14		
Israel (1965)	37	22	−13	15	yes	—
Israel (1969)	42	28	−8	14		
Denmark (1971)	40	18	−10	22	yes	—
Italy (1972)	42	28	−8	14	yes	—
Iceland (1971)	37	28	−13	9	yes	—

198

can be meaningfully included in the definition of the predominant systems. But here Table 26 affords no clear indication. I would say that the interval measurement is indicative only when an electorate is fairly stabilized (and this is, or was, not the case in Chile, France, and Turkey). When this is so, the wide span of the interval helps very much to explain the cases of Norway and Sweden and, in general, of a predominance that does not rest, of necessity, on the absolute majority. Moreover, if the electorate is stabilized and the interval is wide, one can predict with little risk that a given polity will endure as a predominant type of system. And these remarks lead to an underpinning of the time requirement.

How long does it take for a predominant party to establish a predominant system? At this stage of the argument I am prepared to settle for the following criterion: Three consecutive absolute majorities can be a sufficient indication, provided that the electorate appears stabilized, that the absolute majority threshold is clearly surpassed, and/or that the interval is wide. Conversely, to the extent that one or more of these conditions do not obtain, a judgment will have to await a longer period of time to pass. Doubtlessly, this leaves the duration requirement fairly loose. But this is as it should be. At any given point in time a predominant-party system can cease to be such – exactly as can a twoparty system. This is not to say, obviously, that the other party systems are not subject to change as well; it is only to say that the predominant and the twoparty systems share a peculiar kind of fragility: Small differences in returns, or the mere changing of the electoral system, can more easily transform the nature of the system.[129] On the other hand, the *over* time perspective can be different from the perspective *in* time. There is no contradiction in declaring that a given country does not function, *hic et nunc*, as a predominant type of system and yet displays an overall systemic record of predominance.

An additional clarification is perhaps redundant but not entirely superfluous. The predominant-party system is a *type*, not a class. This is to recall that the criterion here is not the number of parties but a particular distribution of power among them. Thus a predominant-party system can arise either from a twoparty format (as in the limiting case of the American Solid South) or from a highly fragmented format,

Table 26 (*cont.*)

The sources – as with Table 25 – are generally the *State Department Reports* or *Keesing's Archives*. France applies a second-ballot runoff; India the single-ballot district system; the other countries PR (with small constituencies, however. in Japan and Ireland). With reference to Norway and Sweden the war period is discounted. The Turkish pattern is disturbed by military interference; otherwise the 1950–1973 period would have been, in all likelihood, one of countinuous predominance (without any coalitions).

as is particularly the case of the Indian Congress party.[130] It is only for the purpose of establishing a continuum that one may consider the predominant-party system as the variant of twopartism in which no alternation in power occurs (de facto) for a considerable length of time.[131] For all other purposes it should be borne in mind that the predominant-party system can just as well be a variant of any multipartism.

With the predominant-party systems we stand at the edge of the competitive area – so much so that some of these systems are erroneously classified as one-party. Therefore, before turning to the noncompetitive area it is well to stress that the predominant-party system is a type of party *pluralism* in which – even though no alternation in office actually occurs – alternation is not ruled out and the political system provides ample opportunities for open and effective dissent, that is, for opposing the predominance of the governing party. In India, Japan, Uruguay, Norway, Sweden, political opposition does or did exist, and the predominant party has or had – on more or less close margins – to compete for power.[132] Competition is so real that Norway, Sweden, and Ireland may well be at the end of their performance as predominant systems.[133] Trends in Japan equally suggest that its predominant Liberal Democratic party (LDP) – which is steadily losing ground – may well be on its way out.[134] It is noteworthy that if the LDP loses the absolute majority of seats, Japan may easily qualify as a polarized system. In 1972 the relevant parties were five, with the following distribution of voting strength: LDP, 46.9 percent; Socialists, 21.9; Communists, 10.5; *Komeito* (a Buddhist party, whose name means "party for clean politics"), 8.5; Social-Democrats, 7.0. The Democratic Socialist party is in fact very close to the LDP, while the Japanese Socialist party tends to be an extremist party. Since *Komei* can hardly be expected to become a major center pole of coagulation, a post-predominant pattern is likely to reinforce a two-bloc, growing polarization.

On the other hand, new entries might be in sight: Pakistan and, with a very big question mark, Bangladesh (but the latter's symptoms have been, from the outset, ominous). At its first, pre-secession universal suffrage election of 1970, two parties outdistanced all the others: the East Pakistan-based Awami League (Rahman) with the absolute majority, and the West Pakistan-based People's party (Bhutto). As a result of the 1972 separation, Pakistan would be 59 percent People's party, and Bangladesh would be all Awani. Since elections in Pakistan have been, in the past, competitive and reasonably free, under normalized circumstances the Pakistan pattern might well come to resemble the one of India.[135] On the other hand, Bangladesh has been, since its inception, increasingly distant from normalization. Rahman was clearly heading toward dictatorial rule when he was killed, in August 1975, in the course of an overnight revolt. And no one knows, at this stage, where the country will go and how its population will survive. Thus far I have also failed to mention Northern Ireland; and this is because, in spite of its devolved parliament, it is not an independent state. However, it cannot be doubted that – if pacified and independent – Northern Ireland would qualify as a predominant polity: For the Unionists have won every election from the first one in 1921 to the one in 1969.[136]

In conclusion, the fact that the predominant-party systems display, in the main, a relatively high rate of entries and exits goes to confirm that they *are* competitive systems with respect to which it can be asserted that, on the starting line, all the parties have equal opportunities. To be sure, equality of opportunity is always relative, for nobody is really equal at the starting line. Furthermore, equal opportunities are not the same as equal resources; and in the predominant systems the disparity of resources between the party in power and the parties out of power is likely to be greater than in the other pluralistic systems. Even when all these fine distinctions are taken into account, the standing fact remains that the parties of a predominant-party system enjoy an equality of opportunity unheard of in, and unknown to, the minor parties of the hegemonic systems.

NOTES TO CHAPTER 6

1 Duverger, *Les Partis Politiques,* op. cit., p. 245 and *passim,* pp. 239–246, 251, 261–265. The idea of a "natural dualism" was theorized in 1926 by Herbert Sultan. For a devastating criticism of Duverger's "eminently superstitious impression that phenomena occur in pairs" see Aaron B. Wildavsky, "A Methodological Critique of Duverger's Political Parties," *JP,* 1959, pp. 303–318. See also the criticism by Hans Daalder, "Parties and Politics in the Netherlands," *PS,* February 1955, pp. 12–13.

2 *Ibid.,* pp. 241, 269. This misapprehension of the entirely different mechanics of the two systems has been followed up to this day. See esp. Giorgio Galli, *Il Bipartitismo Imperfetto,* Il Mulino, 1966.

3 With reference to my earlier essay, "European Political Parties: The Case of Polarized Pluralism" (in LaPalombara and Weiner, eds., *Political Parties and Political Development,* op. cit., pp. 137–176), Lijphart notes that "Sartori does not consistently draw the line between moderate and extreme multiparty systems at the same point" ("Typologies of Democratic Systems," *CPS,* cit., p. 16). He is quite right. At the time I was not clearheaded as to how the parties should be counted, and this explains my oscillations. It should be clear, therefore, that I now place the dividing line not between four and five, but between five and six, parties.

4 Since the central requirement is "interaction," the counting is straightforward if the parties compete in the same space, but less

straightforward (as will be seen *infra,* ch. 10) the more we assume a space of competition to be two- or multidimensional. Presumably, the more-than-five rule becomes less stringent the less the parties interact in that they are placed in separate competitive dimensions.

5 This chapter, and particularly this section, assumes a spatial perception of politics. Therefore, its central concepts – such as ideological distance – are underpinned in ch. 10, *infra,* which is implicitly referred to throughout the discussion of the competitive systems.

6 An analysis bearing on these concepts is Erik Allardt, "Types of Protest and Alienation," in Rokkan and Allardt, eds., *Mass Politics,* op. cit.

7 This is the interpretation of Sidney Tarrow: "Sartori concludes that the PCI is outside the system altogether" ("Political Dualism and Italian Communism," *APSR,* March 1967, p. 40). See also his *Peasant Communism in Southern Italy,* op. cit. esp. pp. 110–101. Since Tarrow builds his case on the argument that the Italian Communist party is not a "devotee or combat party," let it also be clear that nothing of the kind is implied by my notion of anti-system party. Both misunderstandings are unfortunate.

8 To this effect, the most reliable, and most neglected, indicator is provided by a content analysis of the daily press. This indicator cannot be dismissed as bearing on merely verbal behavior. For one thing, it is as verbal as interviews (which are given, instead, the status of reliable and important evidence). Moreover, visible mass politics does hinge, as I shall stress, on verbal behavior.

9 Duverger's thesis that "the center never exists in politics" (*Les Partis Politiques,* cit., p. 245) confuses the various aspects of the problem and should be reversed: A center "tendency" always exists; what may not exist is a center party. But see *infra,* 10.4.

10 It should be noted that while I hold that a political system may be bipolar and not polarized, Duverger identifies (or confuses) polarization with "bipolarity" (see *Les Partis Politiques,* p. 279). Scott C. Flanagan has now devised an "index of polarization" (in Almond, Flanagan, and Robert J. Mundt, eds., *Crisis, Choice and Change,* Little, Brown, 1973, pp. 86–89, 682–684). His measure includes more elements than my conceptualization and has yet to be tested empirically; but we are surely looking at the same problem.

11 The italics emphasize that my center-fleeing competition is measured by the electoral returns. I explain the appropriateness of this indicator in my chapter, "Rivisitando il Pluralismo Polarizzato," in Fabio Luca Cavazza, Stephen R. Graubard, eds., *Il Caso Italiano,* Garzanti, pp. 202–204, 210–211. The point will also be discussed shortly.

12 The complete figures are in Tables 9 (Italy) and 10 (France) in the following section.

13 *Supra,* 4.1, and ch. 4, n. 13. See also my *Democratic Theory,* cit., ch. 11.

14 See esp. his chapter, "Germany: The Vanishing Opposition," in Dahl, *Political Oppositions in Western Democracies,* cit.

15 The point is made, among others, by J. LaPalombara, "Decline of

Ideology: A Dissent and Interpretation," *APSR*, March 1966, pp. 15–16.

16 One may question their ideological nature (*supra*, 4.4) but hardly their ideological tactics and appeal.

17 While the responsibility-irresponsibility dimension is, in my opinion, the major characterizing feature of opposition in the polarized systems, a wealth of ulterior underpinnings can be drawn from Dahl's concluding chapters of *Political Oppositions in Western Democracies*, cit. Let me mention only that the scope of competition varies, and mightily increases, as we pass from low to high ideological distance.

18 H. V. Wiseman, *Political Systems*, Praeger, 1966, p. 115. Wiseman draws from Harry C. Bredemeier, R. M. Stephenson, *The Analysis of Social Systems*, Holt, 1962.

19 I have emphasized this aspect, the organizational encapsulation, in LaPalombara and Weiner, *Political Parties and Political Development*, cit., pp. 144–147.

20 The discussions and investigations on Italian communism are innumerable. An overview of the recent Italian literature is Arturo Colombo, "La Dinamica del Comunismo Italiano," in Luciano Cavalli, ed., *Materiali sull'Italia in Trasformazione*, Il Mulino, 1973. But see esp. Giacomo Sani, "La Strategia del PCI e l'Elettorato Italiano," *RISP*, III, 1973; Juan Linz, "La Democrazia Italiana di fronte al Futuro," in *Il Caso Italiano*, op. cit.; and the special issue "Il Compromesso Storico," *Biblioteca della Libertà*, September 1974. See also: Donald Blackmer, *Unity in Diversity: Italian Communism and the Communist World*, MIT Press, 1968; and Arrigo Levi, *PCI – La Lunga Marcia Verso il Potere*, Etas Kompass, 1971. The notion of negative integration is of Guenther Roth, *The Social Democrats in Imperial Germany*, Bedminster Press, 1963.

21 For the very great variety of oppositions ànd of the views thus resulting, see Rodney Barker, ed., *Studies in Opposition*, Macmillan St. Martin's Press, 1971. In my contribution I try to underpin the notion of constitutional opposition (pp. 33–36).

22 I say the best evidence because I consider very suspect the interviews with leaders. Not only is the interviewed very sensitive to the expectations of the interviewer, but leaders utilize interviews for selling their public image and/or the party line. The point rejoins n. 8, above.

23 The quotation is from Franco Cazzola, "Consenso e Opposizione nel Parlamento Italiano: Il Ruolo del PCI," *RISP*, I, 1972, p. 92. It should be stressed that most of the Italian legislation is directly enacted by the standing commissions of parliament, whose proceedings are closed and entirely invisible. Communist behavior, when bills come to the floor, is far less coalescent.

24 See Alberto Predieri, "La Produzione Legislativa," in G. Sartori ed., *Il Parlamento Italiano 1948–1963*, Edizioni Scientifiche Italiane, 1963. Subsequently, Predieri has directed a vast research on the Italian legislative process and output, *Il Processo Legislativo nel Parlamento Italiano* (Giuffrè 1974–1975, in 5 vols.), from which one can draw a wealth of evidence. A major conclusion of vol. II (Franca Cantelli, Vittorio Mortara, Giovanna Movia, *Come Lavora*

il Parlamento) is that "the legislative activity . . . is mostly administrative" (p. 110) and that "on the major issues relating to
the social life even the governmental coalitions, with their preestablished majority, encounter great difficulties in obtaining the
approval of parliament . . . out of 85 projects of this type only 7
have been enacted" (p. 156). A perceptive appraisal of what this
legislative output adds up to is in Giuseppe Di Palma, *Decision
and Representation: Parliament Parties and Conflict Management
in Italy*, forthcoming, esp. chs. 2 and 5. Extending an index devised
by Jean Blondel, Di Palma finds that while the "average importance" of bills in the UK is 3.2, in Italy it is .99 (Table 13).

25 See in this connection the "illegitimacy scores" and the overall
"magnitudes of illegitimacy" calculated by Ted Robert Gurr and
Muriel McClelland, *Political Performance: A Twelve-Nation Study*,
Sage, 1971, p. 41, where Italy ca. 1957–1966 is found to have the
highest sentiment of illegitimacy of the period. (See pp. 30–48
and esp. Tables 9, 10.)

26 That this conclusion was unwarranted – at least with respect to
Italy – has been demonstrated by the inquiry of Robert D. Putnam,
*The Beliefs of Politicians – Ideology, Conflict, and Democracy in
Britain and Italy*, Yale University Press, 1973, whose major finding
is that "no fact stands out more sharply from this investigation than
the contrast between politicians from the two nations. On nearly all
the various components of the several dimensions of 'ideological' . . .
the Italians score markedly higher than the British. . . . By any
measure, Italians are more ideological politicians" (p. 78).

27 G. Sani, "Mass Perceptions of Anti-System Parties: The Case of
Italy," forthcoming in *British Journal of Political Science*, October
1975, emphasizes – on the basis of two 1968 and 1972 surveys – the
constraints impinging on the elite reconversion of deligitimization
into relegitimization. The point can be pressed further, I suggest,
by looking into what the voters of anti-system parties "expect" from
their victory.

28 John C. McKinney, *Constructive Typology and Social Theory*,
Appleton-Century-Crofts, 1966, is a very useful analysis and discussion of the typology of types. I actually draw from him the concept
of extracted type (esp. pp. 23–25).

29 For the simplicity of the argument I assume that at least the
totalitarian type has been understood as being a polar, not an
empirical, type. That this is far from being the case is shown by the
current controversy over totalitarianism. The issue is taken up
infra, 7.2.

30 *Supra*, 5.3.

31 On Denmark see Alastair H. Thomas, *Parliamentary Parties in
Denmark, 1945–1972*, Occasional Paper 13, Glasgow, University of
Strathclyde, 1973; and Erik Damgaard, "Stability and Change in
the Danish Party System over Half a Century," *SPS*, IX, 1974.
Mogen Pedersen, "Consensus and Conflict in the Danish Folketing
1945–1965," *SPS*, II, 1967, and Damgaard, "The Parliamentary
Basis of Danish Governments: The Patterns of Coalition Forma-
tion," *SPS*, IV, 1969, are also most interesting studies.

32 An excellent coverage of the Netherlands is the chapter of
A. Lijphart in Richard Rose, ed., *Electoral Behavior: A Compara-*

tive Handbook, Free Press, 1974. But see also Lijphart, *The Politics of Accommodation: Pluralism and Democracy in the Netherlands,* University of California Press, 1968; and the writings of Daalder indicated below, nn. 34 and 73.

33 Aside from the 1973 surge of the Progress party, I indicate four to five parties because in the sixties – but not over the whole period – the Justice party entered two coalitions. Basically, however, over the 1920–1971 period Denmark has been a four-party system, even though the combined electoral strength of the four traditional parties has declined from 96.9 to 81 percent (Damgaard, above, n. 31, *SPS,* 1974, pp. 104–107).

34 "Traditionally, five political parties have dominated the Dutch political system. Three religious parties . . . have contested or shared power with two non-confessional parties . . ." (H. Daalder, J. G. Rusk, "Perceptions of Party in the Dutch Parliament," in Samuel C. Patterson, John C. Wahlke, eds., *Comparative Legislative Behavior,* Wiley, 1972, p. 147).

35 According to my counting rules, however, the Netherlands had a six-party format during the 1971–1972 legislature (the sixth party being DS '70, which entered a short-lived cabinet). Only in 1973 did D '66 and PPR (but not DS '70) enter a coalition government, thereby raising the format of that legislature to seven parties.

36 *Infra,* 6.3, Table 21, and 6.5.

37 On Norway see Stein Rokkan's chapter in Dahl, *Political Oppositions in Western Democracies,* cit.; his recent contribution – with Henry Valen – in Rose, *Electoral Behavior,* cit; and Valen and D. Katz, *Political Parties in Norway,* Tavistok, 1964. Harry Eckstein, *Division and Cohesion in Democracy: A Study of Norway,* Princeton University Press, 1966 remains a case study of great theoretical value.

38 Switzerland has been analyzed best, of late, under the consociational democracy theme (*infra,* 6.3, and nn. 73, 82.) For a general overview see ch. 9 of *European Political Parties: A Handbook,* ed. by Stanley Henig, Praeger, 1969. Better yet, see Roger Girod, "Geography of the Swiss Party System," in Allardt and Littunen, *Cleavages, Ideologies and Party Systems,* op. cit., pp. 132–161; and his article "Le Système des Partis en Suisse," *RFSP,* décembre 1964. Also see Jürg Steiner, "Typologiesierung des Schweizerishen Parteiensystems," *Schweizerischen Jahrbuch für Politische Wissenschaft,* 1969, pp. 21–40; and E. Gruner, *Die Parteien in der Schweitz,* Francke, 1969. G. A. Codding, *The Federal Government of Switzerland,* Houghton Mifflin, 1961, still provides a useful general overview.

39 Note that the returns do not measure the importance of religion. The religious observants roughly amount to a 20 percent of the population; and the appeal of religious memories and symbolism remains quite strong in at least one-half of the Israeli people. See esp. Gutmann, below, n. 43.

40 I neglect the Arab population, which represents about one-sixth of the total population (roughly 500,000 Arabs against 3 million Jews) because the Arab vote splits. Thus the so-called Affiliated Arab Lists (which collect about one-half of the total Arab vote) have consistently supported the *Mapai*-led coalitions. The other major

bloc of Arab votes goes, instead, to the Communist lists. See Jacob Landau, *The Arabs in Israel: A Political Study*, Oxford University Press, 1969. This is not to underestimate, however, the future relevance of an Arab population whose rate of growth is higher – within the existing borders – than that of the Jewish population.

41 This is pinpointed by the model of spatial competition *infra*, 10.4 (and n. 71).

42 See Dan Horowitz and Moshe Lissak, "Authority Without Sovereignty: The Case of the National Centre of the Jewish Community in Palestine," *GO*, Winter 1973.

43 On Israel see Benjamin Akzin, "The Role of Parties in Israeli Democracy," *JP*, November 1955; Amitai Etzioni, "Alternative Ways to Democracy: The Example of Israel," *PSQ*, June 1959; Emanuel E. Gutmann, "Some Observations on Politics and Parties in Israel," *India Quarterly*, Jan.–March 1961; Scott D. Johnston, "Major Party Politics in a Multiparty System," *Il Politico*, II, 1965; S. N. Eisenstadt, *Israeli Society*, Weidenfeld & Nicolson, 1967; Leonard J. Fein, *Politics in Israel*, Little Brown, 1967; Martin Seliger, "Positions and Dispositions in Israeli Politics," *GO*, Autumn 1968; S. Clement Leslie, *The Rift in Israel: Religious Authority and Secular Democracy*, Routledge & Kegan Paul, 1971; E. Gutmann, "Religion in Israeli Politics," in Jacob M. Landau, ed., *Man State and Society in the Contemporary Middle East*, Praeger, 1972; Khayyam Z. Paltiel, "The Israeli Coalition System," *GO*, Autumn 1975. I wish to express my gratitude to Professor Landau for his advice and for having checked my figures.

44 The classics on the Weimar Republic are Karl D. Bracher, *Die Aufloesung der Weimarer Republic,* 3rd ed., Ring Verlag, 1960, and Erich Eyck, *Geschichte der Weimarer Republic,* 3rd ed., Erlenbach, 1962, 2 vols. The Weimar system is clearly, if briefly, analyzed in perspective by Gerhard Loewemberg, "The Remaking of the German Party System" *Polity*, I, 1968; and, now, in the ch. of Derek Urwin in Rose, ed., *Electoral Behavior*, cit., pp. 118–126. See also Charles E. Frye, "Parties and Pressure Groups in Weimar and Bonn," *WP*, IV, 1965. The electoral returns are in E. Faul, ed., *Wahlen und Wähler in Westdeutschland*, Ring Verlag, 1960. In Gurr and McClelland, op. cit. (above, n. 25) Germany (1923–1932) obtains a total magnitude of illegitimacy of 19.3, surpassed only by Spain (1932–1936) with 22.0 (p. 40).

45 *Supra*, 6.1. For other or broader interpretations see: Galli, *Il Bipartitismo Imperfetto*, op. cit., and *Il Difficile Governo*, Il Mulino, 1972; Germino, Passigli, *The Government and Politics of Contemporary Italy*, op. cit.; P. A. Allum, *Italy, Republic Without Government?*, Weidenfeld & Nicolson, 1973; Cavazza and Graubard, eds., *Il Caso Italiano*, op. cit. See also the forthcoming book of Di Palma, *Decision and Representation*, cit., esp. ch. 6.

46 For a general appraisal of the effects of the double ballot, see Fisichella, *Sviluppo Democratico e Sistemi Elettorali*, cit., pp. 195–221.

47 The literature on France is extensive but seldom satisfactory from a theoretical standpoint. Nevertheless, see N. Leites, *On the Game of Politics in France*, Stanford University Press, 1959; Jacques Fauvet, *La IVᵉ République*, Fayard, 1959; D. Pickles, *The Fourth*

French Republic, 2nd ed., Methuen, 1958, and *The Fifth French Republic,* 3rd ed., Methuen, 1965; M. Duverger, *La Cinquième République,* Presses Universitaires, 1968 (4th ed.), and *La VI République et le Régime Présidentiel,* Fayard, 1960; Roy C. Macridis, "France," in Macridis and R. E. Ward, eds., *Modern Political Systems – Europe,* Prentice-Hall, 1963; Duncan MacRae, *Parliaments Parties and Society in France 1946–1958,* St. Martin's Press, 1967; P. M. Williams, *The French Parliament 1958–67,* Allen & Unwin, 1968; S. Ehrmann, *Politics in France,* Little Brown, 1969. On the Gaullists the single major source is: Jean Charlot, *L'U.N.R.,* Colin, 1967, and *Le Phénomène Gaulliste,* Fayard, 1970. From my vantage point MacRae is, for the Fourth Republic, the most useful text. For the more recent writings see Vincent Wright, "Presidentialism and the Parties in the French V Republic," *GO,* Winter 1975.

48 At the 1970 presidential elections Allende obtained 36.3 percent of the vote, followed as a close second (34.9, i.e., less than 40,000 votes difference) by Alessandri, the conservative candidate, with Tomic (a leftward-oriented Christian Democrat) coming in third with a mere 28 percent. Note that Allende had already come very close to victory in the three-cornered race of 1958 and that his percentage in 1964, in the two-cornered contest with Frei, was higher (38.6) than the one that gave him the presidency in 1970. As for the conventions of the constitution, there was no precedent of the congress denying election to the electoral front runner.

49 It is worth recalling that on August 22, 1973, the congress voted a statement of "illegality" of the Allende government, which resulted in the resignation of the military members of the cabinet and doubtlessly helped legitimize the military seizure of September 11.

50 Among the nonpolitical conditions I would cite first the fact that is stressed least by most post-coup interpreters, namely, that by the end of 1972 the inflation rate had surpassed 160 percent and that before the coup it had doubled, reaching the catastrophic high of circa 325 percent. While inflation is an indicator of, and results from, many causal factors, beyond the point reached in Chile in 1972 it can be treated as an independent variable.

51 In 1971, e.g., McDonald classified Chile as a "multi-party dominant system," interpreted the 1969 election as a "contraction" of the party system, and gave his chapter the unperceptive title "The Politics of Orderly Change" (Ronald H. McDonald, *Party Systems and Elections in Latin America,* Markham, 1971, pp. 116 ff.). In general, and for the background of my brief presentation, see esp. F. G. Gil, *The Political System of Chile,* Houghton Mifflin, 1966. A pre-downfall appraisal is the issue "Chilean's Chile," *GO,* Summer 1972, which also compares Chile with France and Italy (pp. 389–408).

52 To my knowledge the only exception to this statement (up until the end of 1974) is the excellent chapter on Chile by Arturo Valenzuela, in J. Linz, Alfred Stepan, eds., *Breakdowns and Crises of Democratic Regimes* (forthcoming).

53 *Supra,* 6.1. For other considerations see Erik Allardt, "Social Sources of Finnish Communism: Traditional and Emerging Radicalism," *International Journal Comparative Sociology,* March 1964;

and, more generally, John H. Hodgson, *Communism in Finland,* Princeton University Press, 1967.

54 In general see Jaakko Nousiainen, *The Finnish Political System,* Harvard University Press, 1971. A recent overview is Pertti Pesonen, "Party Support in a Fragmented System," in Rose, ed., *Electoral Behavior,* cit.

55 "The Party System of Spain: Past and Future," in Seymour M. Lipset and Stein Rokkan, eds., *Party Systems and Voter Alignments,* Free Press, 1967, pp. 200–201.

56 The techniques for measuring trends and fluctuations in party strength are outlined by R. Rose and D. W. Urwin, "Persistence and Change in Western Party Systems Since 1945," *PS,* 1970, pp. 287–319.

57 The coefficients have been suggested and calculated by Alberto Marradi, my close collaborator at the University of Florence. I am also indebted to him for drawing the figures.

58 For Italy (1946–1972) they would be as follows: Communists + 1.32; Socialists and Republicans − 0.84; Christian Democrats − 0.34; neo-Fascists + 1.1. In greater detail see Sartori, "Rivisitando il Pluralismo Polarizzato," in Cavazza and Graubard, *Il Caso Italiano,* cit., esp. pp. 203–209.

59 In Figure 18 on Chile the tripartition is among extreme left, center-left, and center-right, given the characteristic center void of Chilean party politics. The inapplicability of the tripartition to France is explained at various points.

60 *Supra,* 6.1.

61 It should be noted that also the 1935–1940 Labor government was a minority government. Nevertheless, in Norway minority governments have been an exception more than a rule.

62 This raises the question whether a party with two seats and 2.4 percent of the total vote should be considered relevant. I would say that this was doubtlessly the case in the 1961 legislature. However, the Socialist People's party played no role in the 1965 legislature (in which the opposition parties had a majority of 53.4 percent of seats) and was not represented in the 1969 *Storting.* This is why I keep the format over time of Norway at five parties. But the problem is posed again by the 1973 elections. As this example goes to confirm, any conventional threshold of irrelevance can be very misleading. See 5.2, *supra,* with reference to the Italian Republican party.

63 The bibliography on Norway has been indicated above, n. 37.

64 On Sweden see Nils Stjernquist, "Sweden: Stability or Deadlock?" in Dahl, *Political Oppositions in Western Democracies,* cit.; Bo Särlvik, "Political Stability and Change in the Swedish Electorate," *SPS,* I, 1966; M. D. Hancock, *Sweden: A Multiparty System in Transition?* University of Denver Press, 1968.

65 One could add the 1939–1945 National government of all the four parties; but this coalition was clearly imposed by the World War II situation.

66 The inference is that single-party government attributes, by now, relevance to the Swedish Communist party, and rejoins the point of n. 62, above.

67 The analysis of the predominant-party systems is pursued *infra*, 6.5.

68 Compare, in Nils Andrén, *Government and Politics in the Nordic Countries*, Almquist & Wiksell, 1964, Tables 3 and 4 on Denmark, 9 on Norway, 11 on Sweden, and Appendix 2 on Finland, which list the respective governments.

69 On the minority government practice see Hans Daalder, "Cabinets and Party Systems in Ten European Democracies," *AP*, July 1971, p. 288, Table 3, which indicates that, between 1918 and 1969, out of the 250 cabinets covered by the study, 74 have not had a formal parliamentary majority. The figure is somewhat surprising, in spite of the fact that it covers a variety of different thresholds, circumstances, and reasons. A very helpful and pertinent account of the nature of the various coalitions – including the less-than-minimal ones – in Weimar Germany, France, Italy, the Netherlands, Israel, Finland, Sweden, Denmark, and Norway, is in de Swaan, *Coalition Theories and Cabinet Formations*, op. cit., pp. 160–283.

70 Among the massive literature on the Federal Republic see, in general, Arnold J. Heidenheimer, *The Government of Germany*, rev. ed., Crowell, 1966; and Lewis Edinger, *Germany*, Little Brown, 1968. More specific and recent is Derek Urwin, "Germany" in Rose, *Electoral Behavior*, cit. For earlier, significant interpretations see K. Deutsch in Macridis, Ward, *Modern Political Systems*, cit.; and Kirchheimer in Dahl, *Political Oppositions in Western Democracies*, cit.

71 Iceland is an exception, perhaps, to this characterization. It is, however, a very minor and peculiar exception (*supra*, 6.1). Since no country is condemned to unchangeability, only time will tell whether Iceland really is a deviant case. If so, it will enter another type. As for the growing relevance of the small Norwegian and Swedish Communist parties, it results from the attempt to maintain a predominant system with insufficient strength.

72 The Netherlands has not abided by the two-bloc alternative coalition pattern on account of the central positioning of its denominational parties, and especially of the Catholic one. However, the decline of the KVP (Table 5) is leading the Netherlands toward a two-bloc competitive mechanics.

73 Concerning the terminology, Lijphart settles for "consociational democracy"; Lembruch speaks of *Konkordanzdemokratie* (and of a system of *amicabilis compositio*); and Lorwin says "segmented pluralism" (in Dutch: *verzuiling*). The terms "ghettoization," *Lagermentalität*, and "compartmentalization" are also fitting, and frequently used, for the Austrian case. Reference is made to the following writings: Hans Daalder, "The Netherlands: Opposition in a Segmented Society," in Dahl, *Political Oppositions in Western Democracies*, op. cit.; Lijphart, *The Politics of Accommodation*, op. cit., and his article, "Typologies of Democratic Systems," *CPS*, cit.; Gerhard Lembruch, *Proporzdemokratie: Politische System und Politische Kultur in der Schweiz und in Oesterreich*, Mohr, 1967, and his 1967 IPSA paper (mimeo), "A Noncompetitive Pattern of Conflict Management in Liberal Democracies: The Case of Switzerland, Austria, Lebanon"; Jürg Steiner, "Conflict Resolution and

Democratic Stability in Subculturally Segmented Political Systems," *Res Publica*, IV, 1969; Val Lorwin, "Segmented Pluralism: Ideological Cleavages and Political Cohesion in the Smaller European Democracies," *CP*, January 1971; Hans Daalder, "On Building Consociational Nations: The Case of the Netherlands and Switzerland," *ISSJ*, III, 1971, pp. 355–370, and "The Consociational Democracy Theme," *WP*, July 1974; Jürg Steiner, *Amicable Agreement Versus Majority Rule*, University of North Carolina Press, 1974. A useful symposium is Kenneth D. McRae, ed., *Consociational Democracy: Political Accommodation in Segmented Societies*, McClelland and Stuart, 1974. After the Netherlands, the country that has been explored most under the consociational searchlight is Austria. See G. Bingham Powell, *Social Fragmentation and Political Hostility*, Stanford University Press, 1970; Kurt Steiner, *Politics in Austria*, Little Brown, 1971; and Rodney P. Stiefbold, "Segmented Pluralism and Consociational Democracy in Austria: Problems of Political Stability and Change," in Martin O. Heisler, ed., *Politics in Europe*, McKay, 1974.

74 "Segmented Pluralism," *CP*, cit., p. 141. I select Lorwin because his brilliant article represents the most general treatment. The other writings (above, n. 73) are generally on one or two countries only.

75 This is, in effect, the issue of the chapter on social classes and cleavages in vol. II. It should be clear that throughout this chapter I deliberately exclude, as independent factors, the nonpolitical variables – among other reasons to ascertain how much mileage is afforded without them.

76 *Infra*, 6.4.

77 *Structure and Process in Modern Societies*, Free Press, 1960, p. 263.

78 Di Palma, *Decision and Representation*, cit., ch. 6. The implication is that the Netherlands and Switzerland are party-crowded but not ideology-crowded: No crowding and extremization of the ideological space follow.

79 "Typologies of Democratic Systems," *CPS*, cit., p. 21. But see, in more detail, his *Politics of Accommodation*, op. cit.

80 The behavioral capabilities required of consociational elites are nothing less than the following: (i) ability to recognize the dangers inherent in a fragmented system, (ii) commitment to system maintenance, (iii) ability to transcend cultural cleavages at the elite level, (iv) ability to forge appropriate solutions for the demands of the subcultures ("Typologies of Democratic Systems," cit., pp. 22–23). This is indeed swimming against the current. On the other hand, cf. the criticism of Daalder esp. in "The Consociational Democracy Theme," cit.

81 On Belgium see esp. Lorwin's chapter in Dahl, *Political Oppositions in Western Democracies*, op. cit.; D. W. Urwin, "Social Cleavages and Political Parties in Belgium: Problems of Institutionalization," *PS*, September 1970; and the chapter of Keith Hill, "Belgium: Political Change in a Segmented Society," in Rose, *Electoral Behavior*, op. cit. J. Meynaud, J. Ladriere, F. Perin, *La Décision Politique en Belgique*, Colin, 1965, rightly stress the "conflict resolution" role played by the party system.

82 This is not to contradict the point that the "traditional consociational system . . . is in the process of disintegrating under the

impact of a fairly sudden shift in the hierarchy of social cleavages"
(James A. Dunn, Jr., "Consociational Democracy and Language
Conflict – A Comparison of the Belgian and Swiss Experiences,"
CPS, April 1972, p. 27). As Dunn points out, consociational
politics works best when the hierarchy of cleavages is (i) religious,
(ii) economic, and (iii) linguistic. See also the pertinent cautions on
the cleavage concept by Eric A. Nordlinger, *Conflict Regulation in
Divided Societies*, Occasional Paper No. 29, Center for International Affairs, Harvard University, 1972; and the last chapter added
by Lijphart to *Politics of Accommodation*, 2nd ed., 1975, op. cit.

83 *A Cross Polity Survey*, MIT Press, 1963.

84 After ten years of violent strife (1948–1958) the Sitges agreement
ratified by a plebiscite established (until 1974) a system by which
the Liberal and Conservative parties alternate in the presidency and
are given – whatever the returns – an equal number of seats (*pari-
dad*) in both chambers. The Colombian settlement does require the
incumbents to fight for their election but testifies only, on all other
grounds, to the fertility of man's imagination.

85 *Political Oppositions in Western Democracies*, op. cit., p. 333. Panama is exposed to coups. Uruguay (below, n. 127) and the Philippines (at the 1969 elections the Nacionalista party obtained 90
seats, and the Liberal party 15, out of 111 seats) are, or were,
characterized by predominance. It is curious that while two
predominant-party systems are included, India is excluded "because
of one-party dominance."

86 *Introduction to Comparative Government*, op. cit., pp. 165–167.

87 A recent suggestion to this effect is to distinguish between "indistinct
bi-partisan system" (USA) and "distinct bi-partisan system" (England). See Jupp, *Political Parties*, op. cit., pp. 8–13. On the other
hand, according to James MacGregor Burns, *The Deadlock of
Democracy*, Prentice-Hall, 1967, "the pattern of national [USA]
politics is essentially a four-party pattern" (p. 257 and *passim*).

88 This applies to the parliamentary and cabinet systems, not to the
American-type presidential system. With respect to the latter the
argument must be rephrased and adjusted. Thus "governing alone,"
i.e., one party government, is replaced by "presidential government,"
whose parliamentary vis-à-vis is an absolute majority of seats alternating between two parties (though not necessarily in synchronism
with the presidency). "Unnecessary" simply means that coalitions
do not, in fact, occur.

89 In Great Britain, e.g., no winning party (in the House of Commons)
has ever attained, since 1935, a 50-percent share of the popular
vote. Moreover, in 1951 Labour won the election with a 0.8 percent
advantage over the Conservatives, while the latter won a comfortable
majority of seats (321 against 295.) On the other hand, in 1964 the
Labour party went up from 258 to 317 seats with a rise in vote of
only 0.3 percent.

90 See esp. Charles Sellers, "The Equilibrium Cycle in Two-Party
Politics," *Public Opinion Quarterly*, Spring 1965, which recon-
structs the cycle back to 1789. For the presidential and congressional
results from 1876 to 1968, see Walter D. Burnham, in Rose,
Electoral Behavior, cit., pp. 676–677, Table 7 (but also Table 4:
"Typology of American Presidential Elections 1844–1968"). The

analyses on American voting behavior are discussed *infra*, ch. 10. On the American party system in general a very good discussion is in Robert A. Goldwin, ed., *Political Parties, USA*, Rand McNally, 1961. See also William N. Chambers, W. D. Burnham, eds., *The American Party System*, Oxford University Press, 1967. For the debate on the reform of the party system see Evron M. Kirkpatrick, "Toward a More Responsible Two-Party System: Political Science, Policy Science or Pseudo-Science," *APSR*, December 1971. With respect to the characteristics of twopartism in general, the skeletal, or coalitional, or diffuse nature of the American parties (to be discussed in vol. II) does not affect my points.

91 Labour won again the Australian 1974 election, obtaining in the Federal parliament lower house 66 seats against 61; but lost the early election of 1975. Currently, therefore, the alternation record has improved.

92 Interestingly enough, the Belgian Liberals and the Australian Country party are both in the 16-percent range. Thus the comparison applies also in terms of the relative size of the third parties.

93 *Supra*, 6.3, and esp. Table 24 on Belgium.

94 On Australia see L. C. Webb, "The Australian Party System," in *The Australian Political Party System*, Angus and Robertson, 1954; J. D. B. Miller, *Australian Government and Politics*, Duckworth, 1964; James Jupp, *Australian Party Politics*, Melbourne University Press, 1968; H. Mayer, H. Nelson, eds., *Australian Politics*, Cheshire, 1973.

95 Under this clause Ireland from 1948 to 1957 cannot be assimilated to Australia and has never had, therefore, a twoparty system. During those ten years the Dublin government alternated between *Fianna Fail* (the dominant party) and a coalitional "interparty government," which broke up in 1957. The Irish experience reinforces, then, the point that a mere alliance does not suffice to establish a twoparty pattern. On Ireland see *infra*, 6.5.

96 Mildred A. Schwartz, "Canadian Voting Behavior," in Rose, *Electoral Behavior*, cit., p. 552. Recall, in this connection, that also Canada suffers an ethnic-linguistic conflict and that one of the strongholds of the *Créditistes* is Quebec. But see below, n. 121.

97 From 1921 to 1974 this has been the case of 8 parliaments out of 17; and since 1957 the Canadian governing parties have lacked a majority in 1957, 1962, 1963, 1965, and 1972.

98 The literature on Canada is extensive. See especially Leon D. Epstein, "A Comparative Study of Canadian Parties," *APSR*, March 1964; G. A. Kelly, "Biculturalism and Party Systems in Belgium and Canada," *Public Policy*, 1967; Hugh G. Thorburn, ed., *Party Politics in Canada*, Prentice-Hall of Canada, 1967, *passim* (and particularly the chapter by Meisel, "Recent Changes in Canadian Parties," which detects a multiparty evolution of the Canadian system); Howard A. Scarrow, "Patterns of Voter Turnout in Canada," in John C. Courtney, ed., *Voting in Canada*, Prentice-Hall of Canada, 1967; Maurice Pinard, "One-Party Dominance and Third Parties," *Canadian Journal of Economics and Political Science*, August 1967 (discussed by Grahan White, "The Pinard Theory Reconsidered," *CJPS*, September 1973); John Meisel, *Working Papers on Canadian*

Politics, enlarged ed., McGill-Queens University Press, 1973, and his *Cleavages, Parties and Values in Canada,* Sage, 1974; and M. A. Schwartz (above, n. 96).

99 Actually the Liberal party had already won 12 seats in 1945 and again in 1966. However, the short parliament of 1974 is the only one of the postwar period in which the Liberals managed to deprive the winning party of the majority (Labour obtained 301 seats, i.e., 15 below the mark). Former minority Labour governments go as far back as 1924 and 1929–1931.

100 Even a highly selective bibliography on Britain would be massive. Let me simply recall the most recent writing of Richard Rose, his chapter in *Electoral Behavior,* op. cit.; and David Butler, Donald Stokes, *Political Change in Britain,* Macmillan, 1969. For the data see F. W. S. Craig, *British Parliamentary Election Results 1918–1949* (1969), and *British Parliamentary Election Statistics 1918–1970* (1971), both of Political Reference Publications. Among the earlier works see esp. Robert T. McKenzie, *British Political Parties,* Heinemann, 1955; and Samuel H. Beer, *Modern British Politics: A Study of Parties and Pressure Groups,* Faber & Faber, 1965.

101 Exception might be taken to this assertion with respect to New Zealand, where a third party, the Social Credit, has contested the elections since 1954. However, its only success has been one seat in 1966 (with 14.5 percent of the vote, which has since declined): the poorest showing among all the third parties of the twoparty systems.

102 On Austria see the books of G. Bingham Powell and K. Steiner (above, n. 73). The Austrian *proporz* system, which was both the cement and the result of the 20-year governmental alliance between the Socialist and Catholic parties, is well illustrated by F. C. Engelmann, "Austria: The Pooling of Opposition," in Dahl, *Political Oppositions in Western Democracies,* op. cit. Since the Austrian *proporz* is, in essence, a meticulous system of division (and duplication) of spoils, in this respect I doubt that Austria really deserves the praise attached to the notion of consociational democracy. At any rate, it is important to note that the two Austrian parties each fall just short of the absolute majority. It is hardly surprising, therefore, that their choice was to govern together (until 1966) with a 95-percent majority rather than alone with almost no majority.

103 This is, in fact, the option of Scalapino and Masumi, *Parties and Politics in Japan,* op. cit., pp. 79–81. The authors concede, however, that Japan can also be typified as twoparty and multiparty. Instead, I place Japan among the predominant systems (*infra,* 6.5).

104 To my knowledge, Germany was the first country qualified as a two-and-one-half-party system (e.g., C. J. Friedrich, *Constitutional Government and Democracy,* Ginn, 1950 ed., p. 414). And Blondel, (*An Introduction to Comparative Government,* op. cit., pp. 157–158), indicates that Belgium, Canada, and Eire can also be considered such.

105 Japan is considered one-party by Michael Leiserson, Jr. (*supra,* ch. 4, n. 20).

106 Aitkin and Kahan in Rose, *Electoral Behavior,* cit., p. 444. Also Jupp, *Political Parties,* op. cit., notes that Australia "has been typi-

fied as two-party, two-and-two-half party, and four party" (p. 6).
107 Rose, *Electoral Behavior,* cit., p. 487.
108 *Infra,* 7.1.
109 For instance, J. A. A. Lovink raises the question "Is Canadian Politics Too Competitive?" (*CJPS*, September 1973) and points to the fact that the competitiveness of the United States and England – when measured in terms of safe seats – is far lower.
110 See Rose, *Electoral Behavior,* cit., p. 484, table.
111 This is well explained in Dahl's chapter, "The American Oppositions," in *Political Oppositions in Western Democracies,* op. cit.
112 On the registration impediment see Stanley Kelley et al., "Registration and Voting: Putting First Things First," *APSR*, June 1967. On the 40–60 million nonvoter pool see Walter Dean Burnham, "A Political Scientist and the Voting-Rights Litigation," *Washington University Law Quarterly,* 1971, pp. 335–358.
113 For other aspects of twopartism that exceed the limits of a taxonomical analysis, see Lipson, *The Democratic Civilization,* op. cit., ch. 11; and Epstein, *Political Parties in Western Democracies,* op. cit., ch. 3 and *passim.* See also V. O. Key, *Politics, Parties and Pressure Groups,* Crowell, 1958 ed., pp. 225–231; and for a pre-Duverger, single-member-district explanation of twopartism, Schattschneider, *Party Government,* op. cit. The Downsian model is analyzed *infra,* ch. 10.
114 Maurice Duverger, "La Sociologie des Partis Politiques," in G. Gurvitch, ed., *Traité de Sociologie,* Presses Universitaires, 1960, vol. II, p. 44; Almond, in Almond and Coleman, eds., *The Politics of the Developing Areas,* op. cit., pp. 40–42.
115 In Almond and Coleman, eds., ibid., p. 480. Coleman, same volume, also finds "dominant" parties in India, Turkey, Mexico, plus Algeria, Nyasaland, Ghana, Tunisia, Malaya, and Mali.
116 Blondel (*Introduction to Comparative Politics,* cit., pp. 157, 166) adds to the "dominant non-dictatorial party" category of Blanksten the class of the "multiparty dominant": Denmark, Sweden, Norway, Italy, Iceland, plus Chile, Israel, India, Venezuela, Colombia. The confusion has not been lessened by the more recent expression "pivotal party," which is even more ambiguous (as confirmed, in my reading, by Dominique Rémy, "The Pivotal Party: Definition and Measurement," *EJPR,* III, 1975).
117 Other criteria may also be involved. Duverger, e.g., considers "dominant" the French Radicals (in the Third and Fourth Republics) on account of their position value, even though he fails to realize it. In his *Introduction à la Politique,* Gallimard, 1964, he again takes up the dominant party only to note that the "notion is . . . fluid . . . and oscillates, in practice, between two poles."
118 The list could be expanded by including the African area and Southeast Asia. My reasons for not doing so are given *infra,* ch. 8.
119 The best, if indirect, source for checking the reliability of electoral returns is provided by the periodic ratings of "Freedom House" in the journal *Freedom at Issue.* The more recent one is "Comparative Survey of Freedom IV," n. 26, July–August 1974, covering 153 countries. For an analysis of various rating criteria, see Leonardo Morlino, "Misure di Democrazia e di Libertà," *RISP,* I, 1975.

120 Since complete returns on Norway, Sweden, and Denmark are supplied *supra* (6.2), the reader can see for himself the merits and drawbacks of averaging these countries. As for Turkey see *infra,* 9.1 and Table 32.

121 *Supra,* 4.3. A comparable case is the firm, 36-year predominance of the Social Credit party in Alberta, Canada, since 1935 (when it ousted the formerly predominant, from 1921, United Farmers) until 1971. Hence Macpherson's *Democracy in Alberta,* op. cit., bears the subtitle: "The Theory and Practice of a Quasi-Party System" – surely an improvement on the American labels.

122 The case in point is especially India, whose elections are not a model of regularity (understandably so, given the size and the nature of the electorate). Nonetheless, the verdicts overwhelmingly favoring the Congress party over its competitors can be assumed to reflect, in the main, the will of the electorate. Whether this will remain the case in the future is, since 1975, a disquieting question.

123 The more recent instance of this drawback is McDonald, *Party Systems and Elections in Latin America,* op. cit., who makes it as simple as that: "By definition a single party dominant system is one in which a minimum of 60 percent of the seats . . . are controlled by one political party" (p. 220). Accordingly, Mexico (hegemonic, in my understanding) goes with El Salvador and Nicaragua (indeed an intermittent party system), while Uruguay, the longest case of predominance, goes with Colombia (above, n. 84) as a twoparty system. By the same yardstick, Japan, Norway, Sweden, and Ireland would be excluded.

124 The limiting case is Denmark: Under the stalemate of the electoral revolution of 1973 (Table 6), in January 1974 a Liberal single party government took office with 22 votes out of 179.

125 The point is discussed, with reference to Norway and Sweden, *supra,* 6.2.

126 The qualifier "unquestionably" relates to the findings of Daalder (above, n. 69) and is introduced to discard the cases in which minority governments are mere caretaker governments.

127 Uruguay is a dubious case not with respect to its record of Colorado party predominance over the Blanco party (almost a century), but with respect to whether Uruguay may not be a twoparty disguise of a multifractional federation of *sub-lemas.* The question is, then, whether its parties (*lemas*) are significant units. Currently, since 1973, Uruguay is a dual military-civilian polity, under indirect military rule. For Turkey see *infra,* 9.1.

128 On Ireland see Basil Chubb, *The Government and Politics of Ireland,* Stanford University Press, 1970; J. F. S. Ross, "Ireland," in S. Rokkan and J. Meyriat, eds., *International Guide to Electoral Statistics,* Mouton, 1969; and the chapter of J. H. Whyte, "Ireland: Politics Without Social Bases," in Rose, *Electoral Behavior,* cit. See also, above, n. 95. The 1973 election brought about a two-vote majority coalition among *Fine Gael* and Labour, which ousted *Fianna Fail* after 16 years of government.

129 Another way to connect twopartism with predominance is to note that each party of a twoparty system can be viewed as an alliance, at the national level, of constituency parties that are, in their safe

constituencies, "predominant." In other terms, a predominant-party pattern is – at the constituency level – a frequent outcome of a plurality single-member district system.

130 On the Congress party see esp. Myron Weiner, *Party Building in a New Nation: The Indian National Congress,* University of Chicago Press, 1967; and Rajni Kothari, *Politics in India,* Little Brown, 1970. In general, see W. H. Morris-Jones, *Government and Politics in India,* Hutchinson University Library, 1964.

131 The positioning is also justified by the limiting case of the "solitary" party, as R. Girod calls it (in Allardt and Littunen, *Cleavages, Ideologies and Party Systems,* op. cit., pp. 137–138). Girod applies the notion to a Swiss canton, but – as noted *supra,* 4.3 – it could apply also to those Southern states in which the Republicans do not even contest elections. A solitary party pattern is a situation in which the opposition happens to be at a subcompetitive level.

132 As Rajni Kothari appropriately suggests, when the interval is very wide the minor parties can be considered "parties of pressure" ("The Congress System in India," *Asian Survey,* December 1964, now in Kothari et al., *Party System and Election Studies,* Allied Publishers, 1967).

133 *Supra,* Tables 21, 22 (on Norway and Sweden) and above (for Ireland), n. 128.

134 The Japanese LDP started, in 1955, with 63.6 percent of the seats in the House of Representatives. It was at 59.3 in 1969 and down to 55.2 in 1972. The trend was confirmed by the 1974 elections to the upper house (House of Councillors). The LDP won just half of the seats (126 out of 252) and maintained a majority by registering 7 members elected as independents. On Japan in general see Scalapino and Masumi, *Parties and Politics in Contemporary Japan,* cit.; F. C. Langdon, *Politics in Japan,* Little Brown, 1967; Robert E. Ward, *Japan's Political System,* Prentice-Hall, 1967, and *Political Development in Modern Japan,* Princeton University Press, 1968. See also, *supra,* ch. 4, n. 50.

135 In spite of having a military president, Pakistan (formerly West Pakistan) qualifies as a quasi-civilianized regime.

136 On Northern Ireland, see Rose, *Governing Without Consensus,* op. cit.

7

Noncompetitive systems

7.1 Where competition ends

The previous chapter deals with the competitive systems; we now enter the area of the noncompetitive systems. Since competition ostensibly affords the major demarcation, in spite of its familiarity the concept deserves elucidation. By and large, a polity abides by the rules of competition when at election time most, if not all, seats are contested in each constituency between two or more candidates for office. And a first ground of inquiry focuses on what might be "optimal competition," as compared with too much or too little competition.[1] Too much competition may overheat the market and verge on unfair competition.[2] But, at this point, the appropriate question is: How minimal can competition be in order to remain significant?

As noted with respect to the predominant-party systems, the minor parties must be truly independent antagonists of the major party. If the seats are contested – that is, if the candidates of the predominant party are opposed without fear and with "equal rights" – then competition is significant, regardless of outcome, and the meaning of "truly independent antagonists" is clear enough. Supposing, however, that the seats are not contested, it does not necessarily follow that the system is noncompetitive: It may be subcompetitive. The distinction between a subcompetitive and a noncompetitive situation may appear thin – yet the difference is crucial.

A *subcompetitive* situation assumes that a candidate is unopposed only because it is not worth the effort to oppose him. If so, the holder of a safe constituency remains exposed to the rules of competition, and this means, in practice, that an opposer can always materialize and that a safe constituency can become, if displeased or neglected, unsafe. Something of the kind is currently happening to the formerly Solid South in the United States. Hence a *noncompetitive* situation cannot be detected solely on the grounds that a candidate wins unopposed. A system is noncompetitive if, and only if, it does not permit contested elections. What matters is, of course, the real, not the legal, ruling. Whatever the legal ruling, competition ends, and noncompetition begins, wherever contestants and opponents are deprived of equal rights, impeded, menaced, frightened, and eventually punished for daring to speak up.

The foregoing brings out that we are actually employing two concepts: (i) competition and (ii) competitiveness. *Competition is a structure,* or a rule of the game. *Competitiveness is a particular state of the game.* Thus competition embraces "non-competitiveness." For instance, a predominant-party system abides by the rules of competition but testifies to low competitiveness, or even to no near-competitiveness. At the other extreme, competition is "competitive" when two or more parties obtain close returns and win on thin margins. Also, a polity is spoken of as being competitive when the electoral contests are unrestrained and bitterly fought. In this latter case, however, the concept is competition. A ferocious engagement in elections surely demonstrates that the rules of competition are fully operative; but only the returns demonstrate to what extent a given system is competitive in the sense of approaching a near-even distribution of strength among its major parties.

The distinction may be pinpointed as follows: Since competition includes competitiveness as a potentiality, *competition* is equal to, and can be defined as, *potential competitiveness.* Conversely, competitiveness presupposes competition (as a structure) and is something to be measured in outcome, on the basis of its effectiveness.[3] Thus competitiveness is one of the properties or attributes of competition.

The importance of drawing a neat distinction between competition and competitiveness is borne out by how far astray one can go once the two concepts have been muddled. Przeworski and Sprague's suggestion of conceptualizing and measuring competition as the "mobilizing effort" of parties in relation to the "exposure" of the citizen nicely illustrates the point. According to this suggestion, "the empirical interpretation of systemic competition is a knock at the door by a party voter." This is a gentle way of putting it; but if the citizenry is brought by force and intimidation to the polls and made to vote openly for the candidate that has been chosen for it, the measuring system in question would still yield maximal and, indeed, perfect, competition. And the authors come very close to this conclusion, for their own conclusion is that "the competitiveness of the party system in the United States is somewhere intermediate between that in Venezuela and that in the Soviet Union."[4] According to Przeworski and Sprague, it makes perfect sense, therefore, to speak of competition in a one-party system and to declare that the Soviet Union is one of the most competitive systems in the world. The authors go to some pains to show that all of this is "perfectly reasonable"; but nowhere do they make the effort to explain how there can be competition under a monopoly and without a market. This omission is so staggering that it can be excused only by noting that

218

a sequel of errors brings the two authors completely off the track. The first error is, clearly, that they say competition when they mean competitiveness. But once launched in the pursuit of a measure, they equally misconceptualize competitiveness and end up with measuring a third, very different thing, namely, mobilization. To be sure, the Soviet Union ranks very high in mobilization; but this has nothing to do with either competition or competitiveness.

Competitiveness – I was saying – is a state or property of competition. This implies that the two things are closely linked, but it does not settle the question as to whether competitiveness is a major, or indeed the central, attribute of competition. The existing research evidence addresses itself to questions such as whether competitiveness – measured by the closeness of the returns and/or by the frequency with which parties take over from one another – correlates with certain kinds of policy outputs, e.g., welfare expenditures.[5] The findings are causally inconclusive, because other variables are very difficult to control. The thing to note is, however, the narrowness of the questions under current investigation. Let us assume that high competitiveness does translate itself into higher welfare expenditures. By the same token, the broader question would be whether higher welfare expenditures might not lead, in turn, to bankruptcy. Another hypothesis could be that high competitiveness nurtures party clientelism and colonization, or that it breeds a demagogic escalation of overpromising, i.e., an inflationary disequilibrium. In any event, the point is that the existing research affords little clue, if any, with respect to the relevance of competitiveness qua property or variable of competition.

Let us be unsophisticated and candid. Competition, viz., a competitive market-type structure, is important as a means of protecting and advantaging the consumer – both the economic and political consumer. Thus the crucial question is: Which is the protective element, or factor, of competition? Is it competitiveness? I think not. At least in the arena of politics, the essential protective benefits of a competitive structure stem, primarily, from the principle of "anticipated reactions," from the anticipation that the consumer will or might react. This mechanism – the retaliation potentialities of a competitive structure – can be blocked or distorted by advertisement, electioneering, canvassing, and mobilization; but it stands independently of these intervening variables. Thus a polity can be competitive without a single knock at the door, simply because it affords market conditions. True enough, there are "costs of entry," and a market system may well end up in a monopoly; but a monopoly *in* the market remains a far cry from a monopoly *without* market – at least in politics.

The clause "at least in politics" reminds us of important differences between an economic and a political market and between the economic and the political consumer. For one thing, the economic market is infinitely more sensitive, and the economic consumer is in a far better position to appraise his utility and to defend himself. With this I am not suggesting that competition is a theoretical construct that political scientists should invent anew. The differences do not detract from the basic fact that in the realm of both economics and politics a competitive structure defends the public. They do indicate, however, that the interest of the public may be served, in each context, by a different combination of mechanisms. Thus competitiveness is more important and more surely beneficial to economic than to political competition. Likewise, an economist might say that a party system is competitive only when there is an electoral market in which the actions of one firm influence, and are counteracted by, the actions of other firms; whereas a political scientist must relax these conditions and concede that even when a party does not actually influence another party, the mere juxtaposition of the two, or the mere possibility that another party could arise, is of consequence and is incorporated into the actual behavior of politicians. And even the economist will concede that in a market (also a monopolized market) freedom of entry entails a firm's keeping its prices as low as is necessary for discouraging new entries. All of this is more easy to intuit than to document and to measure. But what can be measured – competitiveness – should not blind us to how much is accomplished by the potentialities of a competitive structure.

When Brian Barry writes that even "if there were only one party it would not pay it to take unpopular stands because this would encourage political entrepreneurs to enter the market," he pays heed to the current ambiguity of the "one party" notion. Since one party implies no market, the assertion is contradictory and empirically false. But Barry is quite correct when he notes that when there are two parties of unequal size, the larger one has good reason "to behave competitively, since at some point the inertia of the electorate might be broken." Hence "de facto non-voting or dominance by a party need not produce markedly different effects from universal voting or an equal division of electoral support among the parties."[6] And at this juncture it is appropriate to enter – in principle, or in general – a complaint and a plea. The complaint is that we are very much under the spell of a crude operationalism that dismisses "the possible" (what might otherwise be) and thus fails to appreciate the alternatives. The loss of perspective and the misapprehension thus resulting can be enormous. It follows – this being the plea – that we are very much in need of what I call *potentiality analysis*, that is, of an understanding placed in the *context of the alternatives* and comprehending the principle and reality of anticipated reactions.

In this perspective the decisive element is not actual competition, and, even less, high competitiveness, but whether competition is possible. Thus a system remains competitive – structurally – as long as policies are checked by the awareness that a new competitor might enter the market and that large publics might shift their allegiances. Doubtless, at many points along this broad spectrum the balance between a competitive structure and actual competitiveness is suboptimal and unfelicitous. And the same is true – I hasten to add – for the noncompetitive spectrum. If the competitive systems greatly differ among themselves, so do the noncompetitive polities.

With reference to the analytical framework of Hirschman,[7] in a competitive structure the voter must have *both* the options of voice (making himself heard) and of exit (i.e., of leaving one party for another), and the minimal, nonrenounceable condition is free, unfettered exit. Contrariwise, the characteristic of a noncompetitive structure is, at best, that *only one* of these options be permitted, and never in full. In the cases of totalitarian monopoly neither voice nor exit is a feasible option. In other instances, however, withdrawal or half-exit (leaving the party, though not for another party) may be a costless option, or else ample room can be provided for voice in replacement of exit. These and other differences are precisely what we shall attempt to sort out in the sections that follow.

7.2 Single party

Since the competitive area has been analyzed beginning from its extreme end, it is cogent to begin the analysis of the noncompetitive area from its equally extreme end.

In my classification there is no room for equivocating when unipartism is unipartism.[8] One party means, literally, what it says: Only one party exists and is allowed to exist. This is so because such a party vetoes, both *de jure* and *de facto*, any kind of party pluralism.[9] Even by this strict definition the monoparty class is hardly in danger of running out of cases. Between 1962 and 1968 some 33 states held elections resulting in the allocation of all seats in the legislature to one and the same party. This list includes Albania, Bulgaria, China, Czechoslovakia, East Germany, Hungary, Liberia, North Vietnam, Portugal, Rumania, the Soviet Union, Spain, Tunisia, the United Arab Republic, and Yugoslavia.[10] As we shall see, the composition of a legislature is not the only indicator, and the electoral arrangements are also relevant in the matter. For the time being, however, the foregoing enumeration serves the purpose of bringing out the very composite nature of the one-party class. China and Tunisia, Portugal (until 1974) and the Soviet Union, Spain and Albania may equally be (or have been) single-party states – and yet they are definitely not equal in most other respects. In particular, the single-party states are more or less oppressive, more or less pervasive, more or less intolerant, more or less extractive. This is tantamount to saying that the one-party polities vary in intensity of repression, of coercive control. And it is precisely on account of an order of decreasing intensity of coercion, or repression, that the three following patterns can be meaningfully singled out:

1. one-party totalitarian
2. one-party authoritarian
3. one-party pragmatic

The first two subtypes are pretty well established in the literature, and their differences have long been analyzed under the rubric "dictatorship."[11] When the study of parties came to the fore, it did not add much to what had already been discussed in terms of totalitarian[12] or authoritarian dictatorships.[13] There is only one point that needs to be made very clear from the outset – for it is far from clear in the literature. Totalitarian monopartism represents – exactly like polarized pluralism – one of the ends of the party spectrum. It follows, as I have previously argued, that it must be conceived as a polar or pure type, *not* as an empirical type.

Aside from this *mise au point,* for the rest it is sufficient to remember here that totalitarian unipartism represents the highest degree of pervasiveness, mobilization, and monopolistic control of the party upon the total life experience of the citizens. By definition, the totalitarian party is a strongly ideological party. Also by definition, the totalitarian party is a strong party. A good indicator of such strength is "the premium put on membership in the party": For the more powerful the party, the more it tends to restrict membership and to expel, or cyclically purge en masse, its members.[14] By contrast, the authoritarian regime lacks a strong ideology and a comparable mobilizational capability; and its control does not extend, as a rule, far beyond the normal instruments of power – thereby including, however, the judiciary.

While the first two subtypes are underpinned by a considerable literature, the third case, i.e., my "one-party pragmatic" subtype, is far from being established, even though LaPalombara and Weiner detect, in their taxonomy, a third variety, which they call "one party pluralistic."[15] I take up the suggestion – but with two amendments. In the first place I object to the label.[16] Quite aside from the fact that "pluralism" should not be abused, in the case in point the term should be assigned – if at all applicable – to the hegemonic party polities, not to strict unipartism. The second amendment is of substance. In the taxonomy of LaPalombara and Weiner one finds a curious asymmetry: While the competitive systems are classified along the ideology-pragmatism dimension, the dimension disappears as we enter the noncompetitive area. I take it, instead, that the ideology-pragmatism dimension applies nicely to the whole spectrum.[17] Clearly, with only one party it makes no sense to speak of ideological distance (between parties). But each party, taken one by one, is characterized by a different "ideological intensity" and/or by a nonideological (pragmatic) approach. In this latter sense, therefore, the ideology-pragmatism criterion is not only applicable to, but is indeed indispensable for, the noncompetitive uniparty polities. When we come to unipartism, the numerical criterion affords little mileage, for "one" identifies only a highly concentrated, monopolistic power pattern. Therefore, the varieties of unipartism can be sorted out and analyzed if, and only if, another criterion is entered. And if one selects, for this purpose, the ideology-pragmatism criterion, then it behooves us, as we choose our labels, to bring it out.

By calling my third type one-party pragmatic I declare, in effect, my underlying assumption, namely, that the most powerful, single causal factor for determining (and scaling) the extractive-repressive capabilities of the single-party states is the ideological factor. More precisely put, the totalitarian and the authoritarian polities are assumed to reflect different ideological intensities,[18] while the one-party pragmatic polities represent that end of the continuum at which an ideological mentality gives way to a pragmatic mentality. One can equally say that totalitarianism and authoritarianism appear as different points of an ideological scale whose lowest point is called pragmatism.

The ideology-pragmatism criterion is not entirely novel. Thus in the classification of Almond one finds the ideological (absolute value-oriented) type of party contrasted to a pragmatic (bargaining) type; but this distinction is not worked out.[19] On the other hand, the ideology-pragmatism distinction improves upon the more traditional distinction between "doctrine based" and "non doctrinal" parties,[20] which appears far too low keyed. On the basis of the latter distinction one can either argue – as does McDonald – that denominational parties have no doctrine, or – as I do – that any party may respond to the needs of a particular situation, or to the challenge of its competitors, by providing itself with a "doctrine." For example, it makes perfect sense to argue that Roosevelt's New Deal and Kennedy's Fair Deal amount to the doctrine of the Democratic party in the United States. As these divergent interpretations show, the expressions doctrine-based and non-doctrinaire point to a superficial, or too superficial, layer of differentiation; whereas the opposition between ideology and pragmatism refers us, ultimately, to a mentality, that is, to a deep-rooted source of differentiation.

If the distinction between ideology and pragmatism is carried all the way through the party spectrum, it provides a fresh insight with respect to unipartism. We generally assume that the single party cannot materialize without an ideological legitimation of some kind.[21] The "one-party pragmatic" class challenges this view, calling our attention to the *channeling element*.[22] If this class obtains cases, then it testifies to the fact that unipartism can arise or, at any event, survive without any particular kind of ideological backing. Instead of diluting the concept of ideology to a point of meaninglessness, let us face the fact that a single party can exist on pure and simple grounds of expediency. Linz asks, with respect to Spain: "Is the political system the same or different?"[23] In the light of my tripartition, I would reply that in the aftermath of 1939 Spain was an authoritarian one-party polity that has gradually transformed itself into a pragmatic one. On the other hand, Portugal has long been (until April 1974) a clear case of pragmatic unipartism. Liberia, which is – ironically, if one pauses to consider the name – the first and oldest one-party regime, is another pertinent example.[24] And Tunisia's Neo-Destour also qualifies as a one-party pragmatic case.[25]

To be sure, the distinction between ideology and pragmatism also has feeble points. It can be attacked on the grounds that pragmatism is nothing but a state of low affect, of low temperature of ideologism; or it can be challenged by rotating the perspective, that is, by arguing that we speak of pragmatism when the members of a political community share the same ideology, and of ideologism when a political community adheres to different value beliefs. In the first approach the variable is intensity of affect, and pragmatism and ideologism result as the extreme points of a scale bearing on the temperature of politics. In the second perspective the variable is consensus, and the dichotomy between pragmatism and ideologism simply expresses the difference between a consensual and a conflictual political culture, between a homogeneous and a heterogeneous belief system.

Both arguments are subtle and have some truth to them, even though the experience of ideological politics forcibly suggests that ideology is, ultimately, irreducible.[26] At any rate, the relevant point is that both arguments – and especially the second – belong to a genetic explanation and thereby apply in the long run, over time. While dynamics is important, an excess of emphasis on change leads us to neglect the fact that decisions are taken, and events occur, at single points in time. Hence at each point in time not only must we reckon with the difference between an ideological and a pragmatic problem-solving orientation, but this difference carries with it very important associations. There is little doubt, for instance, that ideology is highly correlated with party cohesion. Likewise, ideological coercion markedly differs – for better or worse – from "naked coercion." Moreover, and this is the nexus that matters most in the present argument, a pragmatic party abides by a "natural development," for it is not a goal-oriented party aiming at a novel state of mankind, whereas the more ideological a party, the more it is predicated upon an "imposed development" dictated by a call of the future.[27]

All in all, the case for adopting the ideology-pragmatism criterion is conceptually strong. Its weakness is empirical; and this weakness requires us to search for complementary criteria and indicators. Among these I would definitely select the degree of sub-group and subsystem autonomy.[28] Along this path one encounters, in fact, manageable sub-groups and indicators. For instance, the press can be conceived as a sub-group whose independence vis-à-vis the political authorities can be measured in terms of "press freedom" scores. Reading the index calculated to this effect by Taylor and Hudson, one finds that the maximum of press unfreedom, i.e., the lowest possible score, is that of Albania (−3.50), followed – in my cursory selection – by Rumania, East Germany, China, the Soviet Union, Cuba, Bulgaria, Poland, Czechoslovakia (−2.50), Hungary (−1.57), Portugal (−1.42), Spain (−1.02), Pakistan (−.01), Yugoslavia (.08), India (.98), Chile (1.19), Mexico (1.46), Turkey (1.66); whereas the highest scoring, i.e., the highest freedom, is found in Norway and Switzerland (3.06).[29] There are many oddities in these scores, e.g., the distance between Czechoslovakia and Hungary, the ranking of Yugoslavia, and the counterintuitive low scores of India and Chile. For the time being, if we are not doing well conceptually, we are not faring better empirically. But, no doubt, other tries will give more reliable and helpful measures.[30]

By bringing together the typology of dictatorship, the ideological criterion, and the yardstick of sub-group and subsystem independence, the relevant characteristics by which totalitarian, authoritarian and pragmatic unipartism can be diversified and identified are as follows.

The totalitarian single party is characterized by its attempt at total reach, at total penetration and politicization. Whether or not it pursues the goal of shaping a "new man," the totalitarian regime is bent upon destroying not only subsystem but also any kind of sub-group autonomy. Totalitarianism represents, then, the ultimate invasion of privacy.[31] "If private areas of life do still survive, they do so on sufferance,"[32] and no line can be drawn between state-controlled and private spheres of life. This implies that a totalitarian regime is more easily imposed wherever the individual and privacy are not valued, that is, in non-Western societies. However, a society is fittingly described as totalitarian only if so molded by politics. That is, the concept is abused wherever applied to a communal-type society and, in general, to a culturally molded state of society.

Authoritarian unipartism amounts, instead, to a control system that neither has the power nor the ambition of pervading the whole society.

This type is characterized, then, not by "totalism" but by "exclusionarism," by restricting the political activities of the outs.[33] When the authoritarian single party has recourse to mobilization, the mobilizing effort does not go in depth: It hinges on the charisma of the leader and is generally satisfied by façade effects – mass demonstrations, mass meetings, and mass abductions to the polls. A Chinese type of "cultural revolution" is, for an authoritarian regime, unthinkable. On the other hand, one of the by-effects of exclusionary policies is that a number of sub-groups keep carefully out of politics. And to the extent that this is so, these groups are left, in the main, to pursue their own course.

The pragmatic single party lacks the legitimation of an ideology and thus compares to the other two types as the one with the lesser coercive potentiality. This implies, in turn, that pragmatic unipartism is ill suited for pursuing exclusionary policies and is prompted, instead, to attempting absorbtive policies. The pragmatic single party equally lacks ideological cohesiveness. Also from this angle, then, its relation to outer groups tends to be aggregative rather than destructive. Moreover, its low degree of internal ideological cohesiveness makes the organization of the pragmatic single party quite loose and somewhat pluralistic.[34]

If the various ingredients that enter the identification of the three varieties of unipartism are sorted out, according to the ideology-coercion criterion the results are as follows: (i) the totalitarian single party is strongly ideologized, highly coercive, extractive, mobilizational, and bent upon imposed (political) development; (ii) authoritarian unipartism is a control system of a lesser ideological intensity, with lower extractive and mobilizational capabilities, bent upon exclusionary policies; and (iii) pragmatic unipartism relaxes all the foregoing traits and can be recognized by "inclusionary" or aggregative (as opposed to exclusionary and destructive) policies attuned to a natural development. According to the second criterion – the relation to outer and intermediate groups – the totalitarian pattern is totalistic and, consequently, ruthlessly destructive of both subsystem and sub-group autonomy; the authoritarian pattern impedes subsystem but tolerates, at least *de facto,* some kind of sub-group autonomy; and the pragmatic pattern may be quite open, instead, to sub-group autonomy and may also allow room for some peripheral subsystem autonomy (e.g., for a pressure group subsystem). With respect to the dictatorial nature of these regimes, one could say that the totalitarian dictator (or dictatorial oligarchy) is unbound and unpredictable; that the authoritarian dictator is unbound but confined, nevertheless, within predictable limits of arbitrariness; and that a pragmatic dictatorship is bounded by the constellation of forces with which it must bargain. Finally, with respect to the channeling (and chaining) function, totalitarian uni-partism can be said to canalize by suppressing; authoritarian unipartism to canalize by excluding; and pragmatic unipartism to canalize by absorbing (or attempting to absorb).

The preceding elements can be roughly summarized as in Table 27. The table goes to show, as we read it vertically, that while each criterion, or variable, does not yield by itself a clear-cut identification, none-theless each type, or subtype, of party-state system is well character-ized by a distinctive syndrome, by a unique complex. On the other hand, a horizontal reading of the table reminds us that the three patterns – totalitarian, authoritarian, and pragmatic – represent sub-types arranged along an ideology-pragmatism continuum roughly cor-responding to diminishing coercive capabilities. Not only, then, are these subtypes assumed to blend into each other, but also to transform themselves into one another.

Over time, any polity confronts us with the question: Has it changed, or has it remained the same? The question is more easily answered in the context of the competitive systems, for such systems have built-in mechanisms of change and can be changed simply by electoral verdicts. To the contrary, the question is awkward with respect to the noncompetitive polities, for their mechanisms do not envisage self-change and their structure is largely insensitive to the pressures resulting from environmental change. This difficulty is heightened whenever the question is addressed to a classification, that is, when we have to decide whether a concrete system should be moved from one class to another. For instance, few people would deny that the Soviet Union was, under Stalin, a totalitarian system; but is it

Table 27. *Characteristics of single party states by types and criteria*

Criteria	Totalitarian unipartism	Authoritarian unipartism	Pragmatic unipartism
Ideology	strong and totalistic	weaker and nontotalistic	irrelevant or very feeble
Coercion, extraction, mobilization	high	medium	lower
Policies vs. outer groups	destructive	exclusionary	absorbtive
Sub-group independence	none	limited to non-political groups	permitted or tolerated
Arbitrariness	unbounded and unpredictable	within predict-able limits	bounded

still such? One of the current suggestions is that the Soviet Union should be reclassified as an authoritarian system.[35] But here three cautions are in order. First, if the Soviet Union is reclassified as authoritarian, what happens to other regimes formerly so classified? With reference to a classificatory scheme, the yardstick must be comparative and, in this sense, relative. If the net result of reclassifying the Soviet system (and party) is to make it equal to the Spanish system (and party) under Franco, the net gain is additional confusion. The second caution relates to the nature of classifications. It should be well understood that variations along a dimension of intensity seldom justify a reclassification, for these are deemed within-class variations. Finally, a classification centered on parties cannot be asked to register variations affecting other structures. Whatever the environmental changes may be, the question is whether a given variation affects the party arrangement. For instance, the transformation of a one-man dictatorship into a collegial dictatorship is very significant for a classification of dictatorships, but it may not be significant from the vantage point of the party.

In any event, the less articulated a classification, the less it permits reclassification. Thus one of the advantages of a tripartition over the bipartition between totalitarian and authoritarian monopartism is that my scheme is more sensitive to system change than the traditional one. On the other hand, even my tripartition cannot account for more than two transformations. The situation improves as my classification is extended to the hegemonic arrangement. Nonetheless, we must face the fact that two contradictory requirements are involved, namely, (i) having enough classes for registering change and (ii) having enough cases for each class. Clearly, it behooves us to strike a balance. This entails that we should neither expect a classification to be oversensitive to change nor assume that the permanence in a class means that a polity remains unchanged.

My emphasis is on the coercive and extractive features of the single-party states also because many current performances of intellectual bravura never convey the feeling that – whatever their other virtues – uniparty regimes surely hurt and abuse – to say the least. But it is clear that a more complete understanding requires us to approach unipartism from other angles as well. Thus the one-party state can be analyzed with respect to its (i) goals, (ii) performance and overall policies, (iii) origins and etiology, and (iv) social base or background.

The notions of tutelary democracy, guided democracy, pedagogic dictatorship, and the like, generally relate to the goals – at least the avowed goals – of a number of single-party states. The goal criterion leaves us to skate on thin ice: Promises are not deeds, and deceit is one of the invariables of politics. Nonetheless, lip service is better than lip disservice, goal commitments do matter, and modern autocrats can be, as some of their forefathers have been, benevolent despots. With reference to the policy and/or performance criterion, unipartism can be characterized along this complex dimension(s) in a number of ways: as revolutionary and progressive, or conservative and reactionary; as developmental and modernizing, or immobilistic and traditionalistic; as exclusionary and destructive, or inclusionary and aggregative – etc. It is under this criterion that we often speak of modernizing autocracy and of developmental dictatorship. With respect to the origins of the party-state systems I have already presented my argument.[36] However, causal explanations probe the matter much more in depth – and currently loom large. One approach focuses on the "crises" along a path of political development, and would thus explain the one-party solution as a byproduct of a crisis overload engendered by bad sequencing and excessive acceleration.[37] But most approaches are more socioeconomic in that they tend to explain the rise of single parties with reference to social conditions and economic structures. In this vein Huntington asserts that "successful one-party systems have their origins in bifurcation; the party is the means by which the leaders of one social force dominate the other social force."[38] The problem with the etiological line of enquiry is that the more we pass from proximate to distal causation, the looser and the vaguer the linkages.[39] We then have, fourth, a sociology of dictatorship that relates the performance and the characteristics of the single-party states to the class or vocational origins of the personnel in power. Under this criterion one can distinguish among political, military, and bureaucratic (or apparat) dictatorship; and/or among proletarian, bourgeois, and technical (or managerial) dictatorships. The *caveat* is, here, that the social background is not a powerful explanatory cue of actual behavior.[40]

A final remark concerns the label "revolutionary one party." It is often unclear under which criterion the expression is intended. "Revolutionary" might point to a goal, i.e., the final and total transformation of a society, or to a policy, i.e., the liquidation, physical or otherwise, of the enemy, and/or to the fact that the party has seized power by revolutionary means (or was revolutionary before seizing power). All is well when the meaning intended by the user is specified by an obverse. If revolution is opposed to counterrevolution and restoration, reference is made to grand historical trends. If revolution is contrasted with order and legality, we are referring to conceptions of life, or at least to value beliefs. If a revolutionary mode is opposed to a conservative or moderate mode, we are pointing to policies and styles of behavior. Most frequently, however, the term is either used in a global and muddled meaning, or in asymmetrical pairs – as when "revolu-

229

tionary" is opposed to "exclusionary."[41] Following the destiny of all the words that become fashionable, by now "revolutionary party" suits more the rhetoric than the study of politics.

7.3 *Hegemonic party*

If the single-party class contains only one party, we are left with a variety of arrangements that are *one-party centered* and yet display a periphery of secondary and indeed "second class" minor parties. In the face of this circumstance we either dismiss the subordinate parties as fictitious alibis or, flying as it were to the other extreme, discover that party pluralism is born. To be sure, the second class parties may well be a pure sham, an empty façade – as in East Germany.[42] If so, they are irrelevant and should not be counted. However, these peripheral, subordinate parties may be relevant in some substantive respect. If such is the case, we are still far removed from a predominant-party system, i.e., from a pluralistic sub- or near-competitive pattern, but we do have a *sui generis* pattern that I call hegemonic.

The label "hegemonic party" has been coined for Poland, and I take it from Wiatr.[43] So far, however, the hegemonic party *type* has not entered, as a type, the current party taxonomies. The reason for picking up this label is not far-fetched: There is no better option. The expression "dominant party" covers, and by now hopelessly mixes, three widely different cases: (i) "predominance," as previously defined,[44] (ii) "hegemony" (as I am about to define it) and, moreover, (iii) whatever major party outdistances the other parties in whichever type of party system. Hence the most sensible course is to use "dominant party" in this last, third sense – which makes the label unfit for typological purposes. Predominance and hegemony remain, therefore, as the two unspoiled, or less spoiled, available terms; and, on balance, the latter conveys the idea of a stronger degree of hierarchical control than the former.[45]

The pattern can be described as follows. The hegemonic party neither allows for a formal nor a de facto competition for power. Other parties are permitted to exist, but as second class, licensed parties; for they are not permitted to compete with the hegemonic party in antagonistic terms and on an equal basis. Not only does alternation not occur in fact; it *cannot* occur, since the possibility of a rotation in power is not even envisaged. The implication is that the hegemonic party will remain in power whether it is liked or not. While the predominant party remains submissive to the conditions that make for a responsible government, no real sanction commits the hegemonic party to responsiveness. Whatever its policy, its domination cannot be challenged.

In applying the label "hegemonical party" to present-day Poland, Wiatr asserts that the Polish non-Communist parties – namely, the United Peasant party, the Democratic party, plus three political associations of Catholic denomination – "share governmental and administrative posts at all levels . . . [and] shape public opinion . . . but without attempting to undermine the position of the hegemonical party."[46] Clearly, not only alternation but the very premises of competition are ruled out.[47] Therefore, I cannot follow another Polish author, Zakrzewski, when this pattern is interpreted as a "multiparty system based on cooperation."[48] As the actual working of the Polish system well shows, a hegemonic party system is definitely not a multiparty system, but is, at best, *a two-level system* in which one party tolerates and discretionally allocates a fraction of its power to subordinate political groups.[49] We shall come shortly to the reasons for the establishment of such a system in its possible varieties. Whatever those reasons, the fact remains that the hegemonic party formula may afford the appearance but surely does not afford the substance of competitive politics. It does not allow open contestation and effective dissent, nor does it approach Dahl's "competitive oligarchy."[50] The *out* parties can never become *in* parties, and their opposition is licensed opposition.

If the one-party polities can be divided into three major subtypes, the hegemonic party polities also display different extractive and repressive capabilities and are liable to specification along similar lines. Of course, there can be no "totalitarian" hegemonic party – this would be a *contradictio in adiecto* – but there can be a more or less "authoritarian" kind of hegemonic party. Under the assumption that the more authoritarian variety is likely to be, at the same time, the more ideological variety, the subtypes may be indicated as follows:

1. ideological-hegemonic party
2. pragmatic-hegemonic party

Poland clearly belongs to the first variety. In this case the peripheral parties are truly "satellite parties," and the question is to what extent licensed parties really have a share in basic decision making. To share an office does not necessarily mean that the power is also shared. Even if the satellite parties are given administrative, parliamentary, and governmental positions, they are not participants *optimo jure*, of full right, and their inferiority status vis-à-vis the hegemonic party is bound to affect heavily, indeed very heavily, their chances of independent behavior. However, even if no power is actually shared, nonetheless the Polish type of hegemonic party arrangement can produce a simulated pluralism, a simulated party market, so to speak.[51]

Why "simulate" a party market? One possible answer is that this is not only a psychological outlet and a safety valve of the political system designed to placate opposition, but it is also a means of providing the elite with a flow of information or, at any rate, with more information than the one party is generally able to gather.[52] In this sense it can be argued that the hegemonic party formula allows, somehow, for "expression." However, the expressive function assumes – in my definition – that demands are satisfied in that they are backed by mechanisms of enforcement.[53] I would rather say, therefore, that a hegemonic arrangement enhances the political communication function with respect to the quantity and quality of information intake. The hegemonic party knows more and listens more. Nonetheless, nothing links the demands to their satisfaction. Whatever the information, the hegemonic party can enforce its own will.

Despite these reservations, the case of the hegemonic party deserves to be kept separate from the case of the one party in the strict sense. Even in its ideological and authoritarian patterning, the hegemonic two-tier arrangement recognizes other political groups in their separateness, thereby paving the way to an enlarged network of political units. The role and the relevance of a simulated party market can be assessed best, I believe, in this perspective. And its fruits become tangible especially when we pass from the ideological to the pragmatic type of hegemonic party.

While Poland affords the prototype of the ideological hegemonic party, Mexico stands out, by now, as a pretty clear and well-established case of pragmatic-hegemonic party. Over the past two decades Mexico has been the favorite hunting ground for the scholars in search of a democracy spontaneously emerging from an authoritarian ancestor. The idea of a "one party pluralism," let alone of a "one-party democracy,"[54] is sustained, more than by any other instance, by the Mexican case. Contrariwise, in my argument the Mexican case testifies, more than to anything else, to the poverty and to the sins of the extant typology of party polities. All sorts of conceptual, interpretative, and predictive errors have resulted from our inability to accommodate into an appropriate framework the Mexican PRI – the celebrated *Partido Revolucionario Institucional*, i.e., the Institutional Revolutionary Party.

The Mexican PRI has been operating and shaping its present structure since 1938.[55] It was preceded – from 1929 to 1937 – by the PNR (*Partido Nacional Revolucionario*), which was dissolved and rebuilt in 1938 under the name of *Partido de la Revolución Mexicana* (PRM), subsequently rebaptized PRI in 1946. In spite of the revolutionary myth – expressed by all the successive labels – the PRI is definitely pragmatic, and so inclusive and aggregative as to near an amalgam-type party. It is equally, as I shall now endeavor to show, the sole

232

Table 28. *Mexico, elections 1958–1973 (low chamber)*

	1958 Seats	1961 Seats	1964 Seats	1967 Seats	1970 Seats	1970 % Seats	1970 % Vote	1973 Seats	1973 % Seats	1973 % Vote
PRI	153	172	175	177	178	83.6	83.3	188	81.8	70.5
PAN	6	5	20	20	20	9.4	14.1	25	10.8	14.4
PPS	1	1	10	10	10	4.7	1.4	10	4.4	3.5
PARM	1	0	5	5	5	2.3	0.8	7	3.0	1.8
	171	178	210	212	213	100.0		230	100.0	

Sources: R. H. McDonald, *Party Systems and Elections in Latin America*, cit., p. 243, from 1958 to 1967; *World Strength of the Communist Party Organization*, cit., for 1970 and 1973.

protagonist of a one-party-centered arrangement surrounded by a periphery of secondary parties.

Table 28 shows two things: the enduring, overwhelming strength of the PRI, and the near-immobility of the representation of the minor parties, namely, the National Action Party (PAN) – which exists since 1939, is the only consistent one, and stands to the right of the PRI – the Socialist People's Party (PPS), which stands at the extreme left, and the Authentic Party of the Mexican Revolution (PARM). The ratios between votes and seats are indicated, in the table, only for the last two elections (which suffice for making the point), and are explained by the fact that the single-member district system was corrected, in 1963, by allowing each minority party as many as 20 seats on the basis of given percentages. Prima facie, therefore, the Mexican system has seemingly liberalized itself with the electoral reform of 1963 (as reflected in the 1964 to 1970 distributions of seats). Upon second thought, however, the 20-seat ceiling (lifted to 25 in 1973) assigned to the minor parties amounts to a fixed barrier that freezes the secondary role of the "out" parties. PAN attained 20 seats already in 1964 and is actually penalized by the arrangement: 14 percent of the vote corresponds to 9.4 percent of the seats in the 1970 congress, and the ratio does not change significantly in 1973. True enough, the case is reversed for the other two parties which obtain more seats than votes – but their strength is insignificant. Let it immediately be added that the PRI can be (moderately) generous in the congress because the congress is relatively unimportant.[56] Mexico is ruled, in effect, by a president in a manner that is reminiscent of the Roman-type dictator. As an author puts it, "Mexicans avoid personal dictatorship by retiring their dictators every six years."[57] The truly indicative figures are, therefore, the ones relating to the presidential elections, in which the PRI's candidates have polled, in 1958, 1964, and 1970, 90.4, 89, and 85.8 percent of the total vote.

Below the presidential level, and as a direct emanation of the president's power, all the other important decisions issue from a seven-member central committee of the PRI. And the rules of the game are very clear. PRI must win anyhow. If there is any doubt as to the large margin of the PRI's necessary victory, the ballet boxes are stuffed or replaced.[58] On the other hand, "if cooptation of dissident groups fails, then repression is likely to occur."[59] PAN is not a menace, and in fact it helps keep alive, as an opposition from the right, the revolutionary image of a left-oriented PRI. On the other hand, if groups to the left of PRI were to become a menace, the PRI is fully prepared – at least there is ample evidence of this in the past – to repress them on internal security grounds and/or to make sure that their returns are made to appear as low as they should be.

Lest my brief account be misunderstood, I am only interested in showing that the Mexican pattern fits the definition of a hegemonic system. I am not suggesting in the least, therefore, that free and really competitive elections might oust the PRI. As a matter of fact, there is an overwhelming evidence to the contrary. The point is not that the PRI would lose if it permitted a full-fledged, free opposition. The point is that the hegemonic arrangement keeps the PRI together, and that the passage to a competitive system would endanger its unity because it would remove the prohibitive penalties inflicted by the hegemonic formula on party splits and breakouts. As a democracy, Mexico is, at best, a "quasi" or an "esoteric" democracy.[60] I say at best, because for the time being Mexico is not even a fake predominant-party system, but a clear-cut case of hegemonic party that permits second class parties as long as, and to the extent that, they remain as they are. However, if the Mexican case is appraised on its own grounds, it deserves at least two praises: one for inventiveness and one for its most skillful and successful management of a difficult experiment.

The two cases under consideration – Poland and Mexico – lend themselves, by virtue of their intriguing potentialities, to interesting conjectures. Poland is a test case for the Communist world. After the Russian invasions of Hungary and Czechoslovakia it is futile to speculate where the two countries would have landed had they been permitted to pursue their own courses. Since 1968, and for the foreseeable future, it is fairly clear that any relaxation of the Communist regimes, at least in East Europe, would have to be maintained within the boundaries of a hegemonic kind of arrangement. The attention of Western observers has been monopolized, understandably, by the Yugoslav route to socialism. However, and quite aside from the unique degree of international autonomy enjoyed by Yugoslavia, the fragility of its endeavor should not escape recognition. True enough, the Yugoslav system is currently the only one that accepts "without qualifications two significant political principles: the legitimacy of special interests and the autonomy of social organizations."[61] But the combination of a relatively depoliticized Communist party (the Communist League), a quasi-market, and a quasi-industrial self-management results in a perilous balance maintained by the personal dictatorial rule of Tito – not by safe institutionalized mechanisms.[62] For Yugoslavia the acid test has yet to come. I am not suggesting that Poland is the future of East Europe and, more generally, of a liberalized Communist world. I am simply saying that – under the Soviet doctrine of limited sovereignty – the Polish type of hegemonic arrangement appears a more plausible and tested option, and that we have yet to appreciate its significance and potential in this perspective.

Reverting to the pragmatic variety of hegemonic party we find that, as of 1973, three countries could have been located in this neighborhood: Portugal, Paraguay, and South Korea. The most interesting case was the first. Salazar had already inaugurated a policy of allowing the oppositions to vent some steam; and his successor, Caetano, pursued the attempt in the 1969 and 1973 elections. Under the Portuguese arrangement up until the overthrow of 1974 only one party, the National Popular Action, was legally permitted to exist; but during the one-month preelectoral period independent candidates were permitted to campaign and to present opposition slates. Since this opposition did not have a party status, it was disbanded after the election. On the other hand, during that one month every four years the contestation was far more effective and disturbing to the regime than it has ever been, or could be, in Poland or, for that matter, in Yugoslavia. Nonetheless, Caetano was as unable as Salazar to get this mechanism going. In 1969 the opposition candidates campaigned against the government and polled 12 percent of the vote, but failed, under the single-member district system, to gain any seats. In the subsequent elections of October 1973 the opposition reverted to the tactics already adopted under Salazar: It campaigned, but then abstained, and recommended the abstention, from voting. The 1973 anti-Caetano campaign was unfree by democratic standards (e.g., the colonial problem was out of bounds), but was a free one by Eastern standards: Not only were the criticisms fearless and the demands outspoken, but the press did publish brief summaries of the opposition campaign. It cannot be doubted that the Caetano regime was eager to have opposition candidates running for office, as is confirmed by the penalty of a five-year deprivation of civil rights for the candidates who walked out. The lesson to be learned from Portugal seemingly is that a mild dictatorship is incapable of establishing a hegemonic pattern. When permitted to speak, the opposition demands equal status and refuses the rules and restraints of a two-tier system. It appears, therefore, that a hegemonic party arrangement is accepted, or acceptable, only in the wake of the loosening up of a hitherto strongly coercive dictatorship.

At the totalitarian end of unipartism one asks, in the wording of Aron, how monolithic can a monopolistic party be? At the hegemonic end the question is: How non-monopolistic can a noncompetitive system become?[63] According to the foregoing analysis, the answer to the latter question is not exalting. Beyond Mexico we have candidates rather than actual cases. Yet it would be myopic, I believe, to declare the hegemonic pattern a phantom-like occurrence.

For one thing, it should be borne in mind that a hegemonic-type development is promoted by awareness and that no clear and distinct notion of a hegemonic artifact has yet been sensed – let alone by the scholars – by the polity builders searching for the least monopolistic possibility of a monopoly. In the second place, for dynamic and predictive purposes it remains very important to have a category, such as the hegemonic one, that permits the location of a given polity "in transition to," or at least as "heading toward." In the third place, we should keep an eye on the vast array of indirect military regimes, and/or of dual military-civilian regimes, for which a hegemonic arrangement seemingly represents an ideal solution.[64] Finally, we need a place for the fake predominant-party systems, that is, for the predominant party that de facto impedes effective competition or that owes its victories to crooked elections. More precisely put, when it cannot be assumed that a given party would remain predominant if the "formal" rules of competition were implemented, the case may well be that such a polity qualifies for being reclassified as hegemonic.

A final point bears on the unit of analysis – the party. I have strictly abided by this unit of analysis in order to find out how much mileage it affords. In spite of much vague talk to the contrary, societal pluralism is affected by, much more than it affects, the ideological, strongly coercive and cohesive single party. On the other hand, I have pointed out that the lesser the coercion, the greater the sub-group autonomy. This is tantamount to saying that as the coercion lessens, the impact of spontaneous societal pluralism grows. When we come, therefore, to the pragmatic polities, we are confronted with the point at which the party arrangement and the societal patterning reciprocally interact and penetrate one another. Thus sub-group autonomy and even subsystem independence may not be reflected in the legislative seats or in the governmental posts – which remain a party monopoly – and yet very much affect the nature and the policy of the monopolistic party. This means that the party no longer is, alone, a sufficient or very telling unit of analysis.

As the party yardstick is relaxed, the concrete question becomes this: Does the distinction between the pragmatic single party, on the one hand, and the pragmatic hegemonic party, on the other hand, still hold? In part, no, I grant – but in part, yes. Take Spain (monoparty, at least until 1975) and Mexico (hegemonic). Societal forces and pressures are accommodated and make their way under both arrangements. Nonetheless, had Spain turned to a hegemonic arrangement, it would not have been the same political system. The conjecture is implausible – as the case of Portugal has shown – but points to the lasting value of the distinction. This distinction also goes to pinpoint the prior question of how non-monopolistic a monopoly can become. Judging by the evidence at hand, the elasticity of a monopoly seemingly ends when a pragmatic single party cannot afford, or is incapable of, restructuring itself along hegemonic lines.

According to a broad estimate, a majority of countries and nearly two-thirds of the world population are governed today by single parties.[65] A framework that allows for two major types and five subtypes is hardly redundant vis-à-vis such an order of magnitude. The problem is not that we lack cases – the problem is that a high proportion of cases is too fluid to be classifiable or classified with any assurance.

NOTES TO CHAPTER 7

1 *Supra*, 2.3.
2 *Supra*, 6.1.
3 Measures of competitiveness (high to low) exist by now in a bewildering variety, especially with respect to the United States. See David G. Pfeiffer, "The Measurement of Inter-Party Competition and Systemic Stability," *APSR*, June 1967; R. E. Zody, N. R. Luttbeg, "Evaluation of Various Measures of State Party Competition," *WPQ*, December 1968; A. John Berrigan, "Interparty Electoral Competition, Stability and Change," *CPS*, July 1972; David J. Elkins, "The Measurement of Party Competition," *APSR*, June 1974; and below, n. 5.
4 A. Przeworski and J. Sprague, "Concepts in Search of Explicit Formulation: A Study in Measurement," *MJPS*, May 1971, pp. 199–212. The quotations are from pp. 208, 210.
5 See D. Lockard, *New England State Politics*, Princeton University Press, 1959; Dye, *Politics, Economics and the Public: Policy Outcomes in American States*, cit.; Richard E. Dawson, "Social Development, Party Competition and Policy," in Chambers and Burnham, *The American Party Systems*, cit.; Charles F. Cnudde, Donald J. McCrone, "Party Competition and Welfare Policies in the American States," *APSR*, September 1969, pp. 858–866; and Ira Sharkansky, Richard I. Hofferbert, "Dimensions of State Politics, Economics and Public Policy," ibid., pp. 867–878.
6 Brian Barry, *Sociologists, Economists and Democracy*, Collier-Macmillan, 1970, p. 152.
7 *Exit, Voice and Loyalty*, op. cit. See *supra*, 3.1.
8 To the best of my knowledge the word "unipartism" was coined by James Coleman and Carl Rosberg, eds., *Political Parties and National Integration in Tropical Africa*, op. cit. The term is intended, here, as a synonym for "single party" and/or "monopartism."
9 The point has been discussed at length, *supra*, ch. 2.
10 The list is drawn from Charles L. Taylor, Michael C. Hudson, eds., *World Handbook of Political and Social Indicators*, rev. ed., Yale University Press, 1972, pp. 49–50, and refers to the countries having zero fractionalization of seats in their legislatures.
11 The distinction between totalitarian and authoritarian dictatorship is summarized, e.g., by Ferdinand A. Hermens, *The Representative Republic*, University of Notre Dame Press, 1958, pp. 134–141. Franz Neumann suggested a more elaborate tripartition between (i) simple dictatorship (which corresponds to the authoritarian type), (ii) caesaristic dictatorship (with a charismatic leader and the support of the masses), and (iii) totalitarian dictatorship ("Notes on the Theory of Dictatorship," *The Authoritarian and the*

238

Democratic State, Free Press, 1957, esp. pp. 233–247). For an analytic discussion of the literature on dictatorship, see G. Sartori "Appunti per una Teoria Generale della Dittatura," in Klaus von Beyme, ed., *Theory and Politics – Festschrift für C. J. Friedrich,* Nijhoff, 1971, pp. 456–485. But see esp. the last essay of Linz, below, n. 13.

12 See esp. Carl J. Friedrich and Z. K. Brzezinski, *Totalitarian Dictatorship and Autocracy,* Harvard University Press, 1956 (rev. ed., 1965); C. J. Friedrich, ed., *Totalitarianism,* Harvard University Press, 1954; and Leonard Shapiro, "The Concept of Totalitarianism," *Survey,* Autumn 1969, pp. 93–95, and *Totalitarianism,* Pall Mall, 1972. Of late the concept of totalitarianism has been challenged. See the discussion in C. J. Friedrich, Michael Curtis, and B. R. Barber, *Totalitarianism in Perspective – Three Views,* Praeger, 1969. With specific reference to the Soviet area studies, the revision of the notion is well argued by Frederich J. Fleron, Jr., "Toward a Reconceptualization of Political Change in the Soviet Union," *CP,* January 1969, pp. 228–244. See also the conspectus of Ghita Ionescu, *Comparative Communist Politics,* Macmillan, 1972.

13 The most subtle and exhaustive analysis of authoritarianism – in its contrast to totalitarianism – is in the various writings of Juan Linz on Spain. See esp. "An Authoritarian Regime: Spain," in Allardt and Rokkan, eds., *Mass Politics,* op. cit., pp. 251–275; and "Opposition in and Under an Authoritarian Regime: Spain," in R. A. Dahl, ed., *Regimes and Oppositions,* Yale University Press, 1973, pp. 171–259. Linz has now published a comprehensive, theoretical and comparative study, "Totalitarian and Authoritarian Regimes," in F. I. Greenstein and Nelson W. Polsby, eds., *The Handbook of Political Science,* Addison-Wesley, 1975.

14 Huntington, in Huntington and Moore, eds., *Authoritarian Politics in Modern Society,* op. cit., p. 15.

15 *Political Parties and Political Development,* op. cit., esp. 38–40.

16 *Supra,* 2.3 and 1.2.

17 *Supra,* 4.2.

18 *Supra,* 5.3.

19 In *The Politics of the Developing Areas,* op. cit., pp. 43–44.

20 See esp. Neil A. McDonald, *The Study of Political Parties,* Random House, 1955, pp. 31–32.

21 As C. H. Moore puts it: "All established single parties need to be infused with value to generate legitimacy for their regimes and rulers. But the ideologies of such parties vary significantly . . ." (in *Authoritarian Politics in Modern Society,* op. cit., p. 57). I am unable to make sense, however, of his fourfold typology of one-party ideologies (ibid.) where I find, e.g., Fascist Italy in the same box with Castro's Cuba as seeking "total transformation," in "totalitarian" and "chiliastic" fashion, albeit in terms of an "expressive function."

22 The channeling (and chaining) function of parties is discussed *supra,* 2.1.

23 In Dahl, *Regimes and Oppositions,* op. cit., p. 253.

24 On Liberia see J. Gus Liebenow, in Coleman and Rosberg, *Political Parties and National Integration in Tropical Africa,* op. cit., pp. 448–481.

25 Other African examples could be entered, but – as explained *infra,* ch. 8 – the fluid polities cannot bear evidence with respect to the consolidated ones. Tunisia is a permissible example in that the Neo-Destour party goes back to 1934.

26 The systematic empirical study of Putnam, *The Beliefs of Politicians – Ideology, Conflict and Democracy in Britain and Italy,* op. cit., lends a great deal of evidence to this conclusion.

27 For the notions of natural and imposed development see Blondel, *Introduction to Comparative Government,* op. cit., pp. 70–76.

28 *Supra,* 2.2. This is the line actually pursued by Finer, *Comparative Government,* op. cit., ch. 12.

29 *World Handbook of Political and Social Indicators* (1972 ed.), op cit., pp. 51–52. Table 2.7. The lowest possible score of the index is −4.00, the highest +4.00. The data are from Ralph L. Lowenstein and the University of Missouri School of Journalism.

30 A broader set of indications bearing on sub-group autonomy is offered by the periodical ratings "Survey of Freedom," published in *Freedom at Issue,* on (i) political rights, (ii) civil rights, (iii) status of freedom, and (iv) trends. In the July–August 1974 issue, out of the 153 countries covered, 63 countries are classified as non-free and 46 as partly free – and the countries with a clean record (rated 1) on political rights number only 22.

31 Robert A. Nisbet, *The Quest for Community,* Oxford University Press, 1953, p. 202, and ch. 8 in general. I have pursued the analysis of totalitarianism along these lines in *Democratic Theory,* op. cit., ch. 7.

32 Finer, *Comparative Government,* op. cit., p. 74.

33 I take the term from Huntington, in *Authoritarian Politics in Modern Society,* cit., pp. 15–17. I do not adopt, however, his "exclusionary-versus-revolutionary" dichotomy, for the two terms belong to different dimensions.

34 I would place in this context the notion of "limited pluralism" developed by Linz with respect to Spain in the sixties (see above, n. 13, and in Dahl, *Regimes and Oppositions,* cit., esp. p. 188.) On the other hand, "limited pluralism" has also been applied – and I would say misapplied – to the Soviet system (Boris Meissner, "Totalitarian Rule and Social Change," *Problems of Communism,* November–December 1966, p. 50); and this goes to explain my reluctance vis-à-vis the label.

35 This suggestion is often associated with the dismissal of the totalitarianism-democracy opposition. However, when a dichotomy is simplistic, it does not follow that its terms should be ostracized: They can be reconceived and put to a non-dichotomous use.

36 *Supra,* 2.1.

37 See the chapter of LaPalombara and Weiner in *Political Parties and Political Development,* op. cit., *passim;* but esp. vol. VII of the SSRC political development series, Leonard Binder et al., *Crises and Sequences in Political Development,* op. cit. See also Dahl, *Poliarchy,* op. cit., ch. 3.

38 In *Authoritarian Politics in Modern Society,* cit., p. 15. The obvious reference is, here, Barrington Moore, Jr., *Social Origins of Dictatorships and Democracy,* Beacon Press, 1966.

39 I dwell on this difficulty, with special reference to the sociology of

240

parties, in my chapter "From the Sociology of Politics to Political Sociology," in Lipset, *Politics and the Social Sciences,* op. cit. The point will be taken up in vol. II.

40 This caution is borne out by the many existing studies focused on the social origins of decision makers, generally members of parliament. See in *Decisions and Decision-Makers in the Modern State,* Paris, UNESCO, 1967, the section "Parliamentary Profession," which covers six countries. See also Dwaine Marvick, ed., *Political Decision-Makers: Recruitment and Performance,* Free Press, 1961.

41 Above, n. 33.

42 In East Germany the German Liberal Democratic Party (LDP) and the National Democratic Party (NDP) survive as purely nominal parties, for they have acknowledged, since 1949, "their mission to be, or act, as 'transmission belts,' with the particular purpose of preparing the middle classes for the 'classless society'" (Ghita Ionescu, *The Politics of the European Communist States,* Praeger, 1967, p. 251).

43 In Allardt and Littunen, eds., *Cleavages, Ideologies and Party Systems,* op. cit. (1964), pp. 283–284. See also Wiatr, "The Hegemonic Party System in Poland," in Allardt and Rokkan, *Mass Politics,* op. cit., pp. 312–321.

44 *Supra,* 6.5.

45 Dahl has of recent adopted "hegemony" to indicate a regime, and "closed hegemony" as the opposite of "polyarchy." These categories are defined along the two dimensions of liberalization (contestation) and inclusiveness (participation). See *Poliarchy,* op. cit., esp. pp. 7–8. Clearly, my notion of hegemonic party is much narrower, for it is underpinned in a party context. Once this difference is acknowledged, it can well be said – in Dahl's terms – that the hegemonic party moves away from a "closed hegemony" toward an "inclusive hegemony" along the dimension of greater inclusiveness. In this perspective Dahl's analysis and mine are complementary. I cannot accept, however, the usage of LaPalombara and Wiener: ". . . a hegemonic system would be one in which over an extended period of time the same party, or coalitions dominated by the same party, hold governmental power" (*Political Parties and Political Development,* op. cit., p. 35). Not only is their conceptualization too broad (it goes so far as to include coalitions), but they apply the stronger term for the feebler cases.

46 In Allardt and Littunen, *Cleavages, Ideologies and Party Systems,* op. cit., p. 283.

47 The electoral arrangements amply testify to this conclusion. "Under the hegemonical-party systems, the existing parties and groups form a joint list. . . . The leading role of one party eliminates political rivalry between the various parties. . . . An agreement as to the distribution of parliamentary seats, or seats in local government bodies, is concluded before the elections" (Wiatr, *loc cit.,* n. 46, p. 287). See, in particular, the analysis of the Polish elections of 1957 by Zbigniew Pelczynski, in D. E. Butler et al., *Elections Abroad,* Macmillan, 1959, pp. 119–179; and also J. Wiatr, ed., *Studies in Polish Political System,* The Polish Academy of Sciences Press, 1967, pp. 108–139.

48 In Allardt and Littunen, *Cleavages, Ideologies and Party Systems,*

cit., p. 282. This interpretation has the same plausibility as Franco's claim that Spain is an "organic democracy."

49 The distribution of seats – over the 1965, 1969, and 1972 elections – has remained basically unchanged, with 255 seats (55 percent) to the Communist party, 117 seats to the United Peasant party, and 39 to the Democratic party, plus 49 seats allocated to independents (which include the Catholic groups). The United Peasant and the Democratic party consistently vote with the Communist party. A limited degree of independence exists only among the Catholic independents. The strongest and truly independent Catholic group is *Znak*. However, over the years the *Pax* group, initially suspect of being a Trojan horse, has come to play a useful mediating role between the church and the Polish United Workers' party, i.e., the Communist party. In the 1972 election *Znak* obtained 7 seats and *Pax* 5.

50 *Poliarchy*, cit., p. 7, Fig. 1.2.

51 This seems to me the only acceptable reformulation of Neumann's statement that "even the totalitarian party depends upon a functioning opposition. If one does not exist, it must be assumed" (in *Modern Political Parties*, op. cit., p. 395).

52 I would actually limit to the hegemonic case Neumann's generalization that in a dictatorial system the party "serves . . . as a necessary listening post" (ibid., p. 398). Both the Italian Fascist party and the Nazi party were highly inefficient listening posts, for the dictator was told only what he wanted to hear; and the case was not very different with Stalin.

53 *Supra*, 3.1.

54 *Supra*, 2.3.

55 The literature is extensive. See W. P. Tucker, *Mexican Government Today*, Minnesota University Press, 1957; Robert E. Scott, *Mexican Government in Transition*, Illinois University Press, 1959, and Scott's chapter, "Mexico: The Established Revolution," in Lucian W. Pye and Sidney Verba, eds., *Political Culture and Political Development*, Princeton University Press, 1965; Martin C. Needler, "The Political Development of Mexico," *APSR*, June 1961; L. Vincent Padgett, *The Mexican Political System*, Houghton Mifflin, 1966, and Padgett's earlier article, "Mexico's One-Party System: A Revaluation," *APSR*, December 1957; Frank Brandenburg, *The Making of Modern Mexico*, Prentice-Hall, 1964; Kenneth F. Johnson, *Mexican Democracy: A Critical View*, Allyn & Bacon, 1971. A contradictory study is Pablo Gonzales Casanova, *Democracy in Mexico*, Oxford University Press, 1970, which is, in fact, a description of the authoritarian nature of the Mexican system, and, in theory, a defense of its democratic value.

56 Compared with the Polish Communist party (see the figures in n. 49, above) the PRI is not generous at all. Clearly, the stronger the control of the hegemonic party, the more it can safely allocate seats to the satellite parties. In this perspective the Mexican electoral reform of 1962–1963 indicates greater self-confidence.

57 Brandenburg, *The Making of Modern Mexico*, cit., p. 141. The differences are that the Roman "constitutional dictator" lasted six months only and that it did not appoint – as does, *de facto*, the Mexican President – its own successor. Thus Mexicans do not really

"avoid personal dictatorship" but lifelong one-man arbitrary rule.

58 Most authors gloss over the Mexican elections or are very naïve in this respect (e.g., Barry Ames, "Basis of Support for Mexico's Dominant Party," *APSR*, March 1970). The fact is that returns are uncontrollable, and there is little doubt that, whenever necessary, they are rigged. See Philip B. Taylor, Jr., "The Mexican Elections of 1958: Affirmation of Authoritarianism?" *WPQ*, September 1960. In 1969, when Correa Rachò contested against PRI the gubernatorial office in Yucatàn, the ballot boxes were seized by armed forces under PRI orders, and the PAN candidate "lost." This is still better than in former cases.

59 Bo Anderson, James D. Cockroft, "Control and Cooptation in Mexican Politics," in L. Horowitz, ed., *Latin American Radicalism*, Vintage, 1969, p. 380.

60 See in Finer's chapter on "The Quasi-Democracy" his perceptive overview of Mexico (*Comparative Government*, cit., pp. 468–479). "Esoteric democracy" is, instead, the assessment of Johnson, *Mexican Democracy: A Critical View*, op. cit.

61 Andrew C. Janos, in Huntington and Moore, *Authoritarian Politics in Modern Science*, cit., p. 444.

62 The literature on Yugoslavia is largely unsatisfactory. A recent, unconvincing assessment is M. George Zaninovich, "Yugoslav Party Evolution: Moving Beyond Institutionalization," in Huntington and Moore, ibid., pp. 484–508. See, more in general, Adam B. Ulam, "Titoism," in M. M. Drachkovitch, ed., *Marxism in the Modern World*, Stanford University Press, 1965. On the point whether the Communist League no longer is a party, I trust a participant observer: "By a change in name, by becoming the 'Communist League,' this political organ has not entirely ceased to be a political party (nor has it ceased to be a political party with regard to doctrine . . .)" (Jovan Djordjevic, "Political Power in Yugoslavia," *GO*, January–April 1967, p. 216).

63 For Aron these questions relate to the shift of emphasis from the fifties to the sixties, whereas in my rephrasing they relate to different points along the party spectrum. See "Can the Party Alone Run a One-Party State – A Discussion," *GO*, February 1967, p. 165.

64 My former examples of Paraguay and South Korea belong to, or grow from, this context.

65 This is the estimate of Jupp, *Political Parties*, op. cit., pp. 5–6. See also above, n. 30.

8

Fluid polities and quasi-parties

8.1 Methodological cautions

The typology discussed thus far does not claim worldwide applicability. While it does not exclude the states that are new in the sense of having recently acquired national independence, it does not pretend to include the states that are new in the sense of starting from scratch – as is the case of most African countries. The distinction is not, then, between old and new states, but rather between *formed* and *formless* states. By saying formed states I make reference not only to the modern political systems[1] but also, and more generally, to the political systems whose identity is provided either by an adequate historical record (e.g., South America), or by a consolidation that has occurred prior to their independence (e.g., India). By saying formless states I make reference to the polities whose political process is highly undifferentiated and diffuse, and more particularly to the polities that are in a fluid state, in a highly volatile and initial stage of growth.

Formed and formless are remarkably loose notions—as they are intended to be. Thus, in my usage, "formed" is broader than "structured." For instance, Latin American states are surely formed—i.e., differentiated and characterized by stability of interactions—but one of their subsystems, the party system, has seldom acquired, during its intermittent life cycles, structural consolidation.[2] On the other hand, while my *structural consolidation* is close to the ordinary meaning of *institutionalization*,[3] it is narrower than, and different from, the concept of Huntington. According to Huntington, "the more adaptable an organization or procedure, the more highly institutionalized it is; the . . . more rigid it is, the lower its level of institutionalization."[4] Instead, my notion of structural consolidation lays the emphasis precisely on the viscosity, resilience, and immobilizing impact of structures.[5] In particular, and concretely, a party system becomes structured when it contains solidly entrenched mass parties. Differently put, mass parties – real ones – are a good indicator of a structured party system.[6] And my insistence on the wording "structural consolidation" implies that I intend a simpler and far less ambitious concept than the one of institutionalization – indeed, that I do not wish to get entangled in the latter. At any rate, the immediate point is that the formless polities have been deliberately ignored, so far, by my argument. I must now explain why.

For one thing, there is currently a marked imbalance between the wealth of sophisticated conceptual frameworks developed for the Third World vis-à-vis the poverty of the frameworks retained for the Western world. If only to restore the balance, a reconsideration of the Western or Western-type experience deserves, I feel, high priority. In the second place, and foremost, a separate treatment of the "embryonic states" is strongly justified on methodological grounds. The relative nature of the distinction between formed and formless states does not detract from the fact that near-astronomic distances and heterogeneities have to be accounted for. To say the least, therefore, the inclusion of the volatile polities within the overall context of the formed polities must be handled with a clear cognizance of the comparative problems that are involved. Two related problems call for preliminary attention: how to avoid (i) typological mishandlings and (ii) Euromorphic disguises.

Since the most influential single study on the new states of the Afro-Asian world remains *The Politics of the Developing Areas,* nothing is detracted from the seminal value of the thinking of Almond and of his associates if the typological mishandling is illustrated with reference to their pioneering study. In 1960 Almond classified party systems according to five types: (i) totalitarian, (2) authoritarian, (iii) dominant non-authoritarian, (iv) competitive twoparty, and (v) competitive multiparty.[7] The first two and the latter two types abide by the traditional classification and do not require additional comments. The novelty is provided by the third type, the *dominant non-authoritarian* category. Almond indicates that this type is "usually to be found in political systems where nationalist movements have been instrumental in attaining emancipation."[8] Since this is an entirely novel criterion, one wonders how the category in question enters a classification based on other criteria. A plausible explanation is that the dominant non-authoritarian type is intended, albeit implicitly, as a provisional and residual category for the new states. Provisional in that it is identified by its take off, i.e., according to how the type got started; and residual because the category is, in truth, extraneous to the rest of the classification. However, this interpretation is neatly ruled out by the placement of the dominant non-authoritarian party at the center of the classification. Far from being an ad hoc category for the emerging states, the dominant non-authoritarian party actually amounts to a standing, "omnibus" type, which appears objectionable on two major counts: first, its indefiniteness, and consequently its enormous stretch (all the way from Japan to Ghana in 1957–1960) and, second, its wording in conjunction with its placement. A party that is called dominant non-authoritarian, and placed halfway along the spectrum, conveys the suggestion that it bridges the gap between unipartism and twopartism – a suggestion reinforced by the fact that the book focuses on polities in flux which can, by definition, fluctuate in either direction. This implies that the fuzzy evidence drawn from fluid polities is brought to bear on the formed polities. If so, the entire construction is enfeebled. While it may be misleading to extrapolate from the "finished" states to the formless states, it is surely wrong to extrapolate back from the latter to the former.

The first *caveat* is, then, that the problem of the fluid polities cannot be handled – on typological grounds – by interpolating a new category amid the categories designed for the consolidated Western or Westernlike polities. We cannot classify on an equal footing form and formlessness, the nations that are built together with "nation building." And this implies that we *are* in need of residual and provisional classes and/or types. The *residual* nature of a class can be signified topologically, i.e., by its placement, and this problem can be settled via a simple device. The *provisional* nature of a category poses, instead, more complicated problems to which I shall revert.

One may, however, eschew typological mishandlings and yet stumble over the choice of terms, by which I mean the attributes and properties associated with the chosen nomenclature. This ulterior point is especially relevant with respect to the African area studies – which represent a more compact body of literature than the Near Eastern or South Asian studies – and can be illustrated in connection with another major symposium, *Political Parties and National Integration in Tropical Africa*.[9] In their introduction Coleman and Rosberg lay the emphasis on "general tendencies" rather than on specific classes or types, and they draw a distinction – within the uniparty and "one-party-dominant" African states – between (i) a pragmatic-pluralistic pattern and (ii) a revolutionary-centralizing trend. This is, no doubt, a flexible and cautious approach. But as we look into the attributes carried in their table, we find that "ideology" is the first and foremost diffentiating factor, and that the revolutionary-centralizing trend exhibits nothing less than a "monolithic" organizational aspect characterized as, or by, "high/total monopoly and fusion."[10] This is only a first sample. As we proceed in perusing the literature on African parties, we encounter a number of "mass parties,"[11] just as we find African single parties that are declared "totalitarian"[12] and/or assimilated to "mobilizational systems."[13] In all these instances we are confronted, I believe, with Euromorphic disguises and, in fact, with the error of dressing a naked infant with Western adult clothing.

Having taken, thus far, the ideological factor very seriously, I have strong doubts as to whether ideology can be pushed any further as a major differentiating element. Ideology does not strike roots in all types of soil. And while there is very little evidence to the effect that ideological factors do have empirical relevance in African contexts, it is abundantly clear that most of what is spoken of as ideology is mere political rhetoric and, at the same time, image selling to Western publics.[14] Likewise, when embryonic polities are declared totalitarian, mobilizational, and the like, my feeling is that we have lost all sense of proportion. Something must be wrong with a discipline that simultaneously dethrones the Soviet Union and promotes an African state to the heights of totalitarianism.

The new states – as here defined – had no previous tradition of statehood.[15] To call them states is juridically correct – but the standing fact remains a low incidence of stateness.[16] The new states are not even "nations," at least in the modern sense of the term invented by the romantics and awakened, or created, by the Napoleonic sweep over Europe.[17] On the other hand, the societies over which the new states attempt to rule are much more deeply and minutely structured than "national societies": They are "cellular societies," or mosaic societies, of primary, ascriptive groupings based upon kinship and primordial ties, embedded in tradition, magic and religion, and mapped by territorial imperatives.[18] The nation-centered societies compare with the non-nationalized, cellular-type societies as the Low Countries compare – orographically – with Switzerland. It is only too obvious, therefore, that the "penetration" of the new states faces a formidable resilience. The modernizing and nation-building tasks fall upon politics. But politics, and precisely the politics of statehood, has yet to be learned. In such a predicament the only definite thing about the parties of the emerging states in transition to some future shape is an enormous disproportion between goals and capabilities, words and deeds.

Reverting more specifically to the African single parties, their ambitions can be, no doubt, all embracing; but their means are not. Let it be recalled that in the Western experience the one party came last, and for the good reason, among others, that the real one-party state presupposes an advanced stage of organizational differentiation and specialization. Thus the mere fact that in a number of African states the one party comes in a flash, and that parties and politics are almost conterminous, already suggests that we may be exchanging shades for substance – a suspicion that becomes all the more forceful as we proceed from unipartism in general, or from mere unipartism, to its totalitarian, ultimate perfection. The simple question is: How can a beginner possibly master the skills, and marshal the means, of a totalitarian penetration, let alone a totalitarian fusion? In the second place, and on similar grounds, I would argue that improvised parties cannot possibly amount to "mobilizational systems." The concept implies that a regime engages in a drastic reshaping of the society, and was developed especially by Philip Selznick with reference to the Bolshevik example.[19] In this genealogy, then, a mobilizational system is part and parcel of a totalitarian regime. If, on the other hand, we do not really mean mobilization system, but simply "mobilization," i.e., capacity to mobilize, then let us not say more than we mean.[20] In the third place, I am left to wonder in what meaningful sense the parties of the new states can be "mass parties." Only in a trivial, uninteresting sense is the mass party a party open to all and/or followed by masses of people, i.e., a "big" party. In its theoretically fruitful sense the notion marks the passage from a personalized to an abstract perception of parties. This implies, in turn, that the mass party presupposes, in the public at large, a "capacity for abstraction." Is this the case with the so-called mass parties in Africa and in much of the Third World? If it is not the case I submit that, once again, we are having recourse to a misleading homonymy.

We shall revert to these issues after having inspected the evidence. For the time being, let the warning be repeated and specified as follows: That the more we approach the volatile polities, the more we need a residual and provisional categorizing not only (i) for *classifying* but also (ii) for *predicating*.

8.2 The African labyrinth

At the beginning of 1974 the African continent contained some 55 countries, thereby including the remaining colonial territories or provinces. The independent non-white states numbered 41. Out of these, the Northern African countries are Arabic and number only five: Egypt, Libya, Tunisia, Algeria, Morocco; and Egypt, independent since 1921, can hardly be considered a new state. Thus the bulk of the countries that qualify as new states is represented by the sub-Saharan countries and more precisely by the black, ex-colonial African states that attained independence between 1957 and 1964. In this group Ghana (formerly the Gold Coast) was the first country to become independent in March 1957. By 1964 all the countries of Tropical Africa had followed suit (later additions are negligible).[21]

To the majority of observers the most intriguing thing appeared, as these new states were born, to be the fast rise of one-party rule. Ghana, Guinea (independent in 1958), and Mali (independent in 1960) came immediately to the fore as possessing – it was asserted – totalitarian and/or dominant mass parties: Ghana's Convention People's party (CPP), led by Nkrumah, which was already a single party in 1960; Guinea's *Parti Démocratique de la Guinée* (PDG), led by Touré, and presumably the most ruthless and effective African party; and Mali's *Union Soudanaise,* led by Keita.[22] Tanzania (formerly Tanganyika and Zanzibar) entered the list later, for it took its present shape only in 1964; but the Tanzania African National Union (TANU) and Nyerere, its leader, quickly came to the center of attention and remain to this day the best supported and most open of the African single-party regimes.[23] Thus by 1964 at least two-thirds of Africa's independent states displayed some kind of single-party rule. But already in 1964 the wheel was beginning to turn.

As Tanzania was born, closing the list of the major black African new states, a number of the "older" newborn states were on the verge of changing hands. That is, around 1965 civilian rule – and its counterpart, experimentation with parties – began giving way, in several countries, to military rule.[24] To make an intricate story short, the turn of the wheel from the second half of the sixties onward is synthesized in a table.

Table 29 speaks for itself on a number of counts. Civilian governments have lasted on the average about 5 years – and nowhere up to 10 years – in all the 14 sub-Saharan countries coup struck (for the first time) between 1960 and 1970. As for the North African countries, Algeria and Sudan have performed even worse, while Libya lasted unchanged for 18 years as a partyless traditional monarchy. Setting aside white-controlled South Africa and Rhodesia, the residual colonies or provinces (including the Portuguese ones released at the end of 1975), the traditional partyless states (Ethiopia until 1974, and Morocco), and Egypt (independent in 1951 and already coup struck in 1952), the remaining unchanged African regimes with a population of more than 5 million are five: Tanzania (13 million), Kenya (11 million), Uganda (10 million), Malagasy (formerly Madagascar, 6.5 million), and Cameroun (5.7 million) – whereas coup-struck Nigeria alone has almost 59 million inhabitants, which is a larger population than is contained in all the former French colonies together.

The table also conveys that military seizure has struck the single-party regimes – in spite of their alleged solidity and greater stability – just about as much as it has struck the multiparty systems. If one accounts also for the plots and the failures, then the chances of military intervention are somewhat higher in the more-than-one party pattern.[25] Nonetheless, the contention that the "takeover of power by the military in new nations has generally followed the collapse of efforts to create democratic-type institutions: the military has tended not to displace the single mass-party authoritarian regimes"[26] was never borne out by the evidence. In the multiparty column of the table we find Sierra Leone, Somalia, and Nigeria, and at least the first two countries had, up until their seizure, performed decently. In par-

Table 29. *Coups in Africa (independence to 1975)*

Country	Year of independence	Before coup Dominant/uniparty	Multi-party	Military seizure(s)
Congo (Kinshasa)	1960		x	1960/1965
Congo (Brazzaville)	1960		x	1963/1968
Dahomey	1960	x		1963/65/67/69/72
Togo	1960		x	1963/1967
Burundi	1962	x		1966/1966
Central African Rep.	1960	x		1966
Upper Volta	1960	x		1966
Nigeria	1960		x	1966/1966/1975
Ghana	1957	x		1966/1972
Uganda	1962	x		1966/1971
Sierra Leone	1961		x	1967/1968
Mali	1960	x		1968
Somalia	1960		x	1969
Lesotho	1966	x		1970
Rwanda	1962	x		1973
Niger	1960	x		1974
Chad	1960	x		1975
Sudan	1956		x	1958/1964/1969
Algeria	1962	x		1965
Libya	1951	—	—	1969
Ethiopia	—	—	—	1974

ticular, Sierra Leone was rightly credited with having the longest and strongest democratic tradition among the former colonies; and the coup struck Freetown in 1967 just after a free and fairly counted election had defeated the governing party, opening the way to an alternation in power to the opposition. Still more to the point, the contrast with the Western single-party states is striking. Even if one leaves aside the Communist states, Hitler and Mussolini had to be overthrown by a world war, Franco ruled up until his death, and the Salazar regime outlived its founder until 1974. By contrast, Nkrumah's rule (and charisma) over Ghana lasted only six years (from 1960, when he disbanded all opposition, to 1966), and his allegedly monolithic if not totalitarian party collapsed overnight without a show of resistance. Mali's similar, allegedly strong, regime has displayed the same fragility.

In the face of these and other events, it is not far from the mark to say that black Africa has been, with few exceptions, the Cape Horn of political scientists at sea. The reading of the literature of the late fifties and early sixties almost invariably rings untrue. Writing in 1961 Wallerstein boldly asserted that "the one-party system is often a significant step toward the liberal state, not a first step away from it,"[27] and much of what was written at the time was in the same vein. This wishful forecasting remains credible only for Tanzania (another plausible candidate for the hegemonic-pragmatic pattern, but currently in search of an ideological base). It was too soon for Wallerstein to pick up Kenya, which became independent in 1963; but it so happens that Kenya would have made the best fit for his two-way communication model open to a liberal potential – though by 1965 Kenya's party network was already fading away and by 1969 the liberal experiment was over.

Apart from the surmises, the fact is that the alleged demiurge of nation building – the mass party – has either been short-lived or has not lived up to expectations. According to Clement Moore (in 1966), the following were, or had been, clear-cut mass party regimes: Ghana, Guinea, Ivory Coast, Mali, Nyasaland (Malawi), Senegal, Tanganyika (Tanzania), Tunisia.[28] But the Ivory Coast PDCI (*Parti Démocratique de la Côte d'Ivoire*) had already been allowed to atrophy in the early sixties; and much of the same has since become true for Senegal (led by Senghor) and Malawi. Since Ghana and subsequently Mali have both been coup struck, we are left with Guinea (the clearest African case of outright dictatorship), Tanzania, and Tunisia. Tunisia could also be dropped on the grounds that the Neo-Destour is – by African standards – an old party (created in 1934 and in charge, prior to independence, since 1954) and does not quite fit the argument. In any case, the list shrinks considerably. If the parties in question really qualify under the mass heading, most of them have indeed been flash mass parties. But do they qualify as *mass parties?* The point is that Moore's list simply and literally corresponds to the list of the extant single-party regimes. And here I would argue that as we pass from multipartism to unipartism, the mass party concept gains in deceptiveness and loses in significance. It gains in deceptiveness because it assumes a mass "support" for which a monopolistic system only affords unverifiable evidence. It loses much of its significance, since the concept is reduced to indicating in the main, the organizational spead of the single party. Hence the issue boils down to ascertaining how far and how deep the party replaces – throughout a territory – the preexisting local authorities and notabilities with a network of its own. If this is so, then it is both unnecessary and confusing to involve in the matter a complex concept resulting from, and required for, a mature stage of development of the competitive systems.

Thus far I have overviewed the transplants – ideology, totalitarian and mobilizational systems, mass parties – which are indeed Euromorphic transplants. Another approach is to invent, for the emerging parties of the new states, new categories. In principle, this is correct. In practice, it is no easy path to pursue. Since David Apter stands out as the most inventive, authoritative scholar in the field of modernization, his notions of, and distinction between, "parties of representation" and "parties of solidarity" can well illustrate the point. The parties of representation "act much as voluntary associations in Western countries" and define a pluralist "reconciliation system," whereas the parties of solidarity seek to eliminate the other parties and define a system of monopolistic amalgamation (e.g., Indonesia's USDEK, Guinea, Ghana, and Mali).[29] The distinction is finely drawn. But the party of solidarity is not, in and by itself, convincing. It is closely reminiscent of the "unified" party, the *parti unifié* (as contrasted with the *parti unique*) spoken of in the French literature[30] – except that Apter draws from a towering source, Durkheim, and his concept has far stronger assumptions. One reason that makes the party of solidarity unconvincing is that it rings far too gently. While the term dictatorship is generously distributed across Latin America, it becomes anathema for Africa, even though the difference between Nkrumah (or Touré) and a dictator is imperceptible. But my major difficulty bears on whether the two types can be meaningfully paired and compared. Whatever the shortcomings of a system based on parties of representation, we know that as long as pluralistic competition lasts, the parties operating such a system will remain what they pretend to be, namely, instruments of expression (as I prefer) and/or of representation. But how do we know that so-called parties of solidarity will, in the long or longer run, remain what they pretend to be? The difference between the two types is, then, that a plural system of parties of representation is based upon built-in mechanisms that provide for its maintenance (as a system of representation), whereas the so-called party of solidarity lacks built-in mechanisms for ensuring that the solidarity of today will remain the solidarity of tomorrow. In cybernetic terms, the former type denotes a "self-restraining" system characterized by feedbacks of self-correction, whereas the latter type points, if anything, to a "self-aggravating" system.

In all likelihood the creation of sets of new, ad hoc categories will take time, thoughtfulness, and more methodological awareness than is generally the case today. Meanwhile, a safe course is to focus on historical, as against calendar, synchronisms. That is to say that we should seek for adaptable categories in the initial and earlier stages of the Western evolution of parties. This approach may still appear a variety – albeit a nonflamboyant one – of Western-centricity. But if we regain perspective, we are not liable to be more Western inspired than the Third World polity builders themselves. After all, party symbols, techniques, and arrangements are – for the new states – adaptations of imports.

When political scientists began their landings on African soil, they had given little thought as to when, and under what conditions, political groups become parties, and subsequently parties of different kinds. Clearly, they were observing party infancy. Nonetheless, they seldom asked themselves whether the newborn child was vital and, in the longer run, needed. It is true that things, once invented, can be imitated in haste. But this is far truer of technology than of political artifacts. In any event, if one begins from party infancy, the prior questions in need of careful investigation are: What can be assimilated, to what extent, and how deep below the surface? Now not only were these issues not investigated, but most observers rushed headlong into assuming that parties – and especially the single party – had, or would have, primacy and centrality in African politics, and that their network was, or was destined to be, the structure of the societies they were bent upon reshaping.

To the historically alerted scholar the foregoing assumption is by no means intuitive. When discussing the rationale of the single party-state systems, I pointed out that these systems presuppose a politically awakened, and indeed a politicized, society.[31] Let it be added that politicization presupposes, in turn, the spread of literacy and that a below-subsistence economy of quasi-starvation combined with a cellular, mosaic-type society hinged on primary groups and primordial loyalties represent not only formidable obstacles, but also excellent reasons for *not* having recourse to party canalization and mobilization investments. The intuitive, or more intuitive, conjecture is, then, that in an African-type setting parties are "functional," and indeed necessary, for the power seizure and the initial power-building phase; but their primacy corresponds to, and arises from, the vacuum of the transition from terminal colonial rule to self-rule. Having fulfilled this role, and the more a "new class" establishes itself as the ruling class, the more we must ask ourselves whether a party arrangement is really needed and, at any rate, why it should have centrality and primacy.[32]

By now these questions can be addressed to an accumulating, if yet unconclusive, body of evidence. It is a fact that in a number of countries the organizational setup of the party-founding stage has either faded away (e.g., Algeria, Kenya, Ivory Coast) or has been suppressed by a coup (as, by 1974, in Mali, Nigeria, Somalia, Sudan, Uganda, Niger). In another group of countries the coup-enthroned rulers permit again single parties, though not the ones they have disbanded. Thus Congo Brazzaville, Congo Kinshasa (Zaire), Burundi, the Central African Republic, Sierra Leone, and Togo currently allow one party to exist. But such parties no longer have centrality; they are instrumental to an indirect military rule, and the three attempts of Nasser in Egypt at rebuilding party-like political organizations (the Liberation Rally in 1954, the National Union in 1959, and the Socialist Union in 1962–1963) are a telling indication of the marginality of the party under the aegis of military personnel.[33] We are left with Tanzania, Guinea, and Tunisia. In the first two countries the duration and effectiveness of their respective single-party arrangements hinge on their founding fathers. That is, it remains an open question whether Tanzania after or without Nyerere and Guinea after or without Touré will remain as they are. My surmise is that Tunisia's Neo-Destour is the only consolidated single party in Africa – by now a forty-year-old party – which is likely to endure after or without Bourguiba.[34]

While the body of evidence is still scant, it does suggest a sober reappraisal of the future prospects. With respect to unipartism my feeling is that in the sub-Saharan area the single party as an autonomous, organized network has lost, or is losing, much of its reason for being. The societies over which the new civilian or military rulers rule do not require a party channeling and chaining. Moreover, political activation and the maintenance of a party network nurtures, in the long run, counter-elites and unwelcome sub-group autonomy. This is equally to suggest that the difference between the one-party and the no-party state will be, in practice, far smaller than it results in theory. As regards, on the other hand, multipartism – loosely understood as no one-party enforcement – my guess is that wherever this pattern will be left to develop spontaneously, it will develop in a routine fashion, as an atomized constellation of parties of notables, of patronage, and of clientele, loosely connected by coalition arrangements. And here I rejoin my initial point about historical synchronisms and the related suggestion of putting to use the categories developed for the early or pre-mass stage of party development.

With due allowance to a number of diversities, thereby including the very great diversity among African countries themselves, it seems to me that the routinized performance of most African parties – single or not – comes already very close to the Mexican and South American *machismo* pattern. If so, it can well be perceived and rendered in terms of the familiar "clientele" or "political machine" models.[35] In this connection one should also recall that Africa belongs to the stage of party growth at which the distinction between party and faction – in the classic meaning of the term – remains very thin.[36] And there is more than a kernel of truth in Spiro's contention that the "development of politics" precedes the politics of development and that Africa still faces the problem of developing politics.[37]

8.3 Ad hoc categorizing

We may now revert to the problems of comparability – cross-area comparability, to be sure – raised by the fluid polities. As suggested earlier, a correct comparative treatment of the incipient states requires types and categories that are (i) residual and (ii) provisional. So far, most authors have attempted to deal with the emerging volatile polities by introducing new categories amid the other types – and this is why such categories are not residual. For the residual nature of a category is revealed by its placement: Instead of being interpolated *between*, it is placed *alongside*. However, a residual category is not, in and by itself, or necessarily, a provisional category.

The reason for insisting that the attributes and classes in use for the fluid polities should be not only residual but also provisional, is that short durations and beginnings have properties which cannot withstand long durations and routine. The initial steps of nation building correspond to a state of emergency and of exceptional performance that cannot be long-lived. Speaking in general, the properties of emergency situations differ from the properties of normal, or normalized situations. Marx buttressed his ideal of a stateless direct democracy on the evidence provided by the Paris Commune of 1870–1871. He evidently neglected to account for the fact that *intensity* and *duration* of direct participation are inversely related – the more intense, the briefer – and the subsequent experience of the so-called Communist democracies proved to what extent his mistake was momentous. Much of the current literature on African parties appears to suffer from a similar oversight. Thus a mass or a mobilizational *momentum* has been mistaken for a mass or mobilizational *nature* of parties. And while Marx had good reasons for overlooking the degradation of energy inherent in long durations, political scientists ought to know better.

How do we indicate a *pro tempore* validity, i.e., the provisional nature of a category? A first device is to have recourse to prefixes like *quasi* and *semi* – as the case may be. Thus a number of equivocations can be beheaded simply by speaking of "quasi-party *systems*,"[38] of "quasi-*mass* parties," and, to be sure, of "quasi-*parties*." Admittedly, it would only be pedantic to say semi or quasi all the time; but pedantry is necessary at a typological level of discussion whenever we tend to forget that the road of comparative politics is marked with pitfalls.

We have yet to confront a final difficulty, namely, how do we seize formlessness? The question relates to the fact that inchoate forms not only tend to defy classification, but tend to be misrendered by classifications. The very act of assigning something to a type imposes upon it a definiteness, a fixity, a form. Therefore, with respect to a state of flux, classes and types can be more deceptive than informative. There is no ready-made remedy for this difficulty. One way of counteracting the attribution of premature form to formlessness is, again, to have recourse to the quasi or semi devices. However, the major safeguard consists in selecting, for typological purposes, categories that are sufficiently loose and uncommitted.

The full set of requirements is, then, that the fluid polities are best apprehended by ad hoc categories that are (i) residual, (ii) provisional, and (iii) loose ended. These requirements afford, in turn, criteria for appraising the wealth of labels proposed, over the past 15 years, for the developing or modernizing areas. The point can be illustrated, once again, with respect to the 1960 Almond and Coleman symposium. I have previously objected to the "dominant non-authoritarian" type of Almond on account of its placement.[39] But once the category is given a residual placement, the wording is felicitous not only on account of its looseness but also because it is suggestive of what the consolidated outcome might be – a predominant-party system. (This is, incidentally, also the best way of implying that only a provisional validity is intended.) The merits of the label – dominant non-authoritarian – are further enhanced if it is implemented by its obverse, namely, "dominant authoritarian." The latter label recommends itself on the same grounds, i.e., looseness, and because it points to a possible future consolidation: the hegemonic-party arrangement. And this leads to an ulterior suggestion, namely, that by adding a third type, the "non-dominant" party pattern, we would come very close to having a full-fledged typological scheme that consistently abides by the same pace and has a nice fit for the developing areas.

If one can draw from Almond a tripartition among (i) *dominant authoritarian,* (ii) *dominant non-authoritarian,* and (iii) *non-dominant* party patterns, Coleman outlines in the same volume a very different tripartition, which is based on the degree of competitiveness and yields the following classes: (i) competitive, (ii) semi-competitive, and (iii) authoritarian.[40] While this framework is intended for the underdeveloped areas, there is nothing ad hoc about it; that is, it can well claim worldwide applicability. And this consideration immediately goes to explain its inadequacy. With respect to Africa, which represents the largest group of countries in the table of Coleman, the first class – competitive – obtains zero cases; the semi-competitive class obtains 23 cases; and the third class, 6 cases. The crucial category is, thus, "semi-competitive"; but the countries carried under this class provide no clue as to what the category might mean – except "other," neither competitive nor authoritarian. At any rate, Coleman was writing in 1959. By 1966 the dubious selectivity of his classification was patent, for at that time it was "close to general rule that elections [in Africa] have ceased to be competitions in any meaningful sense and have been turned into predetermined and glorified plebiscites."[41] Let it be added that while the meaning of the crucial category of Almond – dominant non-authoritarian – is intuitive and definable, this is not the case with semi-competition. And the requirement of looseness should be met by new categories, not by obfuscating the ones that have been sharpened.

I have paid little attention, thus far, to the multiparty pattern. Writing shortly before 1966 Rupert Emerson retained in his classification a "pluralistic competitive" type – a type that makes curious reading both with respect to his own statement that, except for Tanzania, elections had ceased almost everywhere to be competitive, and with respect to the only three examples he could find: Nigeria, Kenya, and the Congo.[42] At the time Nigeria was on the verge of downfall, the Congo had banned all parties and was a near synonym for chaos, and Kenya was, at best, and intermittently, dominant non-authoritarian.[43] Turning to the most accurate systematic counting to date, we find that in 26 black African countries (out of a total of 31) more than one party have legally existed, simultaneously or in succession, during the period from independence to 1969 – with Zaire (Congo Kinshasa) and Nigeria having had the highest number (respectively, 17 and 14) and Upper Volta the lowest (2 parties).[44] The question shifts to which of these countries has displayed, at some point in time, a plural party pattern. But this question is more readily answered by the turn of the wheel. By 1969 parties in the plural had been banned or reduced to monopartism in 23 of the preceding 26 countries – the exceptions being Zambia, Botswana, and Lesotho. In 1970 Lesotho was coup struck, and by 1973 Zambia was dominant authoritarian. Hence the only extant more-than-one party case remains Botswana, which belongs to the non-authoritarian dominant type.[45] Thus the more telling indication of the entire set is that only in 4 countries out of the 26 – Guinea, Ivory Coast, Liberia, Malawi (from 1966) – the dominant authoritarian party has been (up until 1974) one and the same. Aside from these 4 cases, almost all the other 26 countries have been in constant flux – so much so that their brief party and electoral history can hardly be followed without the help of a flow chart.[46]

To gain a better perspective on the matter let us first glance at the overall configuration, which is – in the wording of Apter – that "modernizing nations tend to have either a great many parties or a single dominant party that outlaws opposition or only nominally tolerates it."[47] This global configuration lends weight to the suspicion that multiparty patterns may well exist only because no part is strong enough to eliminate its counterparts, that is, simply on account of a situation of powerlessness, of piecemeal fragmentation of power. If so, this kind of multipartism is far removed from what Westerners mean by "competitive pluralism." Political pluralism, I have pointed out, enters history only when sustained by the belief in the *value* of pluralistic structures.[48] *Ex post* we are told that multipartism is unable to meet the problems of nation building and of fast economic growth. Fair enough. But the first, obvious explanation remains that in most of the Third World multipartism lacks roots in congruent beliefs. Had this preliminary fact been duly weighed, many forecasts would have been quite different.

Competitive pluralism is, then, a deceptive category. We are on much safer grounds, if we say, as suggested earlier, "non-dominant" pattern, thereby dismissing any necessary connection with competition and pluralism. Alternatively, one can speak of "plural party system."[49] In either case no assumption is made as to why a polyparty situation happens to exist. Whether this pattern has a pluralistic backbone, or whether it is boneless, is a matter left to investigation. It should be recalled, on the other hand, that the number of parties is not a very telling indicator prior to the structural consolidation of the party system. Therefore, the only significant distinction with respect to a fluid stage of polypartism is between (i) relatively few parties that actually counterweigh one another (i.e., none of which is dominant) and (ii) a pulverized pattern.[50]

Just as the polyparty pattern can be subdivided into few and pulverized, so too the uniparty pattern is amenable to specification. To begin with, it should be understood that unipartism does not necessarily have a tyrannical flavor unless the *ethos* and the virtues of political pluralism are appreciated. Furthermore, the one-party dominant pattern comes close to being a "natural monopoly" wherever an appalling scarcity of skills and of trained manpower implies that no loss of pluralistic potential is actually at stake. Under these premises, two subtypes can be meaningfully sorted out. One is the amalgam or even "package" kind of single party, i.e., the *parti unifié* that generally results from mergers and tends to be characterized by an aggregative outlook. The second is the typically coercive single party, the *parti unique* that has banned all the other parties, tends to be closed, and generally abides by exclusionary policies. To be sure, in a state of flux the amalgam single party can quickly become a coercive and exclusionary single party – and vice versa. For instance, Kenya switched to unipartism aggregatively in 1964 and forcefully in 1969, when Kenyatta confronted the secession of Odinga by subjecting him to arrest and banning his splinter party. But at any given point in time the analyst should be aware of how different the two patterns can be. It also makes a difference whether the single party results from an original unity, or from military takeover and subsequent reinstatement. But these elements can be entered as variables, and I would hesitate to proceed any further – in a magmatic context – on typological grounds.

To sum up, throughout this chapter my intent has been to account for the difference between flux and consolidation, between (relative) formlessness and crystallization. It follows from this difference that the fluid polities require an ad hoc framework. It does not follow, however, that we should end up with two non-convertible, watertight frameworks. Thus my suggestions lead toward two frameworks that are keyed into each other – as showed in Table 30. Clearly, I have paid great attention to the wording, for "to select – carelessly or purposely – terms that confuse or mislead . . . strikes me as unforgivable."[51] But the semantic preoccupation is aligned with a problem of convertibility, of how a fluid pattern can be related to a structured one.

The correspondences indicated in Table 30 are, to be sure, tentative, and hold only under the *ceteris paribus* assumption, i.e., that each inchoate pattern is allowed to develop "naturally" without interference from exogenous variables. The table is arranged in sequence, that is, according to two stages or phases; but its categories are also arranged in a descending order of abstraction, that is, descending from a highly abstract, all-embracing level to less abstract and more specific ones. Therefore, the various categories are linked and convertible into one another according to the rules of transformation along a ladder of abstraction.[52] It will also be noted that the "dominant non-authoritarian" type is placed under the combined jurisdiction of monopartism and polypartism. This is to signify that in a highly inchoate state of play we cannot draw the borders that are established at, and by, the structured stage.

I have spoken of an African labyrinth. Table 31 confirms that the image nears the truth. It also suggests, I believe, that the Ariadne's thread we have been searching for performs decently throughout the maze. The 39 listed countries fit and are fairly well distributed across the categories of the table, with very few uncertainties (Liberia, for understandable reasons, plus Rwanda and Tanzania). Other attributions may be questionable, if for no other reason than that the information is often scant and difficult to decipher. But the framework as such is not harmed by moving around the slices of each country's profile as long as it provides adequate and sufficient classes for the reclassification.

In spite of its complexity the table omits major details – especially the degree of coerciveness and of inanition – displayed by the party arrangements of the various countries.[53] Since these two variables vary considerably over time, there was no way of following them up. I have thus attempted to give some indication to this effect in the next-to-last column (pattern circa 1973–1974). The explanation of the patterns is

Table 30. *From fluidity to crystallization* (correspondences)

Initial stage	Monopartism				Polypartism		
	Dominant authoritarian			Dominant non-authoritarian		Non-dominant	Pulverized
		By force (Exclusionary)	By merger (Amalgamative)				
Structured stage	One-party dictatorship	Hegemonic party		Predominant-party system		Twopartism-multipartism	Atomized

as follows. (1) "Single-party state" indicates that a regime has officially declared itself such: It goes without saying, therefore, that all the other parties are banned. (2) "De facto single-party state" indicates that this pattern is not backed by an official doctrine; and this might imply a lower degree of coercion. (3) "Dominant authoritarian" indicates a looser and more varied pattern of monopartism. Hence it does not go by definition that other parties are outlawed; they might have dissolved themselves, or be atrophied, or might have never materialized de facto. Here I specify, therefore, whether the other parties are banned, or whether they have withered away more or less spontaneously; whereas the lack of specification suggests a relatively higher openness and flexibility. (4) "Indirect and/or dual military rule" indicates that the military has a decisive hand in the matter, even though the government is returned, at least in part, to civilian hands. Of course, indirect military rule is more suggestive of a disguise, whereas a dual military-civil system implies that the two components are both real. However, the distinction is far from clear-cut, and I have relied, more than on any other indicator, on whether the head of the executive was a military. (5) Finally, "dominant non-authoritarian" is clear enough, for it is the fluid equivalent of a predominant-party system.

A recent study of 31 black African countries having had a party start vindicates the appropriateness of the concept of institutionalization by declaring 17 of the polities in question to be "relatively institutionalized" and by producing the probatory evidence that 14 of those 17 party systems "are still in existence" (as of 1972). The 14 countries are (in a decreasing order of institutionalization): Liberia, Ivory Coast, Tanzania, Botswana, Gabon, Mauritania, Malawi, Rwanda, Senegal, Gambia, Niger, Zambia, Guinea, Cameroun. However, Table 31 suffices to question both the evidence and the inference. Actually, only 10 of the aforementioned 14 countries had remained, as of 1972, unchanged; for Gabon, Malawi, Senegal, and Cameroun underwent, during the sixties, violent or very substantial changes. If one adds to the 3 countries already terminated by coup before 1970 (Mali, Somalia, and CAR), Rwanda (seized in 1973), and Niger (seized in 1974), the updated finding is that 9 out of 17 purportedly institutionalized countries have either been "abnormally terminated" or abnormally transformed. It seems very dubious, therefore, that "the pattern strikingly supports the validity of the concept of institutionalization."[54] The feeble point of the demonstration clearly resides in the category "still in existence" – which verges on meaninglessness if a pattern is considered institutionalized regardless of whether a non-authoritarian polity is forcefully transformed into an authoritarian one.

261

Table 31. *Independent Africa: sequences of political patterns in 39 countries*

Countries by year of independence	Polyparty		Dominant non-authoritarian	Dominant Authoritarian		Military rule		Pattern circa 1973/1974	Size (inhabitants millions)
	Few	Many		By force	By merger	Direct	Indirect		
Ethiopia	—	—		—	—	1974–		No party; coup in 1974	25.000
Liberia, 1860	—	—	1860–(?)	—	1860–(?)	—		De facto single-party state	1.200
Egypt, 1921	—	—	1921–52	—	—		1952–	Dual civil-military, party atrophied	30.000
Libya, 1951	—	—	—	—	—	1969–		Military rule, no parties	1.700
Morocco, 1956	1956–63	—	1963–	—	—	—		Parties collateral (outside parliament)	13.000
Sudan, 1956	1956–58 1964–69	—	—	—	—	1958–64 1969–		Military rule, no parties	15.700
Ghana, 1957	—	—	1957–60/1970	1960–66	—	1966–70 1972–		Military rule	8.500
Guinea, 1958	—	—	—	—	1958–	—		Single-party state	4.000
Cameroun, 1960/1961	1961–66	—	—	—	1966–	—		Single-party state	5.700
C.A.R., 1960	—	—	1960–61	1962–66	—		1966–	Military rule with single party	1.500
Chad, 1960	—	—	1960–61	1962–	—	—		Dominant authoritarian (other parties banned); coup 1975	3.700
Congo Bra, 1960	1960–62	—	—	1963–68	—	1969	1970–	Indirect military with single party (other parties banned)	0.950

Countries by year of independence	Polyparty		Dominant nonauthoritarian	Dominant Authoritarian		Military rule		Pattern circa 1973/1974	Size (inhabitants millions)
	Few	Many		By force	By merger	Direct	Indirect		
Congo K., 1960	—	1960–65	—	1968–		1965	1967–	Indirect military with single party (other parties banned)	21.600
Dahomey, 1960	—	—	1960–63 —	1964–	—	—	—	Direct military rule with single party re-established	2.700
Gabon, 1960	1964–67	—	1960–64/1967	1968–		—	—	Single-party state	0.500
Ivory Coast, 1960	—	—	—		1960–	—	—	De facto single-party state	4.300
Madagascar, 1960	—	—	1960–72		—		1972–	Military rule	6.500
Mali, 1960	—	—	—	1960–	1960–68	1968–		Military rule, no party	5.000
Mauritania, 1960	—	—	—	1960–				Single-party state	1.200
Niger, 1960	—	—	—	1960–		1974–		Single-party state (no party in 1974)	4.000
Nigeria, 1960	—	1960–66	—			1966–		Military rule, no party	59.000
Senegal, 1960	—	—	1960–66		1967–			Single-party state	3.800
Somalia, 1960	—	1960–69	—			1969–		Military rule, no party	2.800
Togo, 1960	—	1960–67	—			1967–69	1969–	Military rule with single party	2.000
Tunisia, 1960	—	—	—		1960–			Dominant authoritarian	4.500
Upper Volta, 1960	—	—	1970–		1960–66	1966–70	1970–	Dual civil-military dominant nonauthoritarian party	5.400
Sierra Leone, 1961	1961–67	—	—		—	1967–68	1969–	Dual civil-military, single party	2.600

Table 31 (cont.)

Countries by year of independence	Polyparty		Dominant non-authoritarian	Dominant Authoritarian		Military rule		Pattern circa 1973/1974	Size (inhabitants millions)
	Few	Many		By force	By merger	Direct	Indirect		
Algeria, 1962	—	—	—		1962–65	1965–		Military rule	12.000
Burundi, 1962	—	—	1962–66	1966–			1966–	Dominant authoritarian (other parties banned)	3.500
Rwanda, 1962	—	—	1962–68		1969–(?)	1973–	—	No party	3.600
Uganda, 1962	1962–65	—	1965–69	1969–71		1971–	—	Direct military rule, no party	9.800
Zambia, 1962	1962–68	—	1968–72		—		—	Dominant authoritarian	4.300
Kenya, 1963	—		1963–69	1969–	—		—	Dominant authoritarian	11.000
Malawi, 1964	—		1964–66	1966–	—		—	Single-party state	4.500
Tanzania, 1964	—		1964–(?)		1964–(?)		—	De facto single party/ dominant authoritarian	13.000
Gambia, 1965	1965–66		1966–	—			—	Dominant non-authoritarian	0.350
Botswana, 1966	—	—	1966–72	—			—	Dominant non-authoritarian	0.600
Lesotho, 1966	1966–70		—	1970–			—	Dominant authoritarian (other parties banned)	1.000
Swaziland, 1968	—		1968–	—			—	Dominant non-authoritarian	0.400

Sources: Black Africa: A Comparative Handbook.; Keesing's Contemporary Archives; World Strength of the Communist Party Organizations.

8.4 The boomerang effect

Morrison and associates observe, in their conspectus, that the payoff of the intensive work on African political systems and parties is slight: ". . . the literature is rich in case study material, but lacking in theoretical content, conceptual sophistication and testable propositions."[55] From the angle of my analysis this somber assessment can be rephrased and broadened as follows: that by misaccommodating the fluid polities within the overall context of comparative politics the Third World specialists have undermined not only their own studies but also the discipline as a whole. There are, then, two sides to the coin, and the attention must now shift to the damage that a comparative mishandling of the formless states inflicts upon the formed states.

For a long time Western observers have traveled across the world assimilating the extraneous to the familiar, that is, using blinkers that blinded them to the exotic. This well-known, by now, Western-centric flaw amounts, logically, to a projective naïveté, to a gratuitous extrapolation. But this error is only aggravated and indeed doubled when the familiar is assimilated to, and perceived through, the exotic. There is no gain, but an ulterior loss, in replacing Western centricity with a quixotic Western eccentricity, that is, in carrying back home the flaw we had previously exported abroad. At this point we have the same error magnified in the reverse, i.e., a reversed extrapolation. Thus the discovery of the non-Western areas has been followed by a *boomerang effect* on the Western studies themselves.

To illustrate the mental processes resulting in a boomerang effect let us take the classic Western tripartition among executive, legislative, and judiciary. As we enter the developing areas, should this scheme be dropped or broadened? Almond drops the structural element and broadens the scheme in functional terms. The "output functions" thus resulting are rule enforcement, rule formation, and rule adjudication.[56] This is, in my opinion, a correct treatment. To be sure, the scheme of Almond remains to some extent Western bound and, also, a number of primitive or diffuse polities are not so differentiated. It does not follow that the functional categories in question should be stretched beyond the point at which Almond leaves them; and it follows even less that the comparative scholar should ignore the structural connotation, or properties, when he travels back West. Indeed, if in a Western setting the structural characteristics are not reentered under the functional categories, the whole trajectory results in a serious loss of specificity. "Pluralism" is an even better example. In the case of the tripartition of power the damage has been lessened by a correct beginning, that is, by the fact that Almond *transforms* the original categories; but in the case of pluralism we have simply *stretched* the category into an empty "universal," and indeed into a mere word whose conceptual substance is watered down to a point of meaninglessness. In its all-inclusive, global application pluralism compounds the everythingness of nothingness. And the net result is – in terms of the boomerang effect – that Western societies have lost an important focus for the understanding of their own nature.

But let us take the very notion of party. In his influential study of Africa Hodgkin makes the point that we should "consider as 'parties' all political organizations which regard themselves as parties and which are generally so regarded."[57] So far so good – I mean "party" can well be left undefined and, therefore, indefinite, in a fluid context, i.e., when we actually observe quasi-parties. However, this argument holds only under this premise – whereas it is often extended as follows: Since some parties, somewhere, must be left undefined, the term should never be defined, for any definition would exclude from consideration the parties that are so-called. By the dint of this logic a mere word replaces the "minimal definition,"[58] and the parties that are specialized agencies are assimilated to, and obfuscated by, the parties that are diffuse and polyfunctional. And the more this logic is generalized, the more we feed back shapelessness where structural differentiation exists, formlessness where the forms matter, and statelessness where states are both gigantic and pervasive.

All in all, the boomerang effect mightily concurs – in association with other factors – in the conceptual fuzziness and sloppiness of the discipline. It equally contributes to the current disparagement of classifications and typologies. Finally, and foremost, the boomerang effect is particularly insidious in the context of argumentation, where it supports an abusive witnessing – as when Tanzania testifies to the possibility, if not to the actual existence, of a one-party democracy, or when the placement of the dominant non-authoritarian type between unipartism and twopartism conveys the idea that monopoly and pluralism are convertible into one another.[59] The point is, here, that any inference from the indefinite to the definite, from the fluid to the formed polities, amounts to an *error of reversed extrapolation* and cannot sustain the burden of proof.

In résumé, and to conclude, the polities lacking structural differentiation and consolidation cannot be incorporated under the Western categories, nor can they provide categories for the West. This does not imply that the volatile polities defy investigation, and even less that they are of minor interest. Quite to the contrary, the political scientist has more to learn from a polity in the making than from a ready-made one. But no such progress is in the offing if we give premature shape to chaos (by extrapolating from Western models), feed back shapelessness where shape already exists (by means of reversed extrapolations), or combine both errors.

1 Modern political systems are defined, following Coleman, as the systems in which "governmental and political functions are performed by specific structures" (Almond and Coleman, *The Politics of the Developing Areas*, op. cit., p. 559) or, more precisely, as having a "relatively high degree of differentiation, explicitness and functional distinctiveness of their political and governmental structures" (p. 532).

2 During the period 1951–1973 I have counted 26 successful coups in Latin America. This goes to explain why – from a party system standpoint – I do not treat Latin America as an area and why, as a rule, the single Latin American countries are entered to illustrate particular points rather than in a self-contained fashion (Chile and Mexico being the outstanding exceptions). A valuable collective volume is Martin C. Needler, ed., *Political Systems of Latin America*, 2nd rev. ed., Van Nostrand, 1970. McDonald, *Party Systems and Elections in Latin America*, op. cit., and *Guide to the Political Parties of South America*, by various authors, Penguin Books, 1973, also cover the whole area. Much of the literature on Latin American countries is found in the studies on military regimes. Besides the first systematic comparative analysis of S. E. Finer, *The Man on Horseback: The Role of the Military in Politics*, Pall Mall, 1962, see, more specifically, John J. Johnson, *The Military and Society in Latin America*, Stanford University Press, 1964, and, for the more recent literature, the review article by Abraham F. Lowenthal, "Armies and Politics in Latin America," *WP*, October 1974.

3 As operationalized, e.g., by Janda, *A Conceptual Framework for the Comparative Analysis of Political Parties*, op. cit., pp. 87–89.

3 "Political Development and Political Decay," *WP*, April 1965, pp. 386–430, *passim*. But now see Huntington, *Political Order in Changing Societies*, op. cit., pp. 12–23, where institutionalization is spelled out according to four criteria: (1) adaptability-rigidity, (ii) complexity-simplicity, (iii) autonomy-subordination, (iv) coherence-disunity. It turns out that, at its highest level, institutionalization corresponds to the ideal organization, i.e., to the organization that displays high functional adaptability in spite of being highly complex, autonomous, unified, and coherent. I find no necessary or even likely congruence between the first and the other three properties. The quotation is from p. 13.

5 With respect to party systems, this viscosity, or "freezing," is underlined by Lipset and Rokkan in their Introduction to *Party Systems and Voter Alignments*, op. cit., esp. p. 50; and it is well documented by the survey of Richard Rose and Derek Urwin, "Persistence and Change in Western Party Systems Since 1945," *PS*, September 1970, esp. pp. 306–307 and Table 9.

6 The mass party concept will be treated in vol. II, ch. 12. A pre-

liminary outline is in my "Political Development and Political Engineering," *Public Policy*, 1968, esp. pp. 281, 292–295.

7 *The Politics of the Developing Areas*, cit., p. 40. Almond indicates that the classification makes reference to the area analyses covered in the book, but his subsequent exemplification confirms that Europe is covered as well and that the typology is meant to provide an overall framework.

8 Ibid., p. 41.

9 Coleman and Rosberg, eds., op. cit. The volume appeared in 1964, that is, four years after *The Politics of the Developing Areas*.

10 Coleman and Rosberg, ibid., esp. pp. 4–6.

11 See esp. Hodgkin, *African Political Parties – An Introductory Guide*, op. cit.; Ruth Schachter Morgenthau, *Political Parties in French Speaking West Africa*, Clarendon Press, 1964, pp. 330–358; and Clement H. Moore, "Mass Party Regimes in Africa," in Herbert J. Spiro, ed., *Africa: The Primacy of Politics*, Random House, 1966. Also Morris Janowitz, *The Military in the Political Development of New Nations*, University of Chicago Press, 1964, speaks of "authoritarian mass-parties"; and, more recently, Crawford Young, "Political Systems Development," in John N. Paden and Edward Soja, eds., *The African Experience*, Northwestern University Press, 1970, has both the mass party and the "renewed mass party."

12 E.g., Arthur Lewis, in an otherwise most sensible little book, *Politics in West Africa*, Allen & Unwin, 1965, asserts: "By a totalitarian party we mean . . . a party which claims to be the supreme instrument of society. In Ghana, Guinea and Mali the party is elevated above all institutions . . ." (p. 56).

13 See esp. David E. Apter, *The Politics of Modernization*, University of Chicago Press, 1965, ch. 10.

14 This is, at least, my reading of Paul E. Sigmund, ed., *The Ideologies of the Developing Nations*, Praeger, 1963. This is also the line of criticism of Finer, *Comparative Government*, op. cit., pp. 509–510; and of Henry Bienen, "One-Party Systems in Africa," in Huntington and Moore, *Authoritarian Politics in Modern Society*, op. cit., pp. 103–104.

15 While "new states" is broader than "African new states," generalizations are permissible as long as it is understood that the Communist East Asian regimes, such as North Korea and North Vietnam, do not enter my argument, i.e., do not qualify as formless or embryonic states. For the broader context see the bibliographical overview of David E. Apter, Charles Andran, "Comparative Government: Developing New Nations," in Marian D. Irish, ed., *Political Science: The Advance of the Discipline*, Prentice-Hall, 1968.

16 See J. P. Nettl, "The State as a Conceptual Variable," *WP*, July 1968, esp. pp. 189–191. The institutional fragility, in Africa, of both party and state is well underpinned by Aristide Zolberg, *Creating Political Order; The Party Systems in West Africa*, Rand McNally, 1966.

17 See, among others, the classic work of Frederick Meinecke, *Weltburgentum und National Staat*, 6th ed., Oldenbourg Verlag, 1922.

18 See, in general, Clifford Geertz, ed., *Old Societies and New States*, Free Press, 1963, which contains, *inter alia*, a chapter of Edward Shils, "On the Comparative Study of the New Nations," which is

very relevant to our concerns. See also, for its anthropological and sociological approach, M. Fortes and E. Evans-Pritchard, eds., *African Political Systems*, Oxford University Press, 1940 (1970).

19 *The Organizational Weapon*, Free Press, 1960.

20 The notion of mobilization will be discussed in detail in vol. II.

21 See, in general, Hodgkin, *African Political Parties*, op. cit.; G. M. Carter, ed., *African One-Party States*, op. cit.; Coleman and Rosberg, eds., *Political Parties and National Integration in Tropical Africa*, op. cit.; G. M. Carter, ed., *National Unity and Regionalism in Eight African States*, Cornell University Press, 1966; A. Mahiou, *L'Avènement du Parti Unique en Afrique Noire*, Colin, 1968; Paden and Soja, eds., *The African Experience*, op. cit.; Henry L. Bretton, *Power and Politics in Africa*, Aldine, 1973; Anna M. Gentili, *Elites e Regimi Politici in Africa Occidentale*, Il Mulino, 1974. Apart from the single nation surveys contained in the collective volumes, the pace-setting monographic studies have been Apter, *The Gold Coast in Transition*, Princeton University Press, 1955, followed by *Ghana in Transition*, Atheneum, 1963; and A. R. Zolberg, *One-Party Government in the Ivory Coast*, Princeton University Press, 1964. The best and most recent data source (up until 1971) is Donald G. Morrison et al., *Black Africa – A Comparative Handbook*, Free Press, 1972.

22 On Ghana, after Apter, *Ghana in Transition*, cit., see H. L. Bretton, *The Rise and Fall of Kwame Nkruma*, Pall Mall, 1966; on Guinea, Bernard Ameillon, *La Guinée, Bilan d'une Indépendance*, Maspero, 1964; and, on Mali, Frank G. Snyder, *One-Party Government in Mali: Transition Towards Control*, Yale University Press, 1965.

23 On Tanzania see Henry Bienen, *Tanzania: Party Transformation and Economic Development*, Princeton University Press, 1967; William Tordoff, "Tanzania: Democracy and the One-Party State," *GO*, July–October 1967, pp. 599–614; and *supra*, 2.3, and ch. 2, n. 27. The 1965 Tanzanian elections are described in Lionel Cliffe, ed., *One Party Democracy*, East African Publishing House, 1967.

24 For some of the details see A. Zolberg, "Military Intervention in the New States of Tropical Africa," in Henry Bienen, ed., *The Military Intervenes: Case Studies in Political Change*, Russel Sage Foundation, 1968; W. F. Gutteridge, *The Military in African Politics*, Methuen, 1969; and Anna M. Gentili, "I Militari nell'Africa Sub-Sahariana," *RIS*, IV, 1971, pp. 635–675.

25 See in Finer, *Comparative Government*, cit., p. 528, Table 21. However, R. E. McKown and R. E. Kauffman, "Party System as a Comparative Analytic Concept in African Politics," *CP*, October 1973, reverse the point: "It has been argued that the levels of instability would be higher in one-party states than in multiparty states, but this was not confirmed" (p. 68).

26 Janowitz, *The Military in the Political Development of New Nations*, cit., 1964, p. 29.

27 Immanuel Wallerstein, *Africa, The Politics of Independence*, Vintage Books, 1961, p. 163. In 1966, however, Wallerstein noted in a very different mood that "the curious phenomenon was not the emergence of a one-party system. It was rather its rapid loss of meaning" – thereby concluding that the trend had been toward "inanition" ("The Decline of the Party in Single-Party African

States," in LaPalombara and Weiner, *Political Parties and Political Development*, cit., pp. 207, 208).

28 In Spiro, ed., *Africa: The Primacy of Politics*, op. cit., p. 88.

29 *The Politics of Modernization*, op. cit., pp. 197 ff., esp. pp. 206–216.

30 The distinction was originally proposed by a Mali politician, Madeira Keita (see in Sigmund, *The Ideologies of the Developing Nations*, op. cit., pp. 175–176), with reference to Ghana and Mali, whose *partis unifiés* were assumed to result from voluntary mergers.

31 *Supra*, 2.1 and 2.2.

32 That the attainment of independence imperiled the reason for being of African parties did not escape, in truth, the most perceptive authors. See, e.g., Coleman and Rosberg, *Political Parties and National Integration in Tropical Africa*, cit., pp. 672 ff.; and esp. William J. Folz, "Building the Newest Nations: Short-Run Strategies and Long-Run Problems," in K. W. Deutsch and Folz, eds., *Nation Building*, Atherton Press, 1963.

33 It is also worth pointing out that the pre-coup *Wafd* party was – between 1921 and 1952 – the closest forerunner of what was to be subsequently called the African-type mass party. On the Nasser attempts, see Leonard Binder, "Political Recruitment and Participation in Egypt," in LaPalombara and Weiner, *Political Parties and Political Development*, op. cit., ch. 8.

34 On Tunisia see Clement H. Moore, *Tunisia Since Independence: The Dynamics of One-Party Government*, University of California Press, 1965; and esp. his chapter, "Tunisia: The Prospects for Institutionalization," in *Authoritarian Politics in Modern Society*, cit.

35 See Zolberg, *Creating Political Order: The Party System in West Africa*, op cit., pp. 159–161, and René Lemarchand, "Political Clientelism and Ethnicism in Tropical Africa: Competing Solidarities in Nation-Building," *APSR*, March 1972, pp. 68–71. A related suggestion is to revisit Ostrogorski's description of how the caucus-type party came about in the second half of the nineteenth century. James Scott, "Corruption, Machine Politics and Political Change," loc. cit., is also very much to the point. On the clientele focus in general see *supra*, ch. 4, n. 12.

36 *Supra*, 1.1. The implication is, here, that the factional subunits may well be the real units. See also *supra*, 4.3.

37 *Africa: The Primacy of Politics*, op. cit., ch. 5 ("The Primacy of Political Development"), *passim* and p. 153. Along this suggestion see Colin Leys, *Politicians and Policies*, East African Publishing House, 1967.

38 The label was coined by Macpherson, *Democracy in Alberta: The Theory and Practice of a Quasi-Party System*, op. cit., ch. 8; but it appears more appropriate for the developing areas.

39 See n. 7, above, and 8.1.

40 See *The Politics of the Developing Areas*, op. cit., p. 534, Table 1. "Democratic competitive" and "semi-competitive" are also retained, in 1964, by Janowitz (below, n. 42).

41 Rupert Emerson, "Parties and National Integration in Africa," in LaPalombara and Weiner, *Political Parties and Political Development*, cit., p. 269. See, in general, W. J. M. Mackenzie and

Kenneth Robinson, eds., *Five Elections in Africa*, Oxford University Press, 1960.

42 Loc. cit., pp. 269, 287–293. Janowitz, *The Military in the Political Development of the New States*, op. cit., has a "democratic competitive" class, which is no better (it covered, e.g., Tanzania).

43 In Nigeria all parties have been suspended since 1966, a civil war with Biafra raged from 1967 to 1970, and the country remains, to date, under direct military rule. Congo (Kinshasa) had been plagued by the Tshombe-Katanga secession from 1960–1963, had a coup in 1965, and was soon to enter the 1967 civil war. Kenya is thus Emerson's only plausible case. But its pluralistic competition means only that an opposition can without risking its life speak up against Kenyatta and the dominant KANU (Kenya National African Union) party, which was a de facto single party in 1965 and which maintained its monopoly by force in 1969. On Nigeria see Richard L. Sklar, C. S. Whitaker, "Nigeria," in Carter, *National Unity and Regionalism in Eight African States*, op. cit.; Walter Schwartz, *Nigeria*, Praeger, 1968; Robert Melson and Howard Wolpe, eds., *Nigeria: Modernization and the Politics of Communalism*, Michigan State University Press, 1971. On Zaire and the Congolese "competitive pluralism" see Daniel Biebuyck and Mary Douglas, *Congo Tribes and Parties*, London, Royal Anthropological Institute, 1961; Daniel J. Crowley, "Politics and Tribalism in the Katanga," *WPQ*, March 1963; and Crawford Young, *Politics in the Congo*, Princeton University Press, 1965. On Kenya see Cherry Gertzel, *The Politics of Independent Kenya 1963–68*, Heinemann, 1970; and Carl Rosberg, *Kenya*, Cornell University Press, forthcoming.

44 Morrison et al., *Black Africa*, op. cit., p. 99, Table 8.2. The count includes "all political parties that were legal . . . in this period, whether or not they resulted from mergers or splits." With Ethiopia, partyless, the table covers 32 countries.

45 Note that Botswana and Lesotho became independent only in 1966 and that they are both very small countries with, respectively, about 500,000 and 700,000 inhabitants.

46 Such flow charts are actually provided by the excellent "country profiles" in Morrison et al., *Black Africa*, cit., Part 2. Here one finds also the country-by-country bibliography.

47 Apter, *The Politics of Modernization*, op. cit., p. 194.

48 *Supra*, 1.2.

49 This is the label of Huntington and Moore in *Authoritarian Politics in Modern Society*, cit., p. 517.

50 In Indonesia, e.g., more than 40 political groups (parties) ran candidates in the 1955 elections; and in the Congo there were, in 1960, an estimated 100 parties.

51 J. David Singer, *A General Systems Taxonomy for Political Science*, General Learning Press, 1971, p. 6.

52 These rules derive from the inverse relationship between the denotation and connotation of concepts, and are illustrated in Sartori, "Concept Misformation in Comparative Politics," *ASPR*, 1970, cit.

53 Variables such as moderately to highly centralized, moderately to low democratic, high/low freedom of opposition, can also be usefully entered for ulterior underpinning. See Irma Adelman and

Cynthia T. Morris, *Society, Politics and Economic Development,* Johns Hopkins Press, 1967.

54 Mary B. Welfling, *Political Institutionalization: Comparative Analyses of African Party Systems,* Sage, 1973, p. 38, and Table 5 on p. 33. While I cannot follow the author on her testing ground, the book is introduced by a valuable discussion of the concept of institutionalization (pp. 5–18).

55 *Black Africa,* cit., p. 95.

56 *The Politics of the Developing Areas,* cit., p. 17.

57 *African Political Parties,* op. cit., pp. 15–16.

58 *Supra,* 3.2.

59 *Supra,* respectively 2.3 and 8.1. This latter point is developed *infra,* 9.1.

9

The overall framework

9.1 System change, continuum, and discontinuities

It has become fashionable to speak of continua, and we are thus apt to speak of a *continuum* of party systems. The underlying assumption is that typological constructs ignore the fluidity of reality and that the interlocking of the real world can be recaptured by postulating an endless stream of continuity. The claim is warranted, but its fulfillment demands fine discretion.

In the first place, the concept of continuum cannot remain, in a natural language, exactly what it is in mathematical language. In particular, it cannot be assumed – in the social science usage of the concept – that continua exclude discontinuity by definition. In the second place, we do not seem to be clearheaded as to how a classification relates to a continuum. When we speak of a continuum of party systems, of political systems, of regimes, and the like, we are using a shorthand expression. In effect we are confronted with two distinct logical operations: first, the determination of the polar concepts that define the continuum or, better, the dimension along which we posit a continuum (e.g., consensus–coercion, liberty–oppression, expression–repression, inclusion–exclusion) and, second, the placement of the classes, or types, at different points of the continuum so defined. Strictly speaking, it is incorrect to postulate a "party continuum"; we can only postulate a "conceptual continuum" along which party systems can be approximately located. The continuum is not between party systems, but between polar characteristics; and the kind of continuity or discontinuity that exists in fact among the various party systems is an empirical question that can only be settled empirically.

A third remark is in order. The reason that we are apt to underscore discontinuity is that the idea of continuum appeals to a unidirectional evolutionary optimism. More often than not, the idea that party systems are contiguous, and thereby *convertible* all along the line, goes to suggest that there is a "natural" course of political development that leads – whenever it is not unnaturally deviated – to freedom, party pluralism, and democracy. Setbacks do occur, but they are only setbacks. The so-called liberalization of Communist regimes, together with the instances of Turkey and Mexico, are highly significant cases that uphold the continuum approach; while the relapses into fascism, authoritarianism, and praetorianism, or the advent of Communist regimes, are seldom explained on the grounds that a continuum postulates a two-way direction of change. As Huntington well shows, we have produced a one-sided theory of development pledged to modernization and forgetful of decay.[1] The popularity of the continuum metaphor appears to be – no matter how unwittingly – another manifestation of the same unilinear evolutionism: It breeds "continuists" who breed, in turn, the idea that liberty follows – as a natural *continuation* – from the loosening of the ties of oppression.

The foregoing indicates that the concept of continuum stands on, and falls between, two stools: a methodological concern, and a substantive issue. The methodological concern – to which we shall revert – bears on how we can seize the interlocking of the real world and, proceeding along this path, transform the discontinuities of classifications into a continuity of degrees – if not into the mathematical convenience of "continuity." The substantive issue – on which I now propose to dwell – bears on system change. The question is: How does a concrete political system *pass* into another? No doubt, system change can be approached from other vantage points. Nonetheless, if it is true that our major theoretical problem is how a continuous treatment of the data fits the real world, then it is worthwhile to explore the empirical issue under the searchlight of our methodological preoccupations.

From this angle system change can be said to occur in two major ways: (i) continuously, i.e., by inner development, endogenous transformation, and spontaneous transition and (ii) discontinuously, i.e., via system breakdown. Accordingly, the issue boils down to this question: Granted that political systems undergo "continuous transitions," are we necessarily confronted, at some point, with "breaks of continuity"? This is a fairly simple and straightforward question – provided that breakdown, and more exactly *polity breakdown*, is adequately pinpointed.

While the concept of breakdown evokes the ideas of fundamental and abrupt change, and/or of violence and revolution, there is no necessary coincidence between these terms. For instance, and in the first place, constitutional change abiding by the constitutional rules of change is not a breakdown. Thus England since the early eighteenth century, the United States since the Philadelphia convention, Sweden since 1809, and the Netherlands since 1848 have undergone fundamental and deep changes but have not incurred in breakdowns: They are continuous polities. Taking the problem from the other end, a coup or a palace revolt that changes the personnel in power but leaves unchanged the structures of authority cannot be qualified as a breakdown, for the polity remains exactly as it is. For instance, the Persian, Roman, Byzantine, and Ottoman empires have lasted over the centuries as continuous polities in spite of hundreds of praetorian seizures and assassinations of their rulers. The USSR is an enduring polity since 1918, or 1920, regardless of whether Stalin's death was natural and even though the course of his succession was decided by force and conspiracy. And a military dictatorship remains a military dictatorship whether or not a colonel overthrows another colonel. On the other hand, whenever basic changes do occur in the authority structures of a polity beyond and outside its inner mechanisms of change, then we do have a system breakdown. Thus we have a breakdown when a dictatorship is installed or removed; when free elections are impeded or reinstated; when subservient judges replace, or are replaced by, an independent judiciary; when parties in the plural are permitted or banned.

The foregoing illustration goes to suggest (i) that fundamental change may well occur continuously, that is, according to the constitutional rules and procedures of system transformation; (ii) that the abruptness of a change is not a reliable criterion; and (iii) that disruptive or violent change need not entail the breakdown of a polity.[2] This adds up to suggesting that the breakdown of a political system is jointly identified by the following two criteria: first, whenever a polity passes into another not by virtue of its own rules of transformation, but by repudiating and infringing such rules; and, second, whenever an ousting from, or a seizure of, power does not retain but alters the preexisting structures of authority, that is, the ways and means of rule making, rule application, and rule adjudication. To be sure, a rule-breaking change that changes the rules of change and that also changes the structure of authority generally results, in actual fact, from a revolutionary seizure of power. However, "revolution" is by now a very broad and slippery term. If entered in the definition of breakdown, we must enter first a number of fine distinctions, e.g., between coup and revolution, between revolutionary pressure and actual revolution, and so forth. But these complexities are avoided if the notion of breakdown is defined – as I propose – independently from causal factors, that is, by a specific modality and scope of change.

If breakdown, and thereby break of continuity, are defined, then "continuous transition" is easy to define. The transitions from one type of political system to another type are continuous, spontaneous, or endogenous whenever they can be imputed to the working principles, or to the rules of the game, inherent in that system. In short, continuous change amounts to self-change, to transformations resulting from, and permitted by, the inner constituent mechanisms of each political structure.

We may now revert to the so-called continuum of party systems. The question whether this continuum is "continuous" is, ultimately, a question of fact. However, no question is *only* of fact. When we ask, "Is this a breakdown or not?" the issue clearly hinges on the cutting points with respect to which it is raised. For instance, if all political systems are declared "mixed," no classification follows and a continuity is assumed by definition. And the case is not very different if we are satisfied with the tripartition among one-, two-, and multiparty systems. Since the one-party class actually includes, in the current usage, one-plus-more parties, the issue is beheaded by the poverty of the classification, i.e., by misclassification. On the other hand, if a more analytic classification divides what was hitherto undivided, then we are immediately alerted to the fact that along our continuum there is a point at which the joints appear disjointed. As we know, the critical juncture lies between the hegemonic systems, on the one hand, and the predominant systems, on the other. Hence the pertinent question is: Can these two systems be converted into one another without breakdown, i.e., continuously, via inner transformation? And this is the question of fact. At this juncture the reply lies in the evidence.

As a matter of historical record, the case is unambiguous: The evidence crushingly points to a discontinuity. I cannot think of a single passage from a competitive to a noncompetitive polity that has occurred without violating the constitutional order – to wit, the conventions of the living constitution – usually under the impact of actual or potential revolutionary violence, coups, and military insurgence. Some of these transitions apparently do not violate the constitutional order in that the violation occurs *after,* that is, after a legal or quasi-legal ascent to power. This only means that the alteration of the structures of authority need not coincide, chronologically, with the ascent to power. Hitler suspended the constitution shortly after his nomination. Mussolini proceeded, instead, more gradually; but no free elections were held in Italy under his rule after 1924. The Communist takeover of Czechoslovakia in 1948 followed a similar course in that it was preceded by a legal ascent to power of Gottwald.

If the passage from a competitive to a noncompetitive structure is, without exception, discontinuous, the rule appears less stringent in the other direction, that is, passing from a noncompetitive to a competitive polity. The issue depends on which evidence is deemed pertinent. For instance the Latin American *golpe* pattern is not meaningful – think of Argentina – as long as the military seizure is conceived as a "provisional interruption" that remains open to the reestablishment of the "suspended" constitution.[3] The case of a military interregnum is also very different in that the military can relinquish the civilian power it has seized without losing its own power. The real problem arises, instead, when a hitherto all-powerful political elite finds itself not only deprived of all power but exposed to the retaliation of the new incumbents.

The military case aside, and if one also discards – as one should – the false witnessing drawn from the fluid polities, so far the literature contains only two instances of a somewhat endogenous development from monocentrism to pluralism: Mexico and Turkey. But Mexico cannot prove the point because it has not crossed the boundary: It is a hegemonic party polity.[4] We are left to discuss, therefore, whether the passage of Turkey to democracy in 1945–1946 was spontaneous enough to warrant the thesis that unipartism can transform itself (i) *by itself* and (ii) *successfully*, into a competitive party system.

The modernizing history of Turkey begins in the aftermath of World War I, with Kemal Atatürk proclaiming, in 1923, the republic and establishing the Republican People's Party (RPP). The first remarkable feat of Atatürk was to reestablish civilian rule immediately. That is, the RPP was not, and has never been, under military tutelage. Atatürk also made two attempts at establishing party pluralism by allowing an opposition party to exist: In 1924, and especially in 1930. Both were abortive. The Republican Progressive party, born in 1924, was dissolved in 1925. The Free party, born in August 1930 with the very encouragement of Atatürk, dissolved itself by November 1930 under the charge of harboring too many reactionary members. Atatürk died in 1938, and it was his successor, Inönü, who presided over the advent of a multiparty regime in 1945. Was the transition "spontaneous"? One need not read what was in the mind of Inönü to reply. The facts of the matter are that in 1945, in the face of Stalin's sweep across Europe and of the longstanding Russian drive toward the Dardanelli Straits, Turkey had little choice: Its degree of international autonomy was dangerously low. Whatever Inönü had in mind, his switch to a standard-type democracy was a vital requirement for a small country that desperately needed the protection of the Western democracies. Presumably, Inönü did believe that party competition and pluralism were good things. But the much stronger presumption is that – when the RPP was ousted, after 27 years of uninterrupted office, by the unexpected landslide victory of Bayar's and Menderes' Democratic party – Inönü might well have followed Atatürk in promptly reverting to unipartism, had it not been for the external pressure and the economic, let alone the political, aid that was involved. He could neither risk nor afford to do so. This is not to question – let it be repeated – the democratic goals of the Republican People's party; it is only to explain why Turkey is not a truly "convincing" example of spontaneous transformation.[5] And the subsequent events eloquently testify to the difficulty of what now appears, in retrospect, a semi-continuous transition. After more than a quarter-century Turkey has yet to achieve a convincing democratic viability.

The first striking thing in the competitive history of Turkey is the magnitude of its electoral swings – as shown in Table 32. The RPP, which begins with an 85-percent victory, loses 70 percent of its seats four years later and drops to such a low in 1954 as to make its comeback in 1957 quite surprising. After the 1960 revolution (actually a military coup) the RPP obtains – under optimal conditions – only a small relative majority and is again severely outdistanced in the subsequent elections until its again surprising victory in 1973. These oscillations are magnified by the fact that the figures are in seats[6] and can be explained, in part, by the changes in the electoral system: multimember constituencies with the winning list taking all until the 1957 elections; proportional representation in 1961 and 1965, amended so as to favor the major parties for the 1969 election. The electoral system variable notwithstanding, by its electoral verdicts Turkey would have been (between 1950 and 1973) a clear case of a predominant-party system[7] in which the RPP had only one "aided" comeback – except that the military has not allowed the system to perform "naturally," i.e., according to its own working principles.

In 1960 a military coup eliminated Menderes (who was sentenced to death and hanged) and banned the Democratic party.[8] A new constitution was drafted and the second republic was returned, after a military interregnum of 18 months, to civilian rule. However, at the 1961 elections the Democratic party had already found a successor – in terms of a same rural-based, traditionalistic electoral appeal – in the Justice party. Thus the RPP failed to win in 1961 an absolute majority, and the military again took the matter into its hands: The party leaders were summoned to a meeting with the chiefs of staff and had to agree to elect General Gürsel president and to form an all-party and above-party government of national union. True enough, Demirel and the Justice party have been subsequently permitted to govern – but not for long and seldom unhampered. In 1971 Demirel was forced to resign and was not permitted to resume office for some four years. A marshal law, imposed by the military, lasted 29 months, until September 1973. And in the 1973 election of the president of the republic the military vetoed the Justice party candidate, tried to impose its own candidate, and after a prolonged tug of war a third man was elected.

While we may disagree as to whether Turkey qualifies as a case of "spontaneous" transition from monopoly to competition, the sure thing is that Turkey is still "in transition." In particular, if the passage to democracy occurred without breakdown in 1945, it did end in breakdown in 1960. Since then Turkey has entered, in the main, a dual military-civilian course. Remaining true to the Atatürk tradition the

Table 32. *Turkey: percentages and seats in National Assembly, 1946–1973*

Parties	First Republic				1960 Coup	Second Republic			
	1946	1950	1954	1957		1961	1965	1969	1973
Republican People's Party (Inönü)	84.9 (395)	14.2 (69)	5.7 (31)	28.7 (173)		38.4 (173)	29.8 (134)	31.8 (143)	41.1 (185)
Democratic Party (Bayar, Menderes) banded in 1960	13.8 (64)	83.8 (408)	93.0 (503)	69.9 (421)		—			
Justice Party (Demirel) founded in 1961	—	—	—	—		35.1 (158)	53.3 (240)	56.2 (256)	29.6 (149)
Other	1.3 (6)	2.0 (10)	1.3 (7)	1.4 (8)		26.5 (119)	16.9 (76)	12.3 (51)	29.3 (116)
Total no. of seats	465	487	541	602		450	450	450	450

military permits civilian rule but keeps it under tutelage, with intermittent, direct interventions whenever the party "logic" departs from the "spirit" of the Atatürk revolution. The paradox is that by establishing the single party Atatürk kept the military out of politics, whereas the advent of competitive politics has brought about a system of military guardianship. Given the remarkable leadership of Atatürk, given an even more remarkable tradition of statehood that goes as far back as the thirteenth century, and given that "the circle of rulers and of politically active citizens has broadened gradually and steadily"[9] – given all these favorable conditions, the case of Turkey does deserve the attention it receives, but for a different and better reason, namely, the extraordinary difficulty of entering a democratic experiment under the assumption that a continuity – in this case the continuity of a modernizing course – can and must be maintained. Thus Turkey is still struggling, since 1945, with the basic incongruence of seeking a democracy without the drawbacks of democracy – i.e., without submitting to the people's will. The extant lesson of 1960 is, in effect, that the military decides to what extent the voice of the people – and especially the voice of religion – can have its way.

As the saying goes, history is nothing but a sequel of exceptions. The extraordinary thing is, therefore, that in the case under consideration the exceptions are indeed difficult to find. Perhaps a few are in the offing. Aside from Turkey, there are four countries that have long been under observation as plausible democracies-to-be: Mexico, Portugal, Spain[10], and Tunisia.[11] Portugal crossed the border in May 1974 via a military coup, i.e., discontinuously. Mexico is in the vicinity of the border but has yet to cross it. Spain still was, in the summer of 1974, awaiting for Franco to leave the scene. And Tunisia is simply the most plausible African candidate. In any event, one of these countries may very soon be the testing ground of how an endogenous passing to democracy may occur, of how a monopolistic polity can switch, or revert, to party pluralism under the sheer force of ideals.[12] Yet it remains to be seen whether the transition will occur smoothly, whether the process of transplantation can be kept under control, or whether both the rulers and the rules of the game will be swept away as soon as the new working principles become operative. Even if we account hopefully for future evidence, the counterevidence will remain, in all likelihood, very thin. Furthermore, our scrutiny of the Turkish experience lends some weight to an additional perplexity. Let us assume, for the sake of the argument, that Turkey is a case of endogenous and continuous transition from monopoly to competition.[13] If so, the question is whether this continuity has not been, in the final analysis, self-defeating. The argument could be that the solution of avoiding or diluting over time the breakdown is not, if at all possible, a preferable solution; and this could be so because it leaves a polity to perform under mutually exclusive working principles.

However that may be, the historical record overwhelmingly warrants the conclusion that along the continuum of party polities there is a point at which we are definitely confronted, as a rule, with a break, and thereby with a boundary. While the one party can be easily transformed into a hegemonic party, the step that follows is a most difficult one. The loosening of a monocentric system occurs either in the form of a lessening of coercive control, or by switching from the single party to the hegemonic party arrangement; but the evidence largely confirms that neither is a takeoff position in the direction of pluralism. It is true that when we arrive at the pragmatic variety of the hegemonic party, the system can be very loose. Yet it cannot escape the destiny of all monocentric systems, namely, that the party and the state *simul stant et simul cadent,* stand and fall together. Conversely, the ankylosis of pluralism does not lead us beyond the predominant-party system, for a predominant party has never transformed itself without force or fraud into a hegemonic or single party. Therefore, neither the hegemonic party nor the predominant party can be considered middle-of-the-road formulas that somehow converge and overlap. The "liberalization" of a monocentric system amounts to a lessening of oppression, that is, to a modification of the *same* political system; whereas a free polity requires the establishment of a *different* system, of a system based on entirely different principles and mechanisms.

We are not really dealing, therefore, with a homogeneous continuum but with *two heterogeneous* continua: On the one side the multiparty, twoparty, and predominant-party systems; on the other side the hegemonic and one-party polities. The first continuum denotes the political systems pivoting on a party *system;* the second continuum denotes the political systems centered on the *party-state* identification. The party systems end with the case of the predominant party; the party-state systems begin with the case of the hegemonic party. The former are competitive systems; the latter are not. The first is the continuum of pluralism; the second is not. The two areas are not separated by the good or bad will of the political actors. Whatever the intentions, there is a point beyond which we are confronted with alternative mechanisms based on opposite working principles.

As anyone can see, the conceptual and predictive implications of the issue of continuity versus discontinuity are of no small import. When one hears, for instance, of one-party democracy, the speaker is suspect of being a "continuist." On the contrary, if the discontinuity thesis is warranted, not only is one-party democracy a patent misnomer, but the predictions about the liberalization of the monopolistic polities are subject to far more cautions than the continuist is willing to acknowledge. According to my argument, the notion of continuum is misused either when it rules out discontinuity by definition, or when it becomes a pure and simple metaphor. With respect to system change a continuity (or a discontinuity) is established by the rules of transformation (or of non-transformation) of one political system into another. Where no such rules or procedures exist, there we have a break of continuity.

9.2 *Mapping function and explanatory power*

The idea conveyed by much of the recent literature is that if a one-party polity becomes loose enough, it approaches party pluralism; and that, vice versa, if no alternation occurs within a twoparty system, then it approaches a one-party arrangement. I have taken the view that both ideas are deceptive and unwarranted and that the attempt to bridge the gap between the noncompetitive and the competitive political systems is based on the inadequacy of a classification that fails to sort out the cases. Consequently, the overall scheme represented in Table 33 is divided in two halves.

This basic discontinuity can be highlighted in various ways. At the top of the table "party-state systems" are contrasted with "party systems" to signify that the one-party and the hegemonic party arrangements lack subsystem autonomy and are not, therefore, a system *of* parties whose systemic properties result from parties (in the plural) interacting among themselves.[14] Another way of pinpointing the difference relates to my initial argument that the primary function of parties (in the plural) is expression.[15] Accordingly, at the bottom of the table the area of monocentrism is characterized by a repressive, or coercive, potential, while the area of pluralism (or of polypartism) is characterized in terms of expressive capability. To be sure, repression does not consist of sheer physical force; it should be understood as indicating, more broadly, high mobilizational and extractive capabilities obtained via mass manipulation. In this broad meaning the notion of repression subsumes also the political communication function and, more exactly, the downgoing type of communication flow. Conversely, the more a political system allows for expression, the more it allows for mass pressure exerted from below. This is the same as saying that the notion of expression points to an upgoing communication flow.

While I am stubborn on the discontinuity matter, this is not because I take a Manichean view of the world. Since "intensity" is a decisive variable, I do not quite see why a party-state system should inevitably be intolerable. I have said that the quasi-one party emerging from stark deprivation of qualified manpower is likely to be a necessity. And I am prepared to concede that a pragmatic one party (or hege-

Table 33: *Typology of party polities*

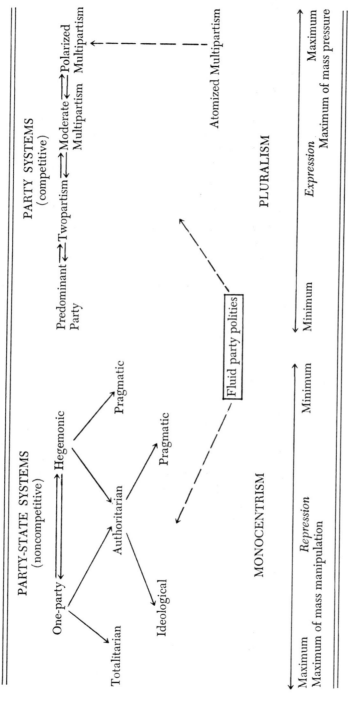

PARTY-STATE SYSTEMS
(noncompetitive)

One-party ⟷ Hegemonic

Totalitarian

Authoritarian

Ideological

Pragmatic

Pragmatic

PARTY SYSTEMS
(competitive)

Predominant ⟷ Twopartism ⟷ Moderate ⟷ Polarized
Party   Multipartism Multipartism

Atomized Multipartism

Fluid party polities

MONOCENTRISM

Maximum   Minimum

PLURALISM

Minimum   Maximum

Repression   *Expression*
Maximum of mass manipulation   Maximum of mass pressure
Maximum   Maximum

monic party) may not only be necessary but even preferable, if the alternative is a chaotic, corrupt, and highly inefficient kind of multi-partism or of atomism. So my concern is with terminological precision. When I say that the single party is not a substitute for a party *system,* no value judgment is intended. Likewise, when I stress that the single party no longer is an *expressive* agency, I only intend to point out that if we wish the expressive function to be performed, then we must be prepared to withstand the drawbacks of party pluralism. And this is, again, a matter of being clearheaded.

It should be understood from the table that the placing of the categories in an order of decreasing intensity of repression on the left side, and of increasing intensity of expression on the right side, is a very loose approximation. I only wish to convey the idea that a one-party structure of the pragmatic variety is less repressive, or less intolerant, than a hegemonic party structure of the ideological variety. On the other hand, the fact that increasing expressive capabilities appear related to the increasing number of alternatives offered to the voter does not imply that a more expressive system is also a more democratic system. Expression is only one of the several indicators that enable us to evaluate a democracy. While the broad lines are roughly represented, the details are, as is inevitable with a scheme, misrepresented. The warning applies equally to the placement of party atomism, which is not meant to convey the suggestion that this situation corresponds by definition to a high degree of expressive capability. Atomized pluralism amounts to a situation in which parties are "labels," loose coalitions of notables that often change at each election and tend to dissolve from one election to another. Since this pattern represents the phase of development of party systems that precedes its structural consolidation, I have placed atomized multipartism at the right end to suggest, very tentatively, that anachronistic prolonged survivals of an atomized configuration are especially conducive to extreme and polarized pluralism.

It should also be understood that by dividing the continuum into halves I do not imply in the least that on the one side we only have repression and on the other we only have expression. Of course not. "Repression" can be defined as a situation in which coercive means of government *prevail* all along the continuum. Conversely, "expression" denotes a situation in which pressures from below *prevail* all along the continuum over coercion from above. Obviously, any situation of repression includes some expression, and conversely any situation of expression includes some repression: In fact, I am pointing to a basic discontinuity of the *same continuum.* On the other hand, the continuities are indicated, in Table 33, by two-way horizontal arrows which signify that within each area – monocentrism or pluralism – the transitions from one system to another occur without breakdown, with-

Table 34. *The simplified structural scheme*

One-party Hegemonic party }	Unipolar systems	Monopartism
[Predominant party] Twoparty Moderate multipartism } Extreme multipartism [Atomized systems]	Bipolar systems } Multipolar systems }	Polypartism

out altering the rules of the game. For instance, the transformation of a predominant-party system into a twoparty or multiparty pattern, and vice versa, is simply left to the voters' choice.[16] Likewise, the passage from the one-party to the hegemonic party pattern, and vice versa, can occur smoothly, as a mere matter of letting go or of tightening (whatever the formal constitution), on account of the highly discretionary nature of the power systems in question.

Finally, the table carries the indication "fluid party polities." This is also to recall that the typology does not apply to the new states whose political processes correspond to a highly diffuse, volatile, and provisional stage of growth. The exclusion is deliberate and has been explained at length. The category is boxed, then, to signify that the fluid polities are included in the table only as a residual category.[17] It should also be clear that the halfway positioning of the category is not meant to suggest that the volatile polities bridge the discontinuity of the continuum, but that their future consolidation will presumably lead them in either one of the two camps.

According to the presentation of Table 33, the major categories are seven. However, when the subtypes are included, the typology consists of ten categories: (i) one-party totalitarian, (ii) one-party authoritarian, (iii) one-party pragmatic, (iv) hegemonic-ideological, (v) hegemonic-pragmatic, (vi) predominant party, (vii) twopartism, (viii) moderate multipartism, (ix) extreme multipartism, and (x) atomized pluralism. For a number of purposes ten categories are cumbersome and unnecessary. When this is the case, the typology can be simplified via successive aggregations. The resulting, more manageable scheme is presented in Table 34.

The table reabsorbs the predominant party by considering this system a possible outcome of any variety of pluralism. Likewise, the atomized systems can be bracketed and considered a likely predecessor of extreme multipartism. We are thus left with five major categories, and these can be aggregated, in turn, into three groups, namely, unipolar, bipolar, and multipolar systems. When the focus is on *structural configurations* (rather than on the number of parties), these latter labels recommend themselves for their straightforward symmetry. In turn, the structural labels help redress the traditional misclassification by indicating that twopartism and moderate multipartism are structurally similar – they are both bipolar systems – and, therefore, that the major division is the one between moderate and extreme multipartism.

The usefulness of a typology of party polities can be assessed in a number of ways. One of these is to ask – very broadly – how much theoretically and predictively relevant information it conveys with respect to the political system as a whole. The question is again answered schematically in Table 35, which relates the party mapping to a number of systemic properties.

Table 35 assumes that the number of parties is the independent variable. There are many reasons for this, on which we have long dwelt. But two reasons stand out at this stage of the argument. The first one is that the number-of-party variable can be operationalized, and indeed measured[18] far better and far more easily than any other variable. And, clearly, many technical advantages follow from disposing of an operational independent variable. The second reason for attributing to the numerical criterion the status of independent variable is that the alternatives easily lead to circular and/or deterministic explanations; e.g., we find that many parties because they reflect that many cleavages. In my argument, instead, the party structures, as indicated by the party numbers, may, but also may not, reflect the societal cleavages, and may either heighten or depress ideological polarization.

The foregoing considerations equally help explain why the ideological factor is conceived as an intervening variable. It is self-evident that the elements carried in the first two columns of Table 35 interact. Thus one might well treat ideology and/or segmentation as the independent variables. If so, however, we would stumble into major operational difficulties, we would easily enter a deterministic and/or a tautological path of explanation and, in any case, the ideological variance would remain totally unexplained.

Be that as it may, the last column of Table 35 indicates where the real trouble might lie. I say "alternative possibilities" because these can be of two kinds: either exceptions, or mixes. The *exceptions*, i.e., the "deviant cases" pointing to a lack of correspondence between the format of the class and the properties of the type, have already been identified and discussed.[19] The methodological point is, here, that whenever we hypothesize a regularity, we must expect events that do not conform to the rule. Does this imply that the rule is contradicted and thereby undermined? This depends on how the rule is conceived. If the rule incorporates the exceptions, i.e., rules over its exceptions by

286

subsuming them under a regularity, then the rule is not undermined by the nonconforming cases. And I have made quite clear all along that the *class* corresponds to the *type* only under the condition that the number of parties (fragmentation) varies in accord with a left–right spread of opinion (ideological distance); whereas parties do not divide only along the ideological left-right dimension, but along other dimensions as well: religious, ethnic, linguistic, and also along a center–periphery and/or a south–north axis. Therefore, even a small ideological space allows, along other dimensions, for a relatively high fragmentation.

In practice, the discrepancy problem hardly arises until we come to the distinction between moderate and extreme multipartism. Hence the rule subject to challenge is actually the following: that a more-than-five party format is an indicator of ideological distance – unless it indicates segmentation. And the argument could be that the rule stands as long as the frequency stands on its side. That is to say that if the finding was that the exceptions are more frequent than the rule, then the rule should be reversed and reformulated as follows: that the format is an indicator of fragmentation – except when it indicates ideological distance. In practice, the reformulation is acceptable, in the sense that my case could be restated accordingly. In principle, however, I would rather put it this way: that the frequency of the exceptions enfeebles the explanatory power of the rule that incorporates them, but does not, in and by itself, reverse the rule – until and unless we find a better rule. For rules should, if they are any good, have a theoretical logic to them.

Deviant cases or exceptions – I was saying – are different from *mixed cases*. The distinction is not as thin as it might appear at first view. To begin with, a given concrete system may be declared mixed because it is *in transit* from one cell to another. This may be called a "dynamic mix" – which is an excellent thing, for it testifies to the sensitivity of a taxonomy to change and dynamics. In this instance, then, a mixed case is by no means a deviant case. The problem arises, instead, with the "static mixes": A given concrete system falls and *remains* between two cells. In this instance, where and when does a mixed case differ from an exception?

This is a good question, especially in that it forces us to recognize that taxonomies serve not only an *explanatory purpose,* but also a charting, *mapping purpose.* Let us assume, for the sake of the argument, that neither the number of parties nor the ideological factor has any causal relevance. Even so, the respective properties of the various kinds of unipartism, of twopartism, moderate pluralism, and polarized pluralism remain as they are. Likewise, if one denies that the format affects the mechanics, one may simply disregard columns I and III,

Table 35. *The overall framework*

(I) Indicator: Number of parties (fragmentation)	(II) Variables: a) Ideology b) Segmentation		(III) Classification	(IV) Typology
	High			One-party totalitarian
			One-party	Hegemonic ideological
1 party (no fragmentation)	Ideological intensity		Hegemonic party	One-party authoritarian
				One-party pragmatic
	Low			Hegemonic pragmatic
2 parties (small/even fragmentation)	Low		Twoparty (format)	Twopartism (mechanics)
3–5 parties		Ideological distance or Segmentation	Limited pluralism	Moderate pluralism
More than 5 parties (high fragmenta-tion)			Extreme pluralism	Polarized pluralism
	High			
1 predominant (high uneven con-centration)			Whatever format	Predominant party system

(V) Constant properties	(VI) Variable properties	(VII) Alternative possibilities
Monopoly	Diminishing coercive-extractive capabilities	
Descending communication		
No subsystem autonomy (or minimal		
	Alternative government	Twoparty polarized
Competition	Moderate politics	
Subsystem automony	Bipolar structure: alternative coalitions	Limited but polarized pluralism
Upgoing com- munication (expression)	Centripetal competition	
	Multipolarity: periphered turnover	Extreme but moderate plural- ism (or semi-
	Centrifugal competition	polarized)
	No turnover Low competi- tiveness	

and begin from column IV, i.e., with the typology. This mental experiment can be pushed to the limit by reading Table 35 from column VI backward. In this case the *causal vector* is lost, but the *associations* remain. For example, if we have alternative government, we find it associated with a competitive system, the centripetal mechanics of twopartism, a twoparty format, a low ideological distance (or a segmentation that does not affect the party system), and, finally, with the small/even fragmentation that results in two relevant parties only. Even when, or if, no causal imputation is made, the charting stands. And from the vantage point of the mapping function of taxonomies the mixed cases serve the same purpose as the pure cases: They equally locate things or events with respect to given parameters.

The mixed cases can be appraised from still another angle. It is true by definition that any scheme does violence to the phenomena it encapsulates. If the concrete cases find an easy fit, in all likelihood this is because the scheme soars at a very abstract level. Conversely, the lower its level of abstraction, and thereby the higher its discriminating power, the greater the likelihood that a number of concrete cases will slip out, to some extent and in some respect, from any single box. From this vantage point the argument could be, therefore, that the mixes accrue to the merits of a meticulous and discriminating scheme of analysis.

Given the enormous variety and fluidity of the phenomena that we attempt to seize, the foregoing intricacies are the least that one can expect. The resulting note of caution is that before assessing exceptions and/or mixes we must know what we demand of a classificatory or typological scheme. With respect to its mapping or charting purpose, mixed cases are just as good and as helpful as the ones that fit into one cell. That is also to say that when a taxonomy manages to disentangle, either within or across neighboring cells, the bewildering maze of real-world phenomena, this is already no mean performance. The mixed cases become troublesome, then, only with respect to the causal and predictive ambitions of a taxonomy. In this latter respect one might argue that if the mixed cases are more frequent than the unmixed ones, then the taxonomy should be reconceived accordingly, that is, should be centered on the mixtures. This is more easily said than done, however. A classification must have a thread – and a consistent criterion that taps on one or more relevant features is no easy thing to construct.

All things considered, I submit that the framework of analysis synthesized in Table 35 passes quite a number of tests. In the first place, the independent variable – the numerical classification of parties – is operational enough and satisfies the logical requirements of yielding categories that are mutually exclusive and jointly exhaustive. Granted that the numerical criterion is not unaided, the assumptions or the constraints to which it is subjected are few, realistic, and surely not far-fetched. And as one proceeds across the various columns, one sees that the categories resulting from the classification also satisfy the requirement of being exclusive and exhaustive "not simply as a logical consequence of the determining criteria, but as a matter of empirical fact."[20]

In the second place the framework seemingly provides a parsimonious balance between the mapping and the explanatory (causal and/or predictive) requirements. While parsimony is not, per se, an unmixed blessing, a balance must be found, for the ease of orientation and the increase of predictive power do not seem to vary together. For instance, the predictive power of the framework would surely be greater and more accurate if three additional intervening variables were entered, namely, (i) the electoral system, (ii) the constitutional structure, and (iii) the degree of international autonomy. But the greater detail introduced by these additional variables seemingly adds an unrewarding complexity into the mapping. On the other hand, with two predictors only (the independent, and the major intervening variable, ideology) the scheme already accounts for a large number of dependent variables and already predicts a variety of trends and outcomes.

In the third place, I submit that the framework under consideration recommends itself on the grounds of being easily intelligible and easy to construct. Our present world moves fast and needs unceasing and easy updating. A framework based on *highly visible* and *elemental* information goes to satisfy, therefore, a vital practical necessity.

A last point deserves mention. The taxonomy developed throughout the second part of the book can be accused of being largely insensitive to the existence of societal strains and tensions. Canada and Belgium are obvious instances. Here we have a limited fragmentation in terms of the number of parties and yet far more strains than, e.g., in Switzerland or even in the Netherlands. But this is as it should be. Across the world we find identical political structures superimposed upon enormously different societal structures. It is only obvious, therefore, that the resulting interactions, tensions, and frictions will be at great variance. And from the vantage point of a science of politics – in its difference from a sociological explanation or reduction of politics[21] – the question is precisely how the superstructure reacts upon the substructures. Cleavages are not "givens" coming out of the blue sky: They may mold, and be reflected in, the polity; but they may equally be polity molded or polity restrained. The United States, with a strong potential of deflagration at the societal level as yet unreflected at the level of its political structures, is a good case in point. Hence the broad question to which I have addressed myself is whether it is a bipolar or

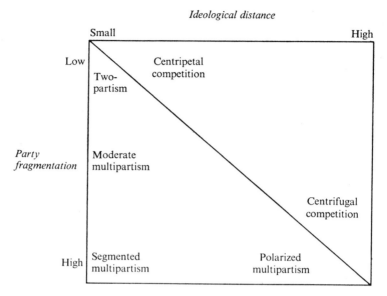

Figure 36. The simplified model

a multipolar structure that lessens or fosters socioeconomic tensions; and my argument has been that a bipolar polity is less exposed and less conducive to polarization, whereas a multipolar system is likely to reinforce and to aggravate polarization. But it is clear that if the polarization of a bipolar system sustains a persistent centrifugal trend, then the polity will not remain, in the long run, bipolar. And this is what we are required to register at the level of the political system.

Let us recapitulate and conclude. From the vantage point of the distinction between mapping purpose and explanatory purpose it can be easily seen that Table 33 outlines the mapping, while Table 35 is indicative of the explanatory and predictive power. Both are somewhat cumbersome schemes. Thus Table 33 has been reduced, in Table 34, to the basic *structural configurations* resulting from my analysis. We are now left to perform a similar simplification with Table 35, that is, to bring out what may be called the *simplified model* (of the competitive systems) – which can be represented in Figure 36.

The first thing to note is that the upper right corner of the figure remains blank. Does this asymmetry point to a flaw? I think not, because the blank stands, in effect, for "breakdown." When a maximal ideological distance engenders a centrifugal competition, a twoparty format is either blown up or paves the way to a civil war confrontation. Hence the figure suggests that extreme multipartism represents – under conditions of maximal polarization – the most likely outcome and, at the same time, the survival solution. The alternative might be, to be sure, a towering predominant party. But a strongly predominant party results from low competitiveness; and if the competitiveness is low, it follows that the variable "ideological distance" does not carry much weight in the electoral arena.

The figure brings forcefully to the fore, in the second place, that my emphasis is on the *direction* of competition, not on *competitiveness*. Since most authors neglect this aspect, it is appropriate to insist on its importance. To be sure, I also account for competitiveness. Thus a predominant-party system can be said to correspond – as I have just recalled – to low inter-party competitiveness. Likewise, the mechanics of twopartism hinges on high competitiveness. However, beyond this point the systemic consequences of competitiveness are not at all clear – as we know.[22] Too much competitiveness – as measured by the close-ness of the margins among the competitors – may be as unhelpful as too little competitiveness; or, alternatively, different degrees of com-petitiveness may not produce any detectable difference either in the behavior of politicians or in the governmental outputs. And this is a first reason why I cannot follow the various attempts at construing "competition" as an independent or central explanatory variable – even though I well understand what prompts these attempts, namely, that competition is a measurable variable and a very attractive one at that.[23] But my major criticism is precisely that our measures cannot sort out the direction of competition and are therefore blind to the one element that surely is of decisive consequence on the overall per-formance of a polity.

9.3 From classification to measurement

There are, conceivably, at least three ways of being displeased with my conceptual analysis. One is the classic objection that classes and types are only abstractions. The second is the argument that classes and types are static, "locational" concepts, while we are in need of dy-namic, "process" concepts. The third and major criticism is expressed, in brief, by the thesis that the logic of classification is superseded by measurement. These objections are not unrelated but are best con-fronted separately.

The first objection is as old as it is unconvincing. Quite aside from the fact that all scientific knowledge deals with generalizations and that all generalization implies abstraction, the Achille's heel of this objection is that it offers – as it stands – no alternative. Granted that classifications cannot follow the shades of reality, that they draw ar-bitrary cuts, it does not follow that we can dispense with classificatory mappings. The world of nature is surely as much a blend as the world of man; yet could a botanist or a zoologist master his field without having recourse to classificatory systems? Actually, the main difference between a zoologist and a social scientist is that the latter needs to be concerned with, and alerted to, classifications much more than the former. The social scientist needs them just as much, but he – unlike the zoologist – cannot be happy with his classifications once and for all: His world being extremely dynamic, he must reclassify, and classify anew, all of the time.

The second objection is as follows: that I have been concerned, in the main, with locational concepts, not with process concepts. This can be readily acknowledged; but not without prior qualifications. The first one is that also locational concepts allow for some dynamics, since the concrete cases can and do move from one box to another. However, some dynamics may not be enough dynamics. For instance, an analysis based on locational concepts – such as structural configurations – suits the nations that are built, but is ill suited for grasping the nation-building process. This has indeed been my view in dealing with the fluid polities, for my warning that classifications can be, in volatile contexts, very misleading, goes to support the view that developmental analysis needs broadly conceived process concepts.[24] Nonetheless, and on the other hand, process concepts too need a frame of reference that must be held constant. Therefore, after we have recognized the difference, and the different appropriateness, of locational vis-à-vis process concepts, in point of method the question remains: Can we grasp dynamics regardless of, or without reference to, statics? This is what I do not believe, and there is something here that we can learn from our philosopher ancestors.

Until Kant, philosophy was largely static. Kant himself was a most meticulous constructor of logical filing systems. Then dynamics followed: Romanticism, classic idealism, and existentialism. With Fichte, Schelling, Hegel, and their descendants we leap from photography to cinematography, from statics to kinetics. Dialectic, fluidity, *Aufhebung*, incessant change, action – these have been for a century the key words in European philosophy. The result has been unintelligible chaos. A reconstruction *ab imis* was necessary, analytic philosophy came to the fore, and most, if not all, of what had preceded was declared meaningless. The reaction of logical positivism, and especially of early logical positivism, was excessive, but vis-à-vis the philosophy of idealism and existentialism the mark was well hit. The dialectical merging of all and any distinction – indeed of analysis itself – was banned, statics was restored.

Where does the analogy come in? It seems to me that a mood of "romantic dialectics" has been creeping into the social sciences. The current recommendations of avoiding dichotomies and logical polarizations, of concentrating on process, change, and the like, have a familiar ring. This is, in fact, the kind of logic that explains that liberty and coercion cannot be distinguished, that freedom is inseparable from oppression, and so forth. Anybody having passed through the experience of Hegelian dialectics, or of its Marxist follow-up, knows where this leads. Soft-pedaling of analytical thinking is dangerously close to confused (and confusing) thinking, just as "process logic" is dangerously conducive to dialectical obscurity. There is one thing that we should learn from what happened to philosophy: how to avoid the same pitfalls. Process concepts, process logic (or dialectics), yield returns; but under the one condition that we do not rush headlong into the Hegelian night in which all the cows appear black. The real world cannot be viewed only as a process–*becoming* – but also, at any point in time, as a state–*being*. With due respect to dynamics, "location" should not be downgraded. And to indict taxonomies of impeding the understanding of "process" is, in principle, no less absurd than to indict a globe of obstructing traveling.

While I am not impressed by the first two objections, the real problem centers on the query: How does the "qualitative science" dealing with *what is* questions, relate to the "quantitative science" dealing with *how much* questions? Bluntly put, how do differences in *kind* relate to differences in *degree?* Or, viewed from the other end, how does pre-measurement relate to measurement? Along this itinerary, which is indeed a long itinerary, it is useful to distinguish among three steps, or phases. First, there is the classificatory treatment of concepts which is, logically, an *either-or* treatment: This *is,* or *is not,* that. If this mode of analysis is called the logic of classification, then the second step can be appropriately identified as a "logic of gradation"[25] consisting of a *more-or-less* (degree) treatment. This second stage is somewhat ambivalent. In no small part the logic of gradation brings about a "quantitative idiom," which is nothing but an idiom largely exposed to abuse[26] (well exemplified by the facile dictum that *all* differences are *only* differences in degree). At the same time, a more-or-less logical treatment is conducive to actual *measurement*, i.e., to attaching numerical values to items. But this is only the beginning of a quantitative science. The third step consists, then, in empowering numbers with their mathematical properties, that is, in bringing our measures under the concepts and the theories of mathematics. At this stage the *quantitative* science is transformed into a *mathematical* science whose ultimate ideal is to discover and express general laws in the form of functional relationships between measured items.

There is no question that this program should be pursued. Thus any researcher must weigh the opportunity of transforming the dichotomous characteristics drawn by the logic of classification into the continuous characteristics demanded by the logic of gradation. And nobody in his right mind can deny that the more we measure, the better. As for the mathematization of political science, what is subject to questioning is whether the mathematics in use suits our problems – not the desirability nor the enormous potentialities of this development. The point of divergence does not bear, then, on the program but on its execution; and more exactly on how the first step, i.e., the either-or (binary) treatment of the logic of classification, relates to the second step, i.e., the more-or-less (continuous) treatment of the logic of gradation. It is here that the issue is joined.

Over the past 20 years the prevalent mood has been to do away with the *per genus et differentiam* mode of analysis under the assumption that the logic of classification was obstructive of, if not inimical to, the quantitative turn of the discipline. Not only was the quantitative science deemed capable of proceeding *without,* or outside of, the qualitative science; but it was further assumed that the quantitative science, as expressed by the logic of gradation, required the actual dismantling and the positive rejection of the classificatory mode of analysis. In my view these are grievous misunderstandings. The first assumption is simply untrue to our actual deeds – as is only obvious, if one pauses to consider that in the domain of politics the qualitative science includes the quasi-totality of our theory. And the second assumption has resulted – in the wake of the recommendation of dismissing the logic of classification – in our building a giant with feet of clay.

Lest my emphasis on the modes of concept formation (classificatory or other) be suspected of privileging the theoretical over the empirical side of the coin, let me take up the question at its data end. Data are "facts" as perceived and dissected by our tools of inquiry, i.e., by the observational concepts of a science. This is the same as saying that data are information processed by, and distributed in, *conceptual containers.* More exactly, data are observations collected and arranged according to how the concepts are shaped and defined by the fact seeker. Therefore, concepts are not only the units of thinking; concepts (observational concepts) are also, and just as much, *data containers.* If so, the crucial question is: What turns a concept into a valid *fact-finding container?*

Without delving into minutiae, let me simply note that the data base of a science is all the more satisfactory the more its data containers (concepts) are (i) *standardized* and endowed with (ii) high to maximal *discriminating power.* If they are not standardized, the information is not cumulative. But standardization is self-defeating unless the data containers are discriminating enough to allow for multipurpose utilization, thereby including utilizations as yet unforeseen. How can these two crucial requirements be met? Here is the rub: because I know of no other technique for meeting both requirements jointly, aside from the classificatory technique. Standardization and sharpening proceed hand in hand if, and only if, a general class (concept) is "unpacked" *per genus et differentiam* into mutually disjoined (either-or) classes that become, as we descend systematically the ladder of abstraction, always more specific – i.e., qualified by larger sets of attributes – and thereby more discriminating.

The point is, then, that research is infinitely wasteful unless it branches out from, and is brought back to, some common backbone. This backbone has long been provided by the logic of classification and the logical discipline thus resulting. If this discipline is relaxed and replaced by undisciplined checklists, each research becomes a fishing expedition that employs different nets and catches different fish. This may be pleasing for the ego of the researcher, but it leaves the science with haphazard, heterogeneous, and overlapping findings that add up – as they are pooled together – to almost nothing. On the other hand, we are hardly better off in turning to the other side of the ledger, for we are left, here, with "omnibus" data containers that hopelessly lack discrimination. Think of our standard categories and variables – social class, occupation, industrialization, literacy, modernization, participation, mobilization, integration, and the like. It is pretty certain that these variables do not measure, across the world, common underlying phenomena, and this quite aside from the reliability of the data-gathering agencies. And the point is, now, that the poorer the discrimination of our data containers, the more the facts are *misgathered* and, therefore, the greater the *misinformation*.

Some years ago the saying was that we were theory rich and data poor. One could equally say, today, that we are theory poor and data cheated. Data cheated – I have said – because our data base is indeed in bad shape. But why theory poor? I mean, can this indictment be imputed to the same cause?

As we revert from the empirical to the theoretical concern, the issue is, in a nutshell, whether our knowledge still needs, as a point of departure, the logic of classification, or whether this first step blocks the others and should be, therefore, ostracized. The dilemma must be faced squarely. Either we take the view that the either-or treatment cannot be bypassed, or we must boldly reverse the itinerary and take the neo-Baconian optics: from the data back to science.[27] This is the dilemma, for the second step cannot possibly sustain the burden of being a founding, initial step. Degrees or quantities *of what?* Clearly, we cannot measure until we know what it is that we are measuring.

297

Clearly, then, *how much* questions – no matter how far they will subsequently lead us – can be sensibly asked only of things and events that belong (with respect to a given property) to the *same class*. The logic of gradation leads to sheer confusion unless a classificatory treatment is presupposed.

As for the neo-Baconian option, if it is true that data are nothing but informations and observations sorted out and processed by ad hoc conceptual containers, then the itinerary "from the data back to science" sounds very much like adding clay to clay. Quite aside from the monumental naïveté of the neo-Baconian epistemology, the facts of the matter are (i) that increasing amounts of research and survey data are matched by their equally increasing lack of comparability and cumulability and (ii) that most of the cheap and dirty data provided by statistical agencies despairingly lack discriminating power. Hence the state of the data base points, if anything, to the vital necessity of improving the quality of the data *at the source*. Computer cleaning is no remedy for hopelessly vague and hopelessly overlapping categories. Yet the neo-Baconian adept has nothing to say on how the fact finder should perform in finding the facts. He is apparently content with re-manipulating "masses of data" – just more of the same mess. The retort is, of course, that we now possess powerful statistical techniques that can do, from the data end, what had to be done, formerly, at the conceptual end: Detect errors and shape or reshape the theory thus resulting. But statistical controls only control the variables in use; multiple regression analysis does not discover for us the variables that might account – once discovered – for the observed correlations; and, likewise, only the indicators that we put in the computer are factored or clustered for relevant dimensions. In short, computer and statistical technology cannot surrogate what an atrophied formation of concepts does not provide.[28]

All in all, it seems to me that in the execution of our program we are throwing away the baby and replacing it with dirty water. A check list is only a poor substitute of a classification; and gradations without prior classification attribute the appearance of precision to imprecision. On the other hand, the limits of classifications can always be corrected by transforming dichotomies into continuous characteristics, while the initial damage resulting from classificatory neglect and sloppiness remains, and is often amplified, throughout the subsequent transformations. Let it be repeated, therefore, that our understanding always and necessarily begins with *what is* questions. If such questions are not refined by a systematic logical treatment, we shall only have the worse of two worlds: a bad qualitative science that reflects itself into a bad quantitative science. The proof of the pudding is in the eating; and the eating that has resulted from taxonomic negligence is dismal – as we have long seen throughout the second part of the book, and as a few ad hoc illustrations help remind.

Take Japan, the United States, West Germany, and Italy. What kinds, or types, of polities are they? As we know, Japan has been considered (i) single party; (ii) twoparty, in that "only two parties have substantial Diet holdings"; (iii) multiparty, in that its parties amount to a "system of loosely structured federations"; and (iv) a one-and-one-half party system.[29] By the same token the United States can be classified as twoparty, as a cyclically predominant system, as a two-and-one-half party system (the half being represented by the Southern Democrats), and as "essentially a four party pattern."[30] The landscape becomes even more confusing when the thread is provided by the pseudoclass of the "dominant" parties.[31] According to Duverger, Italy and West Germany were (in the early fifties) very similar not only because both countries displayed a "marked tendency toward dualism," but also because each was characterized by the presence of a dominant party (which was, for Germany, the currently non-dominant Christian Democratic party).[32] In retrospect one can hardly think of two countries having departed – if we assume they ever had something in common – to a greater extent. But did they ever have anything in common? Likewise, the literature abounds with questions such as this one: "Why has the Mexican PRI been able to retain its domination, while the Turkish RPP was voted out of office . . . ?"[33] A question that opens a whirl of false problems unless we first establish that the PRI is a hegemonic party protected against competitive risks, whereas the RPP has taken its chances, and lost, in a free electoral market – that is, unless we first establish that the two cases belong to different classes.

Clearly, from a comparative and theoretical vantage point this is an impossible state of affairs, in the face of which the condescendence, if not the disparagement, with which we generally greet "mere classifications," is difficult to justify. For one thing – as Friedrich exactly and concisely puts it – "an issue in typology is an issue about the structure of the reality concerned."[34] Moreover, any attempt at understanding patterns and predicting trends is inevitably defeated if we cannot establish, in some warranted and consistent way, which are the countries that can either verify or falsify whatever generalization we are setting forth.

In what follows I propose, therefore, to pursue a quantitative development *within* the guidelines established by the qualitative or nominal science. According to the previously stated views, we are now in an optimal position for moving ahead. Since we have identified the problems, we know what needs to be measured, and we are also able to discern what it is that we are really measuring.

9.4 Measuring relevance

The typology of party polities summarized in the second section of this chapter largely hinges on a numerical criterion, that is, on the number of relevant parties. While I have stressed the limits of this indicator, I have maintained that it cannot be thrown overboard. If we say that the number of parties indicates the *fragmentation* of the party system, then I have remained at the crudest indicator of fragmentation. This is so especially because my focus has been, in the main, on the *relevance* rather than on the *size* (an actually measured size) of the parties. Thus the size element remains, in my argument, tangential. But before turning to size let us first see whether "relevance" can be operationalized and measured better than I have done so far.

The rules for counting the parties are based – for multipartism in general – on two criteria: whether a party has a coalition potential and/or whether it has a blackmail potential.[35] For my purpose – assigning the concrete cases to classes – it was unnecessary, and indeed contrary to the principle of parsimony, to specify these criteria further. But measuring does not permit looseness. Thus in the case of the coalition potential we have a criterion that demands two measures: one for the governing *potential*, and one for the *actual* governmental relevance.

In the first case the measure taps on whichever party either governs, enters a coalition government, or supports a government as a required component of its parliamentary majority at *some points in time*. Two operational problems immediately arise: at which points in time over what time span and, second, which are the concrete majorities (more-than-minimal, minimal winning) and/or how to deal with minority governments. The first difficulty can be solved by establishing that the time unit is the legislature and that one "occasion of relevance" per legislature is sufficient. Supposing (optimistically) that we have also surmounted the second difficulty, we shall obtain a precise figure for each legislature. But this is an incomplete, uninteresting finding, for we are interested in a systemic measure. Presumably, therefore, we shall have recourse to an average. Fine – except that the average can be entirely misleading (if the system has changed), and, in any case, that our value will impute to the system a "false statics," for the time dimension will inevitably be averaged around some past (central) point in time. If one considers, in addition, all the stipulations that are required for the operational underpinning of "majority," it appears that the precision of our values results from a great deal of subjective arbitrariness: It is a false precision which is only an operational artifact. All in all, then, the measure is not worth pursuing. The criterion followed thus far allows us, over time, to drop old parties and/or to enter new ones. Its looseness permits updating. By contrast, the systemic measure seemingly requires an averaging that kills, in turn, whatever dynamics was afforded by the nominal, or more nominal, route. Let it be added, if only in passing, that we face, here, a general methodological problem. Not only must any average value given for a polity assume that the polity in question has remained unchanged – with respect to a given set of parameters – for the time period under consideration, but when we have recourse to averages we must ask ourselves what is the pertinence and/or incidence of the "time span" with respect to what we are measuring. And the truth of the matter is that most comparisons just have to utilize the time series that happen to be on record.

If there is little point in providing a systemic measure of the "potential" relevance of parties, the case is different with respect to their "actual" relevance. In the latter case the criterion can be made very neat: A party is *governmentally relevant* only when it actually governs, enters a government, or supports it at the vote of confidence by giving it that majority that the government demands for taking office. Since each multiparty parliament may produce different coalitional majorities (i.e., majorities that combine a different number of parties), there is no question that the significant time unit is, here, the legislature. Thus the operational basis of the measure is as follows.

First, we do not count the parties that, in a given legislature, have neither entered nor supported (at the vote of confidence) at least one government. If a party votes a government, but its support is unnecessary (beyond the winning point) and rejected by the government, it will not be counted. If, however, a government owes its office to the abstention of other parties, the parties in question will be counted. Second, all the parties that either enter a government or put it in office (as specified) are given the same weight. Third, parties are assumed to behave as units: Therefore, the crossing of party lines is not taken into account. Fourth, each legislature is given the same weight, regardless of its duration – provided that the electoral returns do not produce the immediate calling of another election. Since the duration of the legislature is irrelevant, it also follows that a legislature can be considered even before its termination. Five, the coalitional or governmental relevance of the parties will be averaged, across legislatures, only if, and only when, the characteristics of the coalition game remain constant. Under the foregoing stipulations, let n (the number of legislatures) be at the numerator, and the summation of the c_i's (the coalitional units) be at the denominator. A coalitional unit is attributed to a party every time it takes part in a government or gives it decisive support (if only by abstaining). The measure thus is

$$\frac{n}{\Sigma c_i}$$

The simplest case is represented by a single-government legislature, i.e., by a legislature with only one government. In this instance each governing party (or each party supporting the government in parliament) is given a c of 1. If there are three such parties, for example, the legislature will make a contribution of 1 to the numerator and of 3 to the denominator. However, most legislatures display more than one government. In this case we cannot give a c of 1 to all the parties that enter the various governments, for by so doing we would distort the measure by measuring, in addition, something else: *governmental instability*, i.e., the frequency with which governments fall and partners change. Logically, the problem can be solved in either one of two ways: (i) by giving a c of 1 to all the parties, while making the numerator the number of governments; or (ii) by holding constant the numerator (1 equals one legislature) and dividing the denominator by the number of governments (e.g., with two governments the c_i's will be .5; with four governments, .25). The first option attributes an equal weight to governments of unequal duration; the second option attributes an equal weight to legislatures of unequal duration. Since governmental duration has, in actual fact, a far greater variation than legislative duration, on empirical grounds the second solution appears preferable and is the one adopted in the calculations.

The measure – a function of how many parties have an actual coalition (governmental) relevance, by legislature – is thus disarmingly simple. Since the numerator counts each legislature as 1, and since a single-government legislature equally attributes 1 to the denominator, 1 represents the ceiling of the measure; and the greater Σc_i, the smaller the ratio $n/\Sigma c_i$. So we can immediately test how the ratings perform, across an appropriate selection of countries, over the post–World War II period.

As the title of Table 37 indicates, by measuring how many parties are governmentally relevant we are in fact measuring the fragmentation of governmental coalitions. Note, incidentally, that this is *not* a measure of the "coalition weight" of parties.[36] The second thing to note is that the table excludes the twoparty systems abiding by the mechanics of twopartism. This is right, because my criterion was devised for multipartism. Moreover, the exclusion is necessary because the measure is so defined as to yield, with respect to twopartism, the value 1. And the same is true for the predominant systems. Consequently, Austria is included only for the period (1945–1966) in which it practiced a "grand coalition."[37] And India is included on account of the 1969 split of the Congress party. As for the ratings, their interpretation

Table 37. *Fragmentation of governmental coalitions in 18 countries*
(systemic averages 1946–1974 circa)

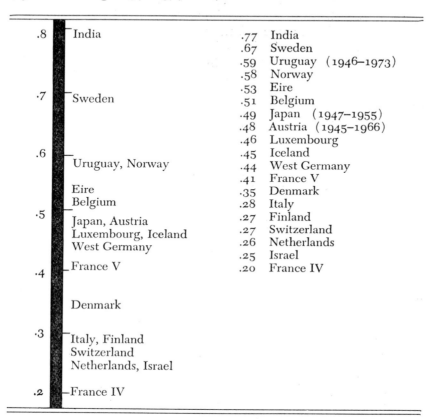

.8	India
·7	Sweden
.6	
	Uruguay, Norway
	Eire
	Belgium
·5	Japan, Austria
	Luxembourg, Iceland
	West Germany
·4	France V
	Denmark
·3	Italy, Finland
	Switzerland
	Netherlands, Israel
.2	France IV

.77	India
.67	Sweden
.59	Uruguay (1946–1973)
.58	Norway
.53	Eire
.51	Belgium
.49	Japan (1947–1955)
.48	Austria (1945–1966)
.46	Luxembourg
.45	Iceland
.44	West Germany
.41	France V
.35	Denmark
.28	Italy
.27	Finland
.27	Switzerland
.26	Netherlands
.25	Israel
.20	France IV

is straightforward. The rating 1 corresponds to a diachronic one-party government, i.e., to a same party governing alone across all the legislatures. The rating .5 corresponds to diachronic two-party governments, i.e., to a distribution centered on coalitions among two parties (presumably ranging from one to three parties). The rating .33 corresponds to diachronic three-party governments, i.e., to a distribution centered on coalitions among three parties (presumably ranging from one to four-five parties).

As one would expect, India ranks highest. Japan is entered only for the period in which it was a system of moderate pluralism. If the entire (1947–1972) period were averaged, the rating would be .71 and would reflect the cancellation of the characteristics of the two systems. The French Fifth Republic rates .41 under the assumption that the Gaullists and the Independent Republicans are best considered as two parties. If they were considered one party, the rating would go up to .62.[38] As we continue to read the table downward, Denmark is a good instance of the difficulties that one encounters along the path of measurement. In 1974 Denmark displayed a Liberal single-party government, with only 21 members in a parliament of 179, which took office under the device of the parliamentary majority voting against the vote of non-confidence.[39] Thus in the 1973–75 legislature our rules compel us to count more than one party. As for the rating of Italy, let it be recalled that we are not measuring the fragmentation of the *party system* but the fragmentation of the *governmental coalitions*. If one considers that in the period under consideration about one-third of the parliamentary votes (the Communists and the MSI) have acquired only in one legislature, in Italy, governmental relevance and, secondly, that the major center party, the DC, has held about 40 percent of the parliamentary seats, then the rating of Italy makes perfect sense.[40]

Whether the measure is useful remains to be seen.[41] What is important, here, is that it highlights how to proceed toward the quantitative science and, conversely, how the operationalization usefully feeds back on the nominal science. The discussion has shown that the broad acceptance of "governmental potential" has nothing to gain from being measured: The drawbacks largely outweigh the advantages. And the point can be extended with even greater reason to an overall systemic measure that would also include the second criterion, i.e., the blackmail potential.[42] On the other hand, the operationalization requires us to distinguish between a broad and a narrow acceptance of the first criterion – and this represents a distinctive gain in clarity. To be sure, even the measure of governmental fragmentation can be accused of producing a false statics and a false precision. But in this instance it was possible to set forth stipulations that minimize both flaws.

9.5 *Numbers and size: the index of fractionalization*

Let us now turn to the size problem. It is intuitively obvious that the number of parties relates to their size and, furthermore, that the size conditions the interplay of the numbers. It now falls due, therefore, to pursue this thread. Our present knowledge suggests two major ways of measuring both number and size. The simplest one may be called the *cumulative percentage* method, as applied to the party topic, among others, by Arend Lijphart and Jean Blondel. A more sophisticated measure is provided, however, by the *index of fractionalization* developed by Douglas Rae.

According to Lijphart "the most objective and straightforward way of comparing the numbers and sizes of political parties in different systems is to examine the cumulative percentages of party strengths in descending order of party size." The technique is tested against five countries – Italy, Switzerland, the Netherlands, Denmark, and Norway – and on the basis of the resulting table, reproduced as Table 38, Lijphart concludes that it is "impossible . . . to make a clear distinction, based on the number and size of parties, between Italy and the other four countries."[43]

In point of fact Lijphart is criticizing an earlier version of my distinction between moderate and extreme pluralism. Since my distinction follows from my counting rules, it goes by itself that if these rules are disregarded no distinction follows. But I am interested, here, in examining the cumulative percentage technique, or method, on its own merits. The question turns, therefore, on whether this method yields returns of theoretical significance.

One may wonder, to begin with, whether the rank ordering resulting from the combined percentages of the largest and next-to-largest parties suggests the likely coalition majorities. In this connection the table would indicate that Italy, the Netherlands, Denmark, and Norway obtain a large (more-than-minimal) majority with twoparty government.[44] It so happens that if the parties in question are identified, this is very seldom the case. The two major Italian parties are, in fact, the Christian Democratic and the Communist, which have never sat together from 1947 to date. In the Netherlands the first two parties are the Catholic and the Socialist, which generally tend to lead alternative coalitions. Norway's first two parties are the Socialist and the Conserva-

Table 38. *Cumulative percentages of selected countries*

	Italy (1963)	Switzerland (1963)	Netherlands (1963)	Denmark (1964)	Norway (1965)
Largest party	38.2	26.6	31.9	41.9	43.1
Two largest parties	63.5	50.6	59.9	62.7	64.2
Three largest parties	77.3	74.0	70.2	82.8	74.6
Four largest parties	84.3	85.4	78.9	88.6	84.5
Five largest parties	90.3	90.4	87.5	93.9	92.6
Six largest parties	95.5	92.6	90.5	96.4	98.6
Seven largest parties	97.2	94.8	93.3	97.7	100.0
Eight largest parties	98.8	96.6	95.6	98.9	

Source: This table drawn from Arend Lijphart, "Typologies of Democratic Systems," is reprinted from *Comparative Political Studies*, Vol. 1, No. 1 (April 1968) pp. 3–44, by permission of the publisher, Sage Publications, Inc.

Table 39. *Average vote and seats of any first two parties (percentages)*
in 24 democracies 1945–1973

	Vote	Seats		Vote	Seats
New Zealand	93	99	India	53	73
United Kingdom	91	98	Sweden	67	69
Austria	89	94	Italy	65	68
Australia	93	90	Iceland	64	68
Turkey	80	89	Norway	63	67
Uruguay	89	89	Ceylon	63	65
West Germany	81	85	France	53	63
Canada	77	85	Denmark	61	61
Eire	74	79	Netherlands	58	59
Belgium	72	77	Israel	53	57
Luxembourg	72	75	Switzerland	49	51
Japan	68	74	Finland	47	49

In seven countries (Denmark, Finland, France, Iceland, Israel, Japan, Sweden) the first two parties change over time. The rank-ordering follows the seats.

tive, which are indeed the mutually exclusive poles of the system. And one can think of many additional cases in which the indication would be no less misleading. For example, during the French Fourth Republic the Communists almost invariably obtained the relative majority of votes, but have never been included, after 1947, in any government. When the Weimar Republic was about to end, in 1932, on the basis of their cumulative returns the Socialists and the Nazis could have governed together with a sufficient majority. Clearly, then, the rank ordering exemplified by Lijphart is blind to ideological incompatibilities and affinities. It equally fails to appreciate the difference between a minor party with a strong coalition-bargaining potential and a relatively large party that counts for little or nothing. In short, the cumulative percentage method gives us no clue about whatever relevance any party might have.

One may ask another question, namely, whether the cumulative percentage does help in establishing significant thresholds. This is notably the suggestion of Blondel, who averages over the period 1945–1966 the combined returns of the two major parties of 19 Western democracies and obtains on this basis the following groups: (i) above 90 percent (United States, New Zealand, Australia, United Kingdom, Austria); (ii) between 75 and 80 percent (West Germany, Luxembourg, Canada, Belgium, Eire); (iii) between 66 and 62 percent (Denmark, Sweden, Norway, Italy, Iceland, the Netherlands); and

(iv) around 50 percent (Switzerland, France, Finland).[45] I have extended this computation to the seats (which were, systemically, far more significant) and to 24 countries over a longer period of time, and – as one would expect – the cutting points disappear (Table 39).

Let us turn, therefore, to the more sophisticated and complete measure that Rae calls *fractionalization* (as opposed to concentration).[46] The measure applies equally to the elective party system (in which the units are the votes) and to the parliamentary party system (in which the units are the seats), and the resulting values yield an interval scale with a fixed zero point (that is, a ratio scale). For the sake of brevity I shall consider only the fractionalization in parliament, i.e., measured in seats (F_p, where F stands for fractionalization, and the subscript p for parliamentary). Rae's index is defined in terms of pairwise disagreement, thereby indicating the likelihood that any two members of a parliament will belong to different parties. More exactly, fractionalization (in a parliament) is the probability that two members drawn at random from the universe belong to different parties. The fractionalization varies from zero (maximal concentration – there is only one party) to a maximum of one (in practice, as many parties as there are seats).[47] A 50–50 split system of perfect parity between two parties is indicated by .5; and the greater the number of nearly equal parties, the greater the fractionalization. The formula is as follows:

$$F = 1 - \sum_{i=1}^{N} p_i^2$$

where N is the number of parties and p_i is the proportion of seats held by the ith party.

Unquestionably, Rae's fractionalization is a measure of how many (number) and, much more, of how large (size) are the parties. However, the measure actually overvalues the larger parties and compresses too quickly the smaller ones – as is obvious, since the party percentages are squared. For example, a 40-percent sized party contributes .16 to the sum of squares, while a 10-percent sized party contributes only .01 (indeed, a disproportionately low value). Let it be clear that I am not objecting to the fact that the index does not increase linearly with the dispersion among a greater number of parties. This is correct, for beyond a certain ceiling of fractionalization a linear relation to the number of parties is more likely to be misleading than informative. The drawback is, then, that the logarithmic performance of the function falls at a far too fast rate – as shown in Figure 40.

The figure indicates a possible correction[48] but hardly a decisive one. Another correction is suggested by Scott C. Flanagan, which he calls "fragmentation index" (FI).[49] The formula is as follows:

$$FI = \sqrt{\sum_{i=1}^{n} V_1^2}$$

For any polity with n parties where the ith contender has a decimal vote share v_i. For no fragmentation – one party – the index value is 1.0; for infinite fragmentation the value is 0.

As anyone can see, Flanagan's index is simply the square root of the complement of the index of fractionalization. But aside from the fact that Flanagan turns Rae's index upside down (no fragmentation, i.e., one party, receives the value 1.0), I fail to grasp in what way the index of Flanagan differs from that of Rae. Both measures are based on the same statistic: The sum of the squared percentages – a sum to which the large parties give a crushing contribution. Since Flanagan only takes the square root of the *sum* (instead of operating on its addends), nothing is actually corrected by his correction. Let us stay, therefore, with Rae, and let us test how his index of fractionalization performs in the real world.

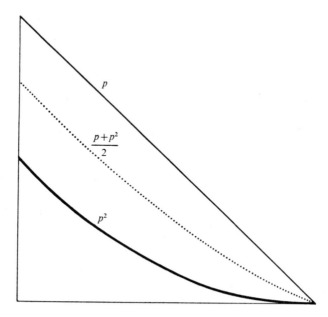

Figure 40. Quadratic performance of F index and possible correction.

The solid curve represents the performance of the F index, while the dotted curve a less elegant but perhaps more realistic formula

$$1 - \sum \left(\frac{p + p^2}{2} \right).$$

9.5 The index of fractionalization

Since Taylor and Hudson have computed the fractionalization for 101 countries,[50] I shall utilize their values and match their coefficients with my taxonomy – as in Table 41. Note that the rank ordering of Taylor and Hudson reflects a single election, and precisely any one election held between 1962 and 1968.

In my reading Table 41 is not only uninspiring but positively misinformative.[51] It is absurd, as implied by my remarks in the last column, to make "blind" runs across the world when we know for sure that our algorithm – in this case, fractionalization – does not control a number of variables that make all the difference, e.g., whether a polity is structured or not, whether the returns are reliable, the distribution preordained, the elections free, the parties under tutelage. Another major flaw of the tabulation is, clearly, that a single-shot value of fractionalization (one election only) assumes an electoral stability that cannot be assumed, in actual fact, for the countries for which I indicate the election year. That is, different electoral occasions would severely alter the overall rank ordering.[52]

The first major flaw can be counteracted by selecting a set of homogeneous countries for which a *ceteris paribus* clause for the non-controlled variables can be presumed. And the second flaw – the one-shot coefficient – can be minimized by taking the mean and/or the median of a sufficient time series. In Table 42 I have thus reduced the number of countries to 25 relatively homogeneous "stable democracies," or continuous polyarchies, over the postwar period. The table computes Rae's fractionalization, ranking the countries according to both their mean and median scores.[53]

The first finding is that the mean and the median do not affect the rank ordering in a way that would justify a clear preferability of one over the other (the median has, however, a larger spread). We are thus left to evaluate what was already very evident in the previous table and remains true – even if to a lesser extent – for the set of homogeneous countries carried over in Table 42, namely, the fact that the ranking and the coefficients bear very little relation to the clusterings of my taxonomy, and thereby to the several systemic properties sorted out by my mapping. To confront the issue more clearly, in Table 43 I cluster the 25 countries according to my typology, carrying over for each country the mean of its corresponding fractionalization score.

Can the patent discrepancies between my clusters, and the corresponding F coefficients, be explained? Clearly, a first explanation is that my taxonomy is especially sensitive to the "position value" of parties, while Rae's index is oversensitive to the "bigness" of the first or two first parties. As a consequence, countries with a very different distribution can receive very similar F scores – as exemplified below:

Table 41. *Party fractionalization (worldwide) compared with taxonomy.*
(See key to this table, p. 312.)

Rank	Country	Fraction- alization (seats)	Structured polities: class and type	New or fluid	Remarks
1	Lebanon (1964)	.945	—	—	Preordained distribution
2	Hong Kong	.900		A	
3	Indonesia (1967)	.877		A	
4	Netherlands	.830	SM		
5	Switzerland	.815	SM		
6	Finland	.803	EM		
7	Israel	.794	EM		
8	Venezuela (1963)	.760	M		Unstable returns
9	Colombia	.753	—	—	Preordained distribution on 50% basis
10	Denmark	.752	SM		
11	Ecuador (1966)	.741		A	Endemic military interference
12	Peru (1963)	.738		ND	
13	Italy	.734	EP		
15	Belgium	.725	M		
15	Ceylon	.725		D	
15	Iceland	.725	EM		
17	Norway	.720	P		
18	Panama	.713		ND	Endemic military interference
19	Sudan (1965)	.709		D	
20	Chile (1965)	.704	EP		
21	Luxembourg	.697	M		
22	Sweden	.693	P		
23	India	.682	P		
24	France	.668	P		
25	Australia	.625	T		
26	Ireland	.624	P		
27	Turkey (1965)	.620	P		
28	Guyana (1964)	.617		ND	
29	Canada (1965)	.616	T		
30	Malaysia	.589		D	
31	Japan	.586	P		
32	West Germany	.582	M		
33	Guatemala	.572		D	
34	El Salvador	.566		D	
35.5	Barbados	.565		D	
35.5	Uruguay (1966)	.565	P		

310

Rank	Country	Fraction-alization (seats)	Structured polities: class and type	New or fluid	Remarks
37	Costa Rica	.541	P		
38	Austria	.535	T		
39	New Zealand	.512	T		
40	United Kingdom	.507	T		
41.5	Honduras	.503		D	Endemic military interference
41.5	Malta	.503		T	
43	Paraguay	.496	H		Unreliable returns
44	Lesotho (1966)	.494		ND	
45	United States	.491	T		
46	Mauritius	.481		T	
47	Jamaica	.479		D	
48	Philippines	.475	P		Unreliable returns
49	Nicaragua	.463		DA	Unreliable returns
50	Trinidad and Tobago	.457		D	
51	Brazil (1966)	.438	P		Indirect military rule
52	Dominican Republic	.430		D	
53	Singapore	.416		D	
54	Uganda (1962)	.414		ND	
55	Zambia (1964)	.402		ND	
56	Gambia (1966)	.401		D	
57	South Africa	.397	P		Limited electorate (18%)
58	South Korea	.387		D	Military influence
59	Rhodesia (1965)	.385		D	Limited electorate
60	Pakistan (1965)	.377		P	
61	Puerto Rico	.370	P		
62	Bolivia (1966)	.358		D	Unstable, military influence
63	Mexico	.303	H		
64	Somalia (1964)	.280		ND	
65	Iran	.276		D	
66	Botswana (1966)	.181		D	
67	Kenya (1967)	.101		D	
68	Malagasy (1965)	.055		D	
.					
.					
.					
85	Poland		H		Wrong

Ruritania	42–36–21	$F = .650$
Belgium, 1946	46–34–11–8	$F = .654$
Kurlandia	49–30–8–7–5	$F = .656$
Italy, 1948	53–23–9–6–3–2–2–1	$F = .653$

In the example two real cases and two fictitious (but perfectly plausible) ones show how highly different distributions (fragmentations) yield F indexes that are indeed very close. Admittedly, these are ad hoc instances for illustrating the point, which do not detract from the overall validity and sensitivity of the F index across a wide range of cases.

In the second place, it is clear that the index of fractionalization does not and cannot discriminate between a *segmented* multipartism and a *polarized* multipartism. If this distinction is set aside, then the first group of countries would run from Finland (.804) to Italy (.721), including Switzerland, the Netherlands, Israel, and Denmark. But the cutting point at .721 appears very thin, and the rank ordering (Finland at the top and Italy at the bottom) is at odds with the systemic properties of the eight countries in question. The situation improves – not surprisingly – if the second group begins with Denmark or Iceland, for here the range and the rank ordering of F correspond fairly well with my perception of this cluster. But as one pursues the comparison, one is bound to conclude that there is no point in trying to patch together things that fall wide apart. That is, we are immediately confronted with another major discrepancy between the values of fractionalization on the one side, and my category of predominant-party systems on the other. The intermingling, here, is hopeless.

Unquestionably, Rae has an excellent case when he claims that "'fractionalization' may be substituted for . . . the theoretically wasteful notion of 'multipartism,' which ordinarily results in the nominal classification of one, two, and multiparty systems."[54] Indeed, with respect to this particular classification the concept of fractionalization does away with annoying questions and measures what the traditional

Key to Table 41, pp. 310–311

Key to Structured Polities:
EP = extreme (format) polarized
      (mechanics)
EM = extreme-moderate (mixed) or
      extreme semi-polarized
SM = segmented (format) moderate
      (mechanics)
M   = moderate pluralism
T   = twoparty
P   = predominant
H   = hegemonic

Key to Fluid Polities:
ND = non-dominant
D   = dominant
DA = dominant authoritarian
A   = atomized

Table 42. *Party fractionalization of 25 democracies (mean and median) 1945–1973*

	Mean		Median	
Finland	.804		.807,5	Chile
Switzerland	.801		.798	Switzerland
Chile	.796		.796	Finland
France IV	.790		.796	Israel
Netherlands	.787		.788	Netherlands
Israel	.784		.770	France IV
Denmark	.755		.743,5	Denmark
Italy	.721		.723	Italy
Ceylon	.716		.716	Iceland
Finland	.716		.708,5	Ceylon
Norway	.691		.692,5	Norway
Sweden	.685		.687	Sweden
Luxembourg	.678		.682	Luxembourg
Belgium	.667		.641	Belgium
Eire	.649		.639	Eire
Japan	.645		.635	Japan
France V	.620		.629	France V
West Germany	.614		.617,5	Canada
Uruguay	.589		.593	Australia
Canada	.574		.585	West Germany
Australia	.565		.580	Uruguay
Austria	.556		.547	Austria
United Kingdom	.512		.518,5	United Kingdom
New Zealand	.494		.499	Turkey
India	.487		.499	New Zealand
United States	.483		.490	United States
Turkey	.461		.449	India

Elections covered: Australia 1946–1972; Austria 1945–1971; Belgium 1946–1971; Canada 1945–1972; Ceylon 1952–1970; Chile 1946–1973; Denmark 1945–1973; Erie 1948–1973; Finland 1945–1972; France (Fourth Republic) 1946–1956; France (Fifth Republic) 1958–1973; West Germany 1949–1972; Iceland 1946–1971; India 1951–1971; Israel 1949–1973; Italy 1946–1972; Japan 1946–1972; Luxembourg 1945–1968; the Netherlands 1946–1971; New Zealand 1946–1972; Norway 1945–1973; Sweden 1948–1973; Switzerland 1947–1971; Turkey 1946–1973; United Kingdom 1945–1970; United States 1946–1972; Uruguay 1950–1971.

lumping "multipartism" hopelessly messes. But the case is enfeebled as the classification is improved. Granted that the fractionalization measure (and similar ones) has attractive mathematical properties, the merits of coefficients must also be weighed against what they fail to give or discern.

Table 43. *Comparison of typology and fractionalization scores (mean) of 25 democracies*

Extreme and polarized (or semi-polarized)		Predominant	
		Norway	.691
Finland	.804	Sweden	.685
Chile	.796	Japan	.645
France IV	.790	Uruguay	.589
Italy	.721	India	.487
		Turkey	.461
Moderate multipartism			
		Twoparty	
Switzerland	.801		
Netherlands	.787	Canada	.574
Israel	.784	Australia	.565
Denmark	.755	Austria	.556
Iceland	.716	United Kingdom	.512
Luxembourg	.678	New Zealand	.494
Belgium	.667	United States	.483
Eire	.649		
France V	.620		
West Germany	.614		

As noted previously, a first limit of the measure is that it cannot discriminate among different kinds of party fragmentation resulting from entirely different causal factors. According to Rae and Taylor, cleavage in a society can be of three types: (i) ascriptive (race or caste), (ii) attitudinal ("opinion" cleavages as ideology or preference), and (iii) behavioral ("act" cleavages elicited through voting and organizational membership.)[55] I do not entirely concur with this tripartition; but it is very much to the point in that Rae recognizes differences that his measure cannot seize. Whether the fragmentation of a party system reflects ascriptive, ideological, or mere "preference" cleavages, the index of fractionalization assimilates these cleavage patterns and actually measures only the "act" cleavages resulting from, and expressed by, voting behavior. Yet the difference between a segmented and a polarized fragmentation is of major consequence for the overall performance of a polity. In this instance I would say, therefore, that far from doing away with a nominal classification the measure is most fruitful *within* its ambit.[56] In the case in point, under the aegis of the distinction between a segmented and an ideologically polarized type of political society the index of fragmentation obtains the discriminating power that it does not have per se.

Rae's measure displays, however, a second limit that cannot be remedied as easily. Here we hit, in general, upon another facet of the continuity versus discontinuity issue. The mathematics in actual usage in the social sciences is not suitable for handling thresholds, and the current effort is precisely to replace nominal with ordinal-to-cardinal scales. Nonetheless, real life hinges on thresholds, confronts us with yes–no binary options, and develops, at some point, through jumps. In particular, major conflicts are such precisely because they display an all-or-none nature and entail zero sum outcomes. With respect to the universe under consideration – the world of voting – the jump, or the all-or-none threshold, is established by the majority principle. Concretely put, the real world of politics – of democratic politics, to be sure – confronts us with two crucial turning points: (i) that majority that wins a share (as opposed to the minorities that take nothing) and (ii) the absolute majority that wins all (as the right to govern alone). And the rub of the matter is that continuous measures are blind to these jumps. At this juncture our indexes and coefficients find, for the time being, their limit. Hence the two routes – mathematical and nominal – must again part company. And their respective merits and defects can be weighed only after having pursued both routes as far as we are able, to date, to pursue them.

9.6 Combining the nominal and mathematical routes

While Rae's approach is comprehended by one concept – fractionalization – my approach falls under two consecutive concepts: Format and mechanics. One may equally say that while Rae performs with one quantitative variable, I perform on the basis of two nominal variables: fragmentation and ideological distance. The very first step is about the same: counting the number of parties. And here we seem to agree to the effect that some parties are more "relevant" than others, i.e., to the effect that we should not count all the parties at their face value. The difference is that Rae's relevance is established by the *quadratic performance* of his function, while my relevance taps on, and is established by, the *position value* of the parties.

The big difference comes, however, with the second step: the size measure. While Rae measures the size with respect to the dispersion of the seats among the parties, my focus is on "natural" *size thresholds*. That is, I do not measure the size but account for it in relation to the majority principle, thereby distinguishing among: (i) a protracted 50-percent or greater majority of one party (predominant system); (ii) two parties nearing the 50-percent majority; (iii) no party nearing the absolute majority and, within this group, either relatively few parties (from three to five) or numerous parties (six and more).

The latter group could be subdivided differently, according to whether the distribution is unbalanced (multipartism with a dominant party) or balanced (even multipartism without a dominant party).[57] However, a "dominance threshold" (below the one that identifies the predominant party systems) is very difficult to draw. In particular, the difference between a major party ranging, e.g., at the 40-percent level, and a major party ranging around the 30-percent level does not appear of great consequence for the systemic properties.[58] Without detracting, therefore, from the usefulness of distinguishing also between an unbalanced and a balanced multipartism, the numerical criterion provides a better clue for sorting out the cases and especially the systemic properties. So we now have a first concept – *format* – and, specifically, four classes of format: predominance, twoparty near evenness, limited fragmentation, and extreme fragmentation. Thus while Rae's measure of the size of parties results in a ratio scale, my underpinning of natural size thresholds leaves me with a (discontinuous) classification.

Since a measure is better than a nominal ordering when it makes a better fit between theory and fact, up to this point I would say that both fractionalization and format are equally useful concepts, neither of which has a winning claim over the other. The mathematical properties of Rae's index are indeed attractive properties; but the "position value" of parties may well establish a more realistic correspondence between theory and fact. Up to this point I would say, therefore, that certain things are best seen discontinuously, i.e., focusing on thresholds, and other things are far better assessed by a continuous measurement. If I have a claim, and if I do pursue the nominal path, this is because of the next step: the linkage between the format and the *mechanics* of a polity. It is here that the measures – if unaided – leave us with little more to say.

Let it be recalled that my construction is endowed with a central assumption, namely, that low or high numbers are indicative of structural configurations that do contain *mechanical predispositions* and do harbor *systemic propensities*. For instance, the number of parties is of consequence for the stability of governments[59]; if the parties are two, immoderate politics is seldom rewarding and centrifugal competition appears suicidal for the system; if the parties range from three to five, we are still likely to find a bipolar configuration conducive to centripetal competition; whereas the very way in which more than five parties interact goes a long way to explain a centrifugal pattern of competition.[60] It should be well understood, therefore, that my counting rules and my size thresholds are placed in this far-reaching perspective. And if one looks at how the format grafts in the mechanics, that is, in an overall systemic performance, then it is fair to say, in general, that the nominal route affords – for all its limits – far more theoretical and predictive mileage than the quantitative and mathematical routes.[61]

In any event, it is here that the issue is joined. And the point can be illustrated with reference to how Taylor and Herman utilize fractionalization and other measures in order to test the influence of the party system upon government stability.[62] Their question is: How much variation in the stability of governments can be explained by variances of the parliamentary party system?

The first finding of the two authors is that while the number-of-parties variable does affect the stability of governments, Rae's index, i.e., parliamentary fractionalization, "explains one fifth of the variation in government stability," that is, twice as much. The authors suggest that this is so because Rae's measure accounts also for the size. I suspect, instead, that Rae's measure performs better than the other variable for a simpler reason, namely, that his function is not monotonic and actually weighs the relevance of parties.[63] However that may be, Taylor and Herman subsequently constrain their data along a left–right dimension, find two measures ("ordinal disagreement" and "variance") that account for the ideological position of the parties, and their conclusion to this effect is that "ideology does not play a very important role in our explanation of governmental stability." But here I cannot agree. Their actual finding is that ideological *sequencing* – in its difference from ideological *distance* – appears immaterial. This is so because their first measure simply orders the parties, and their second measure assumes equal intervals between them. Now the sequencing, or the ideological contiguity of the parties, is a good predictor of governmental coalition making; but there is no reason to assume that, once the partners are given, it has a relevance for the duration of governments (unless we stumble on a rare case of non-adjacent coalition). And the assumption of equal intervals is simply wrong – as is patently revealed by their subsequent and best finding, namely, that "the proportion of seats held by anti-system parties was the best single indicator of governmental stability."[64]

Needless to say, the "best finding" of Taylor and Herman is very pleasing for my taxonomy; but the way they interpret it falls short of the mark. In the first place, it has nothing to do with their previous measures: It is based on the purely "nominal" distinction between pro-system and anti-system parties. In the second place, this distinction has to do (despite their denial) with ideology, for it points to a markedly different ideological distance, or a markedly unequal interval, between two groups (classes) of parties. Hence their best finding actually hinges on the concept of *ideological distance*, which enables them, in turn, to isolate a measurable variable, i.e., the size of the anti-system parties. And these amendments put in a different perspective their final conclusion, namely, that "our best explanation of government stability was the combined linear influence of the size of the anti-system parties and the fractionalization of the pro-system parties."[65] To be sure, the size of the anti-system parties has to be related to the number of pro-system parties. For instance, two large parties only, one anti and the other pro, would be ominous for the stability of the system itself but would surely produce maximal stability of government. Nonetheless, the fractionalization measure plays no special role in the matter: The pure and simple count of the number of relevant pro-system parties would do just as well. Hence the best explanation of Taylor and Herman misses why the anti-system variable turns out to be their best single indicator. In my understanding of the mechanics of polarized pluralism, this is so because the sizable existence of anti-system parties is an indicator of centrifugal strains, if not of centrifugal competition and, thereby, of the likelihood that the pro-system group of parties itself is troubled by excessive ideological distance. Thus the truly explanatory hypothesis is that (i) governmental stability is negatively correlated to the number and heterogeneity of the potential coalition partners (where "heterogeneity" stands for ideological distance between), and that (ii) the best available indicator to date of such heterogeneity is the appeal (measured by the size) of the anti-system parties. Let it be added that the foregoing hypothesis has the further merit of introducing the real problem – which is not the "duration" of governments but their "effectiveness" and efficiency. This is an ulterior problem because it is very dubious whether a long duration is equal to, or grows linearly with, a greater efficiency.

What we learn from the foregoing discussion is how much Taylor and Herman owe to the qualitative or nominal science. Not only are all the contours of the problems they investigate drawn by the qualitative science, but they hit on their best variable because they pick up, along the way, a distinction (between pro-system and anti-system parties) that surely is a typological construct and surely escapes the discriminating power of all their measures. Thus if their explanatory logic is less powerful and stringent than it might otherwise be, this is precisely because they feel the need to take their distance from the nominal science: ". . . the establishment of precise empirical relationships is not materially helped by the use of *mere typologies* [of party systems]. . . ."[66]

By this I do not intend in the least to contribute to the bad relationships between the nominal and the quantitative science. Quite to the contrary, my intent has been, throughout the past three sections, to show how much both camps have to gain by implementing one another. The qualitative science largely remains with the hypotheses it generates and badly needs, therefore, measures that both refine and test these hypotheses. On the other hand, we must beware of a precision that is nothing but an operational artifact. In particular, measures are all the more useful and necessary the more we have first identified the problems, mapped the cases, and suggested causal explanations, that is, the more they are entered under well-circumscribed sets of nominal qualifications and assumptions. Words *alone* beat numbers alone. Words *with* numbers beat words alone. And numbers make sense, or much greater sense, *within* verbal theory.

NOTES TO CHAPTER 9

1 "Political Development and Political Decay," cit., *passim.*
2 See, *contra*, Gurr and McClelland, *Political Performance: A Twelve-Nation Study*, op. cit., esp. pp. 11–13 and *passim*. I am indebted, however, to their lucid analysis.
3 In general we may say – with respect to South America – that most of its party systems are not structured qua systems, but that parties may well remain, even when the military are in control, "visible and functioning political units." As a rule, and even when they cannot participate effectively in the political process, "repressive measures have not been taken against the presence of parties . . ." (Peter Ranis, "A Two-Dimensional Typology of Latin American Political Parties," *JP*, August 1968, p. 798). On Argentina a recent study is Guillermo O'Donnel, *Modernization and Bureaucratic-Authoritarianism: Studies in South American Politics*, Berkeley, Institute of International Studies, 1973.
4 *Supra*, 7.3.
5 See, *contra*, Kemal H. Karpat, *Turkey's Politics: The Transition to a Multiparty System*, Princeton University Press, 1959. In general, see Dankwart A. Rustow, "The Development of Parties in Turkey," in LaPalombara and Weiner, *Political Parties and Political Development*, op. cit., ch. 4; and Clement H. Dodd, *Politics and Government in Turkey*, California University Press, 1969.
6 Up until 1957 (included) no official figures of the voting turnout are available.
7 Until 1973, because at the last elections two consistent third parties have emerged: the National Salvation party, an Islamic formation that obtained 48 seats, and the Democratic party (not to be confused with the one banned in 1960), with 45 seats, exactly 10 percent, a conservative formation – both resulting from breakaways from the Justice party of Demirel. If one considers, in addition, that also the RPP underwent a split, the Republican Reliance party (with 13 seats in 1973), it would seem that Turkey is one of the countries in which the pattern of one-party predominance has come to an end. Given, however, the characteristic elasticity of the electorate, the prediction appears premature.
8 See Walter F. Weiker, *The Turkish Revolution 1960–61: Aspects of Military Politics*, Brookings Institution, 1963.
9 D. A. Rustow, "Turkey: The Modernity of Tradition," in Pye and Verba, *Political Culture and Political Development*, cit., p. 198.

10 On Spain see the writings of Linz, cit. *supra*, ch. 7, n. 13; and, in addition, Juan Linz, "From Falange to Movimiento-Organizacion: The Spanish Single Party and the Franco Regime," in Huntington and Moore, *Authoritarian Politics in Modern Societies*, cit.; and Klaus von Beyme, *Vom Fascismus zur Entwicklungsdiktatur: Machtelite und Opposition in Spanien*, Piper, 1971.

11 In spite of being the last addition to the list, Tunisia was entered more than ten years ago. See Clement H. Moore, "The Neo-Destour Party of Tunisia: Structure for Democracy," *WP*, April 1962, pp. 461–482.

12 Greece does not enter this group of countries, since its military dictatorships (remember that the seven-year dictatorship ended in the fall of 1974 was preceded by the one of General Metaxas in 1936–1941) resemble in many ways the Latin American pattern of being interruptions that do not testify to an "entry" into democracy but more to a "reinstatement" of democracy – albeit a very perturbed one. On the Greek parties see Jean Meynaud et al., *Les Forces Politiques en Grèce*, Montreal, Meynaud Editions, 1965.

13 The more recent reformulation of this argument – to which I equally object – is by Huntington and Moore, *Authoritarian Politics in Modern Society*, cit., pp. 17–22, in the sect. "From Monopoly to Competition: The Democratization of Exclusionary One-Party Systems."

14 *Supra*, 2.2.

15 *Supra*, 3.1.

16 The text implies that the positioning in Table 33 of the predominant party system abides by the logic of establishing a continuum, without detracting, therefore, from the fact that a situation of predominance is unrelated to the format.

17 Which obtains, in turn, a scheme of analysis of its own. See in general ch. 8, *supra*, and especially 8.3, Table 30.

18 *Infra*, 9.4 and 9.5.

19 *Supra*, esp. 6.2.

20 Carl G. Hempel, *Fundamentals of Concept Formation in Empirical Science*, University of Chicago Press, 1952, p. 51.

21 On the autonomy vs. the sociological reduction of politics, see G. Sartori, "What Is 'Politics,'" *PT*, February 1973, esp. pp. 21–23.

22 *Supra*, 7.1.

23 The bibliography on the various measures of competition is in ch. 7, nn. 3, 5. For the importance of measurability see *infra*, esp. 9.3 and 9.5.

24 See Rajni Kothari, *Implications of Nation-Building for the Typology of Political Systems* (mimeo), paper presented at the 1967 IPSA Congress, Bruxelles.

25 I deliberately say "logic of gradation" instead of "logic of comparison." The latter denomination leans on the authority of Hempel (*loc. cit.* n. 20, above, pp. 54–58) and is picked up by, among others, Arthur L. Kallberg, "The Logic of Comparison," *WP*, I, 1966, and by Felix E. Oppenheim, "The Language of Political Enquiry," in Greenstein and Polsby, eds., *Handbook of Political Science*, cit. Nonetheless, it is a misnomer, for also the logic of classification "compares" (this is how differences and similarities are sorted out).

26 Abraham Kaplan, *The Conduct of Enquiry*, Chandler, 1964, p. 13.

27 See, on the point, the perceptive discussion of Robert T. Holt and John M. Richardson, in Holt and John E. Turner, eds., *The Methodology of Comparative Research*, Free Press, 1970, pp. 58–69, of what they describe as "atheoretic approaches to theory development."

28 For a broader treatment of the views expressed in this section see my chapter in G. Sartori, F. Riggs, H. Teune, *Tower of Babel: On the Definition and Analysis of Concepts in the Social Sciences*, Pittsburgh, International Studies Association, Occasional Paper No. 6, 1975.

29 Scalapino and Masumi, *Parties and Politics in Contemporary Japan*, cit., pp. 79–81. The authors opt, in fact, for the last possibility, which can be made equivalent to my predominant type.

30 Burns, *The Deadlock of Democracy*, cit., *supra*, ch. 6, n. 87.

31 That this class amounts to a pseudoclass has been argued *supra*, 6.5.

32 In *Les Partis Politiques*, cit., *supra*, ch. 6, n. 1.

33 Ergun Ozbudun, "Established Revolutions Versus Unfinished Revolutions: Contrasting Patterns of Democratization in Mexico and Turkey," in Huntington and Moore, *Authoritarian Politics in Modern Society*, cit., p. 382. See *supra*, 7.3, Table 28 (Mexico); and 9.1, Table 32 (Turkey).

34 *Man and His Government*, op. cit., p. 28.

35 *Supra*, 5.2.

36 The coalition weight can be measured by counting the cabinet positions held by each party over time both in terms of the percent of cabinet shares, and of the time spent in office.

37 *Supra*, 6.4.

38 France is discussed *supra*, 6.2. See also Table 10.

39 *Supra*, 6.2.

40 *Supra*, 6.1 and Table 9.

41 Party government and coalitions will be discussed at the end of vol. II.

42 Douglas Rae – to whom I am greatly indebted for his very helpful criticisms of this chapter – feels that this conclusion amounts to admitting that my notions of relevance and especially of blackmail potential fail the test of operationalizability. This is true if operationalization is made equal to measurement. However, I disagree with this assimilation (see Sartori et al., *Tower of Babel*, cit., pp. 21–22. On the other hand, Rae does propose a measure that is close enough, in intent, to the one I indicate and that may well be more satisfactory ("An Estimate for the Decisiveness of Election Outcomes," in Bernhardt Lieberman, ed., *Social Choice*, Allan Smith, 1974, ch. 3.3).

43 "Typologies of Democratic Systems," *CPS*, I, 1968, pp. 33–34.

44 Switzerland is hardly relevant to the point, since it has, at the federal level, a preordained system of power sharing and rotation. For the bibliography see *supra*, ch. 6, n. 38.

45 See Blondel, "Party Systems and Patterns of Government in Western Democracies," *CJPS*, June 1968, esp. pp. 184–187; and *Introduction to Comparative Government*, op. cit., pp. 155–160 and Table 10-1.

46 Rae's measure incorporates, in effect, the two variables of Lijphart

and Blondel, namely, the vote (seat) share of the strongest party and the combined vote (seat) shares of the two strongest parties. I have discussed them separately for the clarity of the exposition.

47 See esp. Rae, *The Political Consequences of Electoral Laws*, cit., pp. 46–64; but also D. Rae and Michael Taylor, *An Analysis of Political Cleavages*, Yale University Press, 1970, ch. 2. The formula of Rae (F) has many notations. I reproduce in the text and utilize the one of Taylor and Herman in *APSR*, March 1971, p. 30 (below, n. 62).

48 I owe the suggestion to Alberto Marradi.

49 Scott C. Flanagan, "The Japanese System in Transition," *CP*, January 1971, esp. pp. 234–235.

50 *World Handbook of Political and Social Indicators*, rev. ed., 1972, cit., p. 21 and Table 2.6, pp. 48–50. With respect to the original table I leave out the fractionalization of the vote (which is incomplete), the indication of the source, the date of the elections (except when this information is essential), and all the countries whose fractionalization is .000, i.e., the one-party countries. Taylor and Hudson apply a more sophisticated version of Rae's formula, which accounts more accurately than my notation for the small n's and N's. However, the differences between the two sets of coefficients are almost invariably below the 1-percent level.

51 Rae would presumably concur, for he actually warns against the blind use of his formula in *The Analysis of Political Cleavage*, op. cit., pp. 5, 33–35.

52 This can be seen in Arthur S. Banks, *Cross-Polity Time-Series Data*, MIT Press, 1971, pp. 282–295, where the Rae coefficients are calculated by year.

53 The table draws on the research material assembled and processed, at Stanford, by Andrew Perry, at the time a graduate student of Almond, with the help and under the financial assistance of the Center of Advanced Study in the Behavioral Sciences. I wish to express my deep gratitude to both Andrew Perry and the Center.

54 Douglas Rae, "A Note on the Fractionalization of Some European Party Systems," *CPS*, October 1968, p. 413.

55 Rae and Taylor, *The Analysis of Political Cleavages*, cit., p. 1.

56 This is tantamount to saying that F does measure some part, or in part, what my taxonomy considers.

57 This is not quite the same distinction as the one proposed by Blondel, *Introduction to Comparative Government*, cit., pp. 157–158. In his analysis Denmark, Sweden, Norway, Italy, Iceland, and the Netherlands are "multiparty with a dominant party" (with a mode of 45–35–20); whereas Switzerland, Finland, and France are declared "multiparty without a dominant party." The difference is, then, that Blondel extends his first class to cover also the predominant party systems.

58 The major perceivable difference seems to reside in the greater or lesser share of cabinet posts; unless the major party also enjoys (this being an additional condition) a pivotal positioning.

59 Lijphart disagrees ("Typologies of Democratic Systems," cit., p. 35) but is contradicted, in turn, by Taylor and Herman: "Lijpart's assertion 'that there is no empirical relationship between the number of parties in the system and its stability' seems unwar-

ranted" (see below, n. 62, p. 30). However, their scrutiny bears on governmental stability, while Lijphart's point is more general.

60 These and other systemic properties are discussed in ch. 6 and summarized in Figure 35. See also, *infra,* 10.4.

61 I am again indebted to Rae for pointing out that it is neither fair nor illuminating to compare an index with a theory. It should be well understood, therefore, that my point bears, here, on two broad outlooks, or approaches – surely not on the specific measures selected for illustration.

62 Michael Taylor and V. M. Herman, "Party System and Government Stability," *APSR*, March 1971, pp. 28–37.

63 The measure of governmental fragmentation suggested in 9.4, Table 37, would perform, presumably, even better.

64 Taylor and Herman, loc. cit. The quotations are from pp. 31, 34, 37.

65 Ibid., p. 37.

66 Ibid., p. 30, n. 10. My emphasis.

10

Spatial competition

10.1 The Downsian theory revisited

Anthony Downs' landmark *Economic Theory of Democracy*, published in 1957 but circulated earlier, deals exactly with what the title says. Not only does Downs draw from an "economic" theoretical perspective, but his style – and one might also say his method – is deductive, though not in the rigorous and formalized fashion of current deductive theorizing. Since Downs assumes that citizens in a democracy primarily act to maximize their self-interest and their utility income, that "parties formulate policies in order to win elections, rather than win elections in order to formulate policies," and that the primary objective of politicians "is to be elected,"[1] it is consequential to these premises that a theory of elections is very central to his theory of democracy. Thus Downs can be read and developed along three perspectives: (i) within the general context of theories of democracy, (ii) in terms of a better formal and deductive fit between economic premises and the theory of elections, and/or (iii) by isolating his spatial model of party competition and testing it against empirical findings.

As a theorist of democracy it suffices to note that Downs does not even begin to explain how a democracy comes into being, but that his interpretation appears more convincing the more we read it as an explanation of how democracies inevitably deteriorate and end up performing as meanly as they do. This is, however, the least pursued way of developing Downs.[2] The second reading focuses on his spatial theory of elections, but in the light of more rigorous and mathematically formalized premises. Much of this development hinges, in fact, on rational choice theory of the game-theoretic variety. As has been concisely stated: "Spatial theory is but a particular formulation of elections as a game in the Von Neumann-Morgenstern sense. . . ."[3] The third reading of Downs neglects the premises (the rational-action assumption), does not seek a more formalized model, and tests the spatial model of party competition against the evidence on voting behavior. Donald Stokes was the first to take issue with the Downsian model with reference to its empirical applicability, while Philip Converse has been especially sensitive to its bearing on the interpretation of the data.[4]

My own interest in Downs is very close to the one of Stokes and Converse, except that I shall gradually move away from the U.S. evidence in an attempt to develop the model of inter-party competition where it works least, that is, in multiparty settings. Also for this reason I shall equally leave aside the mathematical approach, since the theorems of the formalized spatial theory are "virtually irrelevant to the analysis of multiparty proportional representation systems."[5]

The first thing to note is that the theme that appears central to most interpreters was not exploited as such by Downs himself, for it is wrapped and somewhat hidden in a chapter whose title is, "The Statics and Dynamics of Party Ideologies." One immediately senses, here, the difficulties that Downs creates for himself in order to be consistent with his premises. Ideologies are difficult to enter, and especially to rationalize, on grounds of economic rationality. Downs contends that "three factors . . . explain how wide ideological variance can develop out of our vote-maximizing hypothesis. They are the heterogeneity of society, the inevitability of social conflict, and uncertainty."[6] Fine for the variance – but how does this explain ideology? Downs actually lays the emphasis on "uncertainty," which is his major intervening variable; and the general thrust of his argument is that with regard to parties ideologies accrue to their distinctiveness, whereas with regard to voters ideologies are "shortcuts" that save them the cost of being informed. This is convincing enough – except that the economic premises lead Downs to conceptualize ideology very narrowly, that is, only from the vantage point of how ideologies are "rationally" put to use and exploited. Nor is a deductive apparatus needed for making the point that ideology is an economizing device for the voters and a "means for getting votes" for the parties.[7]

The backing of an economic theory helps even less the development of Downs' spatial model of party competition as such. It is true that the suggestion comes from two economists, Hotelling and Smithies; but it does not follow that his borrowing of the "spatial analogy"[8] is amenable to an analogical treatment. In 1929 Hotelling sought to explain why two competing stores end up by placing themselves, along Main Street, right next door. In 1941 Smithies improved the argument by pointing out that the demands of the consumers are "elastic" (they may not buy if both stores are too distant, that is, if transportation costs are too high). The implication is that while the two stores will still tend to converge, nevertheless their optimal location (equilibrium) is reached when their closeness does not discourage the hinterland consumers placed at the extreme ends.

Now the crucial issue with respect to the Downsian spatial model is whether a voting space is unidimensional, or whether this assumption is far too restrictive. Therefore, Downs can well proceed by analogy in replacing consumers with voters and firms with parties, but *not* with respect to how a physical space (Main Street or a railroad) relates to a symbolic space. The fact that Main Street is linear cannot testify in the least to the fact that the space of politics (of competitive politics) equally is linear, i.e., unidimensional. We are thus faced with the conclusion that at the most important juncture of his theory of elections Downs fails us precisely because of a misleading economic analogy.

Presumably, Downs realizes that his unidimensionality rests on shaky credentials. The most interesting property of his theory of competition is that leapfrogging is difficult and generally impeded. Adjacent parties can converge or move apart but cannot leap past each other. Downs well understands the centrality of this point but dares not deduce it from, or impute it to, the assumed unidimensionality of his space. What "prevents a party from making ideological leaps over the heads of its neighbours"[9] is explained with the concepts of "integrity and responsibility."[10] So, after having introduced a unidimensional space of competition Downs defends its most important property on entirely different grounds that are, in turn, entirely extraneous to an economic perspective.

For the completeness of the argument it is fair to recall that when Downs assumes that "each stand [of each party] can be assigned a position on our left–right scale," he is actually pursuing another cue, namely, that "the party's net position on this scale is a weighted average of the positions of all the particular policies it upholds."[11] This is in effect the cue picked up by the interpreters interested in the mathematical formalization. However, along this latter route we quickly encounter difficulties that should not block the empirical line of development. Recasting Downs more rigorously, his basic suggestion is that the voter's position over an Euclidean space represents his "utility function." And we know how thorny this concept turns out to be. Along this route we equally and quickly stumble into Arrow's intransitivity of preferences and, moreover, into "equilibria problems" that become very nasty as soon as we move from a two-person zero-sum conceptualization (the case of twopartism) to an *n*-person (multiperson and multiparty) conceptualization of competition that cannot be adequately dealt with in a pairwise fashion.[12]

The superfluity of an economic approach to a spatial theory of interparty competition, and indeed the advantage of separating the two things, can also be highlighted with respect to the very definition of party.

If parties are defined as "vote maximizers," the objection immediately is that this conceptualization is largely untrue to the facts. Likewise, Downs is often criticized because he assumes parties to be "teams," and indeed coherent and unified teams, rather than largely disconnected and multifaceted "coalitions." But let us recall our initial, minimal definition: Party is any political group capable of placing through elections candidates for public office.[13] Now, surely, this definition embraces all the following kinds of parties: (i) witness parties, uninterested in maximizing votes; (ii) ideological parties, interested in votes primarily via indoctrination; (iii) responsible parties, which do not submit policies to maximizing votes; (iv) responsive parties, for which winning elections or maximizing votes take priority; and, finally, (v) purely demagogic, irresponsible parties, which are only vote maximizers. Our minimal definition does not suffer, then, from any "economic" restriction or assumption. Yet if the question, "What do parties compete for?" is raised, it seems quite natural to me to reply: As a rule, for votes – for my definition does imply that parties cease to be such (even though they may survive qua movements, political associations, or pressure groups) when they do not muster votes. This does not mean that parties compete *only* for votes, nor that votes are an end in themselves. Votes are a *means* for staying in the market and a means for enacting policy. Therefore, parties do not necessarily formulate policies in order to win elections; nonetheless, it can well be maintained that *at elections* parties are vote maximizers. Likewise, it is contrary to fact to assume that parties are unified teams; and yet it makes perfect sense to assert that *at elections* even multi-appeal and faction-riddled parties tend to perform as teams.

To sum up, the theory of Downs has actually been furthered in either one of two directions – mathematical and empirical. Along the first route his premises are made stringent and formalized. Along the second route, by giving up the deductive apparatus and relaxing the economic premises his model of party competition overcomes unnecessary objections without suffering – I would add – any loss. This is so because whenever the economic analogies hold, we can still put them to insightful use. Thus the analogue of the witness-type party can well be the firm that does not compete via prices but via high quality, prestige products. At the other end, the analogue of the purely demagogic party is provided by a set of perfectly competitive sales-maximizing firms; while the in-between cases can be assimilated to profit-seeking (though not necessarily maximizing) oligopolies. These analogies help us, in turn, to assess the thresholds at which we either have too much or too little competition – thereby underpinning, among other things, the warning that ever more "competitiveness" is not an unmixed blessing.[14]

10.2 *Issues, identification, images, and positions*

Voting behavior studies provide most of the empirical evidence that substantiates or disconfirms a spatial interpretation of party competition. A disproportionate amount of this evidence is drawn, however, from the U.S. scene or is influenced – when drawn from other countries – by the survey designs originally devised for the American voter. On both counts, for comparative purposes the findings of American scholars are less interesting than their concepts. And three concepts – unknown to Downs and largely articulated after the time of his writing – stand out as being crucial to our understanding of voting: (i) issue, (ii) identification, and (iii) image.

With respect to "issue" the central questions are: To what extent do voters have an issue awareness and an *issue perception?* To what extent do an issue orientation and an issue preference affect their party choice, thereby leading to *issue voting* (or policy voting)? And, in any case, how do voters relate issues to parties and party policies? Moreover, if issues are found to be relevant for a spatial model, then we have a third major connotation of the concept: not only (i) issue perceptions and (ii) issue voting, but also (iii) *issue positions.* What is an issue? Issues are not such unless they are visible and controversial. I equally take issue to mean a bounded set of problems that can be isolated and is indeed perceived in isolation – not only in its distinctiveness but because of its distinctiveness. Brian Barry wonders whether issue should include "group-interest" responses such as "good for the working class."[15] I would definitely reply in the negative. If "good for the working class" is understood as a permissible formulation of an issue, then almost anything can be declared such, and the concept is of no analytical avail.

Issue voters having issue perceptions and issue preferences are often contrasted with "identified voters," i.e., with the voters who identify themselves with a given candidate or party symbol. However, an identified voter can be highly informed on the issues. Conversely, the issue-insensitive voter need not be "identified."[16] Clearly, there are voters who are neither aware of issues nor identified whose motivation for voting may simply be social pressure, or "negative voting" – voting against some feared enemy or outcome.

The foregoing introduces the second concept: identification or, in full, *partisan identification.* Identified voters are supposed to be stand-patters: They always vote for the same candidate or party regardless of what it says or does. This assumes, however, "strong identifiers." Surveys generally distinguish between strong and weak identifiers and assume that the latter are likely to be unstable or defecting voters. But this assumption may well be entirely incorrect. If one accounts, e.g., for negative voting, feeble identifiers may well turn out to be very stable voters. In any event, while we may say that the identified voters are standpatters, the obverse is not true: We cannot really say that all stable voters are "loyalists" identified with "their" party.

Both with respect to issue voting and partisan identification the note of caution is that we often confuse two different things: (i) the actual *variance–invariance* of the voting choice and (ii) the *motivation* for being a switcher or a standpatter. The caution is, then, that from the voting *behavior* we cannot infer the *personality type* of the voter, that is, his motivations. A standpatter need not be "identified" and can indeed be a highly informed, articulate and issue-alerted citizen. Conversely, a switcher may be highly uninformed and issue-insensitive and simply drift randomly or according to some kind of Markovian process.[17] It should be clear, therefore, that issue voting and partisan identification refer to different types of voting motivations, *not* to how many voters do in fact change or split their vote.

Issue voting and partisan identification are best conceived as the opposite ends of a continuum. If so, it is useful to have an in-between concept in which issues and identifications can blend, albeit in very different ways and proportions. Moreover, under the assumption that voters are identified, their way of linking to a given party is obvious; but how do the issue voters link to parties and select among the parties? On both counts we need at least another concept: *party image.* The third concept has been utilized and developed far less than the other two. Yet I take it that parties communicate to mass electorates via party images and that much of their electoral strategy is concerned with building up the appropriate image for the public from which they expect votes.

Party image is not the same thing as *party identification.* Although the two concepts obviously are related to one another, it is quite possible . . . to identify with the same party but to have very different mental pictures of it. . . . Although party image is not as deeply rooted or as stable as party identification, it is likely to be less ephemeral than voter attitudes toward the issues and candidates.[18]

Yes – but there is more to it. An image is – in my understanding – a vague *policy package* condensed in, and rendered by, one word or slogan. "Good for the workers" or, even better, "workers' party" is an image (not an issue). The labels liberal and conservative, progressive and reactionary, left and right, typically exemplify the images for which parties maneuver and outmaneuver one another.

How does one select, then, a given party? If the answer is – as I suggest – via a party image, then the question turns on how the image (not the identification) interplays with the issues. Therefore, from the issue end of the process the question is: How do issue preferences enter the image and eventually alter the identification? Needless to say, our findings do not adequately address these questions. On the other hand, questions necessarily precede the findings.

Issue, identification, and image are thus the major concepts employed for understanding why voters vote as they do. How do these concepts relate to the Downsian model of spatial competition?

In his influential criticism Stokes puts forward three major objections. First, political conflict cannot be reduced to a single dimension, for the findings point to several "dimensions of attitude" toward issues that are independent (inconsistent) from one another. Second, on many issues – such as fighting corruption, promoting prosperity, etc. – parties have exactly the same "position" (they do not offer alternatives: they all oppose corruption); and this entails that "valence issues", as Stokes calls them, cannot be given a spatial ordering even though they play a major role, for one party rather than all takes the blame for past corruption, and only one party is believed, or credible, in promising to fight corruption. Third, it is a fact that "only about one tenth of the electorate [in the 1952, 1956, and 1960 presidential elections] by the loosest definition is found to be using the liberal-conservative distinction or any other ideological concept. By a more reasonable count, the proportion is something like three percent."[19]

The first criticism is somewhat puzzling. Stokes assumes an "issue public" at a time when the findings of his Michigan colleagues were that issue orientations and issue perceptions were weakly related to electoral choices, and that party identifications were the single most powerful motivation of voting behavior in the United States.[20] As Angus Campbell and Converse succinctly put it, "nearly everyone in our samples could be placed in a unitary dimension of party identification"[21] and, "for the public, in sharp contrast to the elite, party preference seems . . . relatively unconnected to issue positions."[22] So why make "issues" the issue? While Stokes seemingly builds up a case that the evidence of the fifties does not warrant, theoretically his point is impeccable, namely, that the Downsian model navigates poorly with respect to, and in terms of, issues.

The second criticism of Stokes brings out the interesting distinction between position issues and valence issues. In essence, a valence issue is a nonpartisan issue, an issue on which there is no disagreement, and yet *is* an issue in that one party accuses another of being untrue to its verbal stands. Pressing the point further we arrive at the question: Why is one party "believed" while another is not? A first reply is that electors are not fooled by what the parties say. But there is more to it. So-called valence issues point, it seems to me, to the juncture at which issue perceptions become largely monitored by party images and identifications. Ultimately, the question hinges on whether identifying with a party establishes – first and above all – "the authorities," indeed the cognitive authorities, on whom mass publics rely for believing, or not believing, in what they are told.[23]

The third criticism of Stokes is that the American voter virtually ignores the left–right spatial imagery, and that even the liberal-conservative mapping is seldom utilized and even more rarely understood. Here Stokes is in keeping with the findings of the Michigan Survey Research Center. So here the blow to the Downsian model appears to be a deadly one. However, at the end of his article Stokes points out that "political conflict *can* be focused on a single, stable issue domain which presents an ordered-dimension. . . . Let us call this the case of *strong ideological focus*. On the other hand, political controversy can be diffused over a number of changing issue concerns . . . the case of *weak ideological focus*."[24] Since this surely is a central point, I propose to take it up in due course. At the moment let us pursue our sweeping review of the American findings.

It was especially Key's *The Responsible Electorate* that attempted to reestablish the cogent connection between voting preference and issues that had been found lacking by the Michigan surveys. Key was motivated by an ethical or at least a practical concern: If politicians "see voters as most certainly responsive to nonsense, they will give them nonsense. If they see voters susceptible to delusion, they will delude them."[25] While I do share Key's concern, let us also bear in mind that democratic controls do not rest only on the *demos* – so that the fairest deal is, perhaps, to ask of an electorate what it can give, and no more. In any event, in the late sixties the fact finders began to search for what Key asked, and the facts themselves underwent a change.[26] The 1964 election revealed a greater ideological awareness and a better perception of party differences. Goldwater did succeed, though not to his own benefit, in moving the Republican party image rightward – just as McGovern succeeded, in 1972, in moving the Democratic image leftward. Concurrently, the 1968 election – with Vietnam, campus, and racial unrest at their heights – did bring these issues to the fore and did increase the amount of "policy voting." In the latest accounts, then, the American voters are found to be more ideologically conscious or at least more motivated by the liberal-conservative image of parties.

To be sure, the recent literature finds more issue voting than before also because it has been searching – with the aid of issue-sensitive measures – for what it has found. Nonetheless, the figures unquestionably speak to a changing pattern. While almost no net change occurred from 1952 to 1964, by 1972 more than one-third of the American electorate turned out to be "independent," that is, non-identified; and only about one-half appeared strongly identified with one of the two major parties. More precisely the independents were about 23 percent from 1952 to 1964, and rose to 29.5 and 35.1 percent respectively in 1968 and 1972. The Democratic identifiers reached a peak of 52.2 in 1964, but were at 41 percent in 1972. The Republican identifiers were about 30 percent in 1956 and 1960, and down to 24 percent in 1972.[27] On the other hand, these changes are hardly surprising if one considers that the 1964, 1968, and 1972 presidential elections were held under a greening America deeply wounded by Vietnam and heated by racial issues. Nor does it appear that any of these elections taken singly was really "critical," i.e., reflected a deep, durable, and fundamental re-alignment.[28] All variations considered, the central conclusion of the Michigan surveys of the fifties still stands: Partisan identifications re-main, despite everything, the single major determinant of American voting behavior. This conclusion holds not so much because the per-centages still remain on its side, but especially because it cannot be disproved by the finding that more people perceive more issues. What matters is the *direction of causality*. Is it the issue orientation that actually determines the voting choice? Or is it the party identification and image that shape the issue perceptions and preferences? One can reply neither or reply both. Yet the problem of which is the indepen-dent variable – to what extent, with respect to what proportion of the electorate – remains. No doubt, partisan identifications may well derive from issue attitudes – but from remote ones, going all the way back to the age and processes of socialization. And, presumably, partisan iden-tifications include policy preferences. However, these conditions will obtain a high consistency between issue preference and party choice that still does not speak to the direction of causation, to the question whether the votes are actually cast *because*, and on the basis of, issues.

The irony of the situation is, then, that when Stokes was – in his first criticism – untrue to his evidence and somewhat unfair to Downs, he was vindicated by the subsequent evidence; and that when he did rest on the findings of the fifties (that the American voter was not located in an ideological space), the findings of the sixties and seven-ties undermined his criticism and vindicated the applicability of the Downsian model. As noted earlier, a spatial model of party competition navigates poorly with issue voters. Conversely, the model applies best under the assumption that voters are ideologically conscious and sensi-tive to the left–right imagery. The intuitive reason for this is that issues can hardly be reduced to a single dimension, whereas the most attractive property of the Downsian model is precisely its unidimen-sionality. Upon further reflection, however, it appears that the voting findings do not easily fit the Downsian model unless an additional (fourth) concept is entered – *positioning* – under two formulations, namely, *position-perception* and *position-image*. The notion of position-perception implies that the voter places himself and the parties in some kind of *spatial ordering*, in a row; and the notion of position-image implies that parties maneuver precisely for conveying to the electorate a *spatial location* of themselves. Given position-perceptions and position-images, then – but only then – can we fruitfully employ the notion of "issue position" in an "issue space."

Having laid out the conceptual framework for organizing the findings, let us outline the full set of conditions under which we should, or should not, expect a spatial model of competition to be serviceable.

1. Where no structured party system exists, the prevalent determinant of voting behavior is some kind of attachment to a notable – and we may thus speak, in short, of *personality voting*. This entails, in substance, that the Downsian model has no bearing on the Third World and until the scene is entered by mass parties.

2. *Policy voting*, that is, a voting choice determined by issues and reacting to the policy stands of parties, is relatively rare; it neither occurs all the time nor can it be easily demonstrated that issue perceptions and orientations are the independent variable. However, when issue or policy voting does occur, it is hardly amenable to a spatial representation, and even less to a single spatial dimension.[29]

3. Whenever politics develops, whenever electorates have a capacity for abstraction, and whenever the party system is structured by mass parties, the strong presumption is that *position-voting related to party images* represents the single, prevalent determinant of the voting choice. And to the extent that voters are *position-oriented,* to the same extent the spatial understanding of party competition is worth pursuing.

4. While voters surely have issue preferences – for otherwise realigning elections would never occur and deviating elections would be difficult to explain – the question hinges on the *defection point*, or the breaking point, that is, the point at which a nondesired issue-policy of the preferred party is perceived and breaks the preexisting image, loyalty, or affiliation of the voter to a given party.

5. Issue voting is easier and therefore more likely within the simpler systems – twopartism – and becomes more unmanageable the more the party system is complicated by an increasing number of parties and especially by coalition governments.

6. Concurrently, issue voting gives way to position-voting as we pass from a feeble to a strong ideological focus, that is, from pragmatic to ideological politics.[30]

The first three points, or generalizations, simply delineate the area of applicability of the Downsian model. The fourth attempts to meet Key's apprehensions by pointing out that neither identifications nor position-voting implies that voters can be fooled to no end, for parties do worry about the defection point. After all, the mechanism through which a voter becomes identified is the party image – and the image is related, in turn, to basic, if vague and elastic, issue orientations. As for the last two generalizations, they simply point to the broad hypotheses to which we shall now turn for closer inspection.

10.3 Multidimensional, unidimensional, and ideological space

The question with which we have yet to come to grips is: What is a "political space"? More precisely: In what kind of space do parties compete? Surely they do not compete in the geographic or physical space of Hotelling and Smithies. Nor is it sufficient to reply that parties compete in a symbolic or figurative space. Furthermore, the transition from a spatial configuration of politics to an ideological type of space is, far more often than not, too easily assumed.

Let us call a left–right arrangement a spatial imagery. Its only property is, as such, to *order* objects side by side (horizontally) in a flat (unidimensional) space. And this is nothing more, in itself, than a *spatial archetype*. How does it enter politics? A spatial translation of political perceptions in terms of left and right was first used during the course of the French Revolution, in perfect keeping with an ideological "development of politics," but with specific reference to the seating arrangements – left side, right side – in parliament. And while value connotations have always been intended, throughout the nineteenth century and well into our century these connotations of praise and blame underwent considerable shifts and, in the aggregate, counterbalanced each other. In an 1848 French dictionary of politics the left-seated members were spoken of as "defenders of the principle of liberty, while the right-seated members were declared "defenders of the principle of power." However, according to the 1848 writer these were "old distinctions" that had lost much of their value, for also within the left many members had become "more concerned with raising themselves to power than with preserving public liberties."[31] With respect to the value connotation, "right" capitalized on the positive association with the legal meaning of the word (the abstract French *droit* and Germany *Recht,* and the concrete English "having a right," let alone "being right") but suffered from the initial association with the king's side and the subsequent one with the Restoration. Conversely, "left" capitalized on the left placement of the heart and on the early association of the word with the constitutional, "republican" politicians, but remained handicapped by the inferiority of left-handedness over right-handedness.

Without pursuing the fascinating developments of, and additions to,

334

these initial associations, it is fair to say that the current victory of "left" – its ever-growing evaluative positiveness – follows from the defeat of the Fascist "rightist" regimes, coincides with the decline of religion (Christ was always painted at the right of God), and currently results in "democracy," "future," and "young" becoming increasingly associated with "left."[32] This victory is of no small consequence, for it renders left the most courted and crucial word in the *war of words* with which political battles are fought. Still more important, as the evaluative imbalance between left and right grows, the emotional element of these labels overcomes their cognitive function. Therefore, this victory brings about what may be called the purely ideological use of left and right. In the Downsian analysis ideologies are devices for "cutting information costs."[33] There is a point, however, at which this "cutting" is so drastic that the "information" element disappears altogether. It is along this shift, then, that a spatial imagery is fittingly spoken of as an *ideological space,* which is all the more ideological the more left and right become sheer laudatory or derogatory epithets. True enough, some associations to some policies remain – but the nicety of spatial images is that they lack any semantic anchorage, that is, any semantic constraint governing their use and abuse. The labels liberal–conservative are often assimilated, at least on comparative grounds, to left–right. Yet the two sets of labels fundamentally differ in that the first cannot be entirely stripped of cognitive-informative content, whereas the latter set consists of empty boxes that can be filled and refilled, in principle, at whim. While there is a semantic impediment against associating "liberal" with Stalinist policies, no such impediment exists for "left." Historically, left–right did enter politics heavily loaded with cultural and religious meaning. But these labels are easily "unloaded" and "reloaded" – for they lack any semantic substratum.

We are now ready to confront the grand debate, namely, whether the space of party competition can be reduced to a single dimension or whether it is inescapably multidimensional. When the Downsian model is utilized for interpreting the data, we are left – across nations – with mixed findings and some results are both puzzling and contradictory. What is pretty certain, by now, is that European (including England) mass publics are able to place themselves, when interviewed, on a left–right scale.[34] But this evidence does not demonstrate, to be sure, that left–right explains, or suffices to explain, the actual voting behavior. A one-dimensional left–right explanation has been found sufficient for Italy[35] and, somewhat more roughly, for Germany[36] and Sweden.[37] England could also be appended to this group.[38] But France is found to be different, in this respect, from Italy.[39] Less surprisingly, the Netherlands and Israel seemingly require two dimensions.[40] And we are now told that Switzerland requires three.[41] As Giacomo Sani rightly emphasizes, much of the controversy on the applicability of the left–right continuum may well hinge on

the different techniques of data-gathering. . . . Thus the conclusions for the American electorate are based on the analysis of open-ended material; in the British case a "screen" question was asked in a preliminary way. . . . In the three continental nations [France, Germany, Italy] the respondents were simply asked to locate parties on a left–right spectrum that was presented to them.

To be sure, it is highly plausible for mass electorates to display – from country to country – "different rates of internalization of different cognitive devices, or labels . . . that assist the average voter in 'making sense' of the party system."[42] But these differences cannot be properly assessed unless we equalize first the data-gathering techniques.

Awaiting more equalized findings, the theoretical argument is that party positioning is a point of intersection that requires, for its determination, not only an abscissa representing the left–right continuum but at least another intervening ordinate: the authoritarian-democratic continuum emphasized by Eysenk[43] and/or the secular –denominational continuum. We may also find ethnic or racial parties that definitely belong to a distinct dimension. Additional dimensions may be construed on the basis of the urban-rural cleavage, and even on the basis of the modernity-tradition cleavage. We quickly end up, then, with some four basic cleavage dimensions, which can be represented as in Figure 44.

Nobody denies that these dimensions of cleavage do exist – in some country or other – that they help organize the issues, and that they

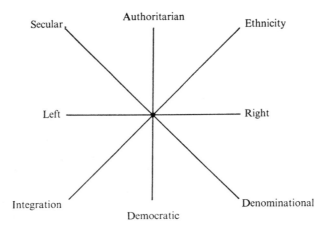

Figure 44. A multidimensional space

enter the party images and identifications. The fact remains that there is nothing much we can do with this multidimensionality – at least in the sense that there is little point in conceiving it as a "space." As Barry observes: "Extending the Downsian one-dimensional analysis to more dimensions does not in itself give reasons for expecting a number of parties nor for the parties to be anywhere except in the middle of the voters as they are distributed over the n-dimensional space."[44] And while more than one dimension generally allows a better fit of the data, nonetheless "evidence that dimensions x, y and z are needed to account for a particular batch of preference orders does not assure that any of the actors are seeing the space in more than one dimension."[45]

We are thus prompted to seek ways of working our way back toward a unidimensional simplification. The first thing to note is that we seemingly find no contradiction in assuming *one* left–right dimension while acknowledging that it actually consists of *multiple* orderings – depending on whether the criterion is economic, socioeconomic, constitutional, populistic, or, in the end, no criterion at all.[46] Under the economic criterion left points to state control (ending with a collectivized economy) and right to a market system based on private property. Under the socioeconomic criterion left favors, and right disfavors, welfare policies and leveling. But there are hosts of noneconomic issues that are equally accommodated under our labels: civil rights, civil liberties, *habeas corpus,* due process, privacy, and so forth – in short, law, safety, and order issues. Here enters, then, what I call (with reference to the constitutional democracies) the constitutional criterion, according to which extreme left and extreme right are used as pointers of an anti-system opposition, and the constitutional left–right differ with respect to how equal laws relate to societal inequalities. However, we also abide by looser criteria. In the fifties left was often equated with "change" and "movement," while right indicated a status quo orientation. But this criterion loses its discriminating power, *inter alia,* in the face of the protective and immobilizing practices of trade unionism. Therefore, on these loose grounds I prefer to speak of a populistic criterion, that is, the pure and simple placing of appeals downward (to the masses, the workers, the deprived) along the dimension of socioeconomic stratification, as against upward or, preferably, at some null point. On similar grounds another criterion is, perhaps, "dissatisfaction." Finally, we end up with no criterion at all, that is, with mere scare and cuss words whose only sense is the one established, following the contingencies, by some Big Brother.[47]

Most of these criteria are, to be sure, strictly Western bound. Indeed, only the economic criterion is able to travel from the democratic to the nondemocratic world. The Soviet Union remains at the left only on account of its state-owned economy – hardly on any other of the aforementioned grounds. Within the Western world, however, the constitutional standard of judgment is no less central than the economic or socioeconomic one, and actually appears to be the crucial criterion at the level of political elite and intra-elite perceptions.[48] Indeed, why should constitutional democracies be such unless they remain a matter of major concern? This is also the reason that upholds my presenting the parties – throughout the volume – in a left-to-right *constitutional-political* sequence. Had I followed a socioeconomic criterion of ordering, the positioning puzzles would have been far greater and a number of parties would have been placed at very different points of the spectrum. No doubt, even under the constitutional-political criterion the positioning of two adjacent parties may well result in being interchangeable, both because the impressionistic nature of spatial assignments is intrinsic to their nature and because two adjacent parties may indeed overlap and compete for the same positioning. But no harm follows by allowing for inverted, contiguous positionings. The case is very different, instead, when the constitutional criterion is replaced by the economic criterion. For instance, under the latter the Gaullists could well be moved, in the fifties, from the far right to a center-left positioning. Likewise, the Italian neo-Fascist party (MSI) represents the extreme right on constitutional grounds but could be placed at very different points of the spectrum under socioeconomic criteria. And similar instances are afforded by a number of multiparty countries.

At first sight multiple orderings complicate rather than simplify our problem. Upon second thought, however, we discover that the "emptiness" of our left–right boxes facilitates, and indeed prompts, the *squeezing* of a multiplicity of orderings (equivalent to a variety of issue spaces) into one and the same spatial dimension. For instance, the authoritarian–democratic dimension of Eysenk is absorbed by extending the overall left–right space and allowing for different distances between the parties. The foregoing adds up to saying, then, that while people locate themselves and the parties at different points of the left–right spectrum for multiple and often confused reasons, yet they *do* assign – whenever the options or the ideological heating grows – spatial positions.[49] On the other hand, the squeezing process entails that a broad gulf is bound to separate (i) the opinions and overall perception of politics tapped by interviews and (ii) the actual voting choice. Indeed, the greater the squeeze, the broader the gulf. When the citizen speaks, he may have many things to say. But when he is coerced into casting a yes–no vote, he may well have to settle for the "least-distance" solution, that is, to vote for the party (candidate) perceived as closest, on the left–right spectrum, to his self-assigned

10.3 Multi-unidimensional and ideological space

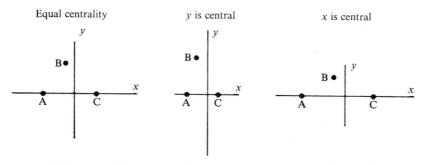

Figure 45. Variations of a two-dimensional party space according to centrality

location on the same spectrum. The difficulties confronting the observer when he attempts to gauge the interview responses to the voting act are the very same difficulties that the voter beheads as he actually votes. Therefore, the observer creates for himself more problems than he can solve unless he accounts for the squeeze and is alerted to the fact that the overall perception of politics of the *citizen* cannot be automatically transferred to the actual ballot of the *voter*.

In spite of the foregoing considerations at least one dimension – the religious one – seems irreducible and encroached upon the actual voting choice. The laical–denominational dimension cannot be absorbed; yet it can be somewhat *compressed*. As Converse ingeniously points out, two dimensions represented in a Cartesian space can be perceived in three very different shapes, according to whether the x and y axes are equal, to whether the x dimension, being more important, is extended and the y dimension shortened, or to whether it is the y dimension that becomes central and extends while the x dimension shrinks – as shown in Figure 45.[50]

Assuming the x axis represents the left–right dimension, and the y axis represents the clerical–anticlerical dimension, if both dimensions are of equal centrality to the voters – as in the first example – the case for unidimensionality is seemingly lost (though not, we shall see, as it stands in the first figure). If, however, the y dimension is dominant, parties A and C become compressed (very close) and we may well argue that this is a case of unidimensional clerical–anticlerical competition between B and A-C in which the left–right dimension plays no other role aside from impeding the coinciding of A and C. In the third case, instead, it is B that is compressed along (in proximity to) the x axis, and the argument becomes that we have here a left–right single dimension of competition in which party B enters the competitive arena only when perceived as an in-between party.

Needless to say, this is the case that fits my argument and can be

339

redesigned so as to represent the competitive status of the Christian Democratic parties of Germany, Italy, France, and Chile. The German CDU does not seek Catholic identifiers (except in Bavaria) nor desires to be perceived as a religious party, and it is almost entirely flattened along the x axis in the pursuit of an absolute majority. The Italian DC capitalizes on Catholic identifiers, but its center (or center-moving-leftward) placement attracts non-Catholic voters as well. The French MRP lost its potential Catholic identifiers by starting, in 1946, too much on the left, and thus failed in terms of both religious appeal and positioning. The Chilean PDC equally failed in stabilizing its support because of its overly fickle swings along the left–right dimension.

The case for unidimensionality can be pressed still further if we are reminded that we are investigating vote hunting, that is, if *competition* is taken seriously. Competition presupposes a common ground on which *two* parties (at least) speak to the same voters. Therefore, just *one* single-claim party – whether religious, ethnic, or linguistic – supported by identified voters does not add another dimension of competition: Actually, such a party is not subject to, or out of, competition. In the first case of Figure 45 (equal centrality of both axes) party B does not testify to a two-dimensional space of competition; it testifies, instead, to an *out-of-running* position. If B is satisfied with its voting pool, it will remain safe – aside from demographic and generational changes.[51] If it seeks, instead, a greater share, then it will have to approach the x axis and attempt to compete, for better or for worse, along the left–right dimension, as indicated in the third case of Figure 45. To be sure, a religious ordinate (the y axis) helps explain, say, why a left-oriented Catholic is not a Marxist Socialist; but this element is discounted, or taken for granted, in the bidding arena. That is to say, in general, that the reasons for the fragmentation of the party system do not translate themselves *eo ipso* into a multidimensional space of competition.

Thus a two-dimensional competition remains plausible especially with respect to Israel, for here we do have two to three denominational parties that compete among themselves on religious grounds.[52] It does not appear warranted, on the other hand, for Italy, Germany, France, or Chile.[53] In particular, the Israeli *Misrachi* (National Religious party) can freely float along the left–right dimension precisely because its identifiers are interested only in the religious payoffs of whatever alliance pays. Contrariwise, the Italian DC has been maneuvering not in another space, but in the same space as all the other parties.[54] Had the DC believed it could gain votes in terms of religious proselytism, it would not have sought, over the past 20 years, a center-left image. The same considerations apply to the ethnic parties. The Swedish People's party in Finland can be located, spatially, anywhere or, better, nowhere: It represents an ethnic out-group that neither loses nor gains votes in a competitive space. On the other hand, the current predicament of Belgium can well be interpreted as a two-dimensional splitting of a formerly simpler space.

Overall, it seems to me that the feeble case might well be the case of multidimensionality. While a unidimensional simplification may oversimplify the elementary case (twopartism), yet it becomes a more realistic representation the more we proceed toward the muddled cases. This is so under two assumptions: first, that position-perceptions become more useful and, at the limit, unavoidable the more the number of parties increases; second, that a left–right space is all the more likely the more we pass from pragmatic to ideological politics.

The argument hinges, then, on *how many* are the parties of a given system. With two parties only, the elector can orient himself without a spatial perception of the left–right type, and there is no compelling reason for a space of competition to be an "ideological space" – as has been the case in the United States.[55] Yet the British pattern is already a different one. For one thing, labels make a difference, and the dichotomy Democratic-Republican is far more anodyne and easily conducive to overlapping than the Labor-Conservative dichotomy. Furthermore, class politics does enter the British-inspired twopartism. On both counts the English-speaking voter is more sensitive than the American-speaking one to a left–right perception of politics.[56] Nonetheless, electorates that are amenable, albeit to a different extent, either to the liberal-conservative or to the labor-conservative squaring of politics, markedly differ from the electorates that plainly abide by the left–right squaring. As already noted, the labor-liberal-conservative distinctions are anchored, semantically, to a cognitive substratum – even if mass publics are unable to articulate it – while the left–right distinction can stand and float as a purely emotional symbolism. And this difference forcibly comes out when we compare – glossing, for the moment, over the three-to-four party systems – twopartism with extreme multipartism. When the voter is confronted with five or more parties, the information costs and the indeterminacies multiply exponentially, and some drastic simplification becomes a sheer necessity. In this context the average voter should be a kind of computer if we expect him to relate – following Stokes – several dimensions of cleavage to several issue performances, and these performances to the issue platforms of several parties.[57]

Around the five-party turning point we are confronted, however, with the bifurcation between segmented and polarized polities.[58] Here we can think of two interpretations. We may argue that the more numerous the parties, the more we either have a multidimensional space (the segmented societies) *or* an ideological space (the polarized societies) of competition. Alternatively, we may argue – this being my option – that while the segmented polities surely require a multi-dimensional explanation for the party *identifications*, it does not automatically follow that their *competition* is multidimensional also.

The broad hypothesis is, then, that the more the parties, the more their competition tends to spread along a linear, left–right type of space; that this is more surely the case the more a party system displays an ideological patterning; but that the space of competition may well be unidimensional also in the segmented polities with low ideological focus, for a party stepping out of line into another dimension runs the risk of being left to play a solitary and, over time, losing game. Hence the presumption of multidimensionality is strong only for the countries in which another "unsqueezable" dimension calls for two parties (at least) to compete among themselves in such a way as to operate a distinct subsystem. The question could be why the left–right dimension is assumed to prevail over the other dimensions. I would answer that in a mass communicating world characterized by mass politics a maximum of visual simplicity coupled with a maximum of manipulability represent an almost unbeatable combination.[59]

10.4 *The direction of competition*

In attempting to show that the Downs' model has been too readily dismissed on overly perfectionistic grounds or on the assumption that issue voting is more decisive than it actually is, I may have gone to the other extreme. In principle, however, models *are* drastic simplifications whose purpose is not to represent reality. A model (in the Downsian sense) purports to bring into prominence some basic feature that otherwise gets lost in the complexity of descriptive accounts.

Not only models are, in themselves, drastic simplifications, but the preceding discussion brings out that it is not on the Downsian premises that we can explain why voters distribute and align themselves as they do. It follows that the Downsian model is best defended and furthered by narrowing the issue, that is, by interpreting it as a theory of *the impact of party positioning upon voting behavior*. Still more narrowly, my interest will be focused on the *rewarding tactics of inter-party competition by the party leaders*. In this perspective, policies and issues are formulated in such a way as to convey to the electorate at large *position-images*, and the competitive preoccupation of party leaders bears precisely on the *position maneuverings* that are believed not to disturb the party's identifiers and, at the same time, to attract new voters (or to retain potential defectors).

The issue having been narrowed, let it be immediately stressed that its elements are more complex than the ones envisaged by Downs. In and by itself, left–right amounts only to an *ordinal space* whose only property is a unidimensional sequencing. If so, it is very tempting to assume that its objects stand at equal intervals. However, as left–right is transformed into an *ideological space,* new properties are added. Parties not only stand side by side but must also be assumed to be placed at *unequal intervals;* and a third property, *space elasticity* – how far and how much the space extends – becomes, I shall argue, even more crucial.

Parties are neither perceived by the public nor by the politicians as simply placed – with respect to the positioning of each actor – rightward or leftward. They are also perceived as being more or less "alien," more or less "extraneous." For the voter this means that some parties are acceptable as second and/or third choices, whereas other parties are simply non acceptable. Thus only a segment of the spectrum allows for *vote transferability:* Each voter moves, or is willing to move, along the spectrum, only up to a point of no-transfer.[60] Likewise, legislators and politicians do not simply abide, in their coalitional maneuverings, by a contiguity principle: They too encounter, or may encounter, a no-coalition point. If these perceptions are recast in spatial language, they point to different *spacings* between the parties – if not to a *disjointed* space. Unequal intervals mean, then, that in an ideological space parties are separated by different distances – distances that can in fact be highly distant.[61]

Space elasticity is best conceived as a third property – rather than as an implication of different in-between spacings – in that it addresses the question: How does the number of parties relate to a space of competition? Most authors seemingly assume the overall space of competition to be fixed, or inelastic. In this perspective, two parties slice among themselves the same "linear size" of competitive space than, say, six parties. But this is a highly unplausible assumption. Whatever the reasons for the proliferation of parties – and there are many – once several relevant parties exist, the assumption supported by the evidence is that their existence is correlated with a more extended space of competition. I am not arguing, then, that several parties exist *because* the space is more extended – for it can be equally held that the space is extended by the parties. I am only pointing out that we have yet failed to translate in spatial terms the otherwise acknowledged differences between homogeneous and heterogeneous (or fragmented) political cultures, or between consensual and conflictual societies. If we speak, as we do speak, of an "integrated" versus and "unintegrated" party system[62] and if – as I have contended all along – party systems differ in being bipolar and multipolar, non-polarized and polarized, the unidimensional spatial representation of all of this is that the various systems display different overall linear distances.

In any event, the pure and simple existence of unequal intervals between the parties brings forcefully to the fore that competition cannot be assumed to have only one, natural tendency – convergence. In other words, an ideological space squarely raises the problem of the *directions* of competition. In the Downsian model parties basically compete centripetally, and the problem is the extent to which their converging is counteracted. Downs indicates two major counterpulls that impede an excessive overlapping or even coinciding of the parties: the abstention of the voters (either of the extreme voters or of the ones who do not care to choose among parties without "differential"), and/or the rise, at the extremes, of blackmail parties.[63] On these premises, Downs suggests that parties find an "equilibrium" among themselves, that is, an optimal position along the spectrum at which they tend to remain or to revert, for, by moving away, they would lose votes. Nonetheless, the thrust of his argument definitely is that competition occurs – within the aforesaid restraints – in one direction only.[64] However, if some parties are perceived – and perceive themselves – as being alien and extraneous, why should they compete centripetally? Moreover, and in general, there is no point in hunting for the non-transferable votes; and the transferable ones may well be located at the outer ends, not in the middle area, of the spectrum.

An ideological space gives equal weight, then, to *two* possible directions of competition, either centripetal or centrifugal. In this perspective a center-fleeing trend is not simply a *pro tempore* reversal of a basic centripetal drive, but an alternative, independent competitive strategy. And if this is so, we have here an entirely new problem with which neither Downs nor his interpreters have yet come to grips. Let us attempt to pursue it.

As is prudent on highly tentative grounds, the cue will be simplified to the utmost – as will be seen by glancing at Figure 46, which is merely intended as a crude visual aid for making one point only: why it is that two-, three-, and four party systems happen – as the empirical evidence abundantly confirms – to be characterized by centrality, by a centripetal drive. The point may appear, in itself, obvious; but it is less obvious when the alternative possibility – center-fleeing competition – is borne in mind. Moreover, and in particular, I shall attempt to explain this centripetal drive in *purely mechanical terms*, that is, simply on the basis of the interactions between the number of parties, on the one hand, and the extension of the space of competition, on the other hand. I am not trying to explain, that is, how and why a given system comes into being, but only how it operates once that it is given. Whatever the reasons why parties are two, three, four (or more), I am simply saying: If they are two, *then;* if they are three, *then* – and so forth. Therefore, it is precisely because each pattern "works" as sug-

10.4 The direction of competition

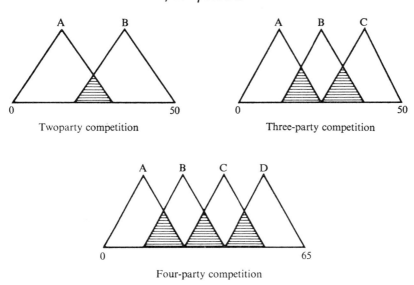

Twoparty competition

Three-party competition

Four-party competition

Figure 46. Schemes of centripetal competition

gested, that it remains as it is. In particular, if in a two-, three-, or four party system the prevailing pull is not centripetal, this means that the pattern in question is in transition either to the one that follows or ultimately to the centrifugal pattern. As for Figure 46, the shaded overlaps indicate the voters for whom the parties compete among themselves; and I use triangles instead of curves because my argument does not presuppose any particular curve of the voters' distribution of preferences.

Twoparty systems have been examined in detail,[65] and here Downs is at his best. Therefore, the first design in Figure 46 hardly needs comment. In twopartism either the contestants converge – for the area of rewarding competition is between A and B – or the system becomes dysfunctional and eventually falls apart. Hence "centrality" is the very essence of the system – *unless* one of the two major parties begins to fear that it has no chance of winning in the foreseeable future. This condition – which is seldom made explicit – calls our attention to two points, namely, how the parties of twopartism should be counted and, second, how the notion of winning should be defined.

I need not dwell on the first point. Let me simply recall that two parties are not the same as a twoparty *system*. A first possibility is that one of the two parties appears confined – either in fact or in fear – to a somewhat permanent minority status. In this case – predominance[66] – there is no compelling reason for the minority party to compete centripetally – it may well try the opposite strategy. A second possibility, albeit an extreme one, is for two parties to belong to entirely different dimensions (e.g., one black and one white, with strong sanctions against trespassing). In this case, however, we simply have a stalemate, not a state of competition – and that is that. Finally, and this we well know, a twoparty *system* may well contain third parties. In this case twopartism differs from three-partism as, or as much as, single-party government differs from coalition government. Pulling these threads together, the Downsian model of twoparty competition may be said to apply under the four following conditions: (i) that the undecided or floating voters are center located, that is, moderates; (ii) that the classification is correct, i.e., that the party system is not a predominant system; (iii) that the two parties compete in the same space; and (iv) that at least one party is able to win a plurality.

Turning to the second point, attention should be called to the fact that the vote-maximizing assumption takes on, in twopartism, an entirely different meaning than in multipartism. In the twoparty context "winning" means a plurality, and whoever does not win a plurality simply loses. In the more-than-two party systems, instead, "winning" means gaining votes or seats – and, furthermore, a party may be more interested in winning in terms of positioning than in terms of returns. And there is a world of difference between the winner-takes-all and the greater-share notions of winning.

These considerations redress the harsh criticism, among others, of Hirschman: ". . . hardly ever was a hypothesis [vote maximizing] so cruelly contradicted by the facts as were the predictions of the Hotelling-Downs theory by the Goldwater nomination."[67] Since the Republicans had reason to fear, at the time, a permanent minority status, from this angle it was perfectly "rational" to attempt a somewhat desperate sortie in search for a realignment. Losing for losing – why not lose with Goldwater?[68] The calculated risk of 1964 – which turned out, to be sure, to be a miscalculation – was to appeal to the pool of the nonvoters.[69] If anything, the "irrational" nomination was the one of McGovern in 1972 (the long-run fears of the Republicans are the long-run hopes of the Democrats), even though it still applies that – failing a plurality – it is rational to lose with the "right" candidate. However, in both instances the *electoral* prediction of the Downs model was entirely correct, for both candidates were in fact severely defeated. Therefore, the Goldwater and McGovern cases deserve scrutiny not because they disconfirm the model, but for the better reason that they prompt us to look at the intra-party processes. Our rationalizations notwithstanding, presidential nominations result, in no small part, from bitter fights among rival groups seeking, to begin with, a victory for themselves. Let us keep well in mind, therefore, that the *outer* moves of a party – the inter-party competition – are also a function of its *inner* moves, that is, of intra-party competition. The question turns, then, on whether also the intra-party processes can be interpreted in Downsian terms.[70] My conjecture is that this is very much the case.[71] But this opens up a path of inquiry that cannot be pursued here.

Moving on to the case of three-partism, the banality of the design in Figure 46 has the merit of vividly confronting us with the question: Why should the rewarding tactics of party competition remain centripetal? After all, with three parties we can already have a left, a right, and a *center*. So we can no longer shun the thorny issue of what is meant by center. The distinction between a center *placement* – resulting from a spatial configuration of politics – and so-called center *opinions* (doctrines, ideologies, and the like) should be, by now, well established. Yet it is well to know *whose* placement. And the ultimate question remains: How is a center placement *perceived as such?*

As regards the first question, the actor, or the subject, can either be a party – the so-called center party – or a portion of the electorate. And I have maintained that while any polity contains a center-placed electorate, only some polities display center-placed parties, i.e., parties that can be meaningfully said to occupy the middle area of a competitive space.[72] No doubt, along this route we may be confronted again with the problem of what center means "mentally" (ideologically or otherwise). But this is not a crucial matter for our purposes. We may leave it at saying that center is, in itself, a broad spectrum containing reasonableness, balancing of pros and cons, moderation, but also pure and simple mental abstention, a know-nothing or a do-nothing (undecided) attitude.

Thus the crucial question is: How and when does the perception of "center" arise with respect to a party that is perceived as "occupying" the center? Here enters the notion of space elasticity, for the perception of a center is a function of the length of the space. A short space does not allow, or does not facilitate, the perception of a center: It has, so to speak, no room for it. A short space is defined simply by its ends – left and right. A third point of reference – the *central point* – becomes meaningful and perceivable only as the space extends, and particularly when the ends of the space are perceived as being two poles apart.

The secret of the centripetal convergence of three parties resides, then, in the linear distance of the abscissa, which remains – in the figure – as it was in the twoparty case. There is no reason to assume, in fact, that three-partism calls for a larger competitive distance than twopartism. If England adopted proportional representation, it would immediately become a three-party system (at least), whereas if the German Federal Republic adopted the single-member district system, its Liberal party would disappear – with the distribution of political preferences remaining unchanged. Assuming, then, that the space of competition does not include – being short – sizable extremized sectors of opinion, parties A and C do not run the risk of being outflanked. Moreover, the fewer the parties, the more each party has a chance of having access to power and is, therefore, governing oriented.[73] On both counts A and C will both try to gain votes by converging toward the central area, for by departing they would leave a vacant space for the expansion of party B. As for party B, it can either attempt to resist on both sides or to attack on one side. What it cannot do – since it is not perceived as a center party and cannot capitalize on the fear of extremism – is push apart its neighbors via a double-front, centrifugal expansion. If anything, the in-between party of a three-party system tends to be squeezed into being the smaller party. Note, also, that with three parties the near evenness of twopartism tends to wither away. Therefore, the competitive interplays may actually take three configurations: not only A and C converging upon B, but also A and B both moving toward C or, conversely, C and B both going in the direction of A. All of this adds up to saying – in my previous terminology – that three parties do not make for a tripolar system: The competitive configuration of three-partism remains *bipolar*.

A four-party system as designed in the figure does not raise any problem. It is merely a subdivided, or doubled, representation of the twoparty scheme. The only difference is that I now assume the space of party competition to be larger – as indicated by the abscissa running, conventionally, from o to 65. There is no necessary reason for this extension. Two parties may slice themselves into four parties simply because a single-member system is replaced by proportional representation. Even so, as the restraints of the single-member system are removed, two things change: The hitherto blackmail parties can well materialize as additional parties, and, in any event, the extreme (not extremized) opinions acquire a leverage. So the odds are that a four party system will either reflect, or help produce, a wider linear space than the one allowed by twopartism. However, the fact that the counterpulls acquire greater force does not detract from the fact that no four-party polity actually displays an extremized or polarized pattern. This confirms, then, that four parties can still interact centripetally either with three parties converging against one (as in Sweden), or in a two-against-two contest for the in-between floating voters.[74]

The step that follows – five parties or more – appears to be the critical step. Here it is imperative to recall that "five" is defined by my counting rules.[75] Moreover, for our purposes we must also account for multidimensionality, thereby discarding the parties that have been declared, in the previous section, out of competition. That is, the five or more parties that enter a unidimensional model of competition must all compete along one and the same line.[76] With these provisos, we may turn to Figure 47, which comes closer to portraying a "model" than the mere visual aids of Figure 46. It should also be noted that we are now representing five specific parties and/or more-than-five parties clustered into five groups. The argument now is that when the critical threshold is bypassed, it makes little difference whether the parties competing along the left–right line are six, eight, or even ten – provided that they are "real parties," that is, that we are not misled by a situation of party atomization.

Downs may be right when asserting that any given distribution of voters in a given electoral structure allows for a certain number of parties and no more.[77] The trouble is that this argument verges on circularity, for the actual distribution results, in no small part, from how many are the parties and is, therefore, shaped by the parties themselves. It is safer, therefore, to pursue the argument only in terms of space elasticity. To be sure, the extended space represented – in Figure 47 – by an abscissa running from o to 100, implies that we are envisaging polities that display a strong ideological focus, low consensus, and high polarization. But this leaves the actual distributions to be investigated empirically.

The arrows in the figure indicate that we now have a competitive pattern that is no longer centripetal but centrifugal. How is this reversal to be explained? The crucial element is – according to my earlier suggestion – that when the extreme ends of the spectrum are so far removed as to be two poles apart, then the center becomes not only a highly visible *point* but also a *pole* endowed with strong leverage. Now a center positioning is perceived by the non-extremized electorate as the *safe position*, the position that best secures the survival of the existing democracy. We may equally say that the center position now incarnates a "center logic" of defense against the extremes. Hence the system is now tripolar or, eventually, multipolar. This entails that a

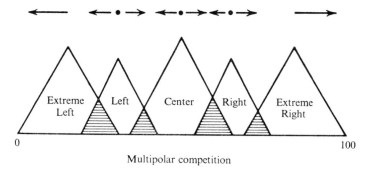

Multipolar competition

Figure 47. Centrifugal competition

349

centrifugal push is started at the very metrical center of the spectrum, for the center party (Italy) or parties (Weimar, Chile) acquire a hitherto unprecedented appeal – so much so that they attempt to expand with the "oil stain" technique, that is, on both sides. And while a simultaneous war on two fronts may not succeed, this logic of expansion is reflected in, and revealed by, the inner, centrifugal tensions of the center party itself. In any event, the central area is now physically occupied in a very real sense, namely, that the moderate electorate no longer is the floating electorate *par excellence:* Indeed, it turns out to be, under the circumstances, a highly stable electorate. To be sure, the "eccentric" push of the center party (or parties) is somehow counteracted by a centripetal competition of the moderate left and the moderate right. But the (pro-system) left is outflanked on its left side, and the (pro-system) right is equally outflanked on its right side. That is, the wings that are loyal to the system have also a problem of competing centrifugally vis-à-vis the unloyal (anti-system) oppositions. This means that their positioning does not allow them to exert any decisive influence on the ultimate trends of the polity.

The final say is left, therefore, to the extremized parties. Since the "extreme extremes" are not exposed to outflanking, one may well wonder why they should not converge. But let us recall the second property of an ideological space – unequal distances. In the case in point we are confronted with very "distant" parties that are perceived, and perceive themselves, as alien, if not as foes. Hence the extreme left and the extreme right neither desire nor have much to gain, in competing centripetally. Their goals are best furthered by tearing the system apart. To be sure, successful anti-system parties are office-holding parties, especially at the local and regional levels. But their holding office does not mean that they are "integrated" into the system; it may equally testify to the system's "disintegration." Even when anti-system parties soft-pedal their anti-ideology, their primary strategy is to make the system collapse by emptying it, that is, by means of a draining leading to a bimodal distribution or to a unimodal one peaked in the proximity of one of the ends of the spectrum.

In sum, the basic idea conveyed by the model that applies to the systems that I call of extreme and polarized pluralism is, first, that the leverage acquired by a center *pole* discourages, and actually impedes, centrality; and, second, that the extreme parties of such systems prosper on more, not on less, polarization. No doubt, this pattern is so precarious, and so unfelicitous, that the iron arm can hardly last indefinitely. Over time, counter-trends may well begin to prevail. This means, or implies, that the space of competition cannot be extended indefinitely: Either a polity squarely collapses or its competitive space will, at some points in time, begin to shrink. The point remains that we do need a model which accounts for the competitive trends of the "unstable," non-working democracies. The fact that most of them have died out is not a reason for forgetting them. It is precisely because they are dead that it becomes crucial to understand why.

Two concluding remarks are in order. The first is that models – as here understood – are supposed to predict *trends,* not single elections. The second one is that the best defense of the approach pursued here is in the point made by Downs himself (in spite of his deductive theorizing), namely, that models "should be tested primarily by the accuracy of their predictions rather than by the reality of their assumptions."[78]

NOTES TO CHAPTER 10

1 *An Economic Theory of Democracy,* cit., pp. 28, 30.
2 This is so also because, after Downs, more insightful approaches to the theory of democracy have been provided by Dahl (*A Preface to Democratic Theory,* cit.), James Buchanan and Gordon Tullock (*The Calculus of Consent,* University of Michigan Press, 1965), and Olson (*The Theory of Collective Action,* cit.).
3 Peter C. Ordeshook, *The Spatial Theory of Elections: A Review and Critique,* ECPR paper, Strasbourg, 1974, p. 3.
4 D. Stokes, "Spatial Models of Party Competition," *APSR,* June 1963 (also reprinted in *Elections and Political Order,* below, n. 16). With reference to Converse see esp. "The Problem of Party Distances in Models of Voting Change," in M. Kent Jennings and L. Harmon Zeigler, eds., *The Electoral Process,* Prentice-Hall, 1966.
5 Ordeshook, cit., p. 21. Within the boundaries of two-candidate contests a recent example of mathematical treatment is R. W. Hoyer, Lawrence S. Mayer, "Comparing Strategies in a Spatial Model of Electoral Competition," *AJPS,* August 1974.
6 Downs, op. cit., p. 100.
7 Ibid., pp. 98, 96.
8 Ibid., p. 115.
9 Ibid., p. 122.
10 Ibid., pp. 103–113.
11 Ibid., p. 132.
12 These difficulties are pointed out by Barry, *Sociologists, Economists and Democracy,* cit., ch. 5, *passim;* and they are acknowledged on more technical grounds, among others, by Ordeshook, loc. cit.
13 *Supra,* 3.2.
14 *Supra,* 7.1.
15 *Sociologists, Economists and Democracy,* cit., p. 143.
16 Also on account of these conceptual ambiguities, issue voting can hardly be assessed with respect to how many voters are identified, and it has in fact been assessed on the basis of the "normal vote." See P. E. Converse, "The Concept of a Normal Vote," in Angus Campbell, Converse, and Warren E. Miller, eds., *Elections and the Political Order,* Wiley, 1966.
17 For a development see Douglas Dobson, Duane A. Meeter, "Alter-

native Markov Models for Describing Change in Party Identification," *AJPS*, August 1974.

18 Donald R. Matthews, James W. Prothro, in Jennings and Zeigler,
The Electoral Process, cit., pp. 149–150.

19 Stokes, "Spatial Models of Party Competition," cit., p. 370 and
passim.

20 See A. Campbell, P. E. Converse, W. E. Miller, D. Stokes, *The
American Voter*, Wiley, 1960, esp. chs. 6, 8.

21 Ibid., p. 127.

22 P. E. Converse, "The Nature of Belief Systems in Mass Publics,"
in D. E. Apter, ed., *Ideology and Discontent*, Free Press, 1964,
p. 229.

23 Reference is made to the "authority beliefs" of Milton Rokeach,
The Open and Closed Mind, Basic Books, 1960, esp. p. 44 and
passim.

24 "Spatial Models of Party Competition," cit., p. 376. I gloss over
the specifically methodological criticisms of Stokes, for they appear
immaterial – it will be seen – to my subsequent argument.

25 V. O. Key, *The Responsible Electorate, Rationality in Presidential
Voting 1936–1960*, Harvard University Press, 1966 (a posthumous
publication edited by Milton C. Cummings), p. 6.

26 The findings of the sixties are well recapitulated and discussed in
the articles of Gerald M. Pomper, Richard W. Boyd, Richard A.
Brody, Benjamin I. Page, John H. Kessel, in *APSR*, June 1972,
pp. 415–470. See also N. H. Nie (with K. Andersen), "Mass Belief
Systems Revisited: Political Change and Attitude Structure," *JP*,
August 1974.

27 These figures are summarized by Peter Nissen, *Party Identification,
Issues and Images as Components of Electoral Decision: An Analytic Model*, ECPR 1975 London paper, mimeo, Table 1.

28 The notion of "critical election" – first developed by Key – is probed
by W. D. Burnham, *Critical Elections and the Mainsprings of
American Politics*, Norton, 1970. Its baseline, or "null model," is
provided by Converse's underpinning of the "normal vote" (above,
n. 16), which equally provides the parameter for "deviating" and
"reinstating" elections. On the basis of the 1952 to 1960 elections
Converse estimates the American normal vote to be 54 percent
Democratic. Elections are classified as maintaining, deviating, and
realigning, in *Elections and Political Order*, cit., by Campbell.

29 To be sure, some issues, such as birth control, are nicely related to
the left–right dimension. But when all issues are taken together, or
when issues are constantly changing, the overall structure of voting
is unlikely to fit a single dimension.

30 This hypothesis may also be stated as follows: That a strong ideological focus is likely to produce congruence between issues and
the left–right dimension. This reformulation actually reinforces the
case for unidimensionality.

31 *Dictionnaire Politique*, 3rd ed., prefaced by Garnier-Pagès, Pag-
nerre Editeur, 1848, the entry *Gauche*, p. 425.

32 For additional considerations see Jean A. Laponce, "The Use of
Visual Space to Measure Ideology," in Laponce and P. Smoker,
eds., *Experimentation and Simulation in Political Science*, Toronto
University Press, 1972, pp. 52–53; and Rokkan, *Citizens, Elections,*

Parties, op. cit., pp. 334–335. I am indebted to Laponce for many penetrating comments on the ms. of this chapter.

33 Downs, op. cit., p. 113.

34 A 1973 survey in nine European countries found the following percentages of left–right self-locations: Germany, 93; Netherlands, 93; Denmark, 91; Italy, 83; Great Britain, 82; Ireland, 80; France, 78; Luxembourg, 78; Belgium, 73. See R. Inglehart, H. D. Klingemann, *Party Identification, Ideological Preference and the Left–Right Dimension Among Western Publics,* mimeo, Table 1. The paper will appear in Ian Budge and Ivor Crewe, eds., *Party Identifications and Beyond,* Wiley, forthcoming.

35 S. H. Barnes, "Left–Right and the Italian Voter," *CPS,* July 1971; Giacomo Sani, "Fattori Determinanti delle Preferenze Partitiche in Italia," *RISP,* I, 1973, and "A Test of the Least-Distance Model of Voting Choice: Italy 1972," *CPS,* July 1974.

36 H. D. Klingemann, "Testing the Left–Right Continuum on a Sample of German Voters," *CPS,* April 1972.

37 Bo Särlvik, "Sweden," in Rose, *Electoral Behavior,* cit., esp. pp. 424–426.

38 According to Rokkan, his sample indicates that the countries that "come nearest" to an arrangement along the left–right dimension are England and Sweden (*Citizens, Elections, Parties,* cit., p. 300).

39 Converse definitely finds, in France, a left–right plus a clerical–anticlerical dimension (see Converse and Georges Dupeux, "Politicization of the Electorate in France and the United States," now in Campbell et al., *Elections and Political Order,* cit., ch. 14; and Converse, "Some Mass-Elite Contrasts in the Perception of Political Space," mimeo, IPSA Paris meeting, January 1975). But see Emeric Deutsch, D. Lindon, P. Weill, *Les Familles Politiques,* Minuit, 1966; and Roy Pierce, S. Barnes, "Public Opinion and Political Preferences in France and Italy," *MJPS,* November 1970, whose conclusion is that "public opinion in the two countries is most closely related to left–right ordered party identification for religious and religious related issues" (p. 658).

40 The reason will be explained shortly. However, while Israel surely is two-dimensional, this is less the case with the Netherlands.

41 R. Inglehart and Dusan Sidjanski, "Dimension Gauche–Droite chez les Dirigeants et Electeurs Suisses," *RFSP,* octobre 1974.

42 Sani, "A Test of the Least-Distance Model," loc. cit., p. 194. The U.K. study referred to in the quotation is David Butler, D. E. Stokes, *Political Change in Britain,* St. Martin's Press, 1969.

43 H. J. Eysenk, *The Psychology of Politics,* Praeger, 1955, ch. 4.

44 *Sociologists, Economists and Democracy,* cit., p. 139.

45 Converse, "The Problem of Party Distances," loc. cit., p. 196. Converse goes on to suggest that "it may be surmised that such perceptions instead of being interpreted as a function of a complex space which all voters perceive in the same way, may be interpreted as a function of simpler perceptions within spaces which differ from voter to voter" (p. 197). I understand this observation to run counter to the "fixed structure" assumption of Stokes (loc. cit., pp. 371–372).

46 It should be well understood that these criteria are articulated at the elite level, not at the level of mass electorates.

47 For instance, I am unable to find any criterion under which a Western leftist should be pro-Arab and, in particular, under which truly feudal sovereigns who should be denounced – in the left optics – as supercapitalistic parasites become untouchable.

48 This is well confirmed by our evidence on coalition governments, which shows that the adjacency principle holds far better in terms of the constitutional than the socioeconomic ordering. De Swaan, *Coalition Theories and Cabinet Formations,* op. cit., creates unjustified difficulties for his best explanation ("closed," i.e., adjacent coalitions) by assuming a priori a socioeconomic ordering. Also the studies on the left–right positionings assigned to the parties by legislators reveal an overriding prevalence of the constitutional criterion.

49 As will be specified shortly, this generalization applies to the more-than-two party systems but can be extended to twopartism with reference to elite groups (below, n. 55).

50 "The Problem of Party Distances," cit., pp. 198–199. My figure simplifies the one of Converse, which is referred to the French party system and carries six parties.

51 Over time party B will have the problem of keeping its followers removed from the dimension in which competition does occur and is likely to lose to it. This is, e.g., the current predicament of the Dutch Catholic party.

52 On Israel see *supra,* 6.2. The Netherlands is a less convincing case, for its Catholic and Calvinist major parties do not really compete against each other: Their respective voters are identified.

53 The well-established fact – at least in the case of France – that the position of the voter on the clerical–anticlerical dimension is the best single predictor of his voting choice is not a counterevidence, for there are many reasons (largely inextricable ones) that make for a good predictor.

54 This is confirmed by the intra-party factional strife (*supra,* 4.4), which occurs exclusively in terms of left–right outflankings.

55 This applies to normal voters, not to elite populations. Thus American and Canadian university students are perfectly able, like all other Western students, to locate themselves on a left–right continuum. See Jean A. Laponce "Note on the Use of the Left–Right Dimension," *CPS,* January 1970; and David Finlay et al., "The Concept of Left and Right in Cross National Research," *CPS,* July 1974.

56 Austria (*supra,* 6.4) is the extreme case, i.e., the more definitely ideological one, of the twoparty category.

57 It is especially at this end that the methodological critiques and assumptions of Stokes appear vitiated by what I call the "microscope fallacy" – a variant of the fallacy of misplaced precision.

58 *Supra,* 6.3.

59 Let it be added that the decline of religion brings about a "religious left," which produces, in turn, a congruent ordering of the religious and economic dimensions, thereby reinforcing the left–right perception of politics.

60 This is well confirmed by Michael Laver, "Strategic Campaign Behavior for Electors and Parties: The Northern Ireland Assembly

Election of 1973," *EJPR*, March 1975, with reference to the introduction, in Ulster, of the single transferable vote. Laver makes his
research a test of the Downsian model.

61 Converse ("The Problem of Party Distances," loc. cit., pp. 184–
193 and esp. Figure 2) analyzes the French and Finnish evidence
finding, with reference to the "perceived distances" between the
parties, that "in both cases the gulf between the two main parties
of the left (Communists and Socialists) is very nearly as large as
the length of the segment occupied by all the non-Communist parties together" (p. 191). With respect to the Netherlands a sophisticated research of H. Daalder, Jerrold G. Rusk, "Perceptions of
Party in the Dutch Parliament" (in Patterson and Walke, *Comparative Legislative Behavior*, cit., esp. pp. 169 ff.) reports "a clear
differentiation between parties regarded as potentially *in* the system
. . . and parties *outside* the system" (p. 180), indeed a significant
finding for a system with comparatively low polarization (*supra*,
6.2). Denmark is covered on similar grounds by Mogens N. Pedersen, E. Damgaard, P. Nannestad Olsen, "Party Distances in the
Danish Folketing," *SPS*, vol. 6, 1971. On Norway, see Converse
and Henry Valen, "Dimensions of Cleavage and Perceived Party
Distances in Norwegian Voting," *SPS*, vol. 6, 1971.

62 See, among others, Helmut Unkelbach, *Grundlagen der Wahl-
systematik*, Vanderhoeck, 1956, pp. 36–41.

63 Downs, op. cit., pp. 127–132. Enfranchisement may well be a third
"tearing apart" factor (exemplified by Downs, with reference to
England, p. 129, Figure 6), but it is an exogenous factor whose
influence disappears as all the parties readjust to the new distribution.

64 With reference to multiparty systems Downs simply allows that
they provide "no incentive for parties to move toward each other
ideologically" (ibid., p. 126), with the sole consequence that the
party "differentials" will remain neat.

65 *Supra*, 6.4.

66 *Supra*, 6.5.

67 *Exit, Voice and Loyalty*, op. cit., p. 71.

68 This is, in part, the argument of William C. Baum, *APSR*, September 1965, p. 693, in response to the one of Converse, below.

69 Converse et al., "Electoral Myth and Reality: The 1964 Election,"
APSR, June 1965.

70 Sjöblom, *Party Strategies in a Multiparty System*, op. cit., pp. 163–
164, briefly goes into this problem from the angle of party cohesion
and shows well how the Downsian model can be redesigned so as
to account for the intra-party distribution of preferences.

71 Remember, in this connection, that party members are far less
multidimensional, in their reciprocal outmaneuverings, than electorates at large, and that they make a much greater use of left–right
epithets. Other supportive considerations can be drawn from ch. 4,
supra, on party fractions. For instance, "factions of interest" are,
for themselves, pure vote maximizers.

72 *Supra*, 6.1.

73 Even the smaller party must have a governmental role to play, for
otherwise we have, by definition, a twoparty system.

74 For the details and the evidence supporting the three cases over-viewed in the text, reference must be made to ch. 6, *supra*.
75 *Supra*, 5.2.
76 This remark helps settle the dubious cases that have been long dis-cussed in ch. 6, *supra*, namely Switzerland, the Netherlands, and Israel.
77 Downs, op. cit., p. 126.
78 Ibid., p. 21.

Index

abstraction, levels of, 57, 259
activation and political development, 41
Adelman, I., 271
Adrian, C. R., 110
Afghanistan, 40
Africa: and boomerang effect, 265–7; cellular societies, 247; coups, 249; mass parties, 246, 248, 250–2; multiparty pattern, 254, 257–8; patterns in thirty-nine countries, 262–4; single parties, 246–8, 253–4
Aitkin, D., 213
Akzin, B., 206
Albania, 221, 225
Alessandri, J., 159, 207
Algeria, 248, 249, 250, 253, 264
alienation vs. protest, 132–3
Allardt, E., 119, 202, 205, 207
Allende, S., 141, 145, 159, 160, 207
alliance(s), cross-party, 91
Allum, P. A., 206
Almond, G. A., 37, 38, 52, 53, 56, 67, 192, 202, 214, 223, 245, 256, 257, 265, 268
alternation in twopartism, 186–8, 192, see also turnover
Ameillon, B., 269
Ames, B., 243
Andersen, K., 352
Anderson, B., 243
Andran, C., 268
Andrén, N., 209
antiparty state, 40
anti-system party: defined, 132–3; and ideological distance, 317–18, 350; and polarized pluralism, 132–4; and re-legitimization, 144; and revolutionary party, 133; and system survival, 140–1, 144–5
apparat-state, 45
Apter, D., 52, 68, 252, 257, 268, 269, 271, 352
Argentina, 276
Aristotle, 13
Aron, R., 236, 243

Arrow, K. J., 38
Atatürk, K., 277, 280
atomized: party, 75; party system, 125–6, 284
atomized pluralism, 284, 285
Australia, 185, 187–8, 190, 306
Austria, 180, 185, 186, 190, 213, 302, 306
authoritarian-democratic continuum, 336
authoritarian unipartism, 222, 225–6, 227–8
authoritative communication, 57–8, see also repression
autonomy, see sub-group and subsystem autonomy
Axelrod, R., 130

Baerwald, H. H., 112–13, 115
Bagehot, W., 34, 38
Balfour, Lord A., 16
Bangladesh, 200–1
Banks, A. S., 185, 322
Barber, B. R., 239
Barghoorn, F. C., 53
Barker, Sir E., 44, 52
Barker, R., 203
Barnes, S. H., 67, 115, 353
Barry, B., 108, 220, 238, 328, 337, 351
Bartholomew, D. J., 108
Barton, A. H., 130
Baum, W. C., 355
Bayar, C., 277
Beer, S. H., 213
Belgium, 173, 178, 180, 182, 183–5, 187, 188, 291, 306, 341
Bernard, J., 34
Berrigan, A. J., 238
Berrington, H. B., 108
Beyme, K. von, 34, 239, 320
Bhutto, Z. A., 200
Biebuyck, D., 271
Bienen, H., 268, 269
bifactionalism: balanced vs. unbalanced, 85; as twopartism, 87
bilateral oppositions, 134, 179

Index

Index

delegitimization, 143, 144; and anti-system parties, 132–3
Demirel, S., 278, 319
democracy(ies): and conflict, 15–16; Downs theory of, 324–7; and expression, 284; intra-party, 71, 105; and one-party pluralism, 47–51; and parties, 23; stateless, 255; and theory of elections, 324, 331; Turkey's transition to, 277–80, *see also* one-party democracy
democratic centralism, 96
Denmark, 146, 147, 149, 150, 151, 173, 178, 182, 190, 194, 196, 197, 304, 305, 306, 312
Deutsch, E., 353
Deutsch, K. W., 35, 56, 67, 209, 270
development: endogenous, 274, 277, 280; imposed vs. natural, 224–5; of politics, 254
developmental analysis and process concepts, 294
dictatorship(s): African, 252; hegemonic, 234; sociology of, 229; totalitarian and authoritarian, 222, 226, 228, 238
differences of kind vs. degree, 295
Di Palma, G., 181, 204, 206, 210
direction: of competition, 293, 344–5; of communication, 57
discontinuity: of party vs. party-state system, 281–2; of same continuum, 284–5
discriminating power, 296–7
disequilibrium, inflationary, 140
dissent: horror of, 13, 39; and pluralism, 16
distributive system, proportional and per capita, 101
Djordjevic, J., 243
Dobson, D., 351
Dodd, C. H., 319
dominance threshold and predominance, 316
dominant party: countries with, 192–3; criticism of, 194–5, 197; defined, 193; vs. predominant system, 192, 195, 197, 198, 199
Douglas, M., 271
Downs, A., 38, 123, 130, 191–2, 324–7, 342, 344, 345, 349, 351, 353, 355, 356; criticism of, 330–3
Drachkovitch, M. M., 243
dualistic blinders, 131
Dunn, J. A., 211
Dupeux, G., 353
duration: of coalitions, 318; of fractions, 80; of governments, 92, 302, 317–18

Durkheim, E., 146, 252
Duverger, M., ix, x, 36, 48, 54, 58, 60, 66, 67, 71, 106, 114, 131, 192, 201, 202, 207, 214, 299; laws of, 95, 98; on one-party democracy, 48
Dye, T. R., 111, 238
dynamics and statics, 294–5

East Germany, 221, 225, 230, 241
Easton, D., 53
Eckstein, H., 68, 70, 205
economic left-right ordering, 337–8
Edinger, L., 209
Egypt, 248, 250, 254
Ehrmann, S., 207
Eisenhower, D. D., 186
Eisenstadt, S. N., 206
Elazar, D. J., 109
Eldersveld, S. J., 71, 106
elections: credibility of, 194; theory of, 324
electoral system: and career politician, 97; intra-party impact of, 95, 97–100; in Italy and Japan, 93; and laws of Duverger, 95, 98
Elkins, D. J., 238
El Salvador, 193, 194
Emerson, R., 257, 270
enfranchisement, *see* suffrage
Engelmann, F. C., 213
Engels, F., 24
England, *see* United Kingdom
Epstein, L. B., 35, 60, 68, 69, 212, 214
Ethiopia, 249, 262
Etzioni, A., 34, 206
Eulau H., 36
Evans-Pritchard, E., 269
exceptions vs. mixed cases, 286–7, 290
exclusion clause, 99–100
exclusionarism, 226, 227
exit and voice, 221
explanatory function, 287, 290, 291; and mapping, 282–93
expression, 56–8; and democracy, 284, *see also* communication
expressive function, 27–8, 282
extreme multipartism, 285, 287
extreme pluralism, 126, 131–2
Eyck, E., 206
Eysenk, H. J., 336, 338, 353

Facchi, P., 114
faction(s): as concrete group, 5; criticism of, 73; vs. fraction, 74, 75; of interest, 76–8, 102, 103, 104; and interest groups, 37; in Madison, 11–12; vs. party, 3–5, 25; and power-seeking groups, 59; as party subunit, 72–3; par excellence, 77; from party to, 105–6; power vs. spoils, 77;

Index

Index

Index

Index

Schelling, 294
Schlesinger, J. A., 70, 84, 109, 110, 111
Schumpeter, J. A., 50, 54, 59
science: and classification, 293–4, 297, 298; data base of, 296–7; neo-Baconian, 297–8; quantitative and qualitative, 295–6, 298, 299, 318–19
Scott, J. C., 107, 270
Scott, R. E., 242
Schwartz, M. A., 212, 213
Schwartz, W., 271
sect vs. party, 4
secular-denominational dimension, 336, 339–40
segmentation, 126, 180–1, 287, 341–2; depolarized, 128; and polarization, 312, 314, see also fragmentation
segmented pluralism, 179–85; and moderate pluralism, 180
Seliger, M., 206
Sellers, C., 211
semi-competition, 256–7
semi-polarization, 151, 163
Senegal, 251, 261, 263
Sernini, M., 112
Seyd, P., 108
Sharkansky, I., 238
Shils, E. A., 33, 53, 268
Shubert, G., 38
Sidjanski, D., 353
Sierra Leone, 249, 250, 263
Sigmund, P. E., 268, 270
Sindler, A. P., 110
Singer, J. D., 36, 271
single-member district system, see plurality
single party: African, 246–8, 253–4; and channelment, 42; and democracies, 41; and parties, 39–40; vs. party system, 284; typology of, 221–30, see also one-party, unipartism
single-party government, 186, 187–8
single-party state, see one-party state
Sivini, G., 37
size: and majority principle, 315; measurement of, 304–15; and relevance, 123, 300; thresholds, 315–16
Sklar, R. L., 271
Sjöblom, G., 120, 355
Smelser, N. J., 68
Smith, M. G., 33
Smithies, A., 325, 334
Smoker, P., 352
Snyder, F. G., 269
societal differentiation vs. pluralism, 15
society: cellular, 247; differentiated, 181; plural, 15; pluralistic, 17; politicized, 41–2, 52, 253; segmented, 179–81
socioeconomic stratification, 337, 338
sociology: of dictatorship, 229; of parties, 23–4; of politics, 180, 291
Soja, E., 268, 269
Somalia, 249, 250, 253, 263
Sorauf, F. J., 38
South Africa, 193, 250
South Korea, 194, 236
South Vietnam, 72
Southern politics, 82–8
Soviet Union, 218–19, 221, 225, 227–8, 247, 275, 337–8
space elasticity, 343, 347
Spain, 155, 163–5, 172, 221, 224, 225, 237, 280
spatial archetype, 334
spatial imagery, 334, 335
spatial model of competition, see competition
Spiro, H. J., 254, 268
spoils faction, 78; vs. power faction, 77
Sprague, J., 218, 238
Spreafico, A., 115
stability, 317–18; and duration, 80, 318; and efficiency, 318
Staël, Madame de, 13
Stalin, J., 227, 275
state: antiparty, 40; formed vs. form-less, 244–5; new, 247, 268; one-party vs. no-party, 39–42, 254; and state-hood, 247
stateless direct democracy, 255
states, in the United States, 82–7
statics, 294–5; false, 300
Steiner, J., 205, 209, 210
Steiner, K., 210, 213
Stepan, A., 207
Stephenson, R. M., 203
Stern, A. J., 111, 112, 115
Stiefbold, R. P., 210
Stjernquist, N., 208
Stokes, D., 213, 324, 325, 328–31, 332, 341, 351, 352, 353, 354
structural consolidation, 21–3, 41, 244
structure, 285, 286, 292
structure of authority, and system change, 276–7
structure of opportunities: and finance pattern, 93–5; and fractions of principle, 101; and number of fractions and parties, 102–3; and plurality, 98; and pure PR, 98–100; and visible vs. invisible politics, 95–6; and voting, 96–7
subcompetitive situation, 217–18, see also competitiveness

368